P.55

Young Children

Young Children

Their Curriculum and Learning Processes

Edythe Margolin

Florida International University

Macmillan Publishing Co., Inc.
New York

Collier Macmillan Publishers
London

Macmillan Publishing Co., Inc.
866 Third Avenue, New York, New York 10022

Collier Macmillan Canada, Ltd.

Library of Congress Cataloging in Publication Data

Margolin, Edythe.
    Young children, their curriculum and learning
processes.

    Includes bibliographies and index.
    1. Education, Preschool.   2. Education, Primary.
3. Child study.   I. Title.
LB1507.M28   372.21   75–12656
ISBN 0–02–376010–9

To Rebecca and Hyman, who created love and joy
in their children.

One of their children passed their heritage on

to the precious three, Priscilla, Don, and Sarah,
who amplified that love and joy in their
own unique way.

Preface

This book is written primarily for those who plan to teach or work with young children in early childhood programs. Early childhood education as a field typically includes the study of nursery schools, kindergarten, and the primary (or first, second, and third) grades of the elementary school. Contemporary trends in education, however, reveal an even broader interest as far as the age range under study is concerned.

Early childhood education in current literature encompasses the education of young children from birth to about age eight. This broader perspective has grown out of a national interest supporting the development of more day care centers. It has also happened because of greater awareness by the public that young children's educational development is important to their later academic growth. The increasing numbers of women who work and who want child care services create a serious and urgent problem in the field of education. An implicit obligation on the part of educational institutions arises. More teachers are needed who are fully qualified to work with young children.

Whether babies and young children are cared for in public school centers, in hospital day (and night) care facilities, or in rooms located in the basements of factories where their parents work does not alter the fact that they need well-qualified people to work with them. At the present time that need is not being met in any satisfactory way. Frequent calls to university education departments asking for recommendations of qualified teachers attest to that fact. Owners of day care facilities are also asking for recommendations of people who can be directors for them. Preparation of this kind for the type of personnel needed has not been anticipated in several parts of the country. In place of the application of much needed systematized knowledge in education that they should have had prior to working with groups of young children and babies, they try to adapt, admirably so, the best ways they can. They report, however, that they rarely feel assured that they are moving in the best directions. Few books are available to guide them specifically for the age groups they teach. The number of books available to those who teach elementary education is greater by far than the number needed now for effective educational interaction processes with young children. Effective interaction does not imply formalized measures: it refers to a knowledgeable background in preparation for educational interaction between personnel and young children.

Child development as an area of study has been taught in some universities since the early 1900's. It has also been part of such disciplines as psychology, social psychology, anthropology, and home economics. University students can elect a course or more in child development (or human development, as it is called in some colleges and universities) but they usually take it in the first two years of work toward their degrees and teaching credentials. Frequently, by the time they have courses in curriculum development they have forgotten what they learned in child development. The subject matter areas, such as mathematics, science, or social studies, are taught without reminders of what the characteristics of a real child are. Although there are some exceptions—courses in which students will link child development principles to the subject matter needed for instruction in early childhood programs—this emphasis is still not as widespread as it should be in teacher training institutions throughout the nation.

New child care facilities recently created through federal support share the problem of preparing competent people to work with young children. They receive funds to support their programs, but their need to use consultants to provide in-service training in a brief period of time often dilutes quality. What is typically accomplished in a few years by universities to prepare professional personnel is compressed into pressure techniques. Short cuts and quick tips, however entertaining they might be at the time that they are presented to teacher-trainees, cannot encourage reflective thought. They encourage mechanistic responses. This is in no way the fault of the people involved. They are doing the best they can under the circumstances with what they have available to them. It is simply a result of seeking quick answers to deep problems in an unrealistic time frame. As a result, these workshops bypass and ignore important foundational knowledge.

The responsibility of leaders and educators interested in early childhood education has to be broadened to include not only the development of children in nursery schools, kindergartens, and primary grades, but also the development of children from birth to age four. These children and infants are currently waiting in centers and institutions. They need competent personnel to work with them. Universities need to provide such personnel if young children are to be given the kind of opportunities for growth that are truly available in the United States. Instead of teacher-trainees being introduced for the first time to quick tips, they should be given basic exposure to reasons why children should be taught in particular ways and what some of the basic assumptions underlying those reasons are. They need a greater emphasis on child development courses. They also need to understand and at the same time to question why specific techniques are recommended. They should be given adequate time to discuss their ideas and to criticize their peers and instructors. This should stem from reflective thought, reading, and depth of information rather than a brief acquaintance with the field in premature workshop experiences. The alternative is to allow the systematic acceptance of piecemeal bits of information to flourish and displace what can be done in a sequentially developed plan toward effecting greater enlightenment about young children's educational growth.

The depth of preparation suggested here can be accomplished by universities particularly concerned with providing a viable program of studies for the field. It seems more timely than ever, considering the amount of writing by researchers and others who have been nationally recognized, to call for a broader perspective on the scope and boundaries of early childhood education, however tentative or crude this conceptualization might be at the present time. A conceptual framework of the field can provide rich sources for the direction of present and future students and scholars. Principles of child development, curriculum development, specific subject matter areas, and sociological insight can be brought together into an illuminating set of objectives and principles for planning. This will represent valid recognition of the many contributions evident in those disciplines. It will also expand a limited perspective presently held by many who indicate a desire to know more about this developing academic area.

The present book developed in part as an answer to the requests from administrators of newly funded children's programs needing assistance in teaching techniques, planning, and evaluation procedures, and in part because of a concern for the need to approach the growing field of early childhood education in broader conceptual terms with the new information we have. The book also presents ways to meet increasing problems related to organizations and institutions that are responsible for the development of teachers and/or administrators. Strategic planners of these groups must consider the intricate relationships between child development principles and curriculum development for young children. To neglect one at the expense of the other is to do only part of the educational job.

In final consideration of purposes and concerns that give rise to the book, it becomes obvious that to do justice to all of them would require an encyclopedic tome. Instead this volume will mark its own beginnings in that direction.

E. M.

Acknowledgments

The author wishes to thank the people who helped develop this book. The cooperation of parents, the principals of schools, and the children themselves who allowed us to "invade" their privacy during work periods was very much appreciated. Without their kindness, we could not have enjoyed the experiences photographing them as we did.

To Gerald J. Margolin, an outstanding and sensitive photographer, without whose work a significant charm of the children's expressions would be absent, goes my deepest gratitude. His patience, willingness to cooperate, and enjoyment of children are reflected in the composition of each photograph.

To Eileen Levine, kindergarten teacher, and to William Kennedy, principal of Olympia Heights Elementary School, goes our gratitude for allowing us to photograph children in their school. We also wish to thank the parents of pupils for permission to take pictures of their children.

A teacher, Marilyn Rabin, and principal, Charles Gelfo, of Royal Green Elementary School gave graciously of their time and energies. We are ever indebted to them and to the children who permitted us to photograph while they were involved in their activities. We appreciate the parents' willingness to allow us to use the photographs of their children for this book.

The publication of a book reflects not only the author's work but also the conscientiousness of many people in a publishing company. This author is grateful to all of them and particularly to Lloyd C. Chilton and Dave Novack, who were supportive and sensitive to the content during its preparation for publication.

Contents

Part Two
Curriculum Planning and
General Conceptual Frameworks

Chapter 3
Curriculum Guidelines

Chapter 4
Children Need to Communicate

Chapter 5
The Child, His Family and Society: Social Studies for Young Children
at School

Young
Children

Part One

Philosophical Goals in Early Childhood Education

Whatever the program, whatever its materials, and whichever students are expected to use them, the crucial understructure of the program is its rationale. Typically, the underlying philosophies of programs are related to the nature of a country's political system (e.g., democratic, totalitarian), its cultural orientations (valuing independence, industriousness, cooperation), its cultural habits, and the way the people view their lives.

Where children are concerned, society hopes that life will be better for them than it was for the previous generation. The mistakes of adults are seen as somehow redeemed by the effort to rear the young intelligently, hopefully leading to their becoming better citizens than their predecessors. Being better citizens applies to children learning to become capable, problem-solving individuals who can approach life's conflicts without becoming totally discouraged or fearful. It pertains to being the kind of person who can develop personally and contribute to society at the same time.

The goals of any educational program for children take into consideration their age range, the anticipated outcome, and how it can help them grow academically, socially, physically, and emotionally. The more that educators know about psychological, educational, and sociological research, the more they may try to incorporate this information into their new curriculum plans. Since interest in young children's education has grown rapidly in the past ten years, much more writing and research has been done on the subject than ever before. Writers on early childhood consequently have more references to consult when they want to create viable curriculum materials.

One of the major philosophical questions of early childhood education has been whether children should learn to read before five. Whether they should be given a curriculum of broader interest and variety as opposed to an academically restricted one has been another major concern of educational planners. Formalized approaches to mathematical techniques and substance have also been an issue. Some theorists suggest that an appropriate age of maturation permits easier and more effective learning than premature exposure to difficult concepts. Many traditional early childhood programs were based on a broad, nonsystematic exposure to materials and subject matter areas. Children learned about science through simple activities, but these activities were not programmed in sequential order. They learned about mathematical techniques and substantive data through informal kinds of experiences, less precisely didactic than they are currently.

Throughout the years, the educational argument seemed to proceed from a concern for the child's emotional, academic, and physical readiness to accept formalized academic programs. Some children are ready for them; some are not. When teachers are given curriculum materials specifying exact ways to follow their use with children, this is done. Teachers expect, however, that children should be able to do precisely what has been specified in the directions. This is teaching by an exact framework, allowing little room for individuality.

For youngsters who are not able to understand quickly what is expected of them, school can be the place that tells them early in life they are inept. The discouragement and feelings of failure that set in can persuade them that they are hopeless. Underlying any instruction in the classroom, therefore, has to be a basic understanding by the teacher of the nature of child development and its relationship to teaching. A crucial prerequisite to teaching young children is an awareness of their need for continual emotional support and encouragement. Premature expectations for perfection the first time a child is asked to do something can inhibit his progress and create constant tension and anxiety.

The goals often listed in educational textbooks state that teachers should help each child develop to his maximum: that teachers should be aware of and sensitive to each child's individual problems and abilities. While the teacher can succeed in knowing the pupils and their individual characteristics, she will have a difficult time if she brings rigid perfectionist standards to each child's efforts. Expecting perfection in the child's initial attempts is self-defeating, both for the teacher and for the child. The irritation rather than encouragement brought into the teacher–pupil relationship can be very damaging to the child's future efforts to learn.

This section discusses the foundations and underlying philosophies of programs for young children. It delves into the relationships between the principles of child development, characteristics of young children, and the principles of learning that need to be considered when planning an early childhood program. When educational planners take into account the age range of the children who are the focus of the program and the characteristics of their physical, social, emotional, and intellectual stages of development, and relate these to the various levels of difficulty in subject matter concepts, it is more likely that individual differences may be perceived in the children's actual processes of learning.

Some program designers who are particularly intent on academic depth for learners sometimes forget the nature of the pupils who are expected to follow the program. Although teachers may in theory and spirit want to be of service to children, they can defeat their purpose through excessive zeal for the transmission of specific facts found in curriculum materials.

Later sections of the book present subject matter areas in early childhood programs so that teachers may have at their fingertips specific content (and references to other sources). They usually have to obtain this from different books. Teachers' responsibilities to the parents of their pupils are also discussed as well as their relationships to the community and its various agencies. International understanding is included too, since it is viewed as an important contribution to the individual's life, in both a personal awareness sense and a professional one.

The purpose of Part One is to set the tone for what follows. It presents the contemporary concern to the point of federal funding, and a national readiness for supporting excellence in education and time spent with those starting out in life. Even though the home is still the focal point for human development by virtue of the time spent in it and the proximity of interacting personalities, recent information on early capacities for intellectual development has brought about change in parental and educational viewpoints. Many more possible causes are investigated when a child appears listless, dull, or lethargic. He is no longer labeled as incapable, unintelligent, or uninterested in his surroundings. A greater fund of knowledge is presently available. Infants and children can be helped in developing their intellectual capacities. Emotional stress can cause physical stress, and vice versa. The individual's physical and emotional state influences his perception of ideas. Intelligence as a concept in education has taken on a much broader definition.

The second chapter in Part One focuses on ways that an understanding of child development principles can be woven into the curriculum. It discusses representative ideas. It does not go into lengthy specifics or exhaust all possible ideas by any means. Its intention is to give suggestions and offer techniques that will have a broad range of reference. The reader, however, must adapt individual techniques specific to circumstances in her own pattern of experiences with babies and children.

Chapter

1

Child Care Centers, Nursery Schools, Head Start Programs, Experimental Programs, Kindergartens, and Primary Grades

One look at the sparkle of excitement in a child's eyes when he is absorbed in a particular activity at school and it is easy to understand why people are motivated to go into the teaching profession. The satisfaction of any teacher seeing children involved in work she has planned for them makes all the effort and training for her job worthwhile. The teacher feels as though she is contributing to the welfare of others, is of service, and in turn gives her life added meaning. When children are not excited about learning and seem to avoid the "business" of the classroom, it becomes puzzling that this can happen in a country as rich in human resources and technological advantages as the United States. It is a paradox that this richness in ideal productivity does not translate itself into excellence in educational processes.

This chapter deals with various types of programs currently emphasized in American education. The programs represent an attempt to use the knowledge that researchers and educators have gained through studies financed by national and local sources, public and private. Professional personnel from several disciplines such as psychology, sociology, and education have pooled their energies and ideas to devise contemporary techniques to be used for the benefit of the improved education of young children.

General philosophies of programs are considered first, their differences and similarities are discussed. They represent a groundwork for building a perspective of early childhood education, what that perspective means, and what educators in that area are attempting to do with young children to enhance their development. Next, the chapter involves discussions of goals and objectives in current programs and it ends with a description of ways that some programs are subsidized, what their sources of sub-sidization are, and how these financial aids are obtained. This kind of support is new to early childhood education and epitomizes a different era in relationships between the government and responsibilities for the young.

Philosophical Orientations of Programs for Young Children

As one begins to review the current programs for early childhood education, it becomes fairly apparent that each writer or team of writers has an image in mind as to what they envision the child to be after he experiences the learning activities planned for him. While it is known that no individual ever develops to his maximum potential (a mandate often given to teachers as the guiding spirit in their relationships to children), it is hoped that each person working with the child will at least help the pupil in the direction of becoming the best that he can at any particular point in life. If the educator succeeds to some extent, the child will meet most challenges at each stage of development. Relative to his psychological, emotional and social development, each individual can go beyond what he has attained thus far.

The teacher who works with young children is typically aware of their rapid growth in personality characteristics at given times in their develop-ment. Language, for example, grows rapidly in the first few years of life; patterns of grammar or syntax begin to develop as the child hears words in phrases and complete sentences. While physical growth is remarkable in the first year of life, other traits develop rapidly as well, at least as compared to the middle years after eight.

Programs that are sensitive to individual childhood differences reflect this awareness in their design. Such a program usually includes plans to develop a range of skills and abilities for varieties of pace and style in children's learning patterns. It acknowledges the fact that all children will not be ready for the same complexities at the same time despite chronological identity.

An emphasis on age group occurred when the Head Start programs began early in the 1960's. As educators and other researchers realized that children in indigent neighborhoods were not making gains in language and reasoning needed to succeed at school, more efforts were made to create programs that would benefit children from low-income homes. Children in these programs were of prekindergarten age, typically about four.

Such programs emphasized educational needs to develop a variety of skills, with most placing language development at the top of their priorities. Research by Bernstein [1] and others [2] had indicated that school-children who did not have some minimum level of verbal facility were unable to perform well in many school skills involving communication: discussion with others on school subjects; conveyance of an understanding to the teacher or class of knowledge gained from books; ability to perform well on written tests; ability to express one's feelings well. This does not mean that any of the researchers inferred that the children did not have an innate ability to communicate. They did in their own familiar context with family and friends. But the communication referred to here is formal transmission of information and knowledge academically in class.

Federal programs were produced across the nation. The widespread understanding that young children's educational origins were of crucial importance influenced the creation of many programs throughout the United States. Monies were released for various ideas and curriculum plans intended to help young children learn to express themselves in different ways, to enjoy hearing stories read to them, to enjoy being at school in pleasant surroundings with other children of their own age with adult supervision to guide them. It was hoped that feelings of competence would grow and that children would enjoy functioning effectively at school with others in self-satisfying ways.

Some researchers felt that cognitive development was required for young children more than any other area of development. Several researchers decided that both intellectual and socioemotional development had to be incorporated into their programs' goals. Looking at Figure 1.1 and the direction taken in many programs, the emphasis taken by any one of them can be sharply seen by placing them symbolically or theoretically at one point. Seeing it in that sense gives a broader sense of perspective in the overall consideration of the philosophies of programs.

For example, some schools, symbolically placed at the bottom of the figure, represent an emphasis on physical or safety needs of the child. The teachers of this school concentrate on keeping the child safe from harm, whether it is physical harm from other children or from toys and

[1] Basil Bernstein, "Social Class and Linguistic Development: a Theory of Social Learning," in *Education, Economy, and Society*, edited by A. H. Halsey, Jean Floud, and C. Arnold Anderson (New York: The Free Press, 1961), pp. 288–314.

[2] Martin Whiteman, Bert R. Brown, and Martin Deutsch, "Some Effects of Social Class and Race on Children's Language and Intellectual Abilities," in *The Disadvantaged Child* selected papers of Martin Deutsch and Associates (New York: Basic Books, 1967), pp. 319–335.

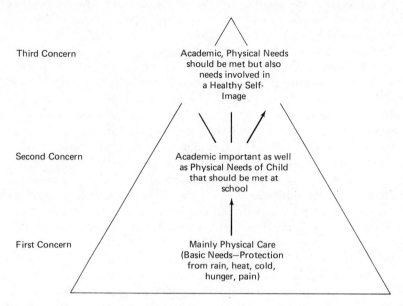

Third Concern — Academic, Physical Needs should be met but also needs involved in a Healthy Self-Image

Second Concern — Academic important as well as Physical Needs of Child that should be met at school

First Concern — Mainly Physical Care (Basic Needs—Protection from rain, heat, cold, hunger, pain)

figure 1.1
Philosophical Emphasis on Children's Programs at School

materials at school. Most of the earlier schools were of this kind. It is referred to as custodial care.

Collective centers were designed to keep children off the streets and were mainly intended for children who were uncared for when their mothers were away from home. They were also planned to provide a service for children whose mothers were very poor. The entire concept of child care has changed from one of merely protecting the young from harm to one of involving them in thoughtful, challenging ways in order to help them develop intellectually.

While people such as Froebel,[3] the Father of the Kindergarten, designed his kindergarten in Germany in 1837 for children as a symbolic, growth-producing (flower-unfolding) concept (as well as a religious-oneness-with-God kind of orientation), the kindergartens that followed in that concept were not as widespread as those developing today in many states. Child care centers were developed in England and in the United States which were conceived mainly for the purpose of serving mothers of low-income neighborhoods; again the concept of education as its major goal was minimally represented.

[3] Friedrich Froebel, *The Education of Man*, translated by William N. Hailmann (New York: D. Appleton, 1889).

It is true that the McMillan[4] sisters in England worked with children of the poor too, as well as some educators in the New York City area who were interested in slum-dwelling children. They did more than feed and protect the children. But the scope of their educational equipment had to be minimized due to lack of funds. Typically, social welfare programs are emergency type procedures planned to at least save the individual from major deficiencies of living, such as adequate food, sleep, and protection from diseases. They want to provide more and to serve in ideal ways, but it is understandable that the money needed to subsidize mass programs for hundreds of children is not inexhaustible.

The history of early childhood education reveals fascinating stories of the ways in which dedicated people acquired help for children.[5] Their zealousness and commitment provided great beginnings for what was realized later to be a respect for the ways that young children grow and learn. Those early advocates for children's welfare could not take for granted the educational development of children that apparently others were willing to do. As more researchers became involved in the study of young children, more began to realize that children were not merely immature adults—that their development occurred in recognizable stages revealing a different kind of intellectual nature at certain age levels.[6] Their thinking and acquisition of knowledge had specific qualities that were not viewed as childishness, foolishness, or simply naïveté, but were abilities developing into mature forms of intellectualism.

Children were not viewed as helpless, unwise humans who were unable to think beyond simple learning tasks. Rather their forms of thought were considered important stages of development in themselves. Adults began to understand how children developed intellectually. The substance of children's speech was given more attention and greater analysis. Instead of laughing at young children's comments and dismissing them as an aspect of immaturity and ineptness, adults began to be intrigued by their meanings in relation to the evidence of thought at certain developmental stages.

In the 1960's and 70's, the awareness of children's age-related intellectualism reached its peak. Social forces were ready for it. Educators and scientists were as well. The curiosity of program planners was tested through various curriculum ideas. One writer, for example, compared traditional kinds of nursery schools with the cognitively oriented ones of

[4] Margaret McMillan, *The Nursery School* (New York: E. P. Dutton and Company, 1921).

[5] Samuel J. Braun and Esther P. Edwards, *History and Theory of Early Childhood Education* (Worthington, Ohio: Charles A. Jones Publishing Company, 1972).

[6] Jean Piaget, *The Language and Thought of the Child* (London: Routledge & Kegan Paul, 1952).

contemporary popularity.[7] This in itself marked a change in the philosophy of a nursery school program, moving away from the emphasis on physical protection and on socioemotional needs of the child as the major goals of the school. He stated: "The major viewpoint in the early education field is that of the traditional nursery school educators. This position is best characterized as child-centered and permissive." [8] The teacher plans the children's programs in terms of her understanding—intuitive and otherwise—of the pupils' needs in relation to child development. The view of planning the program in terms of what is perceived as the child's needs is compared to the more contemporary structured programs that are the inclination of recent educational planners or researchers in education.

One project called the Ypsilanti Preschool Curriculum Demonstration Project tested two programs, one which emphasized language development of young children, and the other which focused on a broader cognitive orientation for learning.[9] The people in the Ypsilanti project also decided to test a traditional type program that emphasized socioemotional objectives and part of the teaching methods assumed to take place in traditional nursery schools. The investigators of the study comparing all three types of programs measured against the gains made by the children in the study found that all three programs were effective with the children. They had thought that the traditional type program would be ineffective with the children of low-income backgrounds compared to the more structured cognitively oriented programs. The traditional types of program were built around the expressed views of the children, their interests and needs as determined or perceived by the teachers.

The writers indicate that while they were occupied looking for the one best program to use with children from low-income backgrounds, it was not any one program that was most successful with the children. Rather the success of programs seemed to depend on the people or teachers who created it, their efforts, their interest, their ways of solving problems as they worked with the children and each other.

As has often been shown, it is the teacher directly involved with the children themselves who creates the successful program and what happens of value with children's progress in learning. The writers concluded that they ought to move from seeking one specific theoretically sound curriculum for effective teaching of the young. They chose instead to view their work in "a much more complex and unexplored goal: How do we draw groups of adults and children together so that each can provide the situa-

---

[7] David Weikert, "A Traditional Nursery Program Revisited," in *The Preschool in Action*, edited by Ronald K. Parker (Boston: Allyn and Bacon, Inc., 1972), pp. 189–215.

[8] Ibid., pp. 191–192.

[9] Ibid., p. 192.

tion with his unique contribution in terms of quality teaching and effective learning?" [10]

In any discussion of the philosophies of programs, it becomes apparent that the identification of philosophies as such can be elusive. Some programs do not state their approaches in clearly philosophical terms. They may weave their ideas into their objectives and goals or state them in the process of describing their plans for the children's activities. Their objectives involve the intentions of the writers who indicate what they hope the child will become as a result of having experienced the program. They state the antecedent conditions for certain consequent conditions. For example, if a child is in an accepting, warm, nurturing environment, then he will be able to learn. This suggests a certain kind of philosophy about the way children will learn.

One may examine and review many sources of educational philosophers who have views about what education ought to accomplish, what it is, and what it can mean in the total perspective of an individual's life. As far as early childhood is concerned, however, the variety of statements about its underpinnings is evident. Some attempt to simplify their philosophy. Since people unfamiliar with the academic structure of the field need information that is readily understandable, many writers try to state their concepts very simply. This is fine. If they are oversimplified, however, this can be misleading. The difficulties of program implementation are often concealed.

Some programs emphasize the importance of developing viable relationships among people. Some stress the need for children to learn how to use the best that is in them, to use their "natural" resources, to develop their own abilities, to discover who they are and what they are able to do well. They are encouraged to develop a satisfying self-concept leading to self-confidence. This engenders wholesome attitudes in learning. A child who has learned to depend on himself in particularly difficult problem-solving situations finds that he is willing to attempt learning in a variety of situations.

Some writers see philosophical foundations as artificial or unduly idealistic, creating impossible goals that human beings cannot achieve. Some see the idealistic foundations as part of education, a necessary torch-bearing stage that must inspire people (teachers as well as others) to want to do almost impossible tasks in order to help children change their self-perceptions from "I am someone who cannot do," to "I can."

Some people interpret philosophical statements as real ideals which should become pure reality, and if these ideals are not pure reality, that is, if the individual finds he does not seem to be behaving in a way that

[10] Ibid., p. 211.

allows him to feel that he is living up to that ideal, he finds it uncomfortable living with himself. And for many who are absolutistic in their conceptualization of ideals and goals, it is painful to fall short in any way.

Philosophical statements may be categorized in terms of the preconditions they include for creating results compatible with the writers' goals. They imply that the presence of one condition will result in another. Given, they may suggest, a classroom in which the atmosphere is encouraging, nonthreatening, and which has a responsive and concerned teacher at its head who is aware of children's developmental needs, children will learn effectively. This is subject to any other cause-and-effect assertion which is oversimplified.

Philosophical statements are also made in terms of an ideal. Viz., if we want a human being who can function effectively in society, who will have confidence in himself, and who will be able to contribute to society, then what must education do to develop that kind of person? How should the child be treated in school? What kind of materials should be presented to him or her? What should the schedule or pacing of the program be?

Philosophical statements can be made in terms of broad philosophies, the pragmatic, in terms of what works, of what is most efficient. If the child is content and seems to be learning, whatever way he learns is fine.

Society generates trends that give rise to certain viewpoints. When higher education was something to which only the upper I.Q. range could aspire, educational philosophy was contemplative and oriented toward the scholarly mind. This was part of an approach that encouraged thinking about the ultimate purpose of life and existence. Ultimate answers are not necessarily intended to build bridges. Engineers and surgeons require more concrete, down-to-earth materials.

In current trends, educational programs have become much more pragmatic. People want something that works right now and that can lead to financial remuneration. "The faster the better" is their slogan. The emphasis on speed, practicality, and money-saving is more obvious in contemporary programs. Parents want their children to learn to read faster and to acquire competence faster. Competitive activity in a society that can award prestige and financial success generates rush, anxiety, and desire by individuals to outdo each other as fast as they possibly can.

Where in the past some classes of people had been suppressed and kept from certain options, a sense of urgency to make up for lost time arises. Understandably, there is a rush to gain as much as possible in a short time. Whatever the reasons, a society that has experienced wars, disasters, political emergencies and deceit, creates an overriding sense of immediacy. Thus, a sense of timing concerning the accomplishment of goals becomes distorted.

Philosophical contemplation about life and the purpose for existence are less frequently reflected in today's education. This has taken on more of an industrial orientation. Results are to be produced in as short a time as possible. Corners are cut; this is sanctioned as long as the student finishes his work quickly and leaves school and gets a job. Quality is less important.

Generally educators are looking to corporation managers and businessmen of factory assembly lines to see how things can be accomplished efficiently. Accountability for the producer (i.e., the teacher or the principal who leads the teachers) is what has become important. The teacher is being paid to produce a good product. If the child does not read, something is wrong with the teacher or the method she uses.

The philosophies of some programs obviously deal with the merits of a structured set of experiences with children rather than self-selected choices. Some programs attempt to fill a perceived identified gap in a child's life. Some writers view language deficits, problem-solving techniques, verbal facility, and auditory skills involving discrimination of sounds as areas that need to be improved if a child is to become an effectively functioning human being.

One notes the efforts of educators to help children in cognitive growth. Intellectual development is, after all, considered to be the educational system's *raison d'être*. Yet in the broad attempt to create knowledgeable and competent people with respect to skills, another segment of society is looking for more concern about individual kindnesses, concern for the feelings and problems of others and less concern for skillful behavior. Consideration, unselfishness, cooperation with others, pleasure from seeing someone else succeed after a persistent effort, emphathizing with the stress of another and wanting to help him deal with it—all these attitudes are desired by some educators.

Many educators talk about "humanizing the human being." This refers to helping man become all that he can, using his potential to develop, to create, to enjoy the company of others, to help his fellow man (and woman), to learn to respond emphatically to the feelings of others. It refers to the affective part of the individual, for the most part. To be human applies to feelings and emotions more than it does to the development of one's skills and abilities in the intellectual or academic sense. The academic aspect may be seen more as mechanistic or impersonally prescribed.

Feelings are assumed to be lost in the mechanistic development of certain skills: those of logic, for example; or of objectivity, when one has to be nonsubjective. This is difficult. One must put aside compassion for others, must be objective and prevent his feelings from interfering with a valid judgment. People who become obsessed with perfection or success can behave in a mechanistic manner. They become irritated with themselves and others if efforts toward that achievement subside in any way.

They want others to have the same intensity as they. If children are in a classroom with a teacher of this kind, they often become frightened or ill.

A Bank Street School program is described by Weber who indicates its intent to develop various plans that can in themselves help to maximize the children's learning potential and improve their physical and emotional wellbeing as well.[11] The program is devised to improve the home environment and to develop other means through which volunteers, nurse's aides, parents and other supplementary personnel can be trained.

Differences between philosophies of the past and present entail primarily the degree of the student's involvement. The pupil is less often in a position of hearing correct answers given to him; but more often he is expected to become involved and to obtain results for himself. The trend is one of fewer lecture methods or reading paragraphs from a book and giving only one right answer on a test of some sort. Alternative answers are sought. The student is more responsible for working toward an answer. It places greater initiative with him to learn what he needs to know. It allows him to pace what he is capable of learning with what he is prepared to do next. His own judgment relative to what he has mastered guides him in taking steps.

The single correct answer is not the end-all in learning. Alternative ways of problem-solving are sought, permitting the student to see that life presents many situations and that there are many ways to answer those problematical situations. What is correct for one person or what satisfies one person's needs may not satisfy another's. Creativity, uniqueness, and originality are encouraged. Of course, where spelling or the pronunciation of a word are concerned, or a correct answer for $2 + 2$ is at issue, one may be creative but a correct answer is still essential. This is different from creating a story that describes feelings which are not expected to be "correct" in terms of any framework provided by a discipline. The human being experiences an endless number and variety of emotions. These are not measured in terms of correctness or incorrectness (even though some teachers try to force conformity here too, unfortunately).

Many programs use terms that suggest a holistic approach, helping children to become "happier" people, to become more aware of their environment and their own abilities to relate well to that environment. This means that more time should be spent by children doing things they enjoy. It is usually difficult to challenge a philosophy that emphasizes ways to help people enjoy life and to maximize their own resources. The methods used to operationalize the philosophy (or to produce the professed ends or desires) are not always those with which people agree.

One often hears that the ends justify the means. Some would argue the point. It makes a difference how children learn—whether they are

11 Evelyn Weber, *Early Childhood Education: Perspectives on Change* (Worthington, Ohio: Charles A. Jones Publishing Company, 1970), p. 77.

motivated to learn so that they are pleased now as well as being better able to help themselves later on, or whether they learn only to receive an external reward of candy or whatever, so that they may develop a habit of learning or cooperating only if they gain something immediately tangible from it. Some short-sighted goals selected for expediency are not necessarily the ones that ought to be emphasized. It is true that human beings do things for rewards. We work for money, recognition, prestige. But children need to develop a spirit of achievement in subject-matter skills that puts an intrinsic satisfaction in overcoming challenges above any potential material rewards.

Looking at Table 1.2, one can see at a glance some of the child development levels that educators consider important. Some educators

table 1.2
*Levels of Children's Development
in Relation to
Philosophies of Programs*

Levels of Accomplishment	Content of Accomplishment	Means of Accomplishment
5	Development of an individual who is oriented toward emotionally sound relationships as well as toward intellectual gain	Teacher provides a variety of activities, consciously gears the child to development, academically and emotionally
4	Skills development become major emphasis of accomplishment	Teacher works primarily on the development of skills in children's activities
3	Self-awareness, self-criticism, knowledge of one's strengths and weaknesses, learning ways to counteract personal problems	Teacher helps child in a knowledge of himself, his strengths, weaknesses; helps child verbalize them
2	Concentration on social skills, functioning effectively in interpersonal relationships	Teacher works on social, interpersonal relationships ("consideration of others") with the children
1	Helping the individual to function at least adequately enough to help himself (to be self-supporting)—these are often the major skills of Special Education teachers	Children participate in experiences they enjoy most; self-discipline is not emphasized (in Special Education children learn to function at minimum levels required to caring for their own practical needs)

concentrate on helping children develop or improve skills commensurate with their age, innate abilities, or desires. The notion here is that if children learn to do well in skills, they will be able to help themselves not only at their present stage, but more importantly will be able to earn a living later on. As a result of such competence, they will be able to function effectively as adults and hopefully to become happy individuals. This kind of person is not a drain on society. He will be a contributor. He can become self-fulfilling and develop a sense of self-worth.

Attaining these goals is important to educators. Self-engagement of the pupil in his progress toward these goals is crucial. If the pupil develops the habit of helping himself, discovering his own resources in seeking answers and solving problems, he will continue this process outside of school. He is developing the kind of self-starting qualities that are needed in a competitive society. The willingness to pursue challenges, to create new ones after former ones have been met, the attempt to reach goals, to set them is a continuous process and a satisfying one. Ultimately the individual is able to help others through his ability, understanding, and skills.

Some of the programs referred to here may be found in curriculum guides of school systems throughout the United States. Some are financed by federal funds and matched by funds from local areas in terms of certain proportions designated by the federal program. With the contemporary trends of the period from the 1960's and 70's moving toward the interest in improvement of young children's educational development, several programs have been funded. Their evaluation comes out publicly in certain sources, professional journals, and other library storage techniques such as microfiche and microfilm. Several directories are available in reference sections of libraries: these give information on research done through various funding agencies.

In some cases funding resources will indicate what they would like to see improved in young children's education. They will specify such interests as bilingual education or language development or reading skills. Researchers respond to this interest and in that way a great deal of research and energy are devoted to certain areas of development.

The comprehensive view of some programs, when a specific set of skills do not need to be focused on for purposes of a research program, emphasizes continuous growth, interaction with people and things, materials and processes upon which the child builds meanings relevant to his particular social and intellectual environment (e.g., family, peers, non-family and other adults around him). Many university laboratory schools have done this. They orient themselves toward idealism and attempt to tap every resource in the individual child.

Goals and Objectives of Contemporary Programs for Young Children

The goals and objectives outlined for programs are typically much more specific than philosophical statements. Goals are similar to expected outcomes that the curriculum or program writers anticipate if their plans are followed by the teachers and children for whom they were devised.

The term *program* as it is used here is conceived in the same way that the term *curriculum* has been used thus far, that is, it refers to a specified set of activities designed for the children to experience at school in order to reach certain goals or to make constructive gains, educationally, socially, emotionally, whatever the curriculum or program writers intended these changes to be. A program usually includes a sequence of activities which is based on a specific rationale. Sometimes the activities are interdependent in the sense that one is built on another; one activity depends on the completion of the preceding one, going from simple to complex skills or concepts.

Sometimes, the activities for children are planned so that the children undergo active energy input in one set of experiences and follow that by a passive activity, such as listening to the teacher tell a story, listening to a recording, or watching an educational film. The timing and pacing of activities are related to children's physical characteristics. Sustained quiet activity for any extended period of time is difficult. Thus it is used with consideration.

Curriculum plans include basic directions intended to give impact to what the teacher will concentrate on in helping the children learn. Once the ideas or objectives are stated, the activities are usually drawn from that basic orientation.

Many years ago, courses of studies defined purposes and goals in such a manner that the implementation of those goals was not clear. Purposes were stated in idealistic terms and in abstract contexts. They did not lend themselves easily to the means that could be used to implement the goals, nor were they intended to be precise enough to be operationalized. Everyone would agree that children should appreciate beauty, justice, originality; but teachers were not told how to put those ideas into practice for children's activities. Since the introduction of behavioral objectives, however—with their emphasis on ways in which a child's behavior would be changed after instruction in a specific lesson— objectives have typically become more structured and precise. Courses of studies now include the kinds of objectives that can be interpreted into a lesson that the teacher can use directly with the pupils.

Program designs themselves in their original form usually have lengthy objectives and a description of a rationale. One would have to obtain those original reports to see the ideas in their totality and context. Fortunately several writers have undertaken the large task of either visiting these programs in various parts of the country and/or have reviewed them in some way.[12] One author discusses programs in her book by dividing the book into age groups of the children who were served by the program—that is, the book includes a section on programs for infants and toddlers, a section on programs for children two to five, and one on primary grades' programs.[13] Another book represents a series of papers given at a conference for conceptualizing preschool curricula,[14] and another gives examples of programs to illustrate various types that exist or have existed in the late 1960's and early 1970's.[15]

Depending on how the authors want to present their materials and which ones they want to emphasize, they will devote more time and space to some aspects and will give greater detail on some programs than on others. In one book, a few statements indicate the rationale and objectives of various programs. Following those statements, the program is briefly described and the authors present important underlying assumptions on which the programs are based. One underlying assumption for example, was, "Teaching should be adapted to the needs of the child." [16] It is essential that readers or students learn to recognize what the underlying assumptions are. In some cases, the writers will make those assumptions explicit as was done above. In other cases, however, the assumptions are not stated, but the writer hopes that they are implied. In any case, the student or scholar should look for these "givens" or underlying bases of programs whether they are stated explicitly or not.

Most writers touch on the kind of organization of experiences that teachers usually use or should use with children. This organization sometimes refers in part to the way these activities are scheduled, paced, or timed in the total school day of the child. This pacing or timing may be referred to as structure or organization of the classroom. The teacher's way of presenting materials, and the question of whether all the children should participate in working with them simultaneously is considered an aspect of structure in the classroom.

Some people think of structure as a restrictive kind of function that controls children in a negative sense. Structure as a concept seems to be one of the most misused words in education. Structure actually denotes preplanned activities and their arrangement in the classroom. By planning to have only four children at a table, having four sheets of paper for them to use at that table, and four chairs at that table, the teacher has

---

[12] Robert D. Hess and Doreen J. Croft, *Teachers of Young Children* (Boston: Houghton Mifflin Company, 1972); Weber, op. cit.; Ronald K. Parker, editor, *The Preschool in Action* (Boston: Allyn & Bacon, Inc., 1972).

[13] Weber, op. cit.

[14] Parker, op. cit.

[15] Hess and Croft, op. cit.

[16] Ibid.

"structured" the use of those materials. She has control for the number of children who will be at that table at one time. The children at that table may have the freedom to participate in the work at that table, but the teacher has structured the classroom before the children even reach it.

Structure can be used wisely. It is part of an organizational process. It should not be considered as a term that is synonymous with rigidity or inflexibility. It should not be confused with lack of freedom in the classroom. Teachers can be noting individual needs. Children can be participating in groups involved in a structure of some kind, yet still be part of a "structured" classroom. What is important to observe is whether the children are learning and whether they reflect a businesslike, matter-of-fact attitude about what they are doing. Most important if they are not to appear tense and fearful, the structure of the classroom should be appropriate to their learning activities and an effective way of participating in them.

Programs vary in terms of the emphasis they choose from among the following areas: visual abilities of young children, auditory skills, motor (or perceptual-motor) skills, language development, problem-solving skills. The programs are similar in terms of the manner or treatment given to those various skills in the implementation of any given program. Depending on the researcher or the research trends, and the background and interests of the directors of the program, the study will take on greater depth in some areas than in others.

Language development has been emphasized to a great extent since the beginning of the Head Start program. Research had shown that children from low-income areas need more practice in language skills such as were typically needed in the previous academic context of schools. They already do have communications skills meaning more to their own groups, who use the same phrases, gestures, and words. The kind of language typically used in conversation at home, parties, or at play is not the same needed for academic problem-solving, logic, or precision with mathematical problems and scientific analysis. More writers in the areas of language have been analyzing situation-specific language, formalized-type language, and individualistic expression, finding that systematic or formalized language arises when an individual feels it is appropriate to use. The more choices one has for any given situation, an interpersonal one, a public or less personal situation—e.g., speaking to someone the child does not know—the better it is for the individual in obtaining what he wants. The greater the repertory from which to draw language expressions, the greater it is to the individual's advantage. He is able to "fit" into many kinds of situations and places. He has an ability to "sell" himself and his ideas when he is able to articulate his views in ways that many people (rather than only those he knows) are able to understand.

One program emphasized language in a systematic format for instruction to young children. The program was written giving exact statements for the teacher to use with the children and also the exact statements that she was to use after certain responses were given by the children. She was not to deviate in any way.[17] Some teachers resented having to repeat statements exactly as written. They felt like automatons not needing to use their own ideas. Where many classrooms emphasize the importance of the teacher's decision-making and responses to the child as crucial to effective classroom teaching, this program appeared to ignore the teacher's need to feel human. She needed to feel that she was doing the planning for the children; otherwise she regarded her contribution to children as valueless. Some programs, in their desire to make a "teacher-proof" product constructed inflexibly with no allowance for deviation, err in forgetting that it is human beings who must disseminate the program—not automatically programmed robots having no feelings.

Another program found in the literature involved itself in planning small units of work based on children's interest and designated its objectives in terms of personality characteristics of the children and on children's interests. Cognitive development itself was not specified, as had been the case with some of the others referred to earlier. Among nine brief objectives were "Ability to stick to a task for increasingly long periods," and "positive attitude toward school." [18] These in themselves suggest that the children will learn in an intellectual sense, but the objectives are not operationalized. This permits broader interpretation of a program. It allows teachers to do what they think is needed with a certain group of children. The decision-making strongly rests with the teacher and her observation of their needs during ongoing activities.

In another program using specifically designed lessons that teachers are expected to follow without deviation, the author indicates that the major goal is for the children to function in a cognitively maximum sense, and that language and cognition will constitute the major emphasis throughout the planned activities.[19] The author explains that the purpose of such precisely designed lessons and insistence on such strict adherence to their outlines is to ensure the teacher's grasp of the program's intent. The teacher needs help in understanding the specific methodology underlying the program. The program itself, its author suggests, represents a departure from the kind of work familiar to the teacher.

The rationale of the program assumes that most low-income children are not deficient in sensory functioning nor in cognitive potential, but rather are not functioning as required because of few traditional experi-

[17] Carl Bereiter and Siegfried Engelmann, *Teaching Disadvantaged Children in the Preschool* (Englewood Cliffs, New Jersey: Prentice-Hall, 1966).

[18] Weikert, op. cit., p. 196.

[19] Helen F. Robison, "Rationale for the CHILD Curriculum," in *The Preschool in Action*, edited by Ronald K. Parker (Boston: Allyn & Bacon, Inc., 1972), pp. 301–336.

ences. Other writers have stated this, indicating that the kind of nonschool experiences a child has makes a difference in his cognitive functioning at school and his understanding of what is expected of him in the pupil role.[20]

Robison goes on to say that even though cognitive functioning is emphasized in the CHILD curriculum, it does not intend to convey the idea that this kind of functioning is over-valued. It is done to balance out the de-emphasis on this aspect of functioning "in the models and forms of guidance at home."[21] In other words, the school program represents an attempt to give the child another kind of context that is not present in the child's home.

A rationale for this program is also presented in twelve statements that indicate why certain activities and the organizational format are included in this program. The activities are formed around eight content areas: music, language, mathematics, science, sociology, geography, and economics—and cognitive skills.[22] Within the language area and the cognitive areas are a separate list of goals. The program is definitive and precise, while taking into consideration that children have different requirements depending on their progress through the program. It allows for a variety of pacing and a respect for individual abilities of each child.

Objectives of any program typically proceed from ideas that are based on an understanding of educational psychology of learning, of motivation, of attitude formulation, of ego development, of self-concept or impressions of self-worth and of child development principles. They have an added emphasis on specificity and the need to identify certain desires or behaviors that the child will attain upon exposure to the program. The behavioral objectives attempt to delineate exactly what the children and the teacher will focus on if certain aspects of a skill or concept are to be mastered by pupils. Along with the necessity for specificity in defining a concept or skill in parts and in sequence or organization as well is the added consideration that educators are dealing with human beings, not automatons that can be clicked, pushed, and pulled into becoming the end-product envisioned by the curriculum writers. As far as young children are concerned, it is very necessary to be aware of young, pliable, easily hurt feelings. Neither are they to be intimidated into conforming or complying with the teachers' wishes, nor are they to be teased into it. The teacher has to help the child in wanting to succeed in certain tasks in ways that build a desire to attempt more of them, and also those of greater difficulty. The child begins to *want* to accept a challenge, rather than being forced.

[20] Edythe Margolin, *Sociocultural Elements in Early Childhood Education* (New York: Macmillan Publishing Co., Inc., 1974).
[21] Robison, op. cit., p. 312.
[22] Robison, Ibid.

While cognitive functioning, problem solving, mathematics, language development, and skills in geography are desired, the child's personality development is also of great concern to a teacher of young children. Building positive attitudes toward learning is important because what happens outside the classroom affects the child as well as his self-impressions inside the classroom. If he feels defeated in the classroom, it is highly likely that he will transfer these feelings to situations outside. Inadequacy arouses feelings of self-hatred, unworthiness, aggressiveness either toward others or toward the self, or both. A willingness to ask questions, to solve problems, to persist in a task should also be the teacher's goal for her pupils—not just following specific step-by-step directions.

Classroom behavior in learning and in interpersonal relationships is important in the schooling process, but most educators see this as part of the socialization process. They want the children to benefit from their education when they are outside of school. One of the ultimate purposes of education is geared to helping the child function at upper levels of his capacity and to have his education at school become one of the major contributing forces to his way of life. It should affect the way he earns a living and his financial status, as well as his enjoyment of life that can be gained from an appreciation of skills, arts, sciences, human relationships.

Along the lines of appreciation and enjoyment follows at least one aspect of a framework for the development of a curriculum which involves an awareness of child development principles. How children grow, and what their anxieties, fears, and problems in physical growth are at certain ages and stages of their lives, are important to consider in curriculum development. Teachers who understand children's problems and stages of growth in a physical, psychological, emotional, or social sense seem to enjoy working with children. They empathize with the children's problems, knowing that those problems are a part of growing and difficult to avoid. The mediation of conflicts between parent and child, and between the child and his peers, involves a great deal of decision-making, feelings, and heartbreak. It is the substance of personality. A teacher can be very crucial to a child's development in the process of resolving conflicts and learning from them so that the self is not completely mortified.

The following chapter deals with child development principles, describing the developmental stages of pupils that teachers will learn to know. Hopefully teachers will better understand the children's behavior as human beings as well as pupils trying to learn.

SUBSIDIZATION FOR PROGRAMS

There are various sources for financing programs planned for young children. Many of them come from the federal government, from offices such as Health, Education and Welfare in Washington, D. C. Several sub-agencies within the Office of Education offer monies from experimental programs under various acts that have been granted through Acts of Congress.

There are public funding agencies, the governmental ones just mentioned, and also private organizations such as the Carnegie-Mellon Institute, the Rockefeller Foundations, the Kettering Foundation, and the Russell Sage Foundations.[23] These institutions offer financing of projects and materials; the terms of such funding have to be obtained directly from their offices.

The National Institutes of Health have agencies designated to allocating funds for various research grants or studies qualified people want to undertake. There is a careful screening of applicants who desire to obtain monies from programs of research. Typically the individual who desires research funds applies through an institution with which he is already affiliated. Typically the individual who is associated with a university or research institute of some kind is familiar with research of various types.

Science foundations of various kinds provide financial support for studies in the science areas. By consulting any university library, one can find the sources that supply financial support, along with the conditions for that support. Most of the time, those agencies designate the content of studies that interest them. Emotionally disturbed children—those with learning disabilities for which the proper treatment has not been adequately determined—may be designated for such support.

An individual interested in early childhood education can do a study that is also focused on learning disabilities or the early identification of learning problems. Often, the interest of competence areas of researchers overlap. An individual can find the appropriate agency to subsidize his study through careful searching in the lists of granting agencies or by asking the reference librarians of colleges or universities.

The writer of programs usually has a background in a few disciplines. It may be in education, psychology, sociology, or mathematics, to mention a few. To study children's learning problems presumes a great deal of knowledge and experience—not only working with children but also a knowledge about them in a disciplinary sense. The writers have usually studied children's development in the academic sense. They also know something about the subject matter area needed for instruction at school. If they did not, their description of the proposed research project would reflect an insufficient knowledge of the field to conduct successful research in it.

Writers usually try to control their problem implementation carefully so that their data collection reflects valid and objective procedures. Researchers try to be aware of their own biases toward what they hope

---

[23] See also the directories of agencies or institutions that offer funding support. These are obtainable in most libraries.

to find in the final conclusions of their work. They are aware that their own premature judgments of the problem being studied can influence what they find and how they report their statistics.

The sponsoring agencies—federal, state, local, public or private— change their focus at different times. Their interests often reflect public problems. Social issues that give rise to discontent often become the concentrated concern of several agencies, which try to have qualified professional people study the problem in a scientific context. For this reason, the funding goes to studies on different problems. Researchers who are interested in those problems are fortunate. Their expertise is appreciated by the funding agency. By the same token, the researcher is elated to have his work supported. If a scholar is interested in obtaining funds, he has to look at the most recent directories or resources for publicizing needs for researchers to study current problems. Most problems seem to have about an eight-to-ten-year span of centralized concern of the entire country.

With television and news media bringing immediate problems of the country to the public, the crucial nature of certain issues is intensified. Crime rates, unemployment, ecological problems, civil rights, violations of many kinds from traffic to building codes, to water pollution and the like, male–female relationships either in family settings or public life, sex discrimination in employment—all these problems come to public attention. Certain consequences of that attention upset people's lives. Civic unrest in a country that is based on democratic principles not only upsets government leaders in a way that threatens their own livelihood and welfare but also offends the moral orientation of people who "believe in" the government of the people, by the people, and *for* the people.

Educators are particularly sensitive to moral issues because they are faced with moral orientations every day. They have to sustain and defend a world of "justice" by giving reasons in which not only they themselves can believe but also that they want the children to believe. Working with young children who are fresh to a new life and open to some neutral issues in a sense, the teacher has an excellent opportunity to help children develop optimistic and sensitive attitudes toward their country. At the same time, children can learn about the opportunities their own country can afford for them, the ways they can contribute to it, and the ways in which they can build their own society in a highly constructive manner. For this reason, educators of young children must have valid information and workable solutions to build into the activities and experiences they plan for young children in the classroom. Government offices have several agencies to provide funds for schooling of the young that can help children become optimistic perceivers of their society and to anticipate a productive life in it. The major issues that face those involved in providing children with the best education possible lies more in how to use those funds to best advantage—that is, how to discover the best ways to provide children with the kind of education that can make them "believers" of their own worth in an outstanding society of their own making.

Newsletters of organizations ready to fund certain projects are circulated constantly. Somehow or other the individual who has an exciting project to "sell" in request of funds to implement it is typically able to find a sponsoring agent or agency. The university, college, or institute receives many announcements daily of offers to support research or other experimental projects. It becomes a matter of listening, seeking, and asking about possibilities specifically for the researcher's concerns.

It is true that federal funds (as everything else related to financial matters) have become more restricted, less available in large amounts than was true in the early 1960's. But never in the history of education has the federal government taken so much a part in the provision of nationwide support for education of its schoolchildren. Funds still come from the government and from private philanthropic organizations; they are, however, dispensed in a more competitive manner than they were before.

Looking at the years between the 1960's and early 1970's, one notes how much has happened in a productive sense due to federal assistance. Never have so many materials been available to use with young children to help them in their educational development. Parents too are geared toward thinking of educational toys for their babies. They realize that the young mind has a capacity for learning that will be applied to academic subjects in school when the child becomes older. Counting, saying simple rhymes, singing, and moving to music are all aspects of the curriculum that will be exposed to the child when he goes to school.

The obligation of those who are the recipients of this massive amount of material for young children's activities at school is to examine, to be constructively critical, and not to passively accept what is given to them. Thus, while research projects, funds, materials, and activities are currently thriving, the people working with young children are the crucial testers of the recommended activities. The researchers do not claim—or I would hope not—to have all the answers. Their work needs to be tested. It needs to have the longevity test with many different children. Evaluation of those attempts need to be disseminated at the university level, the elementary school level, and at the researcher's laboratory level, more so than is currently being done.

It is important that people who are unfamiliar with research and reading the findings realize that what is true for some of the subjects or children used in the study is not true for all. Students who are not aware of what is involved in the conduct of research are also not familiar with ways to interpret the findings of a study. Each study has a certain percentage of error, in its implementation, in its statistical calculations, and in the way the statistics are interpreted and related to the actual theoretical implications of hypotheses presented at the beginning of the study. This means that even though certain claims are being made for the success of a given project, there are some subjects (or pupils) for whom the study has not been successful. Students too often assume when they hear about research using some techniques with schoolchildren that a positive report about it indicates total success for everyone in the study. This is rarely true. For this reason, the person studying young children's educational development should look cautiously at research findings. It is wise to examine the study, its description, means of testing findings, and the like. Each person should consider himself critically important in viewing any programs given for use with children.

summary

This chapter has pointed out various philosophies underlying contemporary programs for young children in the United States. Philosophies differ not only in the way they are stated, but in whether they are stated explicitly at the outset of the program. Sometimes the reader is expected to assume a certain philosophy exists after they read the program. Often programs emphasize the desire to help the "whole" child. This typically refers to the child's emotional, social, and physical development as well as his intellectual development. Several programs have been concerned mainly with the child's academic or cognitive growth. In the last 14 years, this has been the major emphasis. Prior to that, the children's development in nursery schools and kindergarten had been articulated as social and academic, but the stress was not as delineated in academic terms or cognitive sequences as it is today.

The tendency in education seems to swing from one end of the spectrum to the other. In one period of American life, adjustment to a group and to other people seemed important (e.g., after World War II in the 1940's). When it became obvious that children from low-income areas were not receiving the appropriate curriculum geared to their abilities and interests, an emphasis on learning to read, an emphasis on cognitive development, was evident in the curriculum for young children in the late 1960's. In the early 1970's, however—and even before that in the late 1960's—an absence of warmth in interpersonal relationships (in part because of what people saw happening with drug abuse and with local and world unrest) has led to a call for humanism in the schools. A concern for conveying academic knowledge coupled with humanistic awareness is the essence of the 1970's. It reminds one again of an emphasis on "getting along" with one's group, an outgrowth of World War II problems. Present-day orientation in education differs in one important sense from the 1940's, however. It differs in terms of the focus—or the locus—of student identification.

The current emphasis on empathy, compassion (not only on the teacher's part but the children's as well), and consideration of other's feelings leads to self-identification for the student. It does not place the group in a superordinate position above the students, who each have a unique identity. The emphasis in contemporary American education is on the needs of the individual, less on what is good for the total group as recommended in curriculum guides of some countries. This also reflects more accurately the principles of democratic foundations found in documents containing American philosophies, historically, and in contemporary popular literature.

Goals and objectives are typically much more specific than philosophies are. Objectives in current education are written so that they specify ways of implementation. They are an outgrowth of the justification or rationale. They indicate the kind of activities that should be used with the child if their program goals are to be achieved.

Students need to examine the objectives side by side with the activities to see whether they do in fact seem to support the objectives. Choices of ways that objectives should be met are important to the heart of education. Some programs show that almost anything is all right to use so long as the children learn. In other words, short-term goals, quick, instantaneous learnings seem to be sanctioned, with little regard for longer-term effects on the child's personality.

The last part of the chapter described sources for gaining financial support for research or experimental programs. Federal subsidization of grants for studying young children's educational development has declined somewhat with the condition of the nation's economy. It never had been as prominent, however, in the financial efforts to improve young children's education as it has been in the last ten years. A strong beginning in the further development of studies for young children has been made. Contemporary workers in education have benefited greatly from this. Even though national priorities may change in terms of where monies will be allocated, people who are currently working with young children can continue to define problems and refine the processes used to improve education generally.

topics for discussion

1. What kind of philosophy would you plan for the underlying orientation of a program for young children if you were given the opportunity and funds to create an outstanding curriculum for children from three to five years old?
2. Interview someone who was part of the inception of Head Start programs, a teacher, a supervisor, or someone who was in the planning process. Ask

that person whether he or she has seen changes in the educational environment from that point to the present. Find out what some of the earlier
purposes of the program were.
3. Visit a program for children, under three, and find out what the objectives
are for them. Observe for one and one-half hours, and note to what extent
the teachers are carrying out the goals of the program as they, the teachers,
interact with the children and adults in the program.
4. What kinds of problems do you see as blocks to an outstanding program for
young children, five and below?
5. What gains might be made by perceiving early childhood education as a
total growth cycle between birth and eight years of age?

selected bibliography

Bereiter, Carl, and Siegfried Engelmann. *Teaching Disadvantaged Children in
the Preschool.* Englewood Cliffs, N. J.: Prentice-Hall, Inc., 1966.

Bernstein, Basil. "Social Class and Linguistic Development: a Theory of Learning," in *Education, Economy and Society.* A. H. Halsey, Jean Floud, and
C. Arnold Anderson, eds. New York: The Free Press, 1961.

Braun, Samuel J., and Esther P. Edwards. *History and Theory of Early Childhood Education.* Worthington, Ohio: Charles A. Jones Publishing Company,
1972.

Froebel, Friedrich. *The Education of Man.* William N. Hailmann trans. New
York: D. Appleton, 1889.

Hess, Robert D., and Doreen J. Croft. *Teachers of Young Children.* Boston:
Houghton Mifflin Company, 1972.

Margolin, Edythe. *Sociocultural Elements in Early Childhood Education.* New
York: Macmillan Publishing Co., Inc., 1974.

McMillan, Margaret. *The Nursery School.* New York: E. P. Dutton and Company, 1921.

Parker, Ronald K., ed. *The Preschool in Action.* Boston: Allyn & Bacon, Inc.,
1972.

Piaget, Jean. *The Language and Thought of the Child.* London: Routledge &
Kegan Paul, 1952.

Robison, Helen F. "Rationale for the CHILD Curriculum," in *The Preschool in
Action,* Ronald K. Parker, ed., pp. 301–336. Boston: Allyn & Bacon, Inc.,
1972.

Weber, Evelyn. *Early Childhood Education: Perspectives on Change.* Worthington, Ohio: Charles A. Jones Publishing Company, 1970.

Weikert, David. "A Traditional Nursery Program Revisited," in *The Preschool
in Action,* Ronald K. Parker, ed., pp. 189–215. Boston: Allyn & Bacon, Inc.,
1972.

Whiteman, Martin, Bert R. Brown, and Martin Deutsch, "Some Effects on Social
Class and Race on Children's Language and Intellectual Abilities," in *The
Disadvantaged Child,* Martin Deutsch and Associates, eds., pp. 319–335.
New York: Basic Books, Inc., 1967.

Chapter
2

Principles of
Child Development:
Their
Implications for
Curriculum Planning

An individual's personality is a dynamic force in relationships with other people. Even though parents affect their children's personality characteristics and the way they respond, children affect their parents' behavior too. Considering the forceful nature of personality development as such and the way it facilitates or inhibits learning at school, it is significant that some teachers of young children are not aware of ways that it develops. Watching some teachers, one can easily see that they are oblivious to the children's nonacademic problems.

This chapter discusses the similarities and differences among infants and young children in the hope that adults working with young children will become more sensitive to the intricacies of natural and learned behavior in the process of personality development. One writer points out the myriad combinations of characteristics in a newborn child, "One particular male from a billion plus in the world mates with one particular female from a billion plus . . . no other combination would produce this particular double source of inheritance." [1]

Of all the possible combinations of constitutional differences in human beings and all the potential combinations of social experiences and family

[1] Gordon W. Allport, *Pattern and Growth in Personality* (New York: Holt, Rinehart and Winston, Inc., 1961), p. 4.

29

backgrounds, it is almost staggering to the mind to conceptualize the ultimate differences in human personality. Not only do constitutional differences create mixtures in types of people, but so does the interaction of those differences as they are affected by social and environmental experiences. The social milieu in every generation's background brings strong influences into the individual's life, giving it a virtual "social era" stamp or imprint that remains for a long time. In some cases, those attitudes never change because they are too strong a part of the personality.

Age Range—Personality Characteristics, Physical and Socioemotional

The age range of classifications used here will coincide with those used by the educational institutions that come in contact with young children from the child's first few years of life in infancy through the primary grades, birth through eight years old. The infancy period will be considered as birth to about two years old; the periods between two to three years old and four to five years old will be treated as the pre- and kindergarten age.

Charts can be obtained in which children are classified in terms of what they can do by certain ages or stages of their development. The problem here is that often those descriptions can be appropriate for children of other ages as well as those indicated in one cell of a chart. For example, to say that a child has a short attention span at a certain age suggests that this is unique to only that age group. This is true of people at any age; it depends on what the person is doing relative to what interests him. He will remain with an activity when he is interested in it. In that sense, a chart description can be misleading. A child of four may have a brief interest span in one kind of activity but much longer in another that appeals to him. So much depends on other factors of personality and predispositions at that time. Caution is needed in the interpretation of behavior relative to any age group.

People working with children at the infant stage, birth to two, are working with them in a different way than those at the other end of the early childhood continuum—i.e., eight-year-olds. Those with children under two are involved in the physical needs of babies. Feeding, bathing, cleaning, resting, exercising arms, legs, playing games with the baby are part of the function of any caregiver in an institution responsible for infants.

Physical differences among babies have been noted by several authors. Some babies are more excitable than others. Some are more passive. Some are easier to please and less irritable than others. In any case, the differences among them are part of their own normal development. Walking

Sarah thinks it is great to be able to drink from a glass at six months old. Physical coordination is not easy at this age, but Sarah masters it well.

or talking later than other babies does not necessarily suggest abnormality. Acquiring teeth later than other babies does not mean that a baby is "backward" in his development. As parents compare babies with those of relatives or friends, they sometimes become overanxious if their own child does not function the same way as others.

From a physical standpoint alone, the growth of the baby is most rapid in the first nine months of life. When one considers that a cell in nine months multiplies itself many times and develops into a human being having all the essentials needed to function properly as a self-contained human system, it is incredible. (Of course there are exceptions to this, as any hospital register will show.) The stages of growth and their rapidity change in different parts of the human cycle, but the physical and its relationship to the mental development of the individual is very impressive for the first few years of life.

INFANCY

Infants typically triple their weight during their first year of life. While growth is rapid, it does not have a stabilizing effect in its progression. The infant responds quickly to cold, heat, and other external conditions. His heart beats faster and his temperature rises quickly. Mothers become somewhat accustomed to that, but it is still alarming.

"The first year of the child's life brings remarkably rapid and extensive growth changes. Body length increases over one-third, and weight almost triples, so that by the age of 1, the average baby is about 28 or 29 inches tall and weighs about 20 pounds."[2] The authors go on to comment on body proportions. The infant's legs are about one-fifth the length they will be as an adult and they grow rapidly in infancy. The face and head develop at a slower rate than the rest of the body. "The total length of the head and face of the 3-month-old fetal infant is about one-third of his total body length; at birth this height is about one-fourth; in adulthood about one-tenth."[3]

Infants' bones are soft in the early stages of life. The bones harden at different rates among people and takes place differently depending on the individual's constitutional makeup. ". . . By the end of the first year most children have developed three of their total (i.e., adult stage) complement of 28 hand and wrist bones."[4] Bone ossification in the skeletal structure refers to the degree to which the hardening of the cartilage has taken place. A child's ossification age and development can be evaluated in terms of standard measures that were acquired by taking the measurements of many other children.[5] A child may be considered fast- or slow-maturing ". . . if his skeletal age is 75 to 85 per cent below or above" other children of his own chronological age.[6]

Muscle development is an important aspect of a child's development. It affects his desire to use the muscles, to move around, to enjoy a generally high level of energy in his activities. The weight and capacity of his muscles at birth are expected to increase about 40 times by the time he reaches adulthood.[7] The more his muscles are used, the more the capacity of them builds up greater strength for future use. They become stronger with greater and more frequent activity.

The child learns a great deal as he moves around his environment. Sensori-motor intelligence is affected by what he learns as he discovers things, people, and events around him. He investigates during his movements by tasting, smelling, feeling, pushing, pulling, squeezing, manipulating objects, toys, or household objects that are safe for him to handle.

[2] Paul Henry Mussen, John Janeway Conger, and Jerome Kagan, *Child Development and Personality* (3rd ed., New York: Harper & Row, 1969), p. 146.

[3] Mussen, Conger, and Kagan, Ibid.

[4] James O. Lugo and Gerald J. Hershey, *Human Development* (New York: Macmillan Publishing Company, 1974), p. 147.

[5] Ibid., p. 351.

[6] Ibid., p. 352.

[7] Elizabeth B. Hurlock, *Child Development* (5th ed., New York: McGraw-Hill Book Company, 1972), p. 114.

One-year-old Sarah reaches out to an exciting world that beckons to her as she takes her "earlier" steps in life.

Not only is the muscle capacity and development of the child influential in his desire to move around but so is his nutritional condition. A child who is adequately fed, given a proper balance of food types with its needed proportion of vitamins, minerals, and liquids will be able to maintain a high, active energy level. It is easy to notice a child who does not have a proper diet. He appears listless, uninterested in those about him, and his skin, hair, and eyes appear dull. Of course, skin and hair are not affected only by nutrition, but by cleanliness as well.

The baby learns a great deal in motor activity during his first year. He learns to sit up, to crawl, to hold objects, to feed himself, to stand holding on periodically to something for support. He begins to walk. He typically walks well as he enters his second year of life. The first few months of his second year, he is usually very busy trying to walk. For a child, walking is one of the most exciting experiences in the first years of life. Moving along on his own power is stimulating; and when he begins to walk, this enterprise occupies much of his time and energy.

Motor development proceeds in an orderly and sequential manner. That is not to say it happens at the same time for every individual.

Generally, however, its direction proceeds from head to foot, cephalo-caudally. The baby sits before he stands; he has to lift his head and hold it erect before he is able to sit. His motor growth also takes a proximodistal direction, from the inner area of his body to the outside. He is able to do things with his hands in a gross, crude manner before he is able to manipulate tiny objects with any evidence of having finer control over his muscles. With more practice, more opportunities, and maturity, a child gains greater control over his movements. Mind-body coordination becomes well attuned.

The baby's teeth begin to erupt by the first half year of his life. This varies of course from infant to infant. Some writers state that this occurs about seven months, on the average.[8] Some say it happens between six to eight months.[9] By the age of three, a child has about 20 baby teeth.[10]

The process of teething in the child is accompanied by pain, disturbed sleep, and general discomfort. People around the child have to be patient

There are so many things to touch and smell. One-year-old Sarah stoops down and breathes in loudly and deeply showing her mother that she is smelling the flowers.

[8] Mussen, Conger, and Kagan, op. cit., p. 148.
[9] Hurlock, op. cit., p. 116
[10] Hurlock, op. cit., p. 116.

Sarah seems to be thinking, "Hy, there, everybody. I'm walking by myself!" The skills involved in learning how to walk at the end of the first year and into the second are incredible. The child gathers greater strength and self-control as she practices and constantly challenges her newly discovered skills.

with him. The baby cannot complain, except to behave in a generally irritable manner, restless, and difficult to pacify.

Strong teeth, habits of cleanliness, and adequate nutrition affect a child's general growth. With adequate care, he is able to withstand some of the offsetting problems of cutting teeth and other processes of normal growth. Warmth, protection from a concerned adult, and continuing emotional support of the child through the discomforts he experiences in those early years of development can do a great deal to promote sound emotional, social, and physical growth.

Reactions to stressful situations for a child occur in different ways. Some may vomit, some may break into a rash, some develop a high fever, and some show a flush of red in the skin. These reactions in early life may remain as symptoms in the individual as he matures into adult life. These visceral tendencies reflect his particular way of responding to tensions of various kinds, physical or mental.

One of the most important ways of responding to others or to stressful situations occurs with the learning of language. Infants developing into early childhood stages begin to realize their power in using certain words. The responses of attention, pleasure, or concern they receive from saying, "Mama" or "Dada" quickly let them know the significance of words.

Language learning is one of the most complex aspects of development in the human being. How it occurs, and when and what the optimal conditions are for its development, have been the focal concern of many writers and researchers. Its crucial importance to the individual's personality development has been emphasized again and again. Values of a society are implicit and explicit in language development. If the child is normal in terms of physical and psychological maturity, he will imitate the language of those around him. Regardless of the culture in which he lives, he hears a language of some sort. He hears it and begins to imitate its sounds. The use of those sounds in words and sentences is, of course, what makes language development as individualistic as it is.

Babbling, crying, and cooing are all forms of language development. The child is expressing something to the outside world. Adults around him interpret it in a certain way. The specific child's emotional states are made familiar to the caregiver by the way the child responds. Grunts, gestures, facial expressions combine to give an overall impression.

One writer indicates that sounds made by the baby in his earliest stages of development are based on sucking or swallowing movements.[11] Another writer points out that major language development, including about half of the major elements in language—i.e., phonemes that make up the vowels and consonants of language formulation, emerge in the first year of life.[12] Babies are doing a great deal of experimenting. They are not aware, of course, that this is what they are actually doing. It is the adults around them who capture meanings in the child's vocalizations and indicate to the baby that he is doing something important in his process of development.

Some adults are self-conscious about talking to a baby. They feel that since a baby cannot understand intellectually what they are saying, it is foolish to speak to one. Babies, however, derive a great deal more than just talk from an adult's conversation. The softness or soothing quality of the voice can calm them; a reassuring quality of the adult's voice can provide a baby with some emotional security. The emotional tone underlying the adult's interaction with a baby is important to his direction of development. Comforting tones to the baby, rather than cacaphonous, harsh, irritating ones encourage feelings of stability.

Singing to the baby, too, can help his language development. The rhythmic sounds expose him to various tones, syllables, pitch, high and

[11] Mollie S. Smart and Russell C. Smart, eds., *Children: Development and Relationships* (New York: Macmillan Publishing Co., Inc., 1967), p. 127.
[12] Mussen, Conger, and Kagan, op. cit., p. 188.

low sounds. His ear will become attuned to a variety of sound levels. He will be able to recognize those sounds if he hears them often and will be able to reproduce them in time.

The baby's memory of sounds, of words that are used with him, the degree to which he is able to remember things and the quickness with which he remembers, are all aspects of his intellectual capacity. Intellectual development occurs in many ways. Children inherit certain levels of abilities as a result of genetic constitution. What happens with their original "endowment" depends on the environment, opportunities to use their capacities for certain skills, and the quality of responsiveness they perceive toward themselves from others.

Problem-solving, adaptability, memory, valid reasoning, judgment are valued factors of intellectual development. Experiences in such activities involving those skills are considered more important than genetic beginnings. Individual perceptions and experiences are currently emphasized in the improvement of intellectual and educational skills. With some exceptions, the notion of a fixed, predetermined level of intelligence or absolute stabilized ceiling limit on intellectual capacity is no longer given credence or support. Relative upper limits or levels of intellectual capacity are sometimes defined after repeated tests, in cases of brain damaged children and others. Typically, however, current research findings recommend an openness in helping all children go beyond apparent low capacity levels.

The kinds of activities the baby engages in during his first year of life represent intellectual functioning. He turns his head at the sound of noise, he plays with his hands, toes, and other parts of his body, he reaches for objects, he differentiates among people and things, and generally indicates that his mind is recording sounds, images, and ideas. Memory traces are taking place. Intelligence can be viewed as a construct, an ability to interact effectively with one's environment, and an ability to change one's ways of behaving when they seem appropriate.

Intellectual development in infancy is studied mainly in terms of performance behavior. In adult life, it becomes more abstract through language; that is, motor activity is less paramount than mental activity. In any case, discussions on the nature and definition of intelligence can be found in several books on psychological development. An example of the controversy about its "fixed" or changing nature can be obtained in Stott and Ball's article [13] and in other books on the topic of intelligence in the human being.

Intellectual development is related to emotional tendencies in the individual. The way an individual perceives life and people's responses

[13] Leland H. Stott and Rachel S. Ball, "Intelligence: a Changing Concept," in *Children: Readings in Behavior and Development*, edited by Ellis D. Evans (New York: Holt, Rinehart and Winston, Inc., 1968), pp. 264–308.

toward him and his behavior affects his emotional attitudes toward people and life in general. This will also become instrumental in an individual's *Weltanschauung*. His evaluation of—and impressions formulated in regard to—the responses of others toward him, and toward what he perceives as restrictions or freedom, greatly influence the positive and negative aspects in his emotional development. This in turn affects his condition of mental health. Whether the attitudes of others toward him seem to him fair or not influences his self-appraisal.

The kind of emotional development that occurs in early childhood continues to influence in later childhood the intellectual and social development of the personality. An infant who is comfortable, who feels he is well loved and well protected from harm, is free to pursue many kinds of activities. He senses that his environment is somewhat safe because the people around him will not permit anything to hurt him. This affects what he will reach out for or what he will try to do. The child who is afraid to reach out to things and people will, of course, experience a deprived or barren environment. This is what we want to avoid. We would like to help children become somewhat reasonable "risk-takers"— that is, to risk having a problem when interacting with the environment or with other people. This somewhat selective—rather than impulsive, non-thinking—risk-taking can result in positive growth. The individual has developed degrees of self-trust in his abilities to meet situations. He has also developed attitudes of trust toward the world.

Feelings are powerful motivators toward activity. They can guide the individual toward constructive learning or away from it. They can influence an individual in the way he relates to others. One of the most difficult problems people face in life is the management of their feelings or emotions. Socialization processes instruct people to control their feelings to the point of not damaging others; yet from babyhood on, the individual is taught to operate in terms of constraint, while at the same time being allowed to express feelings of anger, hostility, and jealousy.

Emotional development is in part a way of keeping feelings in tow while using them in constructive ways. Society, defined through closer interaction with our parents, siblings, teachers, and friends teaches us what we should be ashamed of, feel guilty about, and what we should be angry about; at the same time, there are many characteristics and value achievements that we are expected to strive for as well. The reconciliation between these efforts for approval, and avoidance of shameful behavior occupies a great deal of people's emotional development throughout life. Mental institutions have many inmates who were not able to manage this point of reconciliation. Teachers who work with young children are in an excellent position to help them learn how to manage their emotional conflicts. They are in a relatively prime position to help children learn to assuage feelings of guilt that stem from characteristically human behavior. For example, a child who is envious of a baby sister or who is angry about another child performing better in a task than he, can be helped to realize that these are common human reactions. The way we handle these reactions is different, however, from the way we accept ourselves as being human for experiencing those feelings. To realize that they are human does not mean that we are content to continue to behave in the same way by betraying our anger or dissatisfaction in childish "acting out" mannerisms.

Physical appearance is affected by one's emotional state at any time. "Pleasant emotions improve the child's looks. Curiosity leads to an expression of alertness . . . unpleasant emotions distort the face . . . because people are attracted or repelled by facial expressions, the emotions play an important role in social experiences." [14] This is an important point about emotional tone, its physical manifestation, and how it affects social interaction and appearance. This suggests that a child's opportunities for "equal access" to the enjoyment of life will be affected not only by his intellectual capacities but also by the combined results of his emotional and physiological states. His facial expression and physical mannerisms give clues to others about his expectations for getting what he wants. Slumping, dejection, looking as though one has lost everything, do not transmit expectations of success.

Adults have to be aware of taking their own frustrations out on a child. They have to know themselves well enough to know how to deflect their own hostilities and anger from the children with whom they work. They have to consciously avoid inflicting their irritations toward others on the helpless child in their charge. A sensitive adult can learn ways to prevent a dumping-out of his own feelings on babies—who have not yet learned how to protect themselves from adults who are not fair in their treatment of children.

CURRICULUM RELATIONSHIPS TO AN INFANT'S DEVELOPMENT
IN HIS FIRST YEAR

People working with infants in their first year of life need to be thoroughly familiar with the physical and physiological necessities that contribute to their vitality. The babies' physical needs for comfort, safety, security need to be met as far as feeding, sleeping, and protection from cold and heat are concerned. Their needs for warmth, love, and security are essential to their psychological development, as well as its physical concomitants. A comprehensive view of infant development is needed if the child's well being is to mature.

The way a baby is held when he is fed, the way he is touched and the way he is fondled when he is picked up and held close to sense the warmth

[14] Hurlock, op. cit., p. 185.

of human skin, affect his total development. Institutional studies of babies that are not being separately cared for by individual adults who provide the fondling needed for emotional and affectional development, indicate that these babies are deprived. This is revealed by their responses to people and the expressions in their eyes.

Some babies—reared in institutions that did not adequately provide emotional warmth, adult-infant individualistic interaction, and playfulness with the infant—evinced divergences from babies reared in environments that met those needs. "The institutionalized babies vocalized very little; they showed no cooing, no babbling, and little crying. Moreover, they did not adapt their postures to the arms of an adult . . ." [15] The children were described as feeling to the person who held them more like wooden, stiff dolls than relaxed and adapting.

The deprivation that can result from little practice in babbling and cooing sets a child back in his development not only in speech or language but in the emotional desire to try forms of social interaction which relate people to each other. Institutions that work with infants must have a well-planned schedule for adult-infant individualized interaction through games, talking, singing, and generally giving the infant undivided attention. While it has been difficult to measure the extent of a satisfactory emotional relationship between adult and child,[16] the importance of an affectional relationship supersedes what is done, and the emphasis is more on how it is done and whether the child senses that the person cares about him.

Many references for games that can be used for the stimulation of infants have appeared in literature on infant development.[17] They are excellent resources for people and mothers interacting with babies. They provide helpful and easy suggestions for stimulating responses from infants. Popular books on parent-child interaction give recommendations too for the ways that parents can relate to children. Journals on babies, parent education, and family development include articles of this nature as well.

Child development and childhood as an important period of life have become recognized as crucial to personality development and ultimately one's self-support. More materials are being written on parenthood and home life with children. The same things that are recommended for babies at home in their cribs or play pens can be used in institutions. Mobiles, colorful, washable, durable, non-toxic objects that are safe for the baby

[15] Mussen, Conger, and Kagan, op. cit., p. 230.

[16] Edward Tronick and Patricia Marks Greenfield, *Infant Curriculum* (New York: Media Projects Incorporated, 1973), p. 33.

[17] Ira Gordon, *Baby Learning Through Baby Play: A Parent Guide for the First Two Years* (New York: St. Martin's Press, 1970); also Genevieve Painter, *Infant Education* (San Rafael, California: Dimensions Publishing Co., 1968). See also Judith Levey and Gayle Wykle, *Activities for Babies*, Parent and Child Development Center, 601 North Street, New Orleans, Louisiana 70130 (undated).

to touch, taste, squeeze, bang on, bite, or push are available for the baby at different periods of the day. The toys, however, are not intended to replace adult interaction with the baby. The best place for a toy is at the end of the parent's (or the teacher's) arm, encouraging the baby to respond. There are times, too, that the baby will enjoy playing by himself.

The first year of a baby's life is extremely exciting for him and for the adults watching his progress. From lying in a crib most of the time to learning how to sit and to stand, the baby begins his walking efforts around the end of the first year. The year from one to two marks great development in walking and talking. Adults with children in that year of life need to be active because the child moves around very quickly. The healthy child is curious and wants to explore every nook and cranny he sees, especially those that are forbidden. To him, a piece of broken glass is just as interesting to taste as a soft sponge. He is not aware of the danger in splintered glass. For this reason, the adult with a baby that age finds it difficult to do anything else but watch him during most of his waking and active hours.

FROM ONE TO TWO YEARS OLD

The child from one to two is greatly involved in physical activity. His legs and arms are growing longer and his muscular activity supports greater agility and speed in movement. As the child realizes his own resources, he experiments by trying to walk faster, manipulate more objects in the environment, and move beyond boundaries earlier untested. As the child discovers greater locomotor facility, ". . . practice brings improvement . . . in walking and stair-climbing, coordination improves; waste movements are eliminated; steps become longer, straighter, more rapid." [18]

Muscle development varies among children, as do other aspects of their growth; but typically the muscles are gaining strength and increasing in weight. They grow in length, width, and breadth. This growth influences the child's efforts to use those muscles and to be on the go.

In relation to muscle development, sphincter control is difficult for the child. Toilet training, which involves specific coordination of muscles related to control of the bladder and the bowel, is difficult for the child. The parent can watch for cues in the child's behavior which indicate that the child is ready to excrete. Some children learn control by two-and-one-half; some achieve it by four or five. In any case, after they have achieved control, it does not mean that they will not slip back occasionally. This is normal. It may happen when the child is upset, tired, or ill.

The child is typically eating new foods in his second year of life. With more teeth, he is able to chew easily. New foods cause his digestive tract

[18] Mussen, Conger, and Kagan, op. cit., p. 246.

Eighteen-month-old Beatrice appears upset as she tries to handle all three pups that have wiggled themselves hind-side up and sideways almost outside of her stranglehold grasp. This is no easy strategy for a young child coming to grips with another set of young resisting forces.

to react in unusual ways. Mothers have to watch his behavior and general responses to different foods. His diet still needs to be watched carefully.

The middle of the child's second year of life (about eighteen months) is a kind of peak for him. He is using all the skills he has accumulated thus far. They have come rapidly and well compared to the speed of abilities he will discover later in his childhood. Hopefully his attempts to reach out to that world will be encouraged within the margin of safety.

The development of language, a greater facility in its use, greater vocabulary, greater knowledge of words and more meanings, enlarge a child's world. By asking the child to do simple tasks—such as getting something from the table or to bring an object from one place to another —he is learning to follow directions and becoming familiar with different words and what their actions represent. A child is able to understand more words than he is able to reproduce. By the age of two, a child has a vocabulary of about 250 to 300 words. It is typically in the last few

Beatrice seems relieved as all three puppies have righted themselves and can now breathe with their heads up in the air. This was quite a conquest for an eighteen-month-old child.

months of the second year of life—i.e., about 21 months—that the child acquires many words, if his environmental context yields words and language contacts for him.

Language development accompanies emotional, social, and intellectual development. A child's facility with language, and his judgment of the way people respond to him in terms of the words or sentences he uses and the meaning he attempts to attach to them, influence his self-concept, emotional stability, and intellectual development. Even though these aspects of a child's development are discussed separately, they are by no means separate in the way they develop. It is a complicated process, intricate and subtly interrelated.

Intellectual development involves a capacity for and an understanding of skills and concepts needed for reasoning, for problem-solving, number, spatial relationships. Children having interested and responsive adults around them have a better chance of learning certain skills. Adults who like to play with babies, teaching them various games such as pat-a-cake, peek-a-boo, rolling a ball to them and asking them to roll it back, are familiarizing the babies with meanings in language, and providing forms of social exchange needed for healthy development. This does not mean that a child who does not have an adult of this kind around him will not develop in healthy ways. It suggests that a child in that context will have a greater chance for a good start in his patterns of interaction with others and his temperament if such types continue in contact with him.

The child in his second year of life begins to differentiate himself from the environment, realizing that certain requests from others will not always be granted. He expects to have what he wants, however, most of the time. He is not as ready to submit to others either. "The one-and-a-half to two-year-old is considerably more likely to refuse a request than he was when younger or than he will be when he is older." [19] His developing sense of autonomy seems to contribute to this kind of behavior.

A child who has developed well in the 10- to 18-month-old period has acquired a strong start for the foundations of competence. "The one-year-old is poised for fundamental development in social and language development as well . . . increasingly the child seems to assimilate ideas of who he is." [20] In general then the infant developing in his second year of life is acquiring many characteristics of further growth, so that by the time he reaches his second birthday he is ready to take advantage of everything his environment can afford for his further gain. His sense of autonomy, broader areas of locomotion coverage, and his wish to assert himself give the people around him a fairly clear impression of his "intentions" or goals. He is not as much of a mystery as he was in the first year of life.

CURRICULUM RELATIONSHIPS TO A CHILD'S DEVELOPMENT
IN HIS FIRST TO SECOND YEAR

With the knowledge that the child between one and two years old is active, is beginning to talk well, enjoys walking around from place to place, widening his horizons beyond the crib and the highchair, people who work with him need to adapt to the kind of toys, activities and relationships with him that can enrich his development.

It is a joy to work with babies who are involved with life. They are busy testing their own strength and abilities not only in relation to their control over materials but over people as well. In the sense of autonomy and control, children in their second year of life, from 12 to 24 months, enjoy pull-toys. They love to push their own vehicles. They enjoy pushing

[19] Burton L. White, Jean Carew Watts with Itty Chan Barnett, Barbara Taylor Kaban, Janice Rosen Marmor, and Bernice Broyde Shapiro, *Experience and Environment*, Vol. 1 (Englewood Cliffs, N. J.: Prentice-Hall, 1973), p. 235.
[20] Ibid.

their own toys around. The more pliable their dolls are, the better—the easier to do with them what the child wishes. The toy moves easily under the child's grasp, is resilient, and nonresistant to manipulation and squeezing.

Toys need to be safely constructed, because children can pull them apart easily. They may not mean to be rough with them, but their unawareness of cause and consequence—i.e., of what happens when a certain stroke is taken with a toy or doll—results in many accidents. Children have difficulty controlling their muscles, making them less tense or more gentle at any time. For this reason, problems arise when the child in his unawareness of his own muscle strength breaks toys. Parents need to understand that one of the most difficult aspects in a child's development is to discover his own power in muscle control.

A child enjoys playing with a wooden hammer and peg set. This will help him develop hand–eye coordination. He enjoys holding things and throwing them to someone ready to catch them; bean bags, medium-size balls, and stuffed objects are fun to throw to an encouraging adult.

Nesting blocks are fun to place inside each other. Some sensitivity for size, shape, and capacity begins to develop. Hollow wooden dolls that fit inside the other, each a size smaller, are fascinating to manipulate.

The child should be allowed to try to feed himself, dress himself, and to help in any kind of practical function that he is inclined to do. Efforts toward self-help—even though not performed to perfection or quickly—should not be discouraged. The child should be helped in every way to value his own efforts and to learn how capable and bright he is, especially when he initiates the action. Initiative, motivation to try his abilities at tasks or games (except when they are not safe for one reason or another), and curiosity toward learning how to do something within his limits, should be urged, facilitated, and enhanced.

Social interaction is encouraged by game playing, enjoying a happy atmosphere by smiling, mimicking, or mocking in a fun-like manner with the child. The adult who enjoys this kind of play with the child is helping him learn how to respond socially to others. The tempo of happiness and pleasure that is generated by such playfulness can contribute to the child's development of such characteristics. Social responsiveness is partly related to intelligence, to perceptiveness on the part of the child, and a readiness to respond to adults and others around him. Recommendations for games to be used with children to arouse their interest in responding can be found in several resources involved in day care [21] or child development centers as well as in other books mentioned earlier.

---

[21] An example of this would be found in Vol. 2 of *Day Care Serving Infants* (Washington, D.C.: U. S. Department of Health, Education, and Welfare, HEW Pubication No. (OCD) 72-8) n.d., p. 63; see also the appendix of that publication.

FROM TWO TO THREE YEARS OLD

The child's physical build at age two is a predictor in part as to the kind of build he will have later as he matures. "Children tend to maintain their relative standing in height and weight during the preschool period. Those who are tall and heavy for their age at 2 years are likely to be tall and heavy, compared with other 5-year-olds, when they are 5." [22] By the age of two, boys generally weigh about 23 to 35 pounds and their height is in the range of 32 to 37 inches.[23] Some writers suggest that a boy's height at age two is half of what his height is to become as an adult and that a girl's height at two is slightly more than half of the height she will reach by the time she is an adult. The first doubling of height occurs in four years and in 16 years the final height is evident.[24]

At the age of two, the child has a protruding abdomen, even though more muscle tissue is developing—rather than fat as in the infant stage. The head is larger than the trunk and legs in terms of its proportional development later. By the age of three, the child's brain is about 75 per cent the weight it will be at the adult stage of life.

Motor control between ages two and three steadily increases. Since the child's muscles have become stronger and since he has been exercising those muscles in various ways of testing himself, he is able to do many activities that involve muscular control. "The 2-year-old, to whom walking steadily, running, and climbing are thrilling achievements, advances through walking tiptoe, hopping, jumping, tricycling, agile climbing, and stunting to the graceful age of 5." [25]

In many cases, boys are more muscular than girls; but this varies from individual to individual. Boys have greater muscle tissue than fat, unlike the girls. This appears to have a relationship to motor control. Some boys show greater competence in motor control than do girls.

The child between two and three can perform many tasks, such as turning doorknobs, unscrewing tops of containers, putting on shoes and socks, or managing a pencil and crayon. These activities represent greater muscle control, involving finer muscles. Hand–mind coordination develops with facility in this age range. The more the child discovers he is able to do, the more he wants to do.

By the age of two-and-one-half to three, the child has all of his temporary teeth, 20 in all. This, of course, affects his speech, the kind of food he can eat, and his facial expression and appearance. His temporary teeth

[22] Mussen, Conger, and Kagan, op. cit., p. 282.

[23] Smart and Smart, *Children: Development and Relationships,* pp. 98–100.

[24] Mollie S. Smart and Russell C. Smart, eds., *Preschool Children: Development and Relationships* (New York: Macmillan Publishing Co., Inc., 1973), p. 7.

[25] Smart and Smart, *Preschool Children,* p. 27.

will begin to fall out and be replaced by his permanent ones two or three years later, when he is about five.

At the age of two, the child is forming simple sentences. The sentences may contain a verb and a noun, along with the child's expression showing what he means. Between two and three, the child accumulates an additional 600 words. Since the nation became aware of the importance of language development in the child, many studies have been done to investigate its development in children from birth through their school years. For detailed information on the acquisition of language, there are many studies that can be consulted which were done between the 1950's and the 1970's. The factors that affect an individual's rate of language development—physical, emotional, social, and intellectual—are treated in careful detail. Never has the professional literature dealt so specifically with this area of development in a child's life.

The use of language affects a child's intellectual development and the way he will interact with people. In that sense, it affects his emotional and social development. Language—and the use of it—is an extremely important human tool. Language is connected with memory, perception, insight, and cognitive development. The child's interpretation of the world around him—of the people and their reaction toward his behavior—is fed to his brain through language that he utilizes in the explanation. His inner self becomes as much, or even more, a reality to him than the external world. His reactions to experiences are reactions based on the *meanings* he derives from those experiences with others or with things. Thus, his inner reality is greatly dependent on the way he perceives meaning from the environment.

Language is very much affected by the culture in which a child grows up. Besides the fundamental linguistic differences in given words for given objects (e.g., the French word *chien* or the Spanish word *perro* as distinguished from the English word *dog*), cultural attitudes toward the concept affect the general usage. Slang expressions and off-color or sexual connotations affect a child's attitudes toward words. The syntax of a language affects a child's language development differently from one country to another. Understandably, this causes problems when a child has learned one language in one country before five and is then compelled to learn a second language in a new country. Learning that an adjective must precede the noun as required by one language can interfere with learning that the adjective follows the noun in another language.

The child learns of which experiences he is expected to be ashamed. The culture, through the family, siblings, and peers, is transmitted to the child through the socialization processes or general interaction with the child. These processes are greatly dependent on language. The language introduces meaning. The individual soon learns that the meaning of experiences can be described in relative terms. His vocabulary becomes larger and his choice of word usage becomes more selective.

Between two and four years old, the child constructs thought in a somewhat symbolic sense. Much of what he has learned prior to two years was acquired through action: sensori-motor activity provided intellectual schema for the child. This action upon objects in his physical environment yielded information for him on the characteristics of the surrounding world. Between two and three, he is in what Piaget terms the preconceptual or preoperational stage. In this stage of development, a child is able to conceive ideas in relation to words. He does not need to *act upon* objects in order to know something about them. He is familiar with them in terms of their appearance: he recognizes their size, shape, or texture, and he begins to know whether they are pliable, hard, or bristly.

He cannot determine relationships of objects to each other and how they can affect each other or how their appearance can change if they are placed next to each other; this involves reasoning (or operational thought). Piaget terms this stage between two and four years old the preconceptual part of the preoperational stage. The child is formulating concepts about objects as they appear to him, but he cannot in his mind mentally change certain aspects of them. A blue block is always blue to him. Later in his development, he realizes that a blue block has other properties: stiffness, for instance, or size as compared to adjacent objects. It can appear dark blue if it is placed next to a lighter blue block. In short, an object assumes many properties when relationships to other objects are introduced.

The child also finds it difficult to take the point of view of another person when he has already decided to see something in a certain way. "To think egocentrically means on the one hand that one does not adapt oneself to the sayings nor to the viewpoints of other people, but brings everything back to oneself, and on the other hand, that one takes one's immediate perception as something absolute...." [26] It becomes easier to understand why a child between two and three has a difficult time trying to adapt to another person's point of view. What appears as obstinacy is a reflection of the nature of thought and its development in a child of that age.

CURRICULUM RELATIONSHIPS TO THE CHILD'S DEVELOPMENT
FROM TWO TO THREE YEARS OLD

The child from two to three years old—in his desire to move around and to try this hand–eye coordination—enjoys running, playing with balls, rolling and throwing them to someone, sensing his ability to deal with it. He loves to crawl through tunnels made of two large chairs placed upside

[26] Jean Piaget, *Judgment and Reasoning in the Child* translated by Marjorie Warden (Paterson, N. J.: Littlefield, Adams & Co., 1959), p. 136.

down; to crawl under two people forming a bridge with their arms; to swing; and to slide down a smooth ramp or slide. He can learn to ride a tricycle. He can walk a broad plank. He enjoys the development of a sense of balance. With all these activities, an adult notes his comfort or readiness to participate. The child is not forced. If he hesitates, the adults wait until he is ready and involve the child in many other activities that do not arouse anxiety and tension.

Adults who are doing something for children can talk to them while doing it. The teacher may say, "I am getting this ready for you so that you will be able to paint soon." This helps the child in understanding and hearing simple interactional techniques. The teacher is a model in the sense that she provides a language "auditory" model. The child will imitate her speech forms.

Directions are not difficult for the child his age to follow as long as they are given clearly, simply, and without pressure. As long as the child is aware that the adult wants him to cooperate and is patient with him, he will enjoy the relationship as well as the activity.

The child at this age is able to do several kinds of art activities. Finger paint is pleasurable for most children unless they have been advised by their parents "not to get messy." If parents are aware however of the beneficial effects of hand-eye coordination, perceptual-motor development, and explorations with color and paints, they will cooperate with teachers and encourage their children to become involved in many activities at school. Most of the materials used with children are water-soluble, non-irritating, and non-toxic. Teachers must see that materials are safe for children.

If children indicate by their nervousness and anxiety that they do not want to participate in certain activities, messy or otherwise, the teacher does not force them. They are simply led to another activity. Sometimes a child likes to watch another child do what he himself avoids. At a later date, the classmate may bring him to one of the activities that are new to him, and he may want to participate as long as his friend is with him. Teachers have often asked one child if he wanted to join his friend in a certain activity and in this way succeeded in involving the child in a new experience.

The child needs help in understanding his outbursts and sudden change of mood. When he becomes angry, the teacher tries to find out why, then proceeds to offer an explanation. "Perhaps you are angry that John took the shovel from you without asking. I don't blame you. I would be angry too if someone did that to me. Let's go tell John you are angry and that you will let him have the shovel after you are finished with it."

Children need help in verbalizing their feelings. They should not be made to feel guilty or wrong when they do become upset. They are human and have justifiable reasons for being angry. A sensitive teacher can help a child learn how to manage his feelings by explaining them to him. This relieves the guilt and also provides the child with constructive ways to solve problems.

In this regard, puppets that children can make from paper bags and puppets the teachers use for storytelling with children can help them with problems they encounter at play with other children. The puppets become the characters of stories that help children work out elementary conflicts. Children remember the solutions used in stories. Books in general are an excellent source providing information and social interaction, and a habit-forming medium that can serve the child well in the future too. It would not be wise, however, to overdo any one medium to the extent of preventing a child from participating in physical experiences which can also contribute to his reservoir of knowledge, sensory and intellectual. Such experiences can include walks in a park (the woods if available) and a visit to a zoo. These give the child first-hand experiences which contribute to a broader view of life, people, animals, and nature.

FROM THREE TO FOUR YEARS OLD

While the child's growth at this age is not as rapid as it was in the first couple of years of his life, it continues in an obvious manner. It is noticeable. The legs seem to grow longer in relation to the trunk of the body. The head has slowed down its growth rate except for the lower facial part and in general the child's appearance changes almost from month to month. He is able to do many more physical activities than he did when he was younger. His extremities seem to accommodate more of his desires to engage in vigorous activity and play either by himself or with others.

By this age the child's brain is about 75 per cent of its weight at the adult stage of life. Even though the brain weight does not increase as rapidly as other aspects of the child's growth, there is still a great deal of cortical activity occurring.

The child's skeletal structure is not yet as strong as an adult's. The low density of muscle, high presence of cartilage, and loose attachment of muscles and ligaments to the skeletal structure signify that infection or undue pressures in his body can do damage. While the child is not a hot house specimen, he cannot be treated as though his physical being is hardy beyond the point of withstanding undue pushing, pulling by the arm or the hand, or other unusual stressful action by others.

The child in this age range is subject to infection in the ear and throat. The Eustachian tube that extends from the ear to the throat is straighter and wider than it is in adults. Children are highly subject to earaches in their early childhood years.

Children in the three-to-four age range can vary in weight as much as 13 to 16 pounds. Boys are usually more muscular than girls, but there are always divergences. From three to four, boys may show a weight gain of about three to five pounds; girls may gain from four to seven pounds. Height gains of three to four inches can be made by both boys or girls in this year from three to four.

The child in this period of development can perform many gross motor and fine muscle coordinating tasks. He is able to balance more blocks on top of each other than he could before; he can do more of a controlled type of scribbling pattern with crayon or pencil. He can balance himself on one foot for a few seconds. His motor control is becoming specialized and focused.

Hand–eye coordination improves, preference for greater use of one hand than the other in performing various tasks becomes more obvious. Children at this age seem to have more sensitivity to how their performance compares with that of their age mates. They are becoming aware of the behavior of other children with whom they play and interact. They are able to notice the way others respond to them as they perform various activities and tasks. They know when others are pleased with what they are doing and when they are not. They are proud of their own skills.

It is important to the child's intellectual development that he be encouraged to speak, to formulate ideas, to express his feelings, and to establish that what he says and does are important to the people around him. Success begets success. The knowledge that what he does is valued will stimulate the desire to try many activities, even those that involve risk-taking.

The child's development of mental images increases, and he is able to do some types of imaginary play. He can pretend he is driving a truck by using a block, a rock, or nothing at all. He can pretend he is eating when he does not have any food available: his imagination supplies the substance of play. Imagination used in play is the same source used for the creation of impressive ideas for painting, story-writing, and vivid self-expression.

Symbolic thinking is evident when the child acts out roles of people he knows. When he takes their roles, he is identifying with their feelings and he begins to act out what he thinks are their intentions.

As children talk to objects in their environment, they develop facility in language. Choosing appropriate words for given concepts show how they view reality. They are testing an internal reality with an external one, using objects of that externality. This may serve to clarify impressions for them. It can also stimulate new ideas.

Children can be helped in learning how to formulate abstract thought —in other words, to learn how to make language work for them. At the same time, their own practice with words and ideas should not be considered unimportant. To assist in developing children's abilities to think and express themselves effectively, educators have experimented with tutorial programs.[27] In one such program, about 15–20 minutes a day, five days a week, children were tutored in ways that were expected to produce categoristic thinking and cause-and-effect reasoning. The subjects were between the ages of three years and three months to four years and seven months. The program was given for a period of four months. Such a program would have to be tried with a larger number of subjects in order to validate the findings, but the researchers indicate that they found changes in the children which reflected the success of the tutorial plan.

Intellectual development in young children occurs in many ways. It occurs in a sensory dimension—that is, children learn from how things feel, how they appear, how they smell, and how they can be manipulated. It is also true that they need a framework from which to develop and apply thought processes. They need to learn which words apply to which objects, events, and actions. They need to remember these associations as they add to their intellectual schema. An interested adult reinforces correct language and the correct usage of given words when applied as they should be. An interested and sensitive adult, however, also knows how to feed the spiritual of the child—the "free spirit" that permits the child to create silly words and imagine playful themes that represent inner thought.

CURRICULUM RELATIONSHIPS TO THE CHILD'S DEVELOPMENT
FROM THREE TO FOUR YEARS OLD

With the realization that three-to-four-year-old children have acquired greater facility than they had in their third year of life—i.e., from two to three—it becomes an educator's responsibility to help the child obtain as much from those skills as possible. The equipment is available; the art, music, and physical materials are normally found in institutions planned for children. As is true of most kinds of equipment, their advantages depend mainly on the way adults and children choose to use them.

Children are expected to participate often in using equipment, books, puzzles, games, dress-up clothing, in record-playing, singing games, listening to poetry, and telling stories. Since the recognition has been relatively recent in educational history, that little children have intellectual capacities which must be used, children's participation in learning experiences is emphasized more seriously than ever. Children are not to sit passively and listen to the teacher. Instead, they are to be given materials requiring active participation and involvement. The child works with clay,

[27] Marion Blank and Frances Solomon, "A Tutorial Language Program to Develop Abstract Thinking in Socially Disadvantaged Preschool Children," in *Intellectual Development*, edited by Pauline S. Sears (New York: John Wiley & Sons, Inc., 1971), pp. 453–464.

for example, and creates his own product. It is not the adult who does it *for* him or demonstrates step by step how his product should be made.

The child is not like an adult taking an art course who may be interested in learning various techniques for using different materials or media. At this early stage of the child's "educational career," he needs to be given many opportunities to experiment and to find his own way, as long as he does not appear to be frustrated unnecessarily in the process. He needs to know success in working with materials. That success will depend largely on the way the teacher initiates activities for him and the way she responds to him during and at the end of his involvement.

Children at this stage of development have greater facility in language, vocabulary, and the use of sentences, as well as the capacity to enjoy books, puppets, stories, and records. They can be depended upon to follow through when they are asked to respond at certain parts of the story, consequently showing their degree of attentiveness. They clap at a certain word in the story, jump up when the character in the story jumps up. They are no longer infantile in their behavior.

A child at this age should be active, enthusiastic, and able to carry simple directions through to their conclusions. The more he is encouraged to do, the more he will want to do. Teachers should take advantage of the child's desire to be helpful and cooperative and give him every opportunity to find out how much he and his ability can be trusted. Since most children model their behavior by observing adults around them and want to be considered "grown-up," it is most important that they be treated as though they are on their best behavior and performing in a maximum sense.

The teachers often have to help children enrich their experiences by asking purposeful questions. She asks what will be needed for a certain activity the children are planning. One writer gives an example of the teacher catching the child's idea of having a birthday party. After the child told her friends that they ought to have one (in a play situation), the others simply sat. The teacher said that she would like to be at the birthday party too. She asked where she should sit. This initiated more ideas, action, and continued play responses from the children.[28]

Various writers indicate what they consider a critical period in the child's development. Some suggest that it happens at the end of the first year and the beginning of the second, ". . . We have suggested that the 10- to 18-month period of life is in effect a critical period for the development of foundations of competence."[29] The implication is expressed too for the role taken by the child's caregiver and how crucial it is to the

[28] Sylvia Krown, *Threes and Fours Go to School* (Englewood Cliffs, N. J.: Prentice-Hall, Inc., 1974), p. 94.
[29] White and Watts, op. cit., p. 245.

child's foundational development of competence. Some indicate that since the brain has developed about 50 per cent of its total mental capacity by about age four and another 30 per cent by the age of eight, this period of early childhood is critical.[30] No studies have been made, however, to investigate the possibility that more than 20 per cent of one's intellectual capacity may develop after the age of eight.

Despite the fact that brain weight and capacity for mental development can be assessed to an extent by the time a child is four years old, it is important to remember that the number of social roles a child will have to learn is at this point only ten per cent or less.[31] The qualities of personal interaction that the child will yet have to know by the time he is twenty-five represent a challenge to anyone's capacity. Learning social roles involves sensitivity to the way others respond to the individual. It involves emotional assessments both of oneself and the other person(s). It involves greater strain on intellectual and emotional capacities when the individual is doing for the first time something very important to him and is not aware of how he is expected to act.

To be concerned about formalized intellectual activity for young children at school is one part of the problem of educational development. It is also a problem to know how to help them learn to value themselves as people with competence. Since emotions are strongly tied up with the development of attitudes, they are diffuse and difficult to identify at times, especially with young children. The teacher has to be sensitive to the way the child responds to formalized types of learning.

One writer indicates that it is extremely important to help children learn how to be self-starters in their own development.[32] Children have to expect their success as they start any endeavor and have to enter into those activities with that expectation. People who believe that they will succeed do so to a great extent. This belief must be built on some kind of repertoire of experiences. A skillful teacher and a sensitive one can "make a child look good" to himself (which is most important) and to the child's peers as well. It seems fair to say, therefore, that despite the attempt of researchers to identify critical periods of development in a child's life, it is safer to consider all interaction with children critical whenever people come in contact with them for educational purposes or otherwise. An adult has to be ever aware, ever sensitive, and ever knowledgeable about child development and the way it affects a child's emotional and intellectual development. Not to expect too much or too little from a child but to be

[30] Benjamin S. Bloom, *Stability and Change in Human Characteristics* (New York: John Wiley & Sons, Inc., 1964).

[31] Edythe Margolin, *Sociocultural Elements in Early Childhood Education* (New York: Macmillan Publishing Company, Inc., 1974), pp. 39–49.

[32] Jerome Bruner, "Discussion: Infant Education As Viewed by a Psychologist," in *Education of the Infant and Young Child,* edited by Victor H. Denenberg (New York: and London Academic Press, Inc., 1970), p. 115.

supportive at all times, with a variety of equipment and materials for him, can ensure a more positive self-concept for the child and a better conscience on the part of the teacher.

FROM FOUR TO FIVE YEARS OLD

The healthy four-to-five year old is interested in a wide variety of objects, materials, events, and people. He has the physical structure and the build to help himself to a great amount of information. With an active, viable sense of curiosity, he is probing, poking, pushing, and pulling things around. Physical facility is evident as well as intellectual. He typically likes to talk to people and is sociable. His peers are interesting to him, but an adult who manifests responsiveness is equally interesting.

The extremities of the four-to-five year old have developed more than they did in the year before, but soon they will appear to be proportionate to the trunk of the child. Bone replaces the cartilage more and more in the child's skeletal structure, and the bones become harder while their size and number increase.[33] Up to the age of four, the growth of the muscular system is proportional to the body, but after that the muscles develop about 75 per cent so that growth capacity is related to muscle more than it is to weight gain.

Motor skills have been well-developed by the time a child is in the four-to-five year stage of life. Remembering that children vary, one notes that their skills differ in agility, adeptness at performance, and degree of self-confidence. If most of their constitutional endowments have been used to advantage and if they were properly nurtured by those around them, they have generally learned to control many things rather easily.

They run and skip. They pedal a tricycle and they throw a ball a fairly good distance, depending on how much practice they have had. They usually enjoy climbing ladders, jungle gyms, low ledges. They like swings, scooters, and most small vehicles that they can propel, pedal, push, and climb, thereby having active control over their environment.

The child at this age is busily involved in large muscle activity as well as small. He dresses himself, can button, tie, and master small objects fairly well. He can feed himself, and arrange things on a table. Even though their eyes seem at a "far-sighted stage," they manage to do many things accurately. It is however sometimes difficult for them to focus close-up at something and to be expected to differentiate in distinctive ways the differences between small objects.

Many children by the age of five can use about 2500 words; some use more, some less. But generally they are managing language quite well. They enjoy listening to stories and speaking. Most children want to express themselves and are well-equipped to do so. They are reticent

[33] Mussen, Conger, and Kagan, op. cit., p. 283.

mainly when depressed or constrained by elements in the situation that inhibit individual expression.

Four-year-olds can imitate adult behavior successfully. Their perceptions have sharpened considerably; and as they try to imitate their parents' or sibling's behavior in doing ordinary household chores, they are able to complete them in adequate form. They may not always know what to expect in a certain situation—e.g., turning on the garden hose when the nozzle is pointing in their direction not knowng the water will come in their direction. But generally, they can discern how certain simple chores are done if they have had several opportunities to watch them being executed. Their memories have improved so that they are able to recall step-by-step processes in activities, without necessarily knowing why these steps need to be taken. That kind of understanding will develop later.

The child up to the age of four is in the preconceptual stage of the broader preoperational (or prereasoning) stage, according to Piaget. The child has been viewing objects and their nature in terms of the way they appear to him in color, shape, form, or characteristics of pliability. Beginning at this age, from four to about seven or eight, the child shows an intuitive kind of thinking. He appears to imitate adult behavior and in that process appears to understand why he performs certain tasks. When a child indicates his right arm or left one when asked, it does not mean that he understands the broader concept of right- or left-sidedness. It means that he remembers a specific aspect in learning. It is easy for adults to assume that the child truly understands the broader conceptual basis for his answers, even though he does not. Since he is able to see the world mainly from one point of view—his own—he is still not able to de-center his thought sufficiently to conceive of his own language expression from someone else's point of view.

The child uses words that often give the impression he has depth in the knowledge of a given concept. He knows the referents to ideas but does not understand their deeper meanings and the way they relate to a total conceptual system of language, symbols, and ideas in one's culture. Knowing the names of things and actions in relation to them is an important part of understanding the way things work and the kind of systematic framework that one's culture has devised. This knowledge develops through the years. It acquires differentiated meaning for each individual as he matures. It affects interaction with others; it creates a symbolic world of feeling too. Knowledge of names, however, is only part of intellectual development. Yet teachers often read into the child's use of a word their own depth of knowledge regarding its meaning.

It is difficult for a child this age to explain why he did something and how he did it. Sequential thought is difficult for him to reconstruct as it may have occurred to him. He is still not able to view the process objectively—that is, perceiving his own behavior or thought processes outside of himself. He finds it difficult to adapt his answers to the framing of someone else's questions. This is why many of the things he says seem characteristic of *non-sequiturs*.

Children in this age group have begun kindergarten. Typically, they do in the latter part of their fourth year. They have begun an active peer association in the process of school. This can be an exciting and pleasant experience for those who enjoy being with others and who have had experiences at home which contributed to feelings of security. They learn an enormous amount of information about things, people, and non-home environment events. What is important to their social and emotional growth, however, is the way they combine the information and the ways in which it becomes a part of their personalities.

As long as they are in an active environment in the sense that it is planned for their participation in experiences that engender growth, stimulation for their cognitive development will result. Their motor development and perceptual processes will increase in capacity and complexity. The growth of logical thinking is not as obvious, however, as other kinds of motor activities.

The children learn songs and simple dances easily; patterns of repetition greatly facilitate this. Their willingness to participate in different activities encourages the teacher, who wants to create more of them so that the children will have more variety each day. Spontaneity and novelty give vitality to the curriculum; this can increase children's retention of learning as well.

CURRICULUM RELATIONSHIPS TO THE CHILD'S DEVELOPMENT
FROM FOUR TO FIVE YEARS OLD

Knowing that children in the four-to-five-year-old period of life undergo steady growth of the arms and legs suggests that they enjoy physical activity involving large muscles. They can run, jump, hop, throw large balls, bean bags, and move large boxes and blocks. They need equipment that will challenge those abilities and skills in muscle development. Since they are young, they cannot withstand too much physical activity for an extended period of time. They tire after exerting activities. However, teachers who know young children provide a cycle of active, passive, productive, listening experiences in the school day. A balance of activities is one of the elements required of children's programs. This is an important part of the teacher's role—knowing not only how to plan and select the best activities but also how to sense what the children need at different times. It requires knowledge of children's growth patterns and a sensitivity to what children's behavior seems to say.

Children enjoy stories. Beautifully illustrated books which enhance the content of the stories promote the pleasure of language and an ever-growing vocabulary. Pictures are used to stimulate responses from children. Teachers ask the children questions about the pictures relative to what she wants them to study. If the teacher plans a lesson on the ocean, she asks questions not only about the ocean in the picture but also what they think of that goes beyond it: questions about the color of the ocean during the day, at night, when the sun is out, and when it is cloudy; this elicits the subject of the reflection of the atmosphere and the changeability of a body of water. Children talk about trips to the beach, watching tiny insects crawling in the sand and the like. This reinforces their imagery, ideas, of smells, and sounds. It draws the children's attention to the major ideas being studied.

Language experiences of many kinds are important in the child's fourth to fifth year of life, and they continue to be important. At school, there are games involving matching of objects and letters and simple words. Symbols and meanings are central to many activities provided for children. They are a form of "reading readiness" experiences. They are intended to prepare a child for the kinds of concentrated skills that will be required for effective reading in books and on charts.

Puppets, recordings, dolls, and counting games offer the combinations of language, quantitative symbols, and body movement to involve marching and hand-and-arm movement upward and sideward. The child is totally involved in listening, doing as directed, coordinating ideas, actions, and manipulation of objects. He is undergoing the sensory experiences needed preliminary to the understanding of abstract words and concepts which will come in abundance as he matures.

The child is ready for an extended variety of experiences. People who work with him should be aware of the best materials to enhance his development. He can master activities that interest him and those that are not too complicated. The teacher can give him increasingly more difficult activities after success in easier ones. This is why a variety of different kits, activities, and games in the child's environment is important. Children usually find the activity that is manageable for them. Learning centers are planned to provide for the various abilities of children so that they are all occupied at their own levels in achieving success with those activities.

Esthetic experiences such as those in the arts, music, rhythms, movement and poetry or original storytelling are very important to young children. Since so much of what they have to learn in the areas of reading, writing, arithmetic, science, and social studies are geared toward disciplines that involve a systematic order, it is important that they have a counter-balance of self-expressive opportunities. The teacher can learn as much about a child while she observes him expressing his ideas as she can when she sees the finished product.

It is a joy to work with children this age. They are capable of many things and are actively responsive most of the time. Their pleasures are typically obvious. With a skillful teacher, they form a well-integrated "mechanism"; the two reinforce each other. The more enthusiastic the teacher is, the more responsive the children are. Teachers of children in this age group can use all the information acquired at the university prior to their contact with pupils, as well as the infinite variety of knowledge learned from nonformalized experiences out of school.

Cooking, preparing salads, and making bread or cookies involve children in mathematical and scientific experiences. Measuring ingredients, mixing them, and seeing how they change in consistency and substance are concepts of science—i.e., matter and energy. Baking and cooking activities are excellent sources for learning mathematical concepts. Such activities have meaning, first hand, for the children. Many of these activities are an introduction to conceptual foundations of mathematics and science that will be discussed and taught systematically later in school.

Everything that a teacher has learned in relation to sports, sewing, art, and music can be used in the classroom. Children are a responsive audience to anyone who enthusiastically discusses ideas related to those subjects. This information is transmitted to them not in lecture form but as activities for participation. The teacher introduces ideas to help children begin work. They take it from there. Participation, involvement, feeling, sensing, knowing through having gone through the experience— these are emphasized in early life at school. The children learn through many media, through hearing about a science experiment, through seeing it, through looking at it in books, filmstrips, and also performing it themselves.

Young children do simple classification tasks; they do not work with chemicals until they are older. There are many objects surrounding them in their environment that are safe to use for classifying—buttons, wooden pegs, crayons, pencils, tongue depressors, popsicle sticks, lids of jars, boxes of graduated size that can be classified in terms of size, shape, color, and counted as well. Science for young children involves materials safe for handling. Those materials are used, for example, when children examine them under a magnifying glass. They need to touch, to know (the feel of flour), to look at a leaf seeing its veins, a blade of grass, a fruit pit, a drop of water and to become aware of their properties. All these activities are scientific and prepare the child for increasingly more difficult investigative and analytical skills.

While the teacher is planning a comprehensive curriculum so that every child will enjoy something and learn from it, she becomes aware of the ways that subject matter or the disciplines mentioned earlier are included. Science, mathematics, social studies, physical education, health education, language development, reading art, and music are all a part of the program for young children. The secret of effective teaching is in the nature of the experiences offered the children. It is in the way the teacher provides activities from which the children will learn facts, concepts, generalizations, and sensory images to enrich those concepts and generalizations. Many kits have been produced that can be purchased by teachers or schools; [34] these are intended to give a broad variety of opportunities for children to enjoy learning. The teachers can improvise beyond the kits as well and add their own ideas.

FROM FIVE TO SIX YEARS OLD

The child in this age group appears proportionately built in relation to his trunk size and length. His arms and legs have grown beyond the year before and his trunk now appears to be more congruent with the size and length of his extremities. By five years, the child's height typically has doubled that at birth and his weight has increased about five times over his birth weight.

Individual differences in actual height and weight are obvious when children are seen together. Tables on the height of children about five-and-one-half years show the figure 46¼ inches at the 75th percentile of boy's heights. [35] Boys in this age group can be 46¼ inches tall as shown at the 75th percentile; but some, shown at the 97th percentile, can be 48 inches tall. Girls at five-and-one-half years as shown at the 75th percentile can be 45¾ inches tall; at the 97th percentile, girls are represented by a measurement of 48 inches.

Noting the weights of boys in the five-and-one-half year age group, the figures show a weight of 49¼ pounds at the 75th percentile; a weight of 56½ pounds is shown to represent the weight of some boys at the 97th percentile. These figures reflect the disparity of weights among boys in this age range, so that it is easy to see why it is difficult to judge a child's age by looking at him. The weights of girls can be 47¼ pounds at five-and-one-half years as noted in the chart at the 75th percentile, and may be 55½ as noted at the 97th percentile.

The child is beginning to acquire his permanent teeth; he may have about one or two of them by the end of his sixth year. This will affect his physical appearance and self-concept. Temporary teeth should be permitted to fall out when ready, rather than pulling them prematurely. Visits to the dentist are the safest way to ensure proper information on the process and to start sound dental health for the child. Many competent dentists specialize in working with young children. They promote a positive attitude toward dental hygiene and care.

[34] *Peabody Language Development Kits,* American Guidance Services, Inc., Circle Pines, Minn. 50014; *Mathematics Around Us,* a K through grade 6 program, Scott, Foresman and Company, Glenview, Ill. 60025; *DUSO* (*Developing Understanding of Self and Others*), American Guidance Services, Inc., Circle Pines, Minn. 55014.

[35] Smart and Smart, *Preschool Children,* pp. 11–12.

Nutrition is extremely important in this period of life. It is wise for the mother to familiarize the child with many different healthful foods; this helps him acquire a taste for them. The child begins to realize his responsibility in health care. Small amounts of new foods can be given to him. He should not be coerced into eating them; he may be interested some other time. A child can become irritated with foods at one time yet accept them at another. The adult has to be patient, realizing that children will show these extremes in their feelings. This is normal.

At five, the child is sociable. He enjoys people, young and old. He is learning rapidly in many different ways. He senses so much going on that bedtime seems to come too soon, an event that does not appeal to him because it takes him away from a profusion of activity. All of it seems important to him.

Between five and six, the child is typically attending kindergarten or entering the first grade at school. Going from kindergarten to first grade represents great changes for him in the kind of subject matter experiences he has. Learning formats in the first grade are typically much more formalized than in kindergarten. Systems represented in reading instruction and in mathematics are an important and centralized learning focus. Changes from less formalized groupings in kindergarten to the timed sequences of learning segments in the first grade schedules require a new orientation in the child. In some cases where teachers have already begun a formalized schedule for teaching reading and mathematics in kindergarten—and this does occur in some schools—the change is not as radical for the child entering the first grade. It is more or less a continuation for him. But in most kindergartens, the children are not as formally involved in each subject matter area as they will be in the first grade and thereafter.

The child from five to six years old has begun difficult work. He begins to take seriously his role as a pupil, and must become increasingly more accustomed to new kinds of complex experiences.[36] For this reason, it is important that his parents try to sustain a dialogue between him and themselves in order to allow time for him to let them know of his concerns. It is worthwhile to find out what he is thinking and how his experiences at school are affecting him.

Intellectual development has progressed in the five-to-six-year-old child. His powers for using language have increased and his thought processes are proliferating to include a greater use of words representing symbolic thinking. Internal representation has developed to a greater degree than ever in his repertoire of skills. In Piagetian terms, the child is in the middle of his intuitive stage of development under the broader rubric of preoperationalism. It is at around seven or eight years that the child approaches the end of the preoperational stage and is able to see

[36] Margolin, op. cit., p. 59.

things from several points of view. His belief that everyone sees the world as he does—described by Piaget as egocentric—begins to minimize itself. The child realizes that other people have different impressions of reality. This realization has great implications for his developing ability to reason, to explain action in logical terms, to be conscious about his own processes of reasoning.

CURRICULUM RELATIONSHIPS TO THE CHILD'S DEVELOPMENT
FROM FIVE TO SIX YEARS OLD

Since this period of life typically encompasses both kindergarten and the first grade in school, it includes curriculum materials that involve various types of systematization. In some kindergartens, children are still given a wide variety of choice for participation. The teacher may have as many as seven or eight kinds of activities in which a child may want to participate; he may go to them when he wishes without necessarily checking with the teacher.

Some kindergartens are more formally structured than others. Certain half-hours are assigned to a given set of activities. Beginning reading activities are planned in some of them. Half the group may be involved in that reading system while the other half of the class is outside with an aide involved in a game, organized or spontaneous. The children also may be running, playing, or climbing bars or riding tricycles.

Children's experiences in the first grade are more structured for most of the day than those in kindergarten. Much more specific group work goes on. Plans for the day account for each moment more than is true of the kindergarten schedule. Greater flexibility for the children's responsiveness to certain plans is permitted in the kindergarten. Teachers in the first grade, however, are concerned about testing and evaluation of the children. Since accountability of the teacher's behavior has become more of an issue in connection with children's productivity, teachers are more aware of their roles in affecting final assessments made of their pupils. They feel more committed to following certain plans for the children. Plans for achievement of certain objectives are designated in terms of a time sequence. For this reason, teachers know when the children are expected to attain certain objectives and feel greatly responsible for their attainment.

In the kindergarten, the children go from one "learning center" to another. These learning centers include games requiring coordination of hand and eye movements; a listening center or station permitting individual listening by means of a head set to a series of stories and directions to follow; games involving one-to-one matching of letters with pictures symbolizing letters and matching numbers of dots with figures representing that number. The teacher includes walking on the number line to help children "feel" linear measurement and distance from one place to another.

Using the term *learning centers* underscores that games are a learning process. Children used to tell their parents that they just played at school. Educators tried to make learning enjoyable to children by using the "game" technique. When parents asked children what they learned at school, they remembered playing. Now these forms of learning are not called games but centers for learning, and this gives it a more serious connotation.

Since children need many experiences of a concrete and manipulative nature—they need to sense, to feel, to touch, to push, pull objects of different characteristics—they need to be given many opportunities to examine objects that are counted, matched with other things, laid on the table from the smallest to the largest size, and to turn and twist the leaf they are examining under the microscope. This also coincides with Piaget's framework which suggests a child's need for many first-hand experiences, not pictures but the objects themselves. If the child has never smelled the sea, he cannot fully "know it" as a concept. If he has not pushed and poked clay to form an object or a form of some kind, he cannot know clay as a concept. Reading about it before he has contact with it cannot increase his knowledge about it in an abstract sense. Experiences with things in many forms and shapes have to precede a child's understanding of them in the abstract when they learn to read about them.

Children's experiences in the kindergarten should not exclude direct contact with measurement, counting, slicing, cutting, and tasting. Reading about those ideas is not a good substitute. Children are participating in science and mathematical experiences when they have first-hand knowledge in such measuring, smelling, counting, and tasting activities.

Sometimes, in an educator's zeal for the young child's academic progress, the program becomes highly intellectualized. Books, factual stories, and learning-to-read experiences are used for most of the program. It is as though the teachers and parents were college-oriented for the child. Songs, artistic expression, and fingerpainting are regarded as unimportant. Yet those activities are involving the child's ear to rhythmic sounds, attuning his mind's eye to discriminating between high and low, loud and soft tones; paints, artistic experiences provide sensory knowledge that cannot be replaced by a book. The young child needs all these experiences to nurture his personality and his intellectual equipment.

One writer cautions against early formalism in the teaching process with young children. He suggests that if about 75 per cent of the child's mental growth has occurred before he has even been exposed to formalized schooling, and he is supposed to gain about 20 per cent of mental growth between eight and seventeen years old, there seems to be a negative relationship between mental growth and formalized instruction.[37] This would emphasize the importance for a child's need to be involved in first-hand experiences of a wide variety rather than being limited to sequenced language packages and books. Books are not unimportant; they are necessary to a child's learning at school. In the kindergarten that tries to carry out formalized programs that are more appropriate in the first grade, the children are losing out on needed basic learnings.

Teachers need to use all the knowledge at their disposal to help them decide not only what kind of activities are best for young children but also the appropriate or proportionate amounts. It is necessary, too, to remain informed and up-to-date regarding the most recent information and research on young children's development. Journals of professional organizations, the workshops or yearly conferences as well as mid-season meetings all provide updated trends and data in the field. Teachers should avail themselves of all these things. It is also necessary for their own stimulation toward viable relationships with children. It can help sustain a spontaneous, fresh teaching orientation.

SIX-, SEVEN-, AND EIGHT-YEAR-OLD CHILDREN

Children in this age range are still experiencing the early childhood period of their lives. As far as the schools' relationship to them is concerned, they are in the primary grades. Some school systems refer to these grades in a combined sense; they are called a primary block. They represent extremely important beginnings for the child. Later grades such as the fourth, fifth, and sixth represent intermediate grades; and for children's growth experiences generally, that period of life represents later childhood. Authors refer to these stages in different ways. Some call it middle childhood. But in terms of the schools' view, the six-, seven-, and eight-year-old period, when a child is in the first, second, and third grades is seen as early childhood.

Physical growth for the six-year-old slows down compared to the pace prior to that time. He may be about three-and-one-half feet tall and weigh about 47 or 48 pounds. Individual differences referred to earlier indicate a range in weight and height in people of any age.

Muscle tissue continues to increase proportionately to body growth and the child's energies and strength typically increase. Boys usually gain more in muscle mass; girls more in body fat. This varies of course from individual to individual.

Skills in controlling eye muscles have improved in the six-year-old child and continue to accommodate to reading print as the child gets

[37] David Elkind, "The Case for the Academic Preschool: Fact or Fiction?" in *Preschool Children*, edited by Smart and Smart, pp. 184–185.

older. His interest in reading and the concern of adults for him to read well can influence his attitude and consequently his eye muscles in attempting to read. Greater strain in the process can inhibit the child's experiences in learning to read. Tension restricts eye muscles.

Between six and eight, the child can acquire about eight or nine permanent teeth beyond the two he had at six. Teeth falling out and their replacement by permanent ones involves some discomfort in eating certain foods. But in the main—with visits to the dentist and the child's awareness of the process—he can acquire permanent teeth with less pain than he had with his first set of temporary teeth.

Boys and girls are becoming more aware than before about sex differences and about characteristics related to psychosexual development. Sex roles, differences in appearance, differences in acceptable behavior between the sexes, and cultural attitudes toward sexual differences (where those differences should be accented and where they should not) as they are reflected in literature, communication media and commercial advertising are heightened in the child's mind more so than before.

Along with knowledge of sexual behavior and sex-related characteristics in learning various roles, children become more self-conscious of their behavior and private thoughts. They are developing a conscience and are beginning to internalize their parental values to some extent. They feel guilty when they do something their parents told them not to do. While this had begun to develop when they were younger, they are now much more aware of the process; they know when they have deliberately decided to go against their parents' wishes—or those of their teacher, for that matter.

Birth order in a family is responsible for differences in child behavior. The firstborn child is under the constant surveillance of his parents, and they tend to expect more of him. Typically, less is demanded from the younger ones. The parent is too busy with many other household and working tasks to notice details.

The age of the parents and the status of their marriage also affect their attention to the child. The parents' personalities and the number of siblings all influence a child's sex role understanding, what is expected of him, and how satisfied he will be with his own self-image.[38]

This period of life is an important one in terms of a child's understanding of his cultural surroundings. He accepts them as much a part of himself as he does his arms or legs. It is extremely difficult when people visit another country to understand that their own views are not universal, that other people do not value the same things they do. That moral issues, value issues related to personality characteristics and behavior, or eating habits are different from one's own sometimes shocks those who are

---

[38] Margolin, op. cit., p. 135.

deeply engrained in their own society. Speech, social amenities, or phrases used for courtesy surprise newcomers to a country. The child from six to eight is in prime time to absorb his culture. His basic values are built on those given to him from socializing agents (his parents, siblings, teachers and others who transmit cultural views, habits, patterns, norms, and mores).

The child's intellectual development typically advances, depending on his family background and school experiences. His readiness to absorb ideas and to participate in what the schools offer him greatly affect his progress. This in turn is affected by his teacher's attitude toward him and how comfortable he feels being with his peers. Even though his intellectual development is measured by means of various tests, most people are aware that it cannot be as easily separated in the total system of the child. His responses to the environment—even though appearing to be mainly intellectual—are the combined result of many other aspects of his development associated with his environment.

CURRICULUM RELATIONSHIPS TO THE CHILD'S DEVELOPMENT
IN THE SIX-, SEVEN-, AND EIGHT-YEAR-OLD RANGE

Children in the primary grades are experiencing less rapid physical development compared to their earlier years. Their muscle control has begun to acquire greater facility. Their language development has improved to a noticeable extent. They are able to perform many physical tasks and games easily as long as those who work with them take into consideration their age range.

Healthy children in this age range enjoy participation at school as long as they are made to feel that they are competent. They enjoy it when their peers and teachers appreciate what they are able to do and what their special personal qualities are.

Their muscle development and greater strength contributes to their enjoyment of physical activities, so long as these are within their capacities. They enjoy active games; they like to jump rope, to skate, to dance, to play tag and running games.

Since their intellectual development at this stage heightens their sensitivity to the environment, particularly when they are at school, many activities can be presented to them. They continue to learn best, however, by participating in skills development rather than being told about them. They continue to need a variety of experiences to help them learn ways of classifying events, objects, and people in their environment. The wide variety of experiences is needed to accommodate various learning styles of the children in the class. Such diversification can accommodate the different stages of development of the children as pupils, as well as their different stages of achievement in specific subject matter areas.

Influences of the home may facilitate or inhibit what is presented at school. Teachers have to have a broad-based interest in children and an understanding of them as people, as individuals needing respect and care while they are at school competing with others. Teachers can create or encourage a love of learning in pupils who might not have thought that they were competent. This kind of encouragement requires an observant and skillful teacher and one who cares about children and people. She also has to understand herself well in order to give emotionally to others.

summary

This chapter discussed physical, intellectual, social and emotional characteristics of children from birth to about eight years. Since the education of children begins informally from the moment they are born, what happens to them at home or in institutions to make the best of their genetic characteristics is important.

Educational planning has to consider the principles of child development in order to better accommodate effective experiences for young children and babies. The format of this chapter represented the relationship between constitutional or genetic growth characteristics and curriculum planning. It is hoped that this kind of process or framework will be used with planning for children of all age groups.

It is possible to go into much greater detail for each of the stages of development only touched on in this chapter. The growth and maturation of speech patterns, of thought, of emotional and social relationships could comprise an entire book. The purpose here was to reflect mainly the importance of having an understanding of such a relationship, that it exists, is relevant, and makes sense to consider as a rational approach to planning the educational contexts of young children. Even though the subject matter areas were not specified in this section as they must be in kindergarten, first, second, and third grades, they will be discussed later in attempts to delineate the content of disciplines such as mathematics, science, social studies, and physical education. It rests with the teacher's discretion at the final point to know what the children in her age group can learn most effectively and which techniques are most amenable for their maximum development.

topics for discussion

1. In what ways can a knowledge of child development be related to a rationale for a curriculum planned for young children and babies? Why is it important?
2. Visit a day care center and note the science, social studies, and health education activities included in their curriculum. Try to determine what kind of generalizations the children are making about the content of those

activities. Ask the teacher what the major purposes of those activities are for the children.

3. Construct three activities that you think a child of two, three, and four would enjoy using as part of an educational program in a day care center. Try it with children of those ages and evaluate their use of them. Did they seem to learn from them? Did they remain with the activity for a while? Did they permit other children to work with it? What changes would you make in the activities to improve their usefulness?

4. What are the vulnerable areas of stress in young children, i. e., what aspects of their physical and emotional development need to be considered in the timing and scheduling of an educational program for them? Visit a nursery school that you think has considered well the relationships of child development and program planning for the children. Describe their program.

selected bibliography

Allport, Gordon W. *Pattern and Growth in Personality.* New York: Holt, Rinehart and Winston, Inc., 1961.

Blank, Marion, and Frances Solomon. "A Tutorial Language Program to Develop Abstract Thinking in Socially Disadvantaged Preschool Children," *Intellectual Development,* Pauline S. Sears, ed., pp. 453–464. New York: John Wiley & Sons, Inc., 1971.

Bloom, Benjamin S. *Stability and Change in Human Characteristics.* New York: John Wiley & Sons, Inc., 1964.

Elkind, David. "The Case for the Academic Preschool: Fact or Fiction," *Preschool Children: Development and Relationships.* Mollie S. Smart and Russell C. Smart, eds., pp. 180–188. New York: Macmillan Publishing Co., Inc., 1973.

Gordon, Ira J. *Baby Learning Through Baby Play: A Parent Guide for the First Two Years.* New York: St. Martin's Press, 1970.

Gordon, Ira J. *Human Development,* 2nd ed. New York: Harper & Row, 1969.

Denenberg, Victor H. *Education of the Infant and Young Children.* New York: and London: Academic Press, Inc., 1970.

Krown, Sylvia. *Threes and Fours Go to School.* Englewood Cliffs, N. J.: Prentice-Hall, Inc., 1974.

Lugo, James O., and Gerald L. Hershey. *Human Development.* New York: Macmillan Publishing Co., Inc., 1974.

Margolin, Edythe. *Sociocultural Elements in Early Childhood Education.* New York: Macmillan Publishing Co., Inc., 1974.

Mussen, Paul Henry, John Janeway Conger, and Jerome Kagan. *Child Development and Personality,* 4th ed. New York: Harper & Row, 1974.

Piaget, Jean. *Judgment and Reasoning in the Child.* Marjorie Warden, trans., Paterson, N. J.: Littlefield, Adams & Co., 1958.

Piaget, Jean. *The Child's Conception of the World.* Joan and Andrew Tomlinson, trans., Paterson, N. J.: Littlefield, Adams & Co., 1960.

Smart, Mollie S., and Russell C. Smart, eds. *Children: Development and Relationships.* New York: Macmillan Publishing Co., Inc., 1967.

Smart, Mollie S., and Russell C. Smart, eds. *Infants: Development and Relationships.* New York: Macmillan Publishing Co., Inc., 1973.

Smart, Mollie S., and Russell C. Smart, eds. *School-Age Children: Development and Relationships.* New York: Macmillan Publishing Co., Inc., 1973.

Stott, Leland H., and Rachel S. Ball. "Intelligence: A Changing Concept," *Children: Readings in Behavior and Development,* Ellis D. Evans, ed., pp. 264–308. New York: Rinehart and Winston, Inc., 1968.

Tronick, Edward, and Patricia Marks Greenfield. *Infant Curriculum.* New York: Media Projects Incorporated, 1973.

Vincent, Elizabeth Lee, and Phyliss C. Martin. *Human Psychological Development.* New York: The Ronald Press, 1961.

White, Burton L., and Jean Carew Watts, with Itty Chan Barnett, Barbara Taylor Kaban, Janice Rosen Marmor, and Bernice Broyde Shapiro. *Experience and Environment.* Vol. I. Englewood Cliffs, N. J.: Prentice-Hall, Inc., 1973.

Part Two

Curriculum Planning and General Conceptual Frameworks

How the teacher uses children's time when they are in school is crucial to how they will learn and develop positive attitudes toward school. These activities should be carefully planned, with a view to which ones are best for certain children, how much time is to be spent, and when and how often they should be offered.

Educators with a foundation of educational psychology generally consider motivation, principles of developmental psychology and knowledge of substance in planning a program for young children. They know that a child of three needs special activities and materials and has a concentration span that differs from that of a child of eight, who is typically in the third grade, the "top" of the primary grades. Even though both age three and age eight, are part of early childhood, the two are at opposite ends of the growth and development spectrum. The child at three is in nursery school; the child at eight is at the upper end of the early childhood continuum, approaching intermediate childhood and school grades.

This part of the book will discuss some of the conceptual frameworks that serve as general guides for planning programs and/or curriculum materials for young children, ages three to about eight. No single plan for creating a curriculum is ever universally adopted. Theoreticians offering a program design usually emphasize certain aspects that they believe have not been given adequate attention. Some stress a vertically sequenced design, that is, a plan for the ways in which subject matter can proceed instructionally from kindergarten to high school.

Some writers focus on pupils' needs to learn through concept development and generalizations of each subject and how they should be presented at various grade levels. Classroom groups that are organized in teacher teams, or nonspecifically graded classroom groups can use this approach because the content is not "locked into" certain grade levels. Concepts and generalizations of subject matter can be simplified or can be approached at levels of greater complexity. It depends on when the children are ready.

Teachers are given many kinds of kits and programmed materials in packaged "totalities." They can, however, if they have the actual information on available subject matter, design their own curriculum activities or segments of work for the children they know well, in contrast to the program developers who do not know the pupils expected to experience their packaged deals.

Teachers of young children often do not have the confidence they need for planning activities. Too often the activities in programs are planned and written in the format of cartoon characters. Teachers themselves, however, can bring quality to the curriculum if they study the substantive aspect of each of the subject matter areas. Photographs, taken by the teachers themselves have enriched many activities for young children. Filmstrips selected to enhance certain concepts and generalizations in subject matter can be used when the teacher considers them appropriate.

The curriculum guidelines suggested and discussed in the following pages represent the most recent views of educators and researchers generally in education and also some who are specifically concerned about early childhood and elementary education. Each of their curriculum or program designs has merit. Their emphasis or approach differs, but all of them are concerned with maximum educational development.

Part One was a discussion of the means through which some early childhood programs came into existence, how they were (and can be) financed, and what motivated people to do them. It also focused on child development principles for young children in the care of agencies or institutions. People who work with children and see how the principles of child development provide a point of approach for the application of subject matter, should find this second section of the book valuable. It provides information on subject matter needed for the child's educational development.

Teachers are encouraged to plan their own activities comprehensively by using the data brought together in this book. Even though curriculum planning places a greater burden on them, most teachers find it very satisfying and challenging. The more they do it, the more adept they become at it. They do not have to depend as much on purchased programmed materials when they have the necessary insight for planning their own program. In this sense, they are able to provide leadership for their own school staffs and become models for exercising creativity.

Chapter 3

Curriculum Guidelines

After one has spent weeks of writing a research program and after one has been fortunate enough to have it funded, the diligent focus of its implementation begins. Many educators and researchers ask consultants to visit the program site and bring various kinds of expertise to it. People often come from all parts of the country to bring immediate information on ways to give substance to the program. Short- and longer-term recommendations are offered to contribute to the program's success. Since typically the time frame is limited, the need is for quick action.

Between the visits of consultants and the use of their time and knowledge, and also the many commercialized programs that have become plentiful, the plans are enthusiastically set into motion. For the most part, these quick services and materials provide a strong beginning for the teachers and stimulate their interest. Programs come in interesting and attractive packages, and even though some of them may meet with mixed reactions on the part of the teachers who have to adapt to the constraints of a new way of record keeping, they will sell. School systems, too, want to be progressive; they are sometimes in receipt of added monies from federal sources. These funds will be used to purchase new programs.

The actual planning of curriculum frameworks and their implementation does not happen as fast as the construction of new programs. Theoretical foundations for curriculum development typically involve a few years of study, and do not arise in the same profusion as activity programs. Their development requires time and greater depth. Much research must be done before a given theory will be accepted by the academic world. An excellent study in curriculum theory can provide great potential for many programs. Consider, for example, the number of books and programs that have been developed on the basis of Piaget's theories. Although Piaget did not intend it, his work has been used as an educational tool to a great extent.

Points of View on Curriculum Planning for Young Children

There are so many points of view on the best ways to plan a curriculum for young children, that it would require an encyclopedia to explain them. When the issues begin to highlight the logic between a particular set of characteristics of a group of children and a set of goals, the recommendations narrow to relatively fewer ideas. We are not really that certain about what works and what is best for children. We are testing ourselves all the time. This is to our credit. To feel that we have all the answers just because people have explained their ideas well, does not alter the fact that those ideas may still not be producing the best kind of learning in young children.

Since each era has its own special characteristics—wars, ecological disasters, civic and political disorders—teaching orientations differ according to what seems best for children to learn at that specific time. The milieu of society affects what educators think is most important. Looking back through history, one can easily see this emphasis. Social welfare and moralistic concerns were usually relegated to classroom teaching. Schools were expected to preserve morals and ideals as society noted weaknesses in general social behavior.

Curriculum writers refer to that term in different ways. Some consider the curriculum everything that happens to a child at school. Some consider it mainly the experiences and goals that are planned for the children when they are in the classroom and outside in the school yard. Some view it in terms of planned, organized activities but include also some of the spontaneous experiences that arise during the teaching period.

Curriculum organization and design is viewed here as the philosophy, goals, objectives, and experiences planned for the pupils when they are at school. Experiences that arise spontaneously or when the teacher improvises on the spot because she sees a unique opportunity to teach important information, is part of the curriculum. Any activity from which the children learn is considered the curriculum. However, the spontaneous or nonorganized activity because of its improvisational nature cannot be listed in a curriculum guide. It appears when one observes the children with their teacher. In that sense much of what happens in the classroom has not been planned on paper. The written guide differs from its implementation because implementation involves different children and a teacher of specific background and college instruction.

Curriculum guides also include methods of evaluation. This is an extremely important aspect of any work with children. If some kind of assessment is not made, the teacher and educational planners have no way of knowing what was effective and what was not. The type of evaluation used is important to the success of the program in terms of the accuracy, validity and reliability of measurement. It can be simple or complex. In some way, however, the teacher and the children need to have feedback or information on how they are doing.

Children can sense how a teacher feels about them. In this context, children are receiving evaluation of some kind. But the type of evaluation mentioned above refers to letting the children know informally and formally, through test data, how they are understanding what is being taught in the classroom. This aspect of teacher-child interaction will be discussed later in the book.

The development of curriculum with its goals, procedures, activities, and models of evaluation has been examined by many competent professionals. Dewey,[1] Taba,[2] Tyler,[3] and Bruner [4] present philosophical frameworks and indicate the kind of subject matter children should master in order to understand their environment and to help them achieve satisfaction with themselves in a present and future society. They may have a strong part in the making of such a society.

In general, the writers mentioned above are concerned with the way children will be able to function in society. Dewey views the classroom as a microcosm of society. In other words, if the children learn to function in the classroom as society expects them to in later life—i.e., based on democratic principles, on being productive individuals—it is assumed that they will know how to function on their own initiative when they are adults.

Taba is concerned with one of the conditions of society, namely, that

[1] John Dewey, *The Child and the Curriculum and the School and Society* (Chicago and London: The University of Chicago Press, 1963).

[2] Hilda Taba, *Curriculum Development* (New York and Burlingame: Harcourt, Brace & World, Inc., 1962).

[3] Ralph W. Tyler, *Basic Principles of Curriculum Development* (Chicago: The University of Chicago Press, 1950). See also Ralph W. Tyler, "The Organization of Learning Experiences," in *Toward Improved Curriculum Theory*, edited by Virgil E. Herrick and Ralph W. Tyler, pp. 59–67. Supplementary Educational Monographs, Number 71, March 1950 (Chicago: The University of Chicago Press).

[4] Jerome Bruner, *The Process of Education* (Cambridge, Mass.: The Harvard University Press, 1960).

it is not static, it changes. On that basis children ought to be learning how to deal with change by having an astute knowledge of problem-solving and the means for implementing better ideas. This orientation minimizes the memorization of separate, unrelated facts, of learning right or wrong answers as ends in themselves. It emphasizes the ability to find several possible solutions to a problem. It values processes of thinking that involve judging, hypothesizing, exploring, experimenting, inferring. Curriculum development, Taba's work indicates, should be a concentration on helping individuals learn how to find and use resources for solving problems. Their own resources should be increasingly strengthened (a strong point of view of this book) so that they can become independent and trust their own decisions as the right ones for them.

Tyler's work reflects an ambitious attempt to view curriculum development in a total perspective of not only what it is, but how to organize and implement it, and further, how to analyze what it can do. He recommends that educators refer to major ideas presented by those writing on society, and on psychological aspects of the learner's abilities, attitudes, and predispositions, and mental operations generally. With this he suggests that the work of writers on subject matter needed for school instruction be examined; and all should be conceptualized through decisions on whether or not certain subjects or ideas should be taught and, if so, how they should be organized and taught.

Whether or not certain ideas or subject matter ought to be taught is a concern of philosophers of education. The issues of whether or not children should study evolution, various aspects in the history of man, or sexual reproduction are partly philosophical and partly religious. In the main, however, philosophers' writings have helpful ideas for the development of the curriculum. If certain materials are acceptable for instruction, the next question that arises is how they should be taught, when, at what age level, and in what sequence. These are not only broad philosophical issues, but also become the guidelines that provide direction for writers of curriculum frameworks or courses of study.

Bruner's work at one point emphasized the importance of structure in each of the disciplines taught at school. It is assumed that each discipline has its own structure. If children can learn this, they are expected to manage even the most difficult of ideas, because the ideas of greater complexity can be built on those that are simpler. Young children do not need to be taught nonaccuracy of concepts just because they are young and find it difficult to deal with several ideas simultaneously. If the structure of the discipline is known by the teacher, it can be simplified into basic parts that can be understood by children. Structure refers to an interrelationship of parts. The parts refer to concepts and generalizations that are basic to that subject matter area. One of the problems in this approach, however, is that even the authorities who write in the disciplines as spokesmen for their fields do not agree on what that structure is.[5] Some compromises would have to be made in terms of relative points of agreement on what the "real" structure is.

Most writers recommend that the curriculum planners look to the context from which the child comes, that is, to make some observations about a child's society or his environment. An English child in London has different orientations to his family life from one in a Wyoming town. They have similar directions in that their parents want them to be healthy, happy, helpful, cooperative and the like. Their orientations regarding the specifics of what it takes to be a "good" or "decent" person, or a bright, wise one depends greatly on what their parents' impressions are on the subject. There are humanistically similar impressions regarding orientations to one's society and family, but the means that are valued in becoming an admired individual typically reflect the culture in which the person has been reared.

Looking at an individual's society gives the curriculum writer some ideas as to what a child will need to do in order to "survive" or succeed in it, whatever the perspective one wants to take on the topic. But in a society that requires people to help themselves, to think as individuals for the most part, rather than in broad terms for the benefit of a larger group, as certain countries want their inhabitants to do, the child's instruction at school will be different.

A framework recommended in this book (See Figure 3.1) considers the social context of the child, that is, the society or immediate environment in which he lives. It recommends the necessity for knowing the children in terms of developmental principles, or in terms of psychological knowledge about how human beings learn and develop. Specifically, teachers working with young children need to know about the child's psychological development, emotionally, socially, and academically during the ages of three through eight. What happens to children in this age range is important to an understanding of them. A teacher who is aware of young children's fears and anxieties does not make a child feel ashamed of fright, guilt, worries or any other emotion for that matter. It is extremely important that all teachers know what children feel, how they grow, and why they behave as they do. Subject matter is not the only important aspect of teacher preparation for classroom interaction with young children.

After the characteristics of society and the psychological aspect or child growth principles have been considered, the realization that communication among people is important places language and many forms

[5] William T. Lowe, *Structure and the Social Studies* (Ithaca and London: Cornell University Press, 1969).

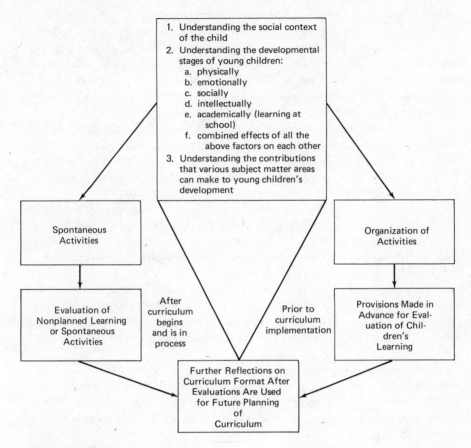

figure 3.1
Framework for Curriculum Planning

of communication as the next step in the framework. Gestures, verbal expressions, written or oral, artistic expression, are all important for children to learn so that they become adept at it as well as knowing why it is important to be able to articulate one's thoughts and ideas well.

Communication is important to an individual's mental health and life's functions for him. If he cannot express himself adequately enough to make his needs or problems understood to friends or professional workers, he withdraws from the environment and locks himself from functioning properly. If he functions effectively, he is able to take care of himself and is not a burden to society or agencies of society. If he cannot communicate effectively in terms of at least his own level of abilities and for his own satisfaction, he may become in an extreme case an individual who needs to be cared for by other people or agencies.

Verbal, oral or written communication is essential to an individual's development. In the functional sense it meets basic needs; in the esthetic sense it enhances the individual's enjoyment of life. For some people it becomes even more important than anything else in life. For them esthetic expression epitomizes life. The joy that good music, art, dance, poetry brings to people creates aspects of personality that cannot be acquired in any other way.

Thus communication forms of many kinds have to be included in the curriculum framework. Educators plan objectives and activities for children that will bring about satisfying experiences and functional abilities for competence in communication. These activities overlap with science, mathematics, arts, social studies, even physical education.

The next aspect of the framework to guide an individual planning a curriculum for young children, is the subject matter areas needed for basic awareness in educational processes. Social studies, physical education, mathematics and science are examples of disciplines usually included in most educational programs.

The social studies include substantive data and techniques from the social sciences, such as sociology, psychology, anthropology, economics, geography, history, social psychology and philosophy. This information is used for writing social studies units for children in primary and elementary grades.

Mathematics for young children draws from major principles of the field and uses techniques appropriate to children's understanding. From simple addition, subtraction, division, multiplication, and the major concepts of the mathematical field, the student learns to comprehend the essence of a mathematical system.

Science includes logical, systematic observation and measurement. It sharpens perceptiveness, explains conflicting data, explains a curious world in which water turns to ice under certain conditions, rain and sand turns to mud. These ideas are fascinating to young children. Experiments and observations help them understand the major principles of science and how those principles can be used as a basis for acquiring more knowledge and accuracy in the field. The logic, the analytical orientation, and insistence on observing the way certain phenomena occur create critical awareness in the child that can be transferred to other situations requiring analytical thought and problem solving.

Art as an area of learning is a way of expressing one's views as well as a way of observing the environment. Principles of art are learned not from reading, the way many other subjects are, but directly from the teacher's ideas for activities. Although some kindergarten pupils are learning to read, their skills in that regard do not carry them far beyond the materials used mainly for learning how to read. For this reason, participation in art is essential if a child is to learn something about it.

Art introduces color, texture, design, tools and techniques that children can use easily if materials are properly presented to them. The major concern of the teacher is that the child use the media, become accustomed to them and develop interest in experimenting with various processes. In essence, the end product is of less importance than the process, particularly in the child's early experience with materials. A satisfying process for a child will encourage him to try again, and this is what is important— that he veer toward the experience rather than away from it.

Music is one of the easiest forms of learning for children. They respond to it emotionally as well as educationally. When they are asked to listen, to imitate, and to move to music in a way that presupposes pleasure and joy, they will like it and not be threatened psychologically by a grim, perfectionistic attitude on the part of the teacher. In that sense, music becomes theirs rather than hers. This is an important goal and a realistic one.

Rhythms or body movement provide a means through which children may express themselves and become familiar with the use of forms, of moving to sounds, to music, and interrelated concepts of both combined. They enjoy movement in which they may be asked to imitate an animal they like, or to skip, hop, and jump to the beat of a drum or accompaniment on the piano. Gradually they perceive, classify, and use various levels of space around them and enjoy arm and leg locomotor movements. Typically they respond well to movement programs. Their quality of responses depends mainly on the skill of the teacher or leader to evoke full participation. The atmosphere of acceptance and joy created by the teacher marks the difference between maximum participation, and fear, unwillingness, or sullenness on the children's part. If the teacher can help children develop greater satisfaction with their own concepts of a "body-image," and greater control over their environmental space, this will carry over to feelings of mastery in other subject matter areas.

After decisions have been made regarding areas that will be included in the curriculum design, the organization and sequence of learning activities has to be decided. Some writers start with the view that an introduction of subject matter can be made if children become involved in something that is familiar to them. An introduction to communication, for example, can begin with the children's writing a letter (or with the teacher's help in writing on the chalkboard, create a class letter) to mail. The activity can lead to discovering more information about a post office, other types of communication, and other ideas that were not familiar to the children. This way of beginning a unit's organization is viewed as answering the psychological needs of the child rather than looking to the discipline itself as a form of organization.

Mathematics and science concepts are introduced to children by using materials they know. Counting or dividing objects usually include pencils, crayons, buttons, colorful sticks. Science experiences involve the use of leaves, flowers, seeds, pits, and magnifying glass that children have seen around them. Fish, birds, hamsters, gerbils are not only pets, but forms of life that help children learn scientific principles and generalizations. Thus, an organization of learning activities proceeds from the familiar to the remote, or ideas that are unfamiliar to the children.

Teachers should realize that abstractions mean little to young children. They are merely empty words if children have not had first-hand experiences to support an understanding prerequisite to abstract comprehension of a concept or generalization. In the teacher's sensitivity to young children's ways of learning, the subject matter is organized into experiences that gradually lead to deeper understandings.

Among the last steps in designing a curriculum, is one of the most difficult, that is, the aspect of evaluation. One of the major obligations of a curriculum writer is to formulate the means for evaluating the effectiveness of it. The problem becomes compounded by the fact that young children cannot read or write with sufficient facility to make group test-taking a dependable factor. It becomes more important to observe them as individuals in their daily routines at school. It becomes important too to notice their individual learning styles. They may know a certain item of information, but if they are not asked the precise question in relation to it, they can appear to be totally unaware.

The curriculum planner has to have some way of knowing whether his ideas are workable and effective for the children expected to experience it. Means of measurement have to be devised. Sometimes they are taken from commercially written tests that have already been devised by testing centers or systems to assess the results of a particular program. But increasingly more teachers are creating their own testing procedures in order to ensure that the concepts they are concentrating on be tested through a format designed specifically for that program.

The conceptualization of frameworks for curriculum planning is usually found in a rationale or statement prior to the curriculum presented. It is sometimes found in the goals or objectives listed in the program. It can also be detected in a summary or set of conclusions in a study plan.

Sometimes the conceptualization of a guide or framework for planning a curriculum sounds ideal as one reads it. But even though the goals, objectives and intentions stated on paper could hardly be objected to by anyone, the manner in which the activities or goals are implemented becomes the crucial problem. How certain ideas are learned by the children, whether the processes valued by the educators or scientists are used in the implementation of the goals is another important aspect of curriculum planning. Whether certain goals are achieved to the sacrifice of other gains is an important consideration.

If the teacher wants the children to have opportunities for esthetic expression while the curriculum in opposition to her personal goals for the pupils, requires formal cognitive gains to account for most of the children's time and energies at school, then the cognitive gains made by the children will not satisfy the teacher's perceptions of what is important for total development in children. If pupils in cognitive programs or systems are fighting over scarce materials, they will not be able to acquire the necessary interpersonal skills regarding sharing. The teacher can work around this problem and use it as a focus for teaching children how to cope with the environment, but this contradiction between goals and their implementation, shows how virtuous intentions for children's educational growth can result in other kinds of inadequate performance levels. Educators and others working with children should be aware of these inconsistencies.

Conceptualizations of a guide or framework for the development of a curriculum are derived from several sources. Writers have a particular approach that they want to stress. Although it may not differ totally from other programs, it may deal more extensively with one area than another. This difference gives it an emphasis because it goes into an area with greater depth. Language development, for example, has never before taken on the importance in a total curriculum that it has recently. If one examines the curriculum guides of school systems about twenty-five years ago, it becomes obvious that the variety of current emphases in the language arts area was nonexistent. Thus, while language development as part of reading was important in the educational process, it was never as significant in curriculum guides as it is in contemporary school programs.

The interest in the improvement of educational experiences for young children who live in low-income areas has opened a new area of research and approaches to curriculum development. While similar frameworks exist for the way education should be provided for young children at school, different orientations are emerging on the basis of new knowledge identified by research. Greater sensitivity has been achieved in relation to the problems of language differences, between the kind of language learned in the informal settings of the home or neighborhood and the language forms, terms, and vocabulary, used in the more objective setting of the classroom. The explanation of facts learned in the classroom is sometimes more difficult than telling people one knows well about an experience.

Language needed by children at school involves an informal style as well as the more formalized one usually seen in textbooks emphasizing accuracy or scientific data. Curriculum writers have not built into the programs for young children well defined areas of concentration regarding levels of skills, e.g., topical sentences, appropriate vocabulary, logical order of thought or ideas required in the processes of learning various language forms. Children are building versatility in language. This objective was not found in older school programs, at least not in the specifically implemented format that is obvious now.

An awareness of what cultural pluralism really means as a concept has only been awakened in the last ten years as far as its benefits to progress in education are concerned. Sociologists and anthropologists have had rich research data in this area of cultural differences and the intriguing implications for life in mixed groups. The vexing problem that blocked the use of knowledge lay in the difficulties usually encountered when one field has to cross over to another and select information that can be applied to its own forces. What seemed to be needed was a deliberate "call" from educators or a commission from the government via research funds to bring the two together. It finally happened.

With the interest in low-income groups of young children and national endorsement of such studies, more research has been stimulated in interdisciplinary studies. Educational orientations are evident too in ethnic and racial traditions, customs, and practices. Because of this broader definition and direction, a healthier comprehension of various groups seems to be increasing. Children learn about various kinds of people who have been reared in cultures different from their own, an important step forward in itself.

The problem of how to have all children, even adults, understand cultural differences while at the same time learning one language, is a challenge to the schools. People have difficulty understanding how they can learn about various cultures without being expected to emulate them. To learn about the customs, traditions, language, values of other cultures does not suggest that one has to adopt the ways of those cultures as one's own. This misunderstanding often arouses problems of identity for individuals.

With an increasing interest in low-income groups of young children, particularly those of varying ethnic and racial origins, and concern that they have a high-quality education, has come conflicting views regarding the time spent in bilingual education at school. Sometimes parents feel that the children will lose racial or ethnic identity that ties families together. Minimizing the use of one's native or informal language spoken at home is often seen as a loss by some parents. Children sense this conflict and are confused about loyalty and alienation.

Parents want children to be successful at school and to be popular with others. They are not always aware, however, that they can impede children's progress when they fear changes in family relationships. Their concern is understandable. The teachers must be cautious when they talk to parents and to the children themselves when new cultural ideas are presented. The teacher needs to help children realize that the ideas learned at school are in addition to what they know. Pupils are not expected to negate their own background or feel ashamed of it. This is not the educational process. Instead, teachers can by their own attitudes show how exciting it is to learn many ideas, language, poetry, stories, songs of different cultures. Not to do so is to close off people from each other and from the total world. This is a serious hindrance to educational goals.

INFLUENCES OF MAJOR CONTRIBUTIONS IN
CURRICULUM DEVELOPMENT

Many contemporary programs reflect the writing of significant curriculum developers. They can be seen in the types of activities offered to children such as the programs which give pupils many opportunities to talk, to discuss, to express their own ideas or experiences. Individual differences in children's learning style have been highlighted for many years in educational literature recommended to university students preparing for teaching. The problem of implementation of those differences in terms of the programs at school persisted, however, in spite of the research and the recommendations evident in the last thirty years of educational history.

The awareness of change in society, of the need for children to learn how to solve problems, and to learn to think are evidence that former curriculum writers' work is being recognized. Words such as process, structure, and comprehension point up the concerns for the way children approach problems rather than stressing only the final answer or a single correct answer. It is as though the teacher is perceived as an overseer to processes of thinking rather than the answer giver. The teacher facilitates the acquisition of knowledge for the children. In fact, even when the teacher has all the answers to the questions asked by the children, she does not give them, but rather asks the child more questions to evoke his desire to pursue the answers for himself. Discovery, probing, seeking endlessly various answers to problems are valued because they lead to a scientific orientation which in itself ensures a constant curiosity for new answers. A child in a nonstatic society will need these abilities and characteristics in his educational and personality development.

Classroom environment reflects a change in educational practices that differ from those in the early 1900's. The desks or tables and chairs used by the children in the classroom are no longer attached to the floor. This permits and encourages versatility in their use. They are changed as the activity changes. In some kindergartens all chairs and tables are pushed aside when the children are involved in a singing game or a rhythms activity. The entire room is cleared of furniture or small rugs so that the children can move freely, with abandon and without fear of bumping into things. The open style classroom has even cleared the walls that separate rooms from each other. Classroom arrangement of furniture, of materials to be used for various activities, of storage areas from which children can obtain for themselves what is needed at a moment's notice,

Classrooms of the past never had reading corners with rocking chairs available for several children as is shown in the classroom here. The relaxation provided by the rocking chairs is rarely legitimized in schools; fortunately it is here. It gives some children an opportunity to enjoy "reading" only if they are looking at pictures as they rock back and forth.

all reflect the contemporary educational planner's view of individualistic learning styles.

Looking at Figure 3.2, one notes the characteristics of a contemporary learning situation which is geared more toward individualism than it ever has been before in education planned for large groups of children. Education in a democratic society is concerned with everyone's education. This is different from older views which favored education for the élite, for those who did not necessarily have to work for a living, and had time to pursue contemplative studies.

The individualistic orientation in education is in part a reflection of Dewey's ideas, of Taba's, of Tyler's and of Bruner's. A recognition of society's changing milieu every few years, an awareness of children's needing to participate in classroom experiences, of children's being ready at various levels for certain concepts and generalizations in subject matter

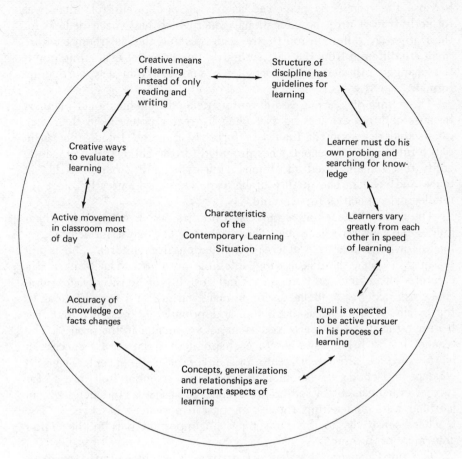

figure 3.2
Interacting Characteristics in a Contemporary Learning Situation

structures, of needing to build on sequences of development are present in curriculum plans for young children today.

Figure 3.2 shows the central aspect at the bottom of the circular entirety or whole of the student's learning; the concepts and generalizations constitute the structure of subject matter. On either side of the circular and interactive learning processes are linking elements. Creativity and accuracy interact; the student is the initiator in his learning. The teacher suggests, the teacher provides information and materials, but the student is the psychological activator in his work at school.

Five concerns in the teaching situation can be noted and studied. First, the nature of the learning situation has changed because the learner is defined differently now. Second, the nature of teaching is different because the teacher is perceived as having a different role than was formerly true. Third, the educational goals which have been defined for the learner are different; fourth, the materials and the classroom environment are different from the past; and fifth, the nature of evaluating pupils has changed. All these differences have emerged from new curriculum formats.

The nature of learning is different as defined by educational planners because children are viewed as having a greater potential in their own intellectual development than was formerly thought. Intelligence is in part a function of the experiences provided for the child. It is not a static entity that remains fixed and unchanging as a child experiences life at home and school. The quality of his experiences will greatly affect his intellectual capacities for learning.

The nature of teaching is perceived now as one in which the teacher guides the children's learning. The teacher is a catalyst for learning, a facilitator, and energizer of creative situations for children. She is not the answer-giver, the all-knowing, infallible absolutist. The teacher is a creature of feeling, of perception and insight, of sensitivity to pupil concerns, anxieties, and needs for human warmth and appreciation. In the teacher's new role as facilitator and provider of best materials for learning, the student is perceived as an active pursuer in the process. The teacher has to bring materials to each pupil that can ensure success in learning which ultimately results in a favorable self-concept. The self-concept in a child's development is seen as an essential "self-starter" for further enhancement in self-oriented goals for success. Independence in learning and goal-setting thrives on past experiences of success. The teacher's sensitivity to this view plays an important part in the child's enjoyment of learning.

The third concern that has arisen from new curriculum formats is the way goals are defined for the learner. The objectives planned for the child involve active participation on his part. He is expected to achieve in several different areas of learning. Objectives are specific, short-term in some cases, longer-term in others. The description of objectives has made major changes in the past ten years or so. Children's learning behavior is measured by successes in small itemized dimensions.

The fourth concern, involving materials and the classroom environment with which children must interact, brings evidence of a greater variety of media in subject matter than was ever available in history. Even though kindergartens of past years had a variety of blocks, puzzles, equipment for climbing and crawling, balls, jump-ropes, musical objects, recordings, books, clay, painting materials, yarn-sewing cards, educational environments of five- and six-year-olds of today have an even larger selection of materials. Since the children have to be the active pursuers in the learning process, they need to experiment with various objects and ideas to ensure success in learning at their levels.

Production of materials has become a self-proliferating enterprise, not only on educational markets but in private business organizations as well. Toy manufacturers employ psychologists to advise them on the best "growth" value of certain toys. Age-appropriate recommendations are given; virtues of intellectual increases in the child if certain toys are used are extolled. In any case, the market has never been as rich with materials ready to be purchased by school systems, teachers, parents and others who come in contact with children in any way. When school systems create their own materials, however, only their own teachers use them; they do not sell them to the public (to other school systems).

The last of the five concerns mentioned as a result of newly defined teaching situations is that of evaluation. Test-taking, while sanctioned and necessary for young children, has been viewed in many more ways than it used to be. More qualities are included in the evaluation of a child's performance. How he responds to materials, to people, to his peers, originality of ideas, initiation of interaction with others, quality and consistency of work are some of the items for consideration that can help to qualify his learning. One or two tests per year are not the major determiners of his progress at school. Much more information is considered in relation to a child's educational performance than a paper-and-pencil test alone. With very young children from three or four to about eight, attitudes toward the means of evaluation have to be more versatile as each educational year advances. Fortunately, educational planners and psychologists, as well as teachers of young children themselves, have responded to a more sensible way of evaluating.

Curriculum development for young children's programs has changed in the past twenty years. Recent scholars have been attracted to the field of early childhood education and have contributed ideas, programs, and formats which are currently available in books and journals. A wide variety of pamphlets from simple ideas to be used in activities with young children, to those of greater depth in reporting research that has been conducted with them, is very much in evidence at book stores and libraries (even in the supermarket). This rise in contributions was made possible in part through government subsidies and national stimulation in support of more research into problems of educational development in early childhood.

Whenever a large number of new materials appear on the market, it is more important than ever that people using them become more critical. One of the precautions to be taken is to protect the flexibility in young children's education. Yet the zealousness of people who want to instantize children's development by using precisely systematic steps in learning expected in a given time (two weeks or so), can inadvertently result in past mistakes of a "lock-step" education which teachers of older students are trying to minimize. The rigidly systematic programs require greater specificity at a given time and at a given "sitting" with the children. It is difficult to avoid this pitfall because educators are trying to be analytical and precise in their work with children.

summary

This chapter dealt with some of the major reasons that curriculum programs are what they are today. Writings in curriculum development are still flourishing; some have made a greater impression than others. For young children, it is necessary to consider major principles in curriculum development and adapt them to various age levels and concomitant abilities of the pupils.

The nature of the teaching situation has changed in the last twenty-five years. Not only has the work of writers in educational psychology, educational philosophy and in subject matter areas made an impact on changing the teaching act and its definition, but so has the current milieu of society.

One of the most important skills that teachers must help children learn is to attack a problem or at least to learn several ways to approach one, i.e., with alternative hypotheses of action. The scientific effort and process of investigation and its attempts to conduct an unbiased approach is highly valued in a complex society. Diversified opinions are useful especially when they are based on fact and expressed well. Children are encouraged to pursue ideas with an effort toward reaching the truth. The memorization of ideas and facts in themselves is not considered as important as it once was. Creative thinking, original ideas, logical thought, and problem-solving are emphasized. Single right or wrong answers are not viewed as appropriate to complicated problems. To expect a simplification of answers when there are many possible solutions is unrealistic. What is right for individuals in one era of history may not be right for others in another era.

American society prizes inventiveness and individuality. Philosophers, psychologists, educators, and academicians, even while discussing the struggle and conflict between freedom for individual expression and the need for social consciousness, suggest ways that individuals should be asserting themselves in the interests of mental health. Various social ills that reflect individual disorders and alienation from social groups indicate the need to be concerned about the educational processes of the young.

If one takes the broad view of curriculum goals, objectives, and implementations for the maximum development of young children at school, it becomes obvious that writers of those programs seek wholesome individualization for children. In one sense some writers are trying to accomplish this by a systematic application of skills that they think children need. Again, people in education must be cautious and not allow methods that seem new or novel to perpetuate the hazards of older ones. The systematic application of techniques and record-keeping, while providing better forms of analysis of what the children can and cannot do, may recreate rigidity in the curriculum.

topics for discussion

1. What are some of the major changes in curriculum development in the last fifty or sixty years? Do you think those changes were warranted? Have they benefited education in any way? Why?
2. Observe teachers at a planning meeting to implement curriculum change. Note some of the difficulties. Do you have some ideas as to the ways you might have responded if you were one of those teachers? Describe them.
3. Bring four courses of study to class that you would recommend. Describe the bases on which you would recommend them. What strengths and weaknesses do you see in them?
4. Give your impressions of a well-balanced curriculum design for three- to five-year-old children. What would it include? Give some of your major objectives for children in each age group. List the activities you would provide in order to meet those learning objectives.
5. How have the subject matter areas changed in terms of the content children study in school? Consider this in the light of ecology, for example, rockets to the moon, scientific innovations.
6. Why is problem-solving perceived as a top priority in contemporary curriculum design? Is it replacing another way of thinking? If so, what is it?

selected bibliography

Biber, Barbara, Edna Shapiro, and David Wickens. *Promoting Cognitive Growth. A Developmental-Interaction Point of View.* Washington, D. C.: National Association for the Education of Young Children, 1834 Connecticut Avenue, N.W., 1971.

Bruner, Jerome. *The Process of Education.* Cambridge, Mass.: Harvard University Press, 1960.

Dewey, John. *The Child and the Curriculum and The School and Society.* Chicago and London: University of Chicago Press, 1963.

Ebbeck, Frederick N., and Marjory A. Ebbeck. *Now We Are Four.* Columbus, Ohio: Charles E. Merrill Publishing Company, 1974.

Featherstone, Helen. "The Use of Settings in a Heterogeneous Preschool," *Young Children,* Vol. XXIX (March 1974), pp. 147–154.

Fein, Greta G., and Alison Clarke-Steward. *Day Care in Context.* New York: John Wiley & Sons, Inc., 1973.

Howes, Virgil M. *Informal Teaching in the Open Classroom.* New York: Macmillan Publishing Co., Inc., 1974.

Lapp, Diane, Hilary Bender, Stephan Ellenwood, and Martha John. *Teaching and Learning Philosophical, Psychological, Curricular Application.* New York: Macmillan Publishing Co., Inc., 1975.

Lowe, William T. *Structure and the Social Studies.* Ithaca and London: Cornell University Press, 1969.

Margolin, Edythe. *Sociocultural Elements in Early Childhood Education.* New York: Macmillan Publishing Co., Inc., 1974.

Margolin, Edythe. "Conservation of Self-Expression and Aesthetic Sensitivity in Young Children," *Young Children,* Vol. XXIII (January, 1968), pp. 155–160.

Margolin, Edythe. "Variety, Vitality, and Response in the Nursery School," *Young Children,* Vol. XXI (November, 1965), pp. 157–160.

Parker, Ronald K. *The Preschool in Action.* Boston: Allyn & Bacon, Inc., 1972.

Prescott, Elizabeth. "Approaches of Quality in Early Childhood Programs," *Childhood Education,* Vol. 50 (January, 1974), pp. 125–131.

Taba, Hilda. *Curriculum Development.* New York and Burlingame: Harcourt, Brace & World, Inc., 1962.

Tyler, Ralph W. "The Organization of Learning Experiences," *Toward Improved Curriculum Theory,* Virgil E. Herrick and Ralph W. Tyler, Ed. pp. 59–67. Supplementary Educational Monographs, Number 71, March, 1950. Chicago: University of Chicago Press.

Weikert, David P., Linda Rogers, Carolyn Adcock, and Donna McClelland. *The Cognitively Oriented Curriculum.* Urbana, Ill.: University of Illinois, 1971.

Chapter 4

Children Need to Communicate

Who am I? Who can tell me?
My mother? My father?
I have to discover for myself
who I am and what I am . . .
and human beings spend most of their lives
trying to discover their identity in relation
to their society.

From the moment a child is born, thoughts are developing inside of him. The way he looks around and the way he kicks his legs and flails his arms reveal inborn sets of mechanisms beginning to assert themselves in relation to the outside world.

When the child is very young his parents may give him books and magazines to play with or look at, either because they are valued for themselves or merely as a device for keeping the child occupied. In any case children always enjoy having the attention and company of an adult who wants to read to them. The interesting and changing tone in the adult's voice when reading to the child or speaking to him is pleasurable. The child is learning from hearing this.

In recent years, more research has been done on the language development of children, especially since its importance to pupil adequacy in functioning at school has been realized. Most of it relating to babies suggests that adults speak to infants whenever they feed, dress, play with or pat them when trying to comfort them. This kind of conversational interaction enriches the child's discriminatory powers in learning sounds, tones, syllables, and intonation of words. It provides them with the needed models for imitation.

Communication, as an area studied in early childhood education, is typically considered in terms of subject matter areas such as language arts, reading, literature, poetry, folktales, and other areas related to either oral and auditory aspects of communication or written expression of ideas, feelings, and factual representations, i.e., expository writing.

Because very young children in the two- to four-year-old group are limited in terms of what they can understand and what they can discuss, communication arts with them include such areas as sharing of ideas, listening to poetry, learning simple poems, doing finger play rhymes, or seeing puppets perform while listening to a story. They like to listen to recordings of stories and games that involve intricate directions for marching, singing, and other activities requiring concentrated listening.

Communication is a form of behavior. It is a complicated aspect of personality growth that involves many kinds of intellectual and emotional elements. Anxiety, hostility, fear or overexcitement can affect a child's production of language at any single instance. The teacher who works

The children enjoy following a story by listening and reading at the same time. The process of combining words with their pronunciation and printed appearance facilitates learning. The children are less distracted by other elements in the classroom when they have earphones to shut out other noises.

with young children has to be very aware of this. Hesitations or fear of disapproval from classmates or the teacher can cause the child to stutter, to mumble, or to produce faulty sounds—breathy, stifled, and incoherent. Because the emotions are closely associated with language behavior, teachers of young children need to learn how to ward off potential fears. The atmosphere of the classroom or other learning contexts must be protected so that children can sense a feeling of acceptance from teachers and others in that environment.

Purposes and Goals in Children's Communication Experiences

Writers of programs in the language arts and reading areas have major goals for children who experience the activities planned for them. They want children to learn how to communicate well, to the maximum of their abilities, and to enjoy the process of communication. A general exposure to written materials, as well as listening to electronic devices, is typical in any program plan. The wider the diversity of the materials and type of activities, the greater is the likelihood of success for the children's participation.

The purposes and goals of various programs for young children in communication arts may be considered in at least four ways. They include concerns for the child's maximum development in areas of listening, speaking, reading, and writing. Within those four areas are several levels of children's intake of information and their output or productivity.

While language facility involves techniques and methods, its development must involve concepts or ideas. The communication process is the means; the content of what is discussed refers to the substance. One of the reasons that it is not easy for the adult to teach language is that it is something that is taken for granted in his own past experiences of development. It becomes so much a part of the individual that it is difficult to separate one's self from it. Separating one's self from one's own language means that he must become self-conscious and aware of sounds, of beginnings, of memories of the way language may have taken on greater meaning in his own life. See Figure 4.1 for these essentials. On the left hand side of the figure is the knowledge and awareness aspect of language development; on the right hand side is the physical aspect in the production of speech sounds. This shows how content knowledge and physical elements and techniques are to be applied interchangeably. It is not an easy process and is built up after many years of practice.

One of the expected rewards or satisfactions in teaching any subject is that the individual who teaches it not only acquires a greater appreciation of it himself, but also enjoys seeing the way children respond to it. It is almost as if a twin process goes into action; there are two types of

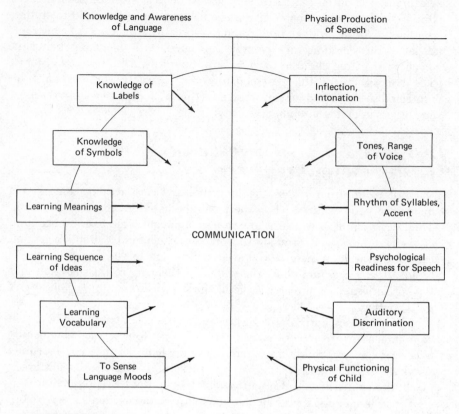

figure 4.1
Beginning Essentials for the Development of Communication

searchers with similar goals—to learn and to maximize the communication system devised by the society of one's environment.

The purposes and goals in activities designed for the development of listening skills involve children's concentration on sounds (and words) in their environment. They are expected to learn how to be discriminating in an auditory sense to differences in sounds and similarities among them, and in a broader sense, they are expected to be aware of the importance of listening to speech in terms of a given message, be it esthetic or functional.

Books devoted to discussions of language arts and reading in young children's development treat the area of listening as one oriented toward skills of comprehension, perception, and discernment of sounds in words, as well as the meanings intended by the speaker. For younger children, in the two- to five-year age range, listening skills, can be encouraged by the atmosphere created by the teacher. This will be discussed later in the section on developmental activities. But for the most part, goals for the development of listening skills should be oriented as much toward learning how to attend to sounds and words as to an understanding of the ideas that those sounds and words are supposed to represent. Meaning is not given the in-depth critical analysis in earlier grade levels in the same way that it will be in later school years. Listening can be geared toward acute hearing and toward a thoughtful understanding, at the child's level, of the written and spoken word.

For children in the primary grades, first, second, and third (or primary block as it is sometimes called), listening skills take on a greater and broader variety as they begin to read. Six-, seven-, and eight-year-old children in those grades have typically increased their abilities in reading and listening. Because individual differences are obvious among children, it is possible to see some five-year-olds performing as well as some seven-year-olds. Critical analyses of reading, or discussion in the case of listening, vary in terms of the children's abilities to reason and to apply logical thought to their ideas.

Listening is extremely important to the reproduction of words and sounds, especially where young children are concerned. The ability to discriminate between the sounds of a "b" and a "d" is needed in learning to read a word, to pronounce it correctly, and to spell it. Many children do not spell correctly because they do not hear the letters in the word and do not recognize them as related to the sound they assume is in the word and the letter that symbolizes the sound. Adults who have never seen certain words spelled but have heard them being used, will often substitute letters that they think represent the sound they have heard. (Some adults have said, "march" in place of the word "month," because they heard it that way and also were not aware of how the word was spelled.) Discrimination between sounds and the particular letter represented for those sounds is almost a lifetime process. It is understandable, therefore, that the listening aspect of a child's language development should receive strong emphasis.

Each writer on language arts as a subject matter area will give a slightly different emphasis to some part of it. Some describe what a good listener is,[1] some suggest what the purposes of listening are from their perspective,[2] and some will discuss the research findings in relation to the

[1] Paul C. Burns, Betty L. Broman, and Alberta L. Lowe Wantling, *The Language Arts in Childhood Education*, 2nd ed. (Chicago: Rand McNally & Company, 1971), pp. 83–84.
[2] Walter T. Petty, Dorothy C. Petty, and Marjorie F. Becking, *Experiences in Language* (Boston: Allyn & Bacon, Inc., 1973), p. 142.

basic kinds of preparedness children should have in achieving auditory skills.[3]

Basically, the children need to develop an awareness and identification of sounds—loud, soft, shrill, etc.—all of which can be done in the classroom. Clapping objects together (books, blocks, opening a window, closing a door), while the children's eyes are closed make them aware of sounds as such. It is this kind of discrimination "exercise" that makes children realize that sound is a separate phenomenon from other things, and that sounds have distinctiveness and meaning relative to speech, words, and other kinds of understanding necessary for basic learning in school.

They need to learn that listening to someone speak can give them information they do not have themselves. This involves a realization of interaction among people, the give-and-take process that enriches social interchange.

Children need to become aware of words that sound alike, that have the same beginnings and endings as well as learning word "families" of similar syllables or root sounds such as "cat," "fat," "rat," "bat," and the like. This is an area of study known as *phonics*, but it is an ear-training activity as well as, later, a reading activity.

Children need to hear sounds of nature, birds, animals, wind, rain and to become aware of the sounds they hear and the ways that sounds can be identified or classified, e.g., as soft, squeaky, harsh, or strong sounds. These associations with sounds and words, and discrimination between them are important to a child's development of sensitivity needed for effective auditory discrimination.

The main purposes of listening programs for children are to help them develop acute discrimination of sounds, of various words, an appreciation of differences and similarities in the language they are going to be using to help them communicate effectively. Not only are they expected to be attuned to the sounds of those words (See Figure 4.1), but also the meaning of those words. Sometimes the same word used in a different context takes on a different meaning. Sometimes words are spelled the same but are different in meaning, sometimes spelled differently (too, two, to) and mean different things.

The area of speaking in a language arts program is another example of the attempt to develop pupil sensitivity to sounds and words, their correct pronunciation and their relationships to ideas and meanings that a child wants to convey. (See Figure 4.1, which suggests some of the important elements involved in the development of communication.)

Children need many opportunities to express themselves, and while

---

[3] Susanna Whitney Pflaum, *The Development of Language and Reading in the Young Child* (Columbus, Ohio: Charles E. Merrill Publishing Company, 1974), pp. 136–144.

they are to be corrected at certain times when they are telling a story, this process of correction should be limited in relation to its effects on the child. Some children will be intimidated or discouraged if they are corrected too often and interrupted mid-sentence by a correction. The teacher should use judgment in this sense. When the teacher says, "Oh, yes, I see you mean —" and continues using the child's words but in correct form, hearing the correction is made less painful to the child. He is far more apt to listen than to close off what is being said because he is hurt by it.

One writer describes effective speech as being ". . . rhythmic; free from many hesitations, repetitions, and interruptions; and produced at a suitable tempo and volume for the content and the audience, with all sounds clearly articulated and distinctly enunciated." [4] This is an ideal toward which the teacher can work with the child. Judgment needs to be used in deciding just when the child's speech will be interrupted for correction or help in improving a child's volume or tempo in his production of speech. A teacher who is sensitive to differences in children will attempt to foster development but not to detract from it by demanding early perfection.

The goals in helping children learn to speak suggest that teachers be aware of the models that they themselves provide when they talk to pupils, remembering to pronounce words clearly, to speak in a rhythmic pattern, use varied tones, and avoid mannerisms or distracting gestures. Since the children are listening to the teacher most of the time, her speaking style is a major source used by them for imitation. The pupils also consider her almost perfect as an individual (especially younger children, who often idolize the teacher) and will feel that it enhances their personalities to speak "like the teacher." They are often, however, not even aware that they are imitating; it becomes "natural" for them. They apparently adopt the style as their own.

Children need to learn how to pronounce about forty-four different phonemes in the English language. A phoneme is the smallest segment of sound, for example, the sound that comes from pronouncing "b" or "d," which distinguishes different words and parts of words from each other. Babies make these sounds, not realizing of course that the sound will be parts of words and have meaning; nevertheless, speech production is developing in their language. They have learned, too, that certain sounds bring certain responses from people. In that sense, they associate sound and meaning, but not with the intellectual meaning that they will know later.

Children in the three- to five-year age range are encouraged to speak, to express ideas, and to share feelings with other people. The teacher's

[4] Petty, Petty, and Becking, op. cit., pp. 109–110.

goals in this context are to provide opportunities for children to obtain a feeling of importance in having something to say to their peers. She is an important element in creating the atmosphere which enhances respect for individuals in that classroom. She shows in her way of listening to each child that what he has to say is of value. The children will begin to expect that kind of attention from others as well. Teachers are more important than they may realize in the process of showing children what their expectations of them are in the classroom. Pupils adapt to those expectations easily. They learn quickly what the social and emotional climate is. This means that the processes of speech need an attentive audience, a sympathetic listener, and ample space, time, and appropriate moments in order to flourish.

As children progress in school they learn more about being responsible for what they say. They learn that before they speak, they should be sure that what they say is true. There are times when people speak for therapeutic reasons; they may be nervous and find that talking can serve as a catharsis to release tension. Children at school can learn the differences between fact and opinion, on the one hand, and angry, prejudiced "personalized," or one-sided statements, on the other. Appropriateness to a given situation is the key to deciding whether factual information is needed, whether emotional and personalized statements are in order (such as in creative writing), or whether the release of anger and frustration are acceptable forms at that time for the expression of ideas.

The children are helped in seeing differences between making accusations stemming from dislike of an individual, and trying to see the truth in the situation. An example of this distinction is a child telling the teacher someone took his pencil, accusing a person he did not like, without being sure the accused person was guilty.

Meaning, responsibility for what one says, making judgments, trying to convey an idea clearly are emphasized as children mature. In the primary grades, however, teachers stress techniques for speaking clearly and well. They make distinctions for pupils by calling attention to elements in speech that are worthy of emulation. With fine literature in the classroom, appropriate to the children's age level, the children have an opportunity to hear rhythmic flowing sounds and words in the expression of ideas. This can be used as a model for their own production of speech and of course can provide beautiful word pictures or imagery.

In the area of reading, which is a complicated developmental process of learning, instructional programs have become very precise in expectations. The psychological and emotional understandings a child needs in learning how to read suggest that the affective qualities, the emotional and feeling tones in the situation, combined with a child's self concept, are crucial in the process. In that sense, some of the decisions that had to be made in identifying the age at which young children should learn to read became a central focus in educational literature.

Systematic reading instruction in the kindergarten was considered taboo for many years. The age of five was considered too young for such instruction. One of the major reasons given for this kind of thinking was that young children's eye musculature was not developed to the point of facilitating the learning of reading. It was reasoned that they could not adjust eye muscles to the size of print most often seen in children's books. The difficulties that children might have in focusing on print and their inabilities to concentrate for extended periods of time on the discussion of ideas seemed to be a barrier to learning to read. The age of six was one that seemed more appropriate to the beginning of instruction in that area. Typically, the child was in the first grade at that age. Thus most programs of instruction seemed better geared toward beginning at age six.

In recent years, programs have been written to introduce reading in the kindergarten. Children are four and five at that time. They are also, in some cases, experiencing school as a process, as a classroom in which they need to learn to interact with several other children. They need to learn many techniques and skills involved in becoming a pupil—how to respond to the teacher, to the subject matter, to objects and materials in the classroom, to procedures involved in routines such as "lining up" to enter and to leave the classroom, learning where to keep their belongings in the cupboards or cloakrooms provided for them, and many other items of schoolroom "policies." Kindergarten teachers are amazed to see the progress of a child who comes in with no awareness of what the routines are and understands them well in so short a time. They are capable of doing this. It must be remembered by adults, however, that the children are learning a large number of school-learning techniques in a short period and are doing so simultaneously.

Purposes and goals of reading programs for children in primary grades concentrate specifically on the techniques needed to learn how to read. It is an extremely important period in young children's lives. In the kindergarten, however, the reading programs concentrate more on beginning skills that involve auditory discrimination and visual discrimination. Hearing and noting differences in sounds and letters is emphasized as well as seeing the way those letters look in relation to the way they sound. This becomes an important part of the ongoing process of learning to read.

Readiness for learning to read goes on all through the day in a kindergarten that has a skillful teacher. It is one in which the children are sensitized constantly to differences in sounds, in pronunciation, and appearance of certain labels, words, songs, tones, intensities. Thus, some of the major goals in any reading program for kindergarten children is to prepare them psychologically, emotionally, socially, and intellectually, as

Story sequences are shown on filmstrips. The child can adjust the pace of the filmstrip to his own desires.

well as academically, for the learning process necessarily involved in reading. Concentration on an idea, focus on a picture, focus on listening for a certain sound or its repetitiveness in speech strengthen a child's visual and auditory acuity. These ideas are also used with musical experiences, so that children can enjoy listening to sounds, high and low, loud and soft, light and heavy, melodious and somber.

One writer suggests that an effective reading program will include an emphasis on the techniques that will increase children's independence in reading: opportunities to read a wide variety of materials of interest to them; opportunities to read aloud to others when the material is of special interest; and listening to the teacher read stories of high quality.[5] The teacher also has the responsibility of listening to the children when they read or speak so that she can know where and when they need help in pronunciation, enunciation, or expressing an idea.

[5] Ruth Strickland, *The Language Arts in the Elementary School* 3rd ed. (Lexington, Mass.: D. C. Heath and Company, 1969), p. 272.

This child seems to be showing that it is sheer joy to relax, rock and enjoy a book, even within the presence of an entire classroom full of children. Open spaces and rocking chairs seem to lift some of the psychological constraints often found in kindergartens.

Nothing like having a friend share the contents of a book with you.

The children enjoy showing each other what they have "written." Their own scribbling makes sense to them.

Learning what the letters look like are part of the first steps in writing and reading.

This girl is learning to sense the difference between an upper case (or capital) "G" and a lower case "g."

This boy has had some experience writing. He does not concentrate "as hard" as other children who find writing difficult.

This girl is not new to the writing process but she proceeds carefully with the assignment.

The children were writing letters to thank the (TV) weather man for visiting them and providing information for exciting discussion periods. The teacher wrote the words on the board that the children needed for their thank-you notes and in this way facilitated some of their concerns for correct spelling.

Children create their own booklets on famous people in history. They write their own stories as well as draw their own illustrations to go with the content.

Sometimes two children like to do a writing project together. While they may write on the same topic, they do independent thinking relative to that topic. They also welcome their teacher's help when they have difficulty.

Most programs help children to acquire skills in the recognition and meaning of words, to develop skills in reading aloud and silently, and to achieve a taste in the enjoyment of many kinds of stories, poetry, and factual material. It is hoped that children will want to read outside the classroom as well as in, thus indicating that their interest in reading is developing in terms of the program's objectives.

Most writers on the subject of teaching children to read suggest that pressures should be eliminated. Children should not be forced to read. If they are ready to read they are typically interested in some elements of reading. It is often the situation of the classroom or something that is uncomfortable at school that turns them away from the teaching process. The problem may be a restricting, overly demanding teacher, some peers that cause discomfort or embarrassment, or parental pressures at home demanding better performances in reading. In any case, what needs to be remembered is that the process of reading involves many kinds of behavior and linkages in the brain to bring successful results. A child has to co-ordinate many skills and physical processes; if he is unwilling for some reason or other to make the effort it will be difficult to force him. Underlying symptoms need to be discovered.

The last area mentioned as part of the language arts program is the acquisition of skills in writing. Not only is the physical act of writing, of learning to formulate letters as those in one's language indicates, demanding when one starts school, but so is the ability to write words, phrases, ideas and sentences of one's own. Most objectives for writing are similar to the areas mentioned already. The children have to begin the acquisition of an extensive vocabulary in order to express themselves as they intend, and have to remember the way the word looks in order to recall the correct spelling of it.

Children between the ages of three and five like to scribble, to try to write their names and have someone look with admiration at what they have done. They like to use a pencil or heavy crayon and relax in trying to reproduce what they think is something they have seen in print or writing. Indeed the writing of adults looks to them like their own scribbling, as it would to anyone not understanding what it said. They rarely do anything of this nature without showing someone what they have done, and they do expect a hearty response of some kind, preferably one of praise and smiles.

In the primary grades, children are learning to formulate manuscript letters, as shown in Figure 4.2. The letters are made up mainly of circles, half-circles, and straight lines. The underlying assumption is made that if children are taught manuscript first, before they are taught cursive writing, they can better make the shift from reading their own writing to reading print in a book which has similar forms. The manuscript writing seems to require less manipulative control than cursive. Also no joining

figure 4.2
Example of Manuscript Writing

of letters is required in the manuscript process. (Note Figure 4.3.) Instruction in cursive writing comes later, toward the end of the primary grades period.

The physical aspect of learning to write is only one part of a child's work at school. It is a gradual process. He learns the shape of letters and gradually puts them together as words. He has to learn how to space words on a page and to leave enough room on the page or line for what he has planned to write. This too is not easy and comes later in the experience of writing.

Earlier in the process of learning to write, however, children copy letters from a chalkboard or from an instructional sheet given out by the teacher. They write simple statements regarding a picture they have drawn. They do not write their own ideas at length, of course, until they are more comfortable in the process of writing in the physical sense as well as the intellectual. They need many experiences in writing before they can feel comfortable in the entire process.

In kindergarten the child has usually seen his ideas written down when the teacher asks him what he would like to tell her about a painting, a drawing, or collage. They learn in this way that their own dictated statements to the teacher represent ideas or words as spoken; these ideas become writing and then reading after they are written.

Children learn to write simple messages such as those in Mother's Day cards (i.e., "I love you, Mother, with love, Ginny"), birthday greetings, Father's Day cards, and other holiday greetings. In the primary grades

abcd

figure 4.3
Example of Cursive Writing

they learn increasingly more complicated means of writing personalized messages. They learn proper punctuation and also begin to understand the forms that are automatically used in letters or brief notes, dates, the salutation form of "Dear Sir," endings such as "Yours truly," or "Sincerely yours." Some school systems use workbooks for writing development exercises with children. The exercises often reflect the more traditional sequence of concentrating on certain letters at certain times and proceed in a systematic letter-by-letter approach.

The goals and objectives in writing programs for young children are directed toward helping them understand the purposes of writing, the worthiness of effectiveness, and the interesting forms of writing employed to express precisely what is intended. It is hoped that gradually children will value their own ideas. The teacher and the program work toward that end. The teacher's goals for the children is to help them enjoy the process and to enjoy a well-written message, idea, story, poetry, and other literary forms.

Developmental Activities for Young Children's Effectiveness in Communication

Since communication is a form of behavior that each child develops, the teacher is in a position to help each one become as articulate as possible. In this process of learning to express one's self well, one important aspect is listening. The child has to have some forms as examples from his environment if he is to imitate what is being said. He has to learn to attune his ear to sounds, nuances, inflections, and various psychological meanings coming from people around him.

Listening is the first component of learning to speak, read, or write. For young children in the three- to five-year-old age range, the teacher provides many stories, recordings, well illustrated books, poems, songs, fingerplay rhymes simple to follow, and musical instruments that sensitize the child to various tones, sounds, intensities, and rhythmic movement.

The teacher draws the children's attention to the way different words sound, beginnings and endings, by merely asking them to listen to certain stories, poems, or songs. Every once in a while, when the teacher hears a play on words in a story she tells the children about it, showing them the interesting effects it creates. Children learn this easily when they hear folktales or rhymes that are repetitive. They will often compose simple stories resembling the ones that were read to them in class.

Fingerplays and simple rhymes catch children's interest. They enjoy repeating them and learn from them as well. A repertoire of poems, stories, and songs provide the child with some confidence in speech. He also learns that rhythmic qualities can be enjoyed in the process. When these rhythmic elements become a part of his memory he can use them for his own ideas in stories and writing later in school.

Kindergarten children can have many opportunities for noticing the pleasurable elements of sound. Many schools have listening centers in which earphone headsets are provided to give children opportunities to listen to stories, songs, or student-participation recordings. The children are asked, for example, to clap their hands, or to sway like an elephant moving his trunk in front of him. There are many recordings of this kind on the commercial market.

In the primary grades, the children learn to listen by learning how to become an audience when a classmate tells them of an experience he or she has had. They learn to ask questions about what they hear. Before a presentation is given the teacher tells the class what they should be aware of, in other words, how to listen for important points in a talk given by a child. The children also learn how to comment on what has been said, to be courteous to the speaker, to wait their turn, and not to interrupt one another.

Children are given many opportunities for games that involve careful listening, such as "Simon Says," which permits the children to follow a given movement by the leader only when the phrase "Simon Says" comes prior to that directed movement. Children who do not listen for that phrase are out of the game. The challenge is to see how long someone can remain in the game. This denotes in part that the child has listened carefully.

The teacher brings various boxes or bags of "surprises" to the children in which articles are hidden. Each child is asked to put his hand in the box and to describe some of the items he thinks are there. Sometimes this is done while the child is blindfolded or places his hands over his eyes. The recognition of sounds or of objects is an important goal in listening; therefore the teacher tries to create as many game-like situations as possible that involve this ability. These things can be done at various times of the day because they have a playful quality. They do not require a great deal of preparation of structuring for the children's participation.

Riddles present a time for perceptive listening. They often have a rhythmic pattern which contributes to the fun of hearing them. The children should be asked to create their own riddles.

Nonsense poetry and humorous rhymes attract children's attention to the qualities of sound and an orientation toward listening for a certain element or point of a poem or story. In other words, the context becomes a lead-up to a significant part of speech or written work. Telling jokes typically involves listening for a punch line, thus children learn to be attentive waiting for a climax in what is being said. They learn to wait for these highpoints.

Following directions to music is an important part of learning how to listen.

The children never seem to tire of singing games, which are both a form of relaxation and of attentive listening.

Many activities that can be used for children in the primary grades are given in books and articles on the subject. The teacher has to constantly search for ideas that can be used for the specific children she has in her class. When she knows the major principles involved in helping children build their acuity skills she can create many activities of her own. Attentiveness which results because of adequately motivated children will go a long way in building skills for listening perceptively. The teacher has to think of ways to entice the children in learning activities, making them curious enough about subject matter so that they will want to listen. Pupils often tell their classmates to "quiet down" so that they can hear what is being said. This is the best kind of evidence that they enjoy their work and are interested in it.

DEVELOPMENTAL ACTIVITIES FOR SPEAKING

Developmental activities needed for helping children learn to speak well are partially a result of their perceptiveness in listening. They can reproduce sounds, words, nuances, or speech patterns which they have heard in the environment, when these auditory aspects are brought to their attention. The school environment is a creative endeavor on the part of the teacher to provide fully for the children's opportunities to express themselves. The key to this set of skills in the teacher is to be aware of the children's developmental levels in speech production at a certain point and to know which activities will best provide for children's progress at that time.

An awareness of individual differences, individual personalities, individual speech styles in young children is essential to teaching. The teacher encourages and urges; she does not push or pressure children, making them feel miserable or unhappy because they cannot meet her expectations in terms of external standards presented in a course of study.

Knowing that children have a larger listening vocabulary than they do of words they use in their own speech, the teacher is patient. She does not tell the child he is not trying; she does not give him the impression that he is deliberately withholding information from her. An emotional atmosphere in the class of rigidity and stiffness on the part of the teacher can only inhibit the child. Some children unfortunately have the feeling that their teacher will not approve of them regardless of what they say. This is obviously very detrimental to children's attempts to learn. For this reason the teacher must provide a nonthreatening environment for them, one in which the children feel accepted.

Pupils need planned opportunities to speak to their classmates, to share ideas and stories with them, to laugh together about experiences they have had and enjoyed. Discussions, choral reading of poetry, recording voices of their peers, role playing, acting out stories they have read, give the children practice in speaking and becoming aware of those

Sometimes children like to be silly and try on wigs. Others join in the fun. School does not have to be a somber place.

These kindergarten boys are having a great time. They built their own private enclosure and are enjoying an uninterrupted conversation.

skills that contribute to doing it well. Games that require talking, telling, giving directions, listening to points requiring participation on the children's part can be found in many books and articles dealing with children's linguistic skills.

Dramatic play is an ideal experience for young children. They become the people they are thinking of and act out many feelings that arise in

114

This is a construction worker building roads and a bridge, as anyone can see. Even while he is doing this, mathematical judgment is in process as well as spatial reasoning.

their own every-day lives involving relationships with others. This is referred to as "taking the role of the other." It involves a kind of thinking in the child that arouses feelings of identification or empathy, as well as anger or release. Trying to place one's self in the position of another person makes the child aware that others have feelings similar to his own. The teacher can use role-playing situations to enhance this kind of awareness. Children may be asked to act out characters in a book, poem or story they have heard. This combines attentiveness and observation skills required in trying to be the first to guess the character correctly. Four-year-olds do an excellent job acting out "Billy Goats Gruff" or "The Three Bears." After hearing the story read to them, knowing they will be expected to act it out, they have usually listened carefully for what they will say if they choose one of the character's parts. They often have to hear segments of the story again.

Telephone conversations in the playhouse area of the kindergarten should be encouraged. The children pretend that they are calling a friend or relative or even calling the doctor to see a "sick patient" in a doll bed. Fantasy, pretending, role-playing, taking the "role of the other,"

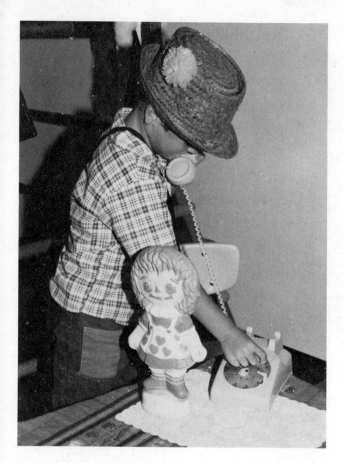

Taking the role of the father or an uncle who is telephoning a message to someone at home is excellent for language development of the young child.

or thinking of one's self in someone else's position, are all excellent ways to help children project ideas relative to the outside world in which they will have to live and cope. Some writers describe this as a kind of role rehearsal. The child is acting out his role or that of the other individual in a role-set (mother to child, son to father, doctor to patient). In any case it serves the purpose of helping the child articulate ways that people speak to each other in daily social exchange. This is necessary for them to learn. There are no specific instructions for this as there are for learning mathematics, science, or spelling.

The teacher learns more about the children, their interests, concerns, anxieties, and misconceptions, as she listens to them speak to playmates in the playhouse area. She learns what happens to the child at home or on his way to school. The teacher who listens to the children's speech in an analytical sense is obtaining ideas for the next steps she will take with the child to advance his development. Breathiness, reticence, and inaudible sounds often reveal symptoms of other problems in a child. Many times they reflect a lack of confidence. The child may feel that what

This busy mother is preparing food for her family, but since she plans to go out soon she has her fancy hat on.

he has to say is not important. The teacher has to establish eye contact with him and listen carefully to what he is saying and has to remember that he needs individual attention more than others when he speaks.

Children are asked to respond to pictures shown to them and to describe what they think is happening. One researcher indicates that children respond with greater complexities in their speech and longer length of sentences when they are asked to describe real objects rather than pictured ones, unconventional incidents in pictures rather than conventional ones, and when they are asked to give their impressions of what is happening in a series of pictures.[6] The teacher has to be ever aware of the great variety of activities and simple experiences that can be presented to children in order to elicit desires to speak.

Musical games help children become aware of tones. The teacher asks them to match tones in the musical scale by singing high and low as she plays the piano, the autoharp, or tone bells. Many kindergarten teachers give their morning greeting to the children in song. The children respond to her in a song, "Yes, I am here," matching her tones.

Sound production, whether in words, notes, or imitation of animals or machine noises (which children enjoy tremendously), provides pupils with opportunities to demonstrate their awareness of auditory discrimina-

[6] Courtney Cazden, *Child Language and Education* (New York: Holt, Rinehart and Winston, Inc., 1972), p. 209.

tion. This in itself gives them information about themselves needed to build that sense of identity which is essential to every person's mental health. The children learn that they can activate events in their environment in ways that arouse social approval. When social approval pays off in feelings of self-worth the child is far more likely to continue in pursuit of such activities that validate those impressions. In other words, to the child it appears to be more fun to do things that receive social approval than it is to be mischievous.

DEVELOPMENTAL ACTIVITIES FOR READING INSTRUCTION

Children often pretend they are reading when they sit next to their parents or teacher and turn the pages of a book. They take on the attitudes and facial expressions of the adult and study the pages, appearing to concentrate with intense interest. This is a start toward the physical attention needed for the highly prized skill in American society.

More has been written recently than ever before in the history of education, on ways to teach reading to young children. Since many adults enjoy reading as a pastime they are surprised and disappointed that children do not. They wonder what is happening in schools and why children are not as excited as they themselves are about books.

Reading effectiveness is not only associated with enjoyment but also with one's livelihood. If the child does not know how to read he suffers in many ways, not only socially but in terms of preparation for a job or profession. This also affects his self image in a negative sense. Success in one's job affects other parts of the individual's life. It transfers to feelings of worthiness, pride, and individual self-satisfaction. If these qualities are not acquired in some measure, the individual has many problems. He turns to other ways of ensuring self-esteem, which may not be in the socially approved categories.

In the age range between three and five, children are seeing pictures in their environment. Parents or siblings tell them what the pictures mean, e.g., the cow on a carton of milk. They learn various word associations by using pictures. They see signs in stores, on the highway, on buses, on trucks. If they are encouraged by answers to their questions, they will ask more. They need this kind of adult exchange if they are to gain information.

Beginning reading occurs in this process of being told the meaning of certain words and pictures. Activities in the kindergarten involve reading labels, seeing other children's names, reading directions, recognizing certain words such as "stop," "go," "exit," "school," "office," and the like. As children realize the importance of noting relationships between letters and words, they pay more attention to differences and similiarities among words and letters.

Instruction in reading in the formalized sense, typically involves groups of children sitting down together and being given the opportunity, one at a time, to read aloud. The teacher attempts to group children who seem to be progressing at similar rates, to minimize the amount of time spent in each group. If an extremely slow child were in a group of pupils that were reading very well, not only would the child be discouraged in that group, but the other pupils would become restless waiting for him to read a sentence or two.

Grouping children in reading units is an issue among educators. Some say that they should be mixed, that the less able should be with those that can do better in order to have a valid model to emulate. The teacher has to use judgment in the way she groups children. Various criteria have to be considered. Academic abilities are one aspect of the child's performance; social and physical skills are also involved in reading. Tension produced by feelings of inadequacy suggests that sometimes the less able child should be with those that permit him to have a more favorable self-concept.

Too few opportunities for success at school can create negative attitudes toward people and all situations at school as well as toward the subject matter in which the child is expected to achieve. Opportunities to succeed are related to the self-concept. This is one of the reasons why the teacher's way of organizing pupils into groups, as well as the kind of experiences she provides, become crucial to the way a child will perceive himself.

One writer indicates that the teacher's power to influence the classroom social system is great, it can increase the interaction among pupils and reduce conflict among them as well as help them increase their self esteem.[7] "Life at school is particularly stressful for the child who, by temperament, is slow to approach new situations or withdraw from them, is irregular in his work habits, is slow in adapting to change in his environment, and is frequently negative in mood."[8]

Thus it is obvious that the teacher has to be not only academically well informed but also sensitive to children's development and their current or daily moods at school. A comfortable way for some children to build confidence is to read something as part of a group, to participate in choral reading. A passage from a book, the chalkboard, or a chart composed by the children can be read with the class, and in this way the child is given some confidence hearing his own voice among others saying the correct words.

In the first grade the children are often composing stories describing a trip they have taken to the zoo, airport, seashore, dairy, supermarket,

---

[7] John C. Glidewell, "The Child at School," in *Modern Perspectives in International Child Psychiatry,* edited by John G. Howells. (New York: Brunner/Mazel Publishers, 1971), pp. 738–739.

[8] Ibid.

The children know what they are expected to do by looking at the chart. Many teachers prepare several charts of this kind so that pupils have enough work to do at any time of the day.

or other community facility. Field trips supply a great deal of information to young children. They visit places with their class and are sensitized before they go toward learning about certain items of information. They are taught to look for significant objects, processes, events, and appearances of various machines they see. When they return to their classroom, they have information for many writing and reading experiences to be done individually and/or as a group. The children can write stories about what they have seen, what their favorite moments were on the trip, and the people they enjoyed the most. They usually draw pictures showing what they had seen. These are linked to their writing and more often than not become part of their own small publications entitled, "What I Liked Best When I Went to the Zoo," or "What I Saw When I Went to the Airport."

The important points in children's having experiences on field trips are that they gain a common source of data to use as ideas for stories, poems, songs, and artistic products from clay, papier maché or rhythms: While a field trip often comes under the heading of a social studies activity, it provides factual material that can be used in any of the techniques for learning at school. Physical education, rhythms, recordings, mathematics, science are related to all of the life's experiences that children have. When they have them as a total classroom group, so much the better. The commonality of the trip on any given day injects spontaneity and zest to the school day as well as to the experiences that follow it.

Reading for children must have a satisfying purpose. They read to discover information. When they write their own stories they are interested in reading them and do not feel apprehensive about knowing the words. They know them because the words are their own.

In the primary grades, from the earliest introduction to reading, children are asked to look for certain facts in passages they are given to read. They obtain information from looking at accompanying pictures. When they do not know the words, they are told to try to recognize the sounds denoted by certain letters in the words. Phonics, a system for sounding out words, is not as prominent in contemporary reading methods as it used to be. If children were to concentrate on one letter at a time, educators reasoned, the pupil's concentration would be on details and would interfere with comprehension. Now children are taught to look at a phrase or a group of words that have meaning in context rather than to focus on certain letters in words. Only when a child's reading slows down because of an inability to recognize a word is he told to look at the letters and sound out what he thinks is the correct pronunciation. Many word games concentrate on word parts, however, and so do beginning programs for young children.

Children have many exercises in seeing families of words, that is, words that have similar parts with only the first letter changing the pronunciation, i.e., "bat," "fat," "cat," "rat," "sat," "pat." Games that have letters on cards and which can be placed next to the other word parts involve the children in word recognition. Bingo word games too have cards with word parts on them which have to be matched to the correct corresponding space.

The essential plans for doing a reading lesson with children includes at least five aspects.[9] First, the teacher should develop a sense of readiness for the lesson by motivating the children. She calls attention to new words they will be seeing and to new ideas in the story. Second, the children are given some clues as to what they can find in the selection to be read and they are asked to look for answers to those questions. Third, they read over again the same materials but they answer more specific questions than they did before. They interpret some of the specific words and concepts by reading certain parts aloud. Fourth, certain skills are emphasized through workbook materials prepared for them in relation

9 Walter T. Petty, Dorothy C. Petty, and Marjorie F. Becking, *Experiences in Language* (Boston: Allyn & Bacon, Inc., 1973), p. 353.

Various beginnings of words are matched with the pictures of objects that the words represent.

to new and review skills in reading; and fifth, enrichment is provided for them by having follow-up work which grew out of techniques and concepts encountered in the reading lesson. The approaches to reading used by teachers are highly varied, as one might guess. Each teacher discovers the techniques that are best for her own pupils.

In all reading lessons, the children are motivated to understand the content of the material. They are assisted before they read the story by receiving information on new words, their meaning, and the way they are used in a sentence. Children are also asked to look for answers to questions about ideas in the reading passages. Pupils read orally the answers to those questions. Follow-up activities are provided to generate more learning from the materials just read. The atmosphere is unhurried and the teacher tries to make the lesson as pleasant as possible.

In one second grade lesson [10] recommended to help the children gain comprehension in their reading, it is suggested that they first read the story to find the main idea in it. Then they select certain details that seem

[10] John J. De Boer and Martha Dallman, *The Teaching of Reading,* 3rd ed. (New York: Holt, Rinehart and Winston, Inc., 1970), p. 217.

122

This chart reminds the children of important facts and ideas that they need to look for in their reading.

more important than others. Finally, they summarize and organize the story by writing a few sentences about it as a group endeavor.

Children have to learn how to recognize words, their meanings, and their many different uses in sentences. Reading skills are complicated. Pupils, however, are able to do many kinds of work regardless of the difficulties involved. With so many games, audio-visual aids, charts, filmstrips, and overhead projectors to show in large size various words, pictures, and inferred meanings, and with new technical machines to help teachers create interesting instructional lessons for children, it seems that the more important human skills that need focusing is the pleasant attitude of the teacher. Pupils who are with this kind of teacher receive a message of faith in them and their abilities to be productive as they possibly can while knowing they will be accepted for those efforts. Self-acceptance becomes the pivotal aspect of drive for the desire to produce.

Many programs have been devised to provide the teacher with systematically organized lessons. They have been geared for certain grade levels beginning with kindergarten. These programs are usually purchased through school systems after various supervisors consider them meritorious enough to allocate funds for their purchase. Sometimes a program is bought and tried out in a few pilot schools. A pilot school is one that is observed for results of a given program. After it has been used in the school and seems to support earlier hunches regarding its worthiness, it is reordered for more schools to use.

The planned lessons are given various names associated with the kind of skills they promise to strengthen in children's language development. Sometimes they are named for the laboratory in which they were produced or written. Regional research laboratories exist in various parts of the United States. Some of these receive federal grants to devise and promote effective language development systems.

Educational corporations affiliated with encyclopedias provide large pictures, posters, lessons, and reading activities that help the teacher create plans for a variety of materials in the classroom. There is no shortage of materials for helping children learn. The teacher, however, has to be aware of developmental levels in each child and how to guide his progress in terms of his learning pace and style. If a teacher is in a school system that does not have a great deal of materials at its disposal, it is not difficult to make them out of cast-off objects such as milk cartons, buttons, plastic containers, or inexpensive five-and-ten cent store items. One writer has suggestions for ways of creating excellent activities using just such materials.[11] Children enjoy learning with materials that are sturdy, do not break easily, and do not cause cuts or scratches from splinters, paint peeling or rusting and the like.

Basal readers have carefully sequenced lessons with activities that are suggested to the teacher as enrichment or follow-up work for the children to do independently. Group plans for the organization of reading depend on the teacher's philosophy in part and also what the administrators recommend at any given time. Some administrators give the teachers complete freedom in the way they want to organize their pupils; some recommend certain formats and may have strong feelings about them. Administrators sometimes study certain programs and subsequently suggest that their teachers try them. In any case, it is not a complicated task to shift children from one group to another if it is obvious that they benefit from it. They need to learn from others, but they also need a period of maintenance time in which they feel that they have mastered the material they are expected to know. In this period they are able to help other pupils. This permits them to have a sense of mastery and self-worth.

Figure 4.4 shows one example of the way teachers organize children into reading groups. Some teachers keep children in those groups when they are doing other subject matter as well as reading, because of psychological reasons. Some teachers feel that certain children do better if

---

[11] Mary Baratta Lorton, *Workjobs* (Menlo Park, California: Addison-Wesley Publishing Company, 1972).

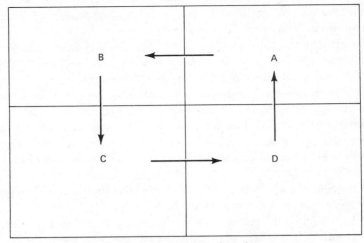

Arrows indicate path of rotation

The teacher works with Group A on a reading lesson.

Group B is working on independent activity at their seats. This activity is related to what they will be reading when she works with them.

Group C is working on matching, word recognition games, discriminating shapes and sizes which are all related to reading skills.

Group D is painting at easels or doing another form of art activity until it is their turn to work with the teacher in reading.

figure 4.4
Reading Groups (An Example of the Way Reading Groups May Be Rotated)

they are not with their closest friends for an extended period of time. Pupils are sometimes distracted from their work if they are close to their best friends with whom they like to talk. As a teacher works with children more frequently and in smaller groups she begins to know them better. About 20 or 25 minutes are spent in each group activity. The teacher decides on the variations when needed. This would depend on the complexity of the activity, the age of the children, and the nature of interaction in the classroom. Some teachers have three groups; others have four or five. Again this depends on how the children are learning.

One writer suggests that children typically read on three descriptive levels.[12] First is the independent level at which most words are known to the child and the content is somewhat familiar to his own experiences. A second level is the instructional level; about 90 per cent of the words

[12] Petty, Petty, and Becking, op. cit., p. 357.

can be recognized by the child and he has about 75 to 80 per cent comprehension. The child who has less ability than those described above is at the frustration level. He needs help.

Children in the third grade or at the top of the primary block of first, second and third grades are moving toward intermediate grade work. Their readiness for difficult materials is evident. They are able to read well, to write, to spell and speak. Variations among children's abilities and skills show that their performances differ. For the most part, however, the children show advancement beyond the six- and seven-year-olds. Most people are surprised at the competence of some children at eight years old. They seem quite mature. Children who were fortunate enough to have had competent and interested teachers and parents who supported them psychologically learn rapidly and begin to show perceptive qualities about people and ways to relate to them.

Pupils in the third grade are given increasingly difficult reading materials. They are, however, still using word attack skills, noting the structural analysis of words, i.e., the endings, beginnings and word parts. They begin to know certain rules in phonetics, sounds of letters before certain other letters (hard and soft sounds); they know that the letters and the position they have in a word affects pronunciation. For example, *circus, cups, city, cabbage,* the letter "c" is given a different sound depending on the letters it precedes.

Children at the age of eight can become much more analytical than they could in the kindergarten, first or second grades. They need confidence and the skills to do so. They need many experiences with the teacher to discuss critical and analytical approaches to the materials being read. They need to have difficult areas pointed out to them. They need to be sensitized to conflicting facts and false information. Their analytical skills can be practiced in both an orientation toward the meaning intended in certain reading passages as well as the structure of words.

Teachers in the third grade need more materials that children can go to after they are finished with their usual assignment. These activities are sometimes called enrichment, supplementary, "extra-credit," or whatever the teacher decides seems most appropriate to her perceptions of what they are and will motivate the children best. But children who do finish their work before others should know that they are expected to do other things. A teacher who has discipline problems is often the one who has not planned enough work for all the children in the class. She cannot always anticipate how long it will take a child to complete an assignment. Activities for those who are finished ahead of others must be available so that they can continue to be involved in learning. Teachers can provide this by taking the suggestions found in many journals and books recommending simple activities for the classroom, and also applying their own initiative and originality to the construction of them. See the bibliography and references at the end of this chapter and others.

Pupils can be given many games and experiences in which they are asked (either on paper or at the chalkboard with the total class, or on cardboard-based cards holding colorful print and pictures) to:

> underline about twenty vowels which are in a list of about twenty words
> unscramble a sentence and place them in logical order
> arrange three words into a sentence
> arrange ten words into as many sentences as they wish
> associate words with meanings in a list of twenty words and twenty meanings
> list as many meanings as they can for five different words
> try to think of as many words as possible that fit the meaning of one word
> find as many prefixes as possible to create meaning for root words in a given list

This list could go on endlessly. The teacher will have materials at hand as well as the books that the children use which often give many suggestions for activities. A creative teacher will find teaching a joy and so will the children who are on the receiving or responsive end in that situation.

The teacher who provides enough activities to give the children opportunities to find out how much they are learning and how capable they are, is the one who enjoys the profession for years, because knowing that she is giving children an important element of self-appreciation seems to sustain her own self-concept as a competent teacher. Seeing children learn to appreciate themselves is exciting. The atmosphere is electric and human. It is a busy, happy one representing growth in action. The competent teacher knows where, when, and how to guide children in this pursuit. The activities are matched with what the teacher perceives is the child's scope of achievement. She attempts to stretch his abilities as he demonstrates a readiness for the challenge. In that way his sense of ego is sustained while he steadily pursues next steps in building his intellectual reserves.

For children who are reading well, the teacher enhances their capacities for analytical skills further by asking them to abstract various meanings from the materials and also to elaborate on the passages. Ideas can be extended in creative ways. Small packets of activities include various purposes. There are few right or wrong answers in this exercise. Open ended, creative answers do not need to be checked against a "correct" key or preconceived answers of any kind.

CREATIVITY AND DEVELOPMENTAL ACTIVITIES FOR WRITING

Helping children learn to compose stories and to do it in ways that are satisfying to them involve effective judgment on the part of the teacher. She has to know what kind of experiences will best develop the children's capacities in that direction. The teacher who observes pupils' behavior astutely can judge their readiness to meet essential challenges in writing.

Class projects help children in writing development. When their work is used as part of a class booklet describing experiences they shared, children feel a sense of participation and identity as pupils. These projects give an excellent start to their awareness of giving a part of themselves, be it in print, in pictures, or in any other way. They are making a contribution in any case.

Kindergarten children learn to write their names and they can also do those of their friends if they wish. They learn the letters of manuscript for lower case and the one capital letter needed at the beginning of the name. They should not be taught to write their names by using capital (or upper case) letters for the total set of letters in their names. It will be confusing for them later when they need to know that capital letters appear only at the beginning of a sentence and of proper names and places. Parents often teach children how to write their names by showing them how to do it, using all capital letters. Teachers can give parents sheets of correct forms of lower case manuscript so that the parent will know what their children are expected to do at school.

In the first, second, and third grades, children are learning to see well-formed writing on the board and they are also noticing punctuation marks and correct format in writing letters, notes, invitations, and directions. A great deal can be accomplished if the teacher is aware that any time something is written on the board, that it be in the form she wants the children to emulate. What the children see in their classroom environment is a model for them. Often they are asked to copy a word or sentence. The teacher therefore must be extremely cautious that it is correct, that it is as she wants them to imitate and adopt as their own habit for the future as well.

Teachers who have not learned to form manuscript letters (or cursive either, for that matter) in the way that children in contemporary education are expected to learn have to practice writing the correct forms. After repeated instances of practice, the teacher will be able to show the children manuscript writing on the board that is worthy of emulation. Learning to write on the board requires different manipulative skills than those needed when sitting down at a desk. It is just a matter of becoming accustomed to standing in front of the chalkboard and controlling the arm muscles in a different way. There are devices for lining up the board, for making straight lines that can be used as basic guidelines.

Most teachers obviate the problem of standing in front of the class while pupils are waiting for an assignment and write the manuscript carefully before the children arrive at school. They have more time to write the letters correctly without having the added responsibility at the same time of worrying about what the children are doing while waiting. They cover the assignment with a large sheet of paper until it is time for the pupils to see it. Directions for their work are ready. The teacher can concentrate on the children and their needs instead of her own.

The teacher's and children's day usually fare well when the teacher has planned as much as possible for the pupils' arrival at school. Pressures are alleviated immeasurably. Typically, the less pressured the teacher is, the less pressured the children are too. Energies and emotions are saved considerably in this way. Planning and organization are important to the skills of a teacher.

Children's early attempts to write stories are encouraged by the teacher's acceptance of them in the sense of realizing that they are not perfect. There will be misspelling, lack of punctuation, missing words; the children's interest in writing a message overrides their abilities to do it correctly. It is their attitude toward the desire to write which must be protected and nourished. Later after the teacher hears the child read the story to her she helps him make some of the corrections that are of major importance. Detailed notes can be introduced much later after the child has had many experiences in writing. In other words, the teacher must use good judgment in knowing when to be critical and when to wait. There will be a next time.

Teachers should have rich files of pictures that stimulate ideas for writing. Children have their own ideas but they need to know how to embellish them. Study prints, i.e., those that can be looked at closely, and larger pictures or photographs that evoke mood and atmosphere for children are extremely useful for the initiation of ideas. Bulletin boards that evoke imagery and word pictures provide a stimulating atmosphere for children. It carries over to their own work. The teacher can see to it that the school room is an attractive, inviting one that urges pupils to work productively and to have a sense of vitality in it.

Children should be encouraged to check their own papers for punctuation, for spelling, for meanings in appropriate forms. They can be likened to editors who look for ways to improve what is written for clarity, sharpness and vividness of image. Color, imagination, and originality are sought in writing. Pupils ought to be encouraged to be different from their peers in the way they express themselves.

Early writing of children is done on unlined paper and heavy, thick pencils are used because they are assumed to be easier to manipulate. As children mature physically and psychologically, they are given writing materials that are appropriate to their abilities. Some authors suggest

This child is cutting out a picture that will illustrate an idea about which she plans to write.

This little girl has already found her illustration, pasted it on its backing, and now proceeds to write in manuscript letters what her picture represents.

130

Children need an interested and patient teacher to help them with early writing efforts. Her concern affects their competence and desires to achieve success in their work.

that about ten weeks of instruction for some children using unlined paper prepares them to manage lined paper. The lines sometimes create implicit pressures for the child who worries about keeping his letters on them. Gradually, however, this problem is managed. Practice in these situations overcomes many concerns. The teacher encourages the pupil not to worry but to keep trying.

In the third grade, children are introduced to cursive writing. When they seem to understand cursive writing and want to do it for themselves they may be ready for such instruction. The joining of lower case letters should be shown first. Some letters can be shown in an easier transitional form from manuscript to cursive. Teachers try to use those as a start whenever possible (see Figure 4.5). In any case, the children who show an interest in it should be the first ones to be introduced to the process. In this way a pleasant orientation is given to it in class. This mood transfers to other children who can enjoy it in a similar way. Teachers have different processes that they like to use in helping children in this transition. At times it is hard to pinpoint exactly where the transition began. Again, this is an area in which teachers have to try out different techniques with children and use what appears to be most effective with their own pupils.

Perfections in writing develop along the way. Proper slant, proper

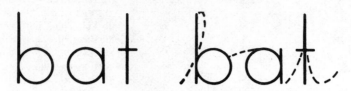

figure 4.5
Transition from Manuscript to Cursive Writing

formation of letters will be emphasized in the process of development. Premature stress on perfection discourages and frustrates any new learner. Teachers have examples of the proper forms for letters and words on the board and on bulletin boards. These examples should be very large so that children can see them from any part of the room. Eye strain, muscle fatigue, and temptation to give up can result when displayed examples of what should be done are too small to see easily.

The teacher should be available for help and should not appear to be annoyed by individual requests for help from children. In this context too the teacher can create for the pupils word files which include well-written examples of words that are often used in story writing. The children have this at their disposal when needed. They are also encouraged to create their own dictionary, which includes words and one or two meanings appropriate for their own use.

If at all possible, at the teacher's discretion, each child should have an opportunity to see his work displayed in an attractive manner on the bulletin board. This does a great deal in encouraging him to continue to produce work which is carefully done. The teacher should know that sometimes children tease each other, and for this reason has to be careful in selecting a child's best work for display.

In the organization of writing materials, children are encouraged to look for main ideas, supporting ideas, interesting details, good endings. They are shown whenever possible exemplary stories in books that illustrate points of organization, sequence of ideas, climactic statements or phrases, and pleasant words of imagery. If the teacher points out the kind of writing she wants them to emulate, they will begin to sensitized to the sound of good writing when they hear it.

While all children are not expected to be literary geniuses they are known to have something important to say. It is the attitudes of people around them who can support this feeling. Pupils' contributions must be respected as such, important to them.

Children should be urged to discuss what they like best about a story. They need help in enlarging their vocabularies of descriptive terms. This can be encouraged in games of matching words with meanings that arouse mental images such as feelings, smells, hurts, anxieties. They need to learn words that create an impact and words that invent moods for people as well as for themselves. Words that permit people to identify with the feelings of the writer or the descriptions that he is trying to convey can create foundations for children in their early writing stages. They begin to realize that in writing, both a listener (or reader) must be kept in mind as well as the writer's intentions for writing.

Teachers can find many activities and games or exercises that can be used to help children develop skills in writing. It is more difficult to help children sustain a desire to write, and in particular, it is difficult for teachers to teach young children how to write. The later the grade, the more activities are available in books and articles for teachers to use with pupils. With the younger child, however, it seems that of greater importance is the teacher's awareness of ways to help him realize that writing is fun, and that he should not be discouraged with first attempts when those attempts meet with some difficulties. It becomes easier as the teacher knows young children better and becomes equally interested in the ways that match the child's attempts with his personality development and his capacity for development of skills in that area.

Many school situations arise in which children are expected to write invitations, birthday greetings, holiday celebrations, or small posters related to significant occasions such as special holidays, contests, special school theme observances. When their writing is done in the context of purpose and usefulness, that too helps the children value what they do. They appreciate making a "real" contribution.

EVALUATION OF CHILDREN'S EXPERIENCES IN COMMUNICATION

Teachers who observe the children carefully, who listen astutely to what they say, and who watch them when they say it are evaluating them constantly. Many testing forms are available for teachers to use with children. Typically, an entire school uses the same language tests in terms of appropriate grade levels. Tests also come with certain kits that have been prepared for the children's use in their daily activities for learning language, reading, writing, and speaking.

Young children find it extremely difficult to take tests in a large group. Indeed, the results, if taken that way cannot be accurate indicators of the child's abilities. Young pupils need assistance in test taking. Even when the teacher goes very slowly, it is difficult for some children to follow directions. If they do not understand what they are expected to do, they merely guess. This does not help the validity or reliability of a test. What is worse, if the teacher takes the results seriously under such conditions and regards the test score as accurate or authentic indicators of the child's abilities, this is a glaring defeat of what evaluation is intended to be.

Effective evaluation procedures give impressions of what the child is able to do, and where he needs help to progress further in his studies at school. It helps the teacher know what next steps for his work should be, what the child is able to master easily, and what is still incomprehensible to him.

Commercial tests evaluate children's skills in reading, vocabulary, comprehension, or phonetic understandings in very systematic ways. Skills are assessed in terms of small segments of a broad idea. Elements of listening are broken down into small parts and checklists to determine children's performance levels in those subareas. Educational testing services have tests already made up for those purposes.[13]

Teachers can provide their own checklists to see whether the children are ready for advancement in reading. Many tests for young children are tests for readiness to go on to more complex work. Journals and associations concerned with children's progress at school provide articles on effective testing techniques and problems to avoid with certain testing procedures.[14]

Various tests that have been used to assess children's skills in reading are: *Lee-Clark Readiness Test, Gates Reading Readiness Tests, The Harrison-Stroud Reading Readiness Tests, California Achievement Tests, Gates Primary Reading Tests.*[15]

Since the writer has not undertaken a systematic evaluation of those tests, none of them is recommended as more worthy than others. This would involve lengthy observations and investigations testing their merit. The teacher and supervisors in any given situation would have to decide which tests were superior to others, why, and in which cases. This again is left to the discretion of educators involved in specific instances with specific children. There are many choices on the market open for selection. What is important in this writer's judgment is more the criteria that educators use in deciding which tests they select. Which test they buy is of lesser importance than which principles that guide them in ways that they make their choice.

The teacher's judgment in many cases can be used to assess readiness of children to proceed with more difficult work. The improvement in many tests made in the last few years is that the methods and techniques for

[13] Sequential Tests of Educational Programs, Princeton, N. J.: Educational Testing Service, 1967.

[14] Robert Farr and Nicholas Anastasia, *Tests of Reading Readiness and Achievement* (Newark, Delaware: International Reading Association, 1969).

[15] J. Murray Lee and Willis W. Clark, *Lee-Clark Reading Readiness Test* (Los Angeles: California Test Bureau); Arthur I. Gates, *Gates Reading Readiness Test* (New York: Bureau of Publications, Teachers College, Columbia University); Lucile Harrison and James B. Stroud, *The Harrison-Stroud Reading Readiness Tests* (Boston: Houghton Mifflin Company); Ernest W. Tiegs and Willis W. Clark, *California Achievement Tests* (Monterey, Calif.: California Test Bureau); Arthur I. Gates, *Gates Primary Reading Tests* (New York: Bureau of Publications, Teachers College, Columbia University).

record keeping have been more systematic than they used to be. In that sense they permit the teacher to be more analytic in looking at the children's progress in reading or communicative arts. Some of the test techniques have made the teacher more aware of details or subsection categories of reading skills and language development in young children.

For those interested in testing that considers individual differences, articles by Kamii [16] and by Cazden [17] may be consulted. In the same volume is also an attempt to conceptualize ways to assess learning in the language arts area from kindergarten through sixth grade.[18] A wealth of information is supplied here for the teacher who wants to evaluate children by combining her own methods with those of some authorities.

Whatever the forms of assessment procedures and whichever the test identified for assessment are, the teacher must remember that tests are not infallible any more than are the people who made them. Norms or standards guide people who create tests; and those who work with young children in the classroom every day must remember that they are referring to human beings whose behavior changes without necessarily giving advance notice of it. Tests, individual differences, teachers' judgments and observations, combined with sensitivity for children's development, can yield results which in themselves may help children progress at school and outside of it as well. It is sincerely hoped that this can become a reality for effectiveness in judgment.

summary

This chapter was concerned with an extremely important aspect of development in young children, their communication skills. Within the area of language arts instruction at school are subdivisions of listening, speaking, reading, and writing. Programs for young children in the language arts vary in terms of their specific goals but in general they help children to become more articulate in the expression of language and their own ideas, and to become proficient or at least functional readers.

The importance of recognizing relationships between children's readiness to participate in certain language activities, and the teacher's awareness of those differences in learning style among young pupils was emphasized. Many activities may be found for the development of precisely

[16] Constance K. Kamii, "Evaluation in Preschool Education: Socio-emotional, Perceptual-Motor, and Cognitive Development," in *Handbook of Formative and Summative Evaluation of Student Learning*, edited by Benjamin S. Bloom, J. Thomas Hastings, and George F. Madaus (New York: McGraw-Hill Book Company, 1971), pp. 281–344.

[17] Courtney B. Cazden, "Evaluation of Learning in Preschool Education: Early Language Development," in *Handbook*, Bloom et al., pp. 345–398.

[18] Walter J. Moore and Larry D. Kennedy, "Evaluation of Learning in the Language Arts," in *Handbook*, Bloom et al., pp. 400–445.

stated skills, and many commercial programs are available for purchase, but the most important focus is that of the sensitive teacher who knows child development and recognizes the need to encourage children in classroom learning activities whatever they may be. The human element is still a major consideration in the teaching act.

topics for discussion

1. Why is language development important in young children's earliest years? How can parents and teachers help in this process?
2. Recall some of your own problems in language development, or that of a sibling or friend. Have they affected you or that individual in obtaining what was wanted at some point in your life? How would your experiences provide some of the needed empathy with your pupils in the classroom?
3. Visit an early childhood unit (kindergarten, first, and second grades in a nearby school or center) and describe their language development program. Include in a folder or card file some of the books and some of the activities used for young children there. What are your general impressions of the program? What do you think would strengthen it? What were its strong points?
4. How does language development and effectiveness in communication affect the mental health of the individual?
5. Describe what you have seen after visiting a classroom in which children are just beginning to read. Note the teacher's manner with the children, their mood of responsiveness, and the specific system emphasized in helping children learn to read.
6. Construct three reading readiness activities for children in kindergarten.

selected bibliography for teachers

Anderson, Paul S. *Linguistics in the Elementary School Classroom.* New York: Macmillan Publishing Co., Inc., 1971.

Anderson, Paul S. *Language Skills in Elementary Education.* 2nd Ed. New York: Macmillan Publishing Co., Inc., 1972.

Applegate, Mauree. *Easy in English.* New York: Harper & Row, 1960.

Arbuthnot, May Hill. *Children and Books.* 4th Ed. Chicago: Scott, Foresman and Company, 1972.

Bloom, Benjamin S., J. Thomas Hastings, and George F. Madeus. *Handbook on Formative and Summative Evaluation of Student Learning.* New York: McGraw-Hill Book Company, 1971.

Brophy, Jere E., Thomas L. Good, and Shari E. Nedler. *Teaching in the Pre-School.* New York: Harper & Row, 1975.

Burns, Paul C., Betty L., Broman, and Alberta L. Lowe Wantling. *The Language Arts in Childhood Education.* 2nd Ed. Chicago: Rand McNally & Company, 1971.

Bush, Clifford L., and Mildred H. Huebner. *Strategies for Reading in the Elementary School*. New York: Macmillan Publishing Co., Inc., 1970.

Carlson, Ruth K. *Literature for Children: Enrichment Ideas*. Dubuque, Iowa: William C. Brown Co., 1970.

Carlson, Ruth K. "Raising Self Concepts of Disadvantaged Children Through Puppetry," *Elementary English* (March, 1970), pp. 349–55.

Cazden, Courtney B. *Child Language and Education*. New York: Holt, Rinehart and Winston, Inc., 1972.

Croft, Doreen J., and Robert D. Hess. *An Activities Handbook for Teachers of Young Children*. 2nd Ed. Boston: Houghton Mifflin Company, 1975.

Darrow, Helen F., and Virgil M. Howes. *Approaches to Individualized Reading*. New York: Appleton-Century-Crofts, Inc., 1960.

Durkin, Dolores. *Teaching Them to Read*. 2nd Ed. Boston: Allyn & Bacon, Inc., 1974.

Ekwall, Eldon E. *Locating and Correcting Reading Difficulties*. Columbus, Ohio: Charles E. Merrill Publishing Company, 1970.

Fedder, Ruth, and Jacqueline Gabaldon. *No Longer Deprived*. New York: Teachers College Press, 1970.

Gilpatric, Naomi. "Power of Picture Books to Change Child's Self-Image," *Elementary English* (May, 1969), pp. 570–74.

Graham, Richard T., and E. Hugh Rudorf, "Dialect and Spelling," *Elementary English* (March, 1970), pp. 363–375.

Greene, Harry A., and Walter T. Petty. *Developing Language Skills in the Elementary Schools*. 4th Ed. Boston: Allyn & Bacon, Inc., 1971.

Glidewell, John C. "The Child at School," in *Modern Perspectives in International Child Psychiatry*. John G. Howells, Ed. New York: Brunner/Mazel Publishers, 1971. pp. 738–39.

Hall, Robert A. *Sound and Spelling in English.* Philadelphia: Chilton Co., 1964.

Haviland, Virginia. *Children's Literature: A Guide to Reference Sources*. Washington, D.C.: Library of Congress, 1966.

Huck, Charlotte, and Doris Young. *Children's Literature in Elementary School*. New York: Holt, Rinehart and Winston, Inc., 1968.

Hughes, Felicity. *Reading and Writing Before School*. London: Jonathan Cape Ltd., 1971.

Inglis, Ruth Langdon. *A Time to Learn*. New York: The Dial Press, 1973.

Johnson, Edna, Evelyn R. Sickels, Frances Clarke Sayers. *Anthology of Children's Literature*. 4th Ed. Boston: Houghton Mifflin Company, 1970.

Kinder, Robert F. *The English Program K–12. The Tree and Its Roots*. Champaign, Illinois: Connecticut Council of Teachers of English, N.C.T.E., 1967.

Ladley, Winifred C. *Sources of Good Books and Magazines for Children*. Newark, Del.: International Reading Association, 1970.

Lamb, Pose. *Guiding Children's Language*. Iowa: Wm. C. Brown, 1971.

Logan, Lillian M., and Virgil C. Logan. *A Dynamic Approach to Language Arts*. Toronto: McGraw-Hill Book Company of Canada, 1967.

Lorton, Mary Baratta. *Workjobs*. Menlo Park, California: Addison-Wesley Publishing Company, 1972.

McKee, Paul. *The Teaching of Reading in the Elementary School*. Boston: Houghton Mifflin Company, 1960.

Meigs, Cornelia, Anne Baxter Eaton, Elizabeth Nesbitt, and Ruth Hill Viguers. *A Critical History of Children's Literature*. New York: Macmillan Publishing Co., Inc., 1969.

Morrison, Charlotte. "A Creative Teacher Shares Notes to Trainees in a Gifted Child Training Program," *The Gifted Child Quarterly* (Summer, 1970), pp. 97–105.

Myklebust, H. R. *The Pupil Rating Scale: Screening for Learning Disabilities*. New York: Grune and Stratton, 1971.

Nelsen, Clarence H. *Measurement and Evaluation in the Classroom*. New York: Macmillan Publishing Co., Inc., 1970.

Petty, Walter T., Dorothy C. Petty, and Marjorie F. Becking. *Experiences in Language*. Boston: Allyn & Bacon, Inc., 1973.

Pflaum, Susanna Whitney. *The Development of Language and Reading in the Young Child*. Columbus, Ohio: Charles E. Merrill Publishing Company, 1974.

Phillips, Gerald M., Robert Dunhem, Robert Brubaher, and David Butt. *The Development of Oral Communication in the Classroom*. Indianapolis: The Bobbs Merrill Co., Inc., 1970.

Possien, Wilma M. *They All Need to Talk*. New York: Appleton-Century-Crofts, 1969.

Robinson, A. Alan. *Reading and the Language Arts*. Chicago: University of Chicago Press, 1963.

Shane, Harold and others. *Improving Language Arts Instruction in the Elementary School*. Columbus, Ohio: Charles E. Merrill Books, Inc., 1964.

Siks, Geraldine. *Children's Literature for Dramatization*. New York: Harper and Row, 1964.

Smith, E. Brooks, Kenneth S. Goodman, and Robert Meredith. *Language and Thinking in the Elementary School*. New York: Holt, Rinehart and Winston, Inc., 1970.

Smith, James A. *Creative Teaching of the Language Arts in the Elementary School*. Boston: Allyn & Bacon, Inc., 1973.

Smith, Nila Banton. *Reading Instruction for Today's Children*. Englewood Cliffs, N.J.: Prentice-Hall, Inc., 1965.

Spache, George D. *The Teaching of Reading*. Bloomington, Indiana: Phi Delta Kappa, Inc., 1972.

Spache, George D., and Evelyn B. Spache. *Reading in the Elementary School*. 3rd Ed. Boston: Allyn & Bacon, Inc., 1973.

Stauffer, Russell G. *Teaching Reading as a Thinking Process*. New York: Harper & Row, 1969.

Strickland, Ruth G. *The Language Arts*. 3rd Ed. Boston: D. C. Heath and Company, 1969.

Tanyzer, Harold, and Jean Karl, Eds. *Reading, Children's Books, and Our Pluralistic Society*. Newark, Del.: International Reading Association, 1972.

Tiedt, Iris M., and Sidney W. Tiedt. *Contemporary English in the Elementary School*. Englewood Cliffs, N.J.: Prentice-Hall, 1975.

Van Allen, R., and Doris M. Lee. *Learning to Read Through Experience*. New York: Appleton-Century-Crofts, Inc., 1963.

Williams, Frederick. *Language and Poverty*. Chicago: Markham Publishing Co., 1970.

poetry

Arbuthnot, May Hill. *Time for Poetry*. Illustrated by Arthur Paul. Glenview Ill.: Scott Foresman, 1952.

Arnstein, Flora J. *Poetry in the Elementary Classroom*. New York: Appleton-Century-Crofts, 1962.

Austin, Mary C., and Queenie B. Mills. Compilers. *The Sound of Poetry*. Boston: Allyn & Bacon, Inc., 1963.

Baruch, Dorothy J. *I Would Like to be a Pony and Other Wishes*. Illustrated by Mary Chalmers. New York: Harper and Row, 1959.

Blake, William. *Songs of Innocence*. Music and Illustrations by Ellen Raskin. New York: Doubleday, 1966.

Blishen, Edward, Compiler. *Oxford Book of Poetry for Children*. Illustrated by Brian Wildsmith. New York: Franklin Watts, 1963.

Brown, Beatrice. *Jonathan Bing and Other Verses*. New York: Oxford University Press, 1936.

De la Mare, Walter. *Rhymes and Verses, Collected Poems for Young People*. Illustrated by Elinor Blaisdell. New York: Holt, Rinehart and Winston, Inc., 1947.

Farjeon, Eleanor. *The Children's Bells*. New York: Walck, 1960.

Field, Rachel. *Taxis and Toadstools*. New York: Doubleday, 1926.

Field, Rachel. *Poems*. New York: Macmillan Publishing Co., Inc., 1951.

Fisher, Aileen. *Like Nothing at All*. Illustrated by Leonard Weisgard. New York: Thomas Y. Crowell, Inc., 1962.

Fyleman, Rose. *Fairies and Chimneys*. New York: Doubleday, 1929.

Howard, Coralie, Compiler. *The First Book of Short Verse*. Illustrated by Mamoru Funai. New York: Franklin Watts, 1964.

Hughes, Rosalind. *Let's Enjoy Poetry*. Boston: Houghton Mifflin Co., 1966.

Japanese Haiku. Translated by Peter Beilenson. New York: Peter Pauper Press, 1955–1966.

Livingston, Myra Cohn. *I'm Not Me*. Illustrated by Erik Blegvad. New York: Harcourt, Brace & World, Inc., 1963.

Merriam, Eve. *There is No Rhyme for Silver*. Illustrated by Joseph Schindelman. New York: Atheneum Press, Inc., 1962.

Sheldon, William, Nellie Lyons, and Polly Rousault, Compilers. *The Reading of Poetry*. Boston: Allyn & Bacon, Inc., 1963.

Thompson, Blanche Jennings, Compiler. *All the Silver Pennies*. New York: Macmillan Publishing Co., Inc., 1967.

Untermeyer, Louis, Ed. *The Golden Treasury of Poetry*. Illustrated by Joan Walsh Anglund. New York: Golden Press, 1959.

Walter, Nina Willis. *Let Them Write Poetry*. New York: Holt, Rinehart and Winston, Inc., 1962.

books for children

Ardizzone, Edward. Author-Illustrator. *Little Tim and The Brave Sea Captain.* New York: Oxford University Press, 1955.

Bemelmans, Ludwig. Author-Illustrator. *Madeline.* New York: Viking Press, 1939.

Beskow, Elsa. Author-Illustrator. *Pelle's New Suit.* New York: Harper & Row, n.d.

Briggs, Raymond. *The White Land.* New York: Coward-McCann, Inc., 1963.

Brown, Marcia. *Stone Soup.* New York: Charles Scribner's Sons, 1947.

Brown, Marcia, *Tamarindo.* New York: Charles Scribner's Sons, 1960.

Brown, Margaret Wise. *The City Noisy Book.* Illustrated by Leonard Weisgard. New York: Harper & Row, 1939.

Brown, Margaret Wise. *The Country Noisy Book.* Illustrated by Leonard Weisgard. New York: Harper & Row, 1940.

Brown, Myra Berry. *Amy and the New Baby.* Illustrated by H. Hurwitz. New York: Franklin Watts, 1965.

Buckley, Helen E. *Grandfather and I.* Illustrated by Paul Galdone. New York: Lathrop, 1959.

Caudill, Rebecca. *A Pocketful of Cricket.* Illustrated by Evaline Ness. New York: Holt, Rinehart and Winston, Inc., 1964.

Cooney, Barbara. *Chanticleer and the Fox.* Thomas Y. Crowell, Co., Inc., 1958.

De Regniers, Beatrice Schenk. *May I Bring a Friend?* Illustrated by Beni Montresor. New York: Atheneum Press, 1964.

Duvoisin, Roger. *Petunia.* New York: Alfred A. Knopf, 1950.

Duvoisin, Roger. *Veronica.* New York: Alfred A. Knopf, 1961.

Elkin, Benjamin. *The Loudest Noise in the World.* Illustrated by James Daugherty. New York: Viking Press, 1954.

Fatio, Louise. *The Happy Lion.* Illustrated by Roger Duvoisin. New York: McGraw-Hill Book Company, 1954.

Flack, Marjorie. Author-Illustrator. *Angus and the Ducks.* New York: Doubleday, 1930.

Françoise, pseud. (Françoise Seignobosc). *What Time Is It, Jeanne-Marie?* New York: Charles Scribner's Sons, 1963.

Frasconi, Antonio. Author-Illustrator. *See and Say: a Picture Book in Four Languages.* New York: Harcourt, Brace & World, Inc., 1955.

Freeman, Don. Author-Illustrator. *The Guard Mouse.* New York: Viking Press, 1967.

Green, Mary McBurney. *Is It Hard?* Illustrated by Luciene Bloch. New York: W. R. Scott, 1960.

Guilfoile, Elizabeth. *Nobody Listens to Andrew.* Illustrated by Mary Stevens. Chicago: Follett Publishing Co., 1957.

Hoban, Russell. *A Baby Sister for Frances.* Illustrated by Lillian Hoban. New York: Harper & Row, 1964.

Hoban, Russell. *Nothing to Do.* Illustrated by Lillian Hoban. New York: Harper & Row, 1964.

Joslin, Sesyle. *Spaghetti for Breakfast.* Illustrated by Katharina Barry. New York: Harcourt, Brace & World, Inc., 1965.

Keats, Ezra Jack. *Jennie's Hat.* New York: Harper & Row, 1966.

Keats, Ezra Jack, and Pat Cherr. *My Dog Is Lost.* New York: Thomas Y. Crowell Co., Inc., 1960.

Kessler, Ethel and Leonard. *Are You Square?* Illustrated by Leonard Kessler. New York: Doubleday, 1966.

Krauss, Ruth. *The Backward Day.* Illustrated by Marc Simont. New York: Harper & Row, 1950.

Kumin, Maxine W. *The Beach Before Breakfast.* Illustrated by Leonard Weisgard. New York: G. P. Putnam's Sons, 1964.

Lipkind, William. *Finders Keepers.* Illustrated by Nicolas Mordvinoff, New York: Harcourt Brace, 1951.

McCloskey, Robert. Author-Illustrator. *Make Way for Ducklings.* New York: Viking Press, 1941.

Minarik, Else. *Little Bear.* Illustrated by Maurice Sendak. New York: Harper & Row, 1957.

Morrow, Elizabeth. *The Painted Pig: A Mexican Picture Book.* Illustrated by René d'Harnoncourt. New York: Alfred A. Knopf, 1930.

Ness, Evaline. Author-Illustrator. *Sam, Bangs & Moonshine.* New York: Holt, Rinehart and Winston, Inc., 1966.

Nic Leodhas, Sorche. *Always Room for One More.* Illustrated by Nonny Hogrogian. New York: Holt, Rinehart and Winston, Inc., 1965.

Petersham, Maud and Miska. Author-Illustrators. *The Box With The Red Wheels.* New York: Macmillan Publishing Co., Inc., 1949.

Politi, Leo. *The Song of the Swallows.* New York: Charles Scribner's Sons, 1949.

Politi, Leo. *Lito and the Clown.* New York: Charles Scribner's Sons, 1964.

Sandburg, Carl. *The Wedding Procession of the Rag Doll and the Broom Handle Who Was in It.* Illustrated by Harriet Pincus. New York: Harcourt, Brace & World, 1967.

Scheer, Julian. *Rain Makes Applesauce.* Illustrated by Marvin Bileck. New York: Holiday House, Inc., 1964.

Slobodkin, Louis. *Yasu and the Strangers.* New York: Macmillan Publishing Co., Inc., 1965.

Tresselt, Alvin. *White Snow, Bright Snow.* Illustrated by Roger Duvoisin. New York: Lothrop, Lee & Shepard, 1947.

Udry, Janice. *Let's Be Enemies.* Illustrated by Maurice Sendak. New York: Harper & Row, 1961.

Ungerer, Tomi. Author-Illustrator. *Snail, Where Are You?* New York: Harper & Row, 1962.

Ward, Lynd. Author-Illustrator. *The Biggest Bear.* Boston: Houghton Mifflin Co., 1952.

Zolotow, Charlotte. *The Quarreling Book.* Illustrated by Arnold Lobel. New York: Harper & Row, 1963.

books for children 4 to 8 years old

Anderson, Hans C. *The Nightingale.* Illustrated by Harold Berson. Philadelphia: J. H. Lippincott & Co., 1963.

Armer, Laura Adams. *Waterless Mountain.* Illustrated by Sidney and Laura Armer. New York: David McKay Co., 1931.

Bannon, Laura. *The Gift of Hawaii.* Whitman, 1961.

Bendick, Jeanne. *Names, Sets and Numbers.* New York: Franklin Watts, Inc., 1971.

Bendick, Jeanne. *What Made You You?* New York: McGraw-Hill Book Company, 1971.

Branley, Franklyn M. *High Sounds, Low Sounds.* New York: Thomas Y. Crowell Company, 1967.

Buff, Mary. *Dancing Cloud, The Navajo Boy.* New York: Viking Press, 1957.

Butterworth, Oliver. *The Oversized Egg.* Little, Brown and Company, 1956.

Carlson, Natalie Savage. *The Family Under the Bridge.* Illustrated by Garth Williams. New York: Harper & Row, 1958.

Cleary, Beverly. *Henry Huggins.* New York: William Morrow and Company, 1950.

Clifton, Lucille. *Don't You Remember?* New York: E. P. Dutton & Co., Inc., 1973.

Cohen, Miriam. *Tough Jim.* New York: Macmillan Publishing Co., Inc., 1974.

Cohen, Miriam. *Will I Have a Friend?* New York: Macmillan Publishing Co., Inc., 1967.

Davis, Lavinia. *Clown Dog.* New York: Doubleday, 1961.

Dobler, Lavinia. *Customs and Holidays Around the World.* New York: Fleet Press Corporation, 1962.

Domanska, Janina. *Little Red Hen.* New York: Macmillan Publishing Co., Inc., 1973.

Estes, Eleanor. *The Hundred Dresses.* Illustrated by Louis Slobodkin. New York: Harcourt, Brace, 1944.

Ets, Marie Hall. *Nine Days to Christmas.* New York: Viking Press, 1959.

Fatio, Louise. *The Happy Lion.* New York: McGraw-Hill Book Company, 1954.

Freschet, Berniece. *Turtle Pond.* Illustrated by Donald Carrick. New York: Charles Scribner's Sons, 1971.

Garthwaite, Marion. *Mario, A Mexican Boy's Adventure.* New York: Doubleday, 1960.

Grayson, Marion F. *Let's Do Fingerplays.* Washington: Robert D. Luce, Inc., 1962.

Griffin, Ella. *Getting to Know UNESCO.* New York: Coward McCann, Inc., 1966.

Hickel, Lorena. *The Story of Helen Keller.* New York: Grosset & Dunlap, 1958.

Hoban, Tana. *Where Is It?* New York: Macmillan Publishing Co., Inc., 1974.

Hoban, Tana. *Push. Pull. Empty. Full.* New York: Macmillan Publishing Co., Inc., 1972.

Hoffman, Robert. *The Indian and the Buffalo.* New York: William Morrow, 1961.

Holling, C. Holling. *Paddle-to-the-Sea*. Boston: Houghton Mifflin Company, 1941.

Holm, Anna. *North to Freedom*. New York: Harcourt, Brace & World, 1965.

Hutchins, Pat. *The Wind Blew*. New York: Macmillan Publishing Co., Inc., 1974.

Hutchins, Pat. *Good-Night Owl*. New York: Macmillan Publishing Co., Inc., 1972.

Ipcar, Dahlov. *The Land of Flowers*. New York: The Viking Press, 1974.

Jeffers, Susan. *All The Pretty Horses*. New York: Macmillan Publishing Co., Inc., 1974.

Jones, Cordelia. *Nobody's Garden*. Illustrated by Victor Ambrus. New York: Charles Scribner's Sons, 1966.

Justus, May. *New Boy in School*. New York: Hastings House, Publishers, 1963.

Keats, Ezra Jack. *Apt. 3*. New York: Macmillan Publishing Co., Inc., 1971.

Keats, Ezra Jack. *Dreams*. New York: Macmillan Publishing Co., Inc., 1974.

Kellogg, Steven. *The Mystery of the Missing Red Mitten*. New York: The Dial Press, 1974.

Kellogg, Steven. *Can I Keep Him?* New York: The Dial Press, 1971.

Kipling, Rudyard. *The Elephant's Child*. Chicago: Follett Publishing Co., 1969.

Klein, Norma. *If I Had My Way*. Illustrated by Ray Cruz. New York: Pantheon Books, 1974.

Kraus, Robert. *Whose Mouse Are You?* New York: Macmillan Publishing Co., Inc., 1970.

Lasker, Joe. *He's My Brother*. Chicago: Albert Whitman & Company, 1974.

Lenski, Lois. *Coal Camp Girl*. Philadelphia: J. H. Lippincott & Co., 1959.

Lionni, Leo. *Fish Is Fish*. New York: Pantheon Books, 1970.

McCloskey, Robert. *Homer Price*. New York: Viking Press, 1943.

McNamara, Louise Green and Ada Bassett Litchfield. *Your Growing Cells*. Boston: Little, Brown and Company, 1973.

Marshall, James. *Yummers*. Boston: Houghton Mifflin Company, 1973.

Mayer, Mercer. *What Do You Do With a Kangaroo?* New York: Four Winds Press, 1973.

Norton, Mary. *The Borrowers*. New York: Harcourt, Brace & World, 1953.

O'Neill, Mary. *Hailstones and Halibut Bones*. New York: Doubleday and Co., Inc., 1961.

Payne, Emmy. *Katy-No-Pocket*. Boston: Houghton Mifflin Company, 1944.

Peet, Bill. *The Wump World*. Boston: Houghton Mifflin Company, 1970.

Pinkwater, Manus. *Fat Elliot and the Gorilla*. New York: Four Winds Press, 1974.

Prather, Ray. *Anthony and Sabrina*. New York: Macmillan Publishing Co., Inc., 1973.

Preston, Edna Mitchell. Illustrated by Leonard Kessler. *The Boy Who Could Make Things*. New York: Viking Press, 1970.

Prieto, Mariana. *A Kite for Carlos*. New York: John Day Co., 1966.

Raskin, Ellen. *Who, Said Sue, Said Whoo?* New York: Atheneum Press, 1973.

Ravielli, Anthony. *The World Is Round*. New York: Viking Press, 1970.

Rice, Eve. *Oh, Lewis!* New York: Macmillan Publishing Co., Inc., 1974.

Sasek, Miroslav. *This Is Historic Britain*. New York: Macmillan Publishing Co., Inc., 1974.

Sauer, Julia. *Mike's House*. New York: Viking Press, 1954.

Sawyer, Rugh. *Maggie Rose, Her Birthday Christmas*. Illustrated by Maurice Sendak. New York: Harper & Row, 1952.

Selsam, Miriam E. *The Carrot and Other Root Vegetables*. New York: William Morrow and Company, 1971.

Selsam, Millicent E. *Peanut*. Photographs by Jerome Wexler. New York: William Morrow and Company, 1969.

Sharmat, Marjorie Weinman. *Sophie and Gussie*. New York: Macmillan Publishing Co., Inc., 1973.

Showers, Paul and Kay Sperry Showers. *Before You Were a Baby*. Illustrated by Ingrid Fetz. New York: Thomas Y. Crowell Co., Inc., 1968.

Showers, Paul. *How You Talk*. Illustrated by Robert Galster. New York: Thomas Y. Crowell Co., Inc., 1966.

Showers, Paul. *Your Skin and Mine*. New York: Thomas Y. Crowell Co., Inc., 1965.

Snyder, Louis L. *The First Book of the Soviet Union*. Revised Ed. New York: Franklin Watts, Inc., 1972.

Solvert, Ronni. *32 Feet of Insides*. New York: Pantheon Books, 1970.

Spier, Peter. *Gobble, Growl, Grunt*. New York: Doubleday, 1971.

Vinck, Antoine de. *Wim of the Wind*. New York: Doubleday, 1974.

Wells, Rosemary. *Noisy Nora*. New York: The Dial Press, 1973.

White, E. B. *Charlotte's Web*. New York: Harper & Row, 1952.

Wiseman, Bernard. *Little New Kangaroo*. New York: Macmillan Publishing Co., Inc., 1973.

Yashima, Taro. *Crow Boy*. New York: Viking Press, 1955.

Zalben, Jane Breskin. *Cecilia's Older Brother*. New York: Macmillan Publishing Co., Inc., 1973.

Zim, Herbert S. *Bones*. New York: William Morrow and Company, 1969.

Zolotow, Charlotte. *When I Have a Little Girl*. Illustrated by Hilary Knight. New York: Harper & Row, 1965.

Zolotow, Charlotte. *The White Marble*. Illustrated by Lilian Obligado. New York: Abelard-Schuman, 1963.

Chapter 5

The Child, His Family and Society: Social Studies for Young Children at School

If ever there were a group of human beings interested in the world around them and eager to learn about it, it is young children. The guidance and points of view they receive about that world are given to them second-hand by parents, siblings and teachers. As they mature, however, they acquire their own thoughts about that society in which they live. It is the school's obligation to give them as much factual information as possible to help them acquire accurate data.

What more interesting phenomenon is there to study but man and his daily interaction with others, and in a society we are trying to understand? This in essence is part of the focus of social studies, the study of man and his society. The term *man* is used in its broadest sense, to include men, women and children.

As one might expect, writers in the field of social studies view it in various perspectives. Their perspectives will affect the way they approach the field. In any case, most of them desire that children understand the world in which they live so that they can function effectively in it. It is hoped that children will realize that the world has acquired its technology and medical advances through the minds of men dedicated to their work. Exciting forms of progress are not magical; people work for them. Social studies can help children understand how humankind has shaped and affected the environment.

145

The subject of social studies might sound too advanced in its symbolic sense for young children in the primary grades or in kindergarten. All one has to do, however, is to think of social studies as synonymous with the concept, society, or context. Then it is easy to understand why a child's environment is not too advanced a concept for him. Children have a context of their own society whatever their neighborhood, region, city, or state happens to be. Social studies content in the primary grades and kindergarten draws its facts and generalizations from the social sciences. These include anthropology, sociology, economics, political science, history, geography, social psychology (some include generalizations and facts from philosophy too).

The information from those social sciences is not transmitted to the children in the same format as it is to adults in high school or higher educational institutions. The facts that are used are accurate. They are taught to children at appropriate levels of children's development in abilities to understand the content. For example, when young children study generalizations from sociology, they are learning about the way people live in communities and how certain services in those communities are provided. The services have to be paid for by somebody. Firemen, policemen, librarians and the like need to be paid for their work that serves people in various communities. Children obtain generalizations from sociology in this elementary sense.

This chapter will discuss some of the major purposes and goals of various courses of study planned for young children in the age range of four through eight; this includes the kindergarten, first, second, and third grades. Following this discussion of purposes and goals of social studies will be suggestions for developmental activities that should be used with children in the age categories mentioned. Sources and means for the evaluation of children's work in this subject matter area are presented; this is followed by lists of professional books that can be used by the teacher to find more information on the social studies.

Purposes and Goals in the Social Studies

One of the major purposes in the instruction of social studies for young children is that pupils learn the dynamics of their society, that is, the ways in which man has contributed to and benefited by it. The norms, traditions or mores that have developed through years of interaction among men create some bases for valuing certain kinds of behavior more than others. Cooperation, responsibility for one's actions, desire to be considerate of others and to enjoy being helpful are some of the traits and characteristics that facilitate constructive ends among people. Diversity in the context of nonviolent action is also regarded as valuable in that it creates change and sometimes influences progress. We should remember that change and progress are not synonymous terms. Change for its own sake does not necessarily mean progress. Whenever changes are made, the values inherent in the means for bringing about change have to be considered in terms of the values of a society.

Children are expected to learn certain values, attitudes, habits, and skills that affect higher levels of performance as members of a society. American society, as others, has its predominant values; society however represents people, it represents *humankind*. It is not an artifact presented to us from a world outside our own (see Figure 5.1). Some of society's values are transmitted from people generations before this one. Nobody experiences a world, when he is born, that is totally his. It is a double world, one of double contexts; his own and the adults who are caring for him. In this dually perceived world, the child gradually takes on his own views which have greater significance for him than those of others. This see-sawing back and forth, this constant attempt to balance, learning whose norms to sanction, or whose "rules to play by," the adults or his peers (and his own) represent a reservoir of constant shifting and re-evaluating.

People's values stem from the general philosophy, both political and humanistic, of a society. Since the American society is based on democratic beliefs, it encourages individuality, independent thought, creativity, and willingness to think through one's position on a given belief or set of values.

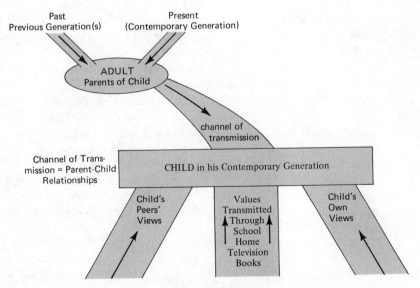

figure 5.1
Acquisition of Social Values (or Values of One's Society)

Through the social studies, children are expected to learn how to make effective decisions, what criteria to use in the process of making them, and how to evaluate what they hear others say about issues that are critically important. They learn to assess and weigh carefully what they hear, even when they become part of a heated debate and people become emotional about their points of view. In fact, pupils are taught that the more irritated an individual becomes in delivering his ideas, the more the listener needs to be cautious in accepting what is said.

Children are expected to value the search for correct information or truth in any issue. They can learn to use initiative in the way they think and to find creative ways of obtaining the truth. They can learn a great deal from the inferences made in reading materials. Originality and creativity are highly regarded in an intellectual sense; scientific contributions often represent just such originality. Children's social studies activities and books should constantly generate lively classroom discussion in which pupils learn to present their ideas, to listen to others present theirs, to separate opinion from fact, to learn how to defend or refute a position taken on a certain problem. In other words, leadership as well as cooperation is sought as children function in the roles of contributing members to a classroom group. Both kinds of behavior and attitudes are needed in a democratic society.

Substantive materials in the social studies are planned for the appropriate developmental level of the children. For example, children in the kindergarten would not be expected to study lengthy units on Latin America or the United States, as children in the intermediate grades (fourth, fifth, and sixth) do. The units for young children in kindergarten or nursery school, or first and second grades are on transportation, the study of harbor facilities, airplanes, trains, or community services and agencies such as the post office, fire department, the bakery, the dairy, and the security or protective services in a community.

Community zoos, a circus when it is available to the children, or any community processing plant that is safe for children to visit indicates ways that people earn a living and also demonstrates how raw materials may be processed for the consumption of people in that community and those in the vicinity. Processing dairy foods, clothing, frozen foods, or cereals show children how men of a past generation and the contemporary one have devised ways to use raw materials in their own environment and have changed them into something useful for people to enjoy, buy, and value.

In studies of societies or communities, children discover that man has helped himself, that people provide for their needs. While some people may decry an overmechanized society or an overly materialistic one, children nevertheless need to know that the goods and services are planned by men and women. Those materials are not there simply because they were dropped on earth by an outside force. Some children, who do not yet know about the cow and the milk it gives, think of milk as coming from a carton (as the major productive source), that one finds in the store. They are not aware of the sequence that goes on between the cow's contribution and the dairy before the milk carton ever appears on the supermarket shelf.

Pupils can learn about sophisticated concepts, but these concepts will not be learned unless the activities planned to produce learning are appropriate to the abilities of a given age group. The teacher has to be sensitive to where pupils are in their hierarchy of concepts. If the children are introduced to difficult concepts without a basic foundation they will not understand them. It is difficult, for example, for young children to know what social justice is. They can understand equity among themselves (particularly if they feel that they have been treated unfairly). They seem to have a grasp of what is equitable. A decision based on "being fair" is often understood. Whenever the teacher tries to help children think in objective terms, at least where one child should have his opportunity (a turn) to do something if others have had it and he has not, the children respond well. But social justice, which is an abstract and less personalized idea and has less direct meaning for children, will require more time and experience for their comprehension, emotionally or intellectually.

Many books have been published on the social studies plus independent courses of study in school systems. The choices that are made for children to use will reflect personal philosophies of the professional group that has been asked to write the social studies for any specific school system.

Social studies used to include, in some states, only the subjects of history, geography, and civics. The contemporary orientation, however, is broader than that. At least since about the 1950's the direction has been to draw generalizations and selected facts from the social sciences (see Figure 5.2). The disciplines overlap at times and tend to move in similar directions.

Social studies units are done on the production of goods, for example, how clothing is manufactured, how textiles are created, how milk is produced from the cow to the time it reaches the consumer, how bread is made, from the wheat to the finished product, and the like. The language is such that the children are able to comprehend complex steps in the development of a product. The stories, the books, recordings, and films on those processes are appropriate to the pupils' levels of understanding and styles of learning.

In each of the social studies units there are goals, objectives, or purposes that relate specifically to the content. If the unit is about a given group of people, children will study ways that individuals work together

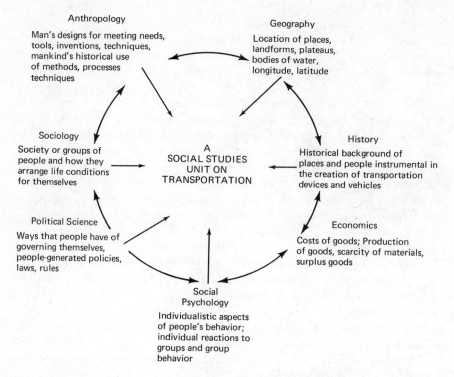

figure 5.2
Social Studies Concepts and Generalizations and Their Sources

to produce necessities, comforts, and needs of benefit to all of them. It is intended to show how people use their ingenuity and physical energies to function smoothly as an organized group. This should not be taken to mean that people function as groups with no conflict; their behavior is another matter. But as far as necessities for food, shelter and sustenance are concerned, groups sense their own needs. A group may be the Americans in an industrialized environment, the French people, rural or urban environments, an Indian group; it may refer, instead of to a people, to a country, a given state, or a town.

Any group, whether from South America, Africa, or one of the European countries, have values that influence the direction they take for themselves and their children in their daily lives. American children studying one of those groups learn about the value orientation of those groups, their religious practices, learn how they live, how they earn a living, what occupations and professions are important to them, what they eat, how they secure their food, how children are raised and educated, i.e., what kind of schools they attend, what they have to study, and so forth.

Any of these groups studied by the children as content for the social studies units include sociological aspects, historical, and geographical ideas related to the country of the people. Principles of anthropology, political science, economics, and social psychology are included in any materials that children study because those ideas were created by humankind to explain, organize and categorize thoughts in a scientific context (see Figure 5.2).

In one course of study designed by Bruner, the major questions and topics are presented in broad terms.[1] If possible the reader should refer directly to the course itself. The interrelationships of ideas are noted, as the directing group of questions focus on how mankind developed and what the important tools and techniques for that development were. Bruner approaches the study of mankind through a concentration on characteristics and ideas that humanize people. He suggests that the humanizing forces include language, tool making, social organization, child rearing, and world view. While these ideas were used in a unit for fifth grade instruction, the major concepts mentioned could be included at any grade level. It all depends on the way activities are planned for the children to learn about these concepts. (Note the activities planned in Figure 5.4.) The teacher makes the major decisions. She plans activities that are appropriate to the levels of understanding of several groups of children in the class. She introduces several ideas at different levels of complexity congruent with various intellectual capacities of children in that classroom.

Recommendations for studying a region are given as guidelines to obtain comprehensive approaches to any area throughout the world.[2] By dividing the conceptualization of a region into a physical and a human component at the start, the pupils see and learn about the region's landforms, water features, climate, location on the map or globe and its proximity to other countries. They obtain a sense of what affects people, their growth, and the way they earn a living. The means for earning a living are often affected by the location of a country or state. A location near water, an ocean coastline, mountains, or desert, influences what people can do for a living, how to obtain food, water, and other life-sustaining essentials.

The religious, philosophical, and esthetic orientations are affected by the physical location and political and geographical boundaries as well.

---

[1] John U. Michaelis, Ruth H. Grossman, and Lloyd F. Scott. *New Designs for the Elementary School Curriculum.* (New York: McGraw-Hill Book Company, 1967), p. 250.

[2] Ibid., p. 252.

Children learn a great deal about principles that other people use to guide their lives. They also learn how to apply some of those principles to themselves. It does not mean that pupils use ideas of the Eskimo and apply them directly to their own lives, for example, but that the techniques used by people for purposes of gathering food or of being paid for something that one does for others can be applied to any group. Eskimoes in the northern part of the world with severely cold climate and accessibility to only certain types of food and raw materials for clothing to protect them, differ from southern people, South American, for example. The differences comprise fascinating units of study. Children learn to conceptualize relationships between countries and people, and their decisions to live as they do. As they perceive relationships, they are learning to think in mature terms. They can see the logic in the ways that the context of people's lives affects their livelihood, their beliefs, and the quality of life they endure or they enjoy.

Some people confuse the term, "social studies" with social education. Social education refers to the interrelationships among children in the classroom and with people generally. The social studies includes more than interpersonal behavior in groups. It refers to concepts, generalizations, facts, and techniques, that are taken from the social sciences such as geography, history, anthropology, political science, economics, social psychology, and philosophy. Even though interrelationships among people are important in social studies, the disciplines mentioned provide the major substance of those studies. If social education were the major concern and the concentration were mainly on interpersonal relationships, social studies would be emphasizing psychology. Psychology, however, is only one discipline out of the total number that comprise social studies.

The substantive aspect of the social studies include techniques used by social scientists; this involves writing questionnaires, interviews, or first-hand reports that researchers design to obtain their data. These data are needed for statistical tests to determine whether certain assumptions could be supported by hypotheses stated at the beginning of the study. Even though young children do not do statistical testing, their teacher can guide them in counting how many people are in favor or not, of a certain idea. Children learn some of the rudiments in judging, counting, estimating how people feel or think, or what values they uphold. They are helped in realizing that their opinions may truthfully reflect their own feelings, but may not always be valid or factual. Impressions of what may be commonly perceived as truth are often found to be unsupported when these ideas are subjected to research or a systematic count of people who subscribe to certain values, beliefs, or ideas.

It is important to remember that the academic age of pupils influences how much they can retain or understand about concepts that have associative conditions or significant relationships. These relationships are

figure 5.3

Means Through Which Pupils Learn About the Social Studies

Learning About It Through Reading Materials	Expressing Ideas About It	Bringing the Community Into It
Reading Stories about it	Writing Stories About It	Inviting Informed Resource People to Class to Talk to Pupils
Reading Articles, Pamphlets, Magazines (National Geographic)	Creating Plays Related to the Information Obtained on It	Bringing in Community Agents Affiliated with Ideas Studied in Social Studies Unit (i.e., city planners, engineers)
Noting Advertisements Related to It	Painting Pictures About It	Inviting Artistic People in the Community to Discuss Work Related to the Social Studies Unit
	Doing a Group or Class Mural	
	Doing a Rhythms Activity Representing the Information	
	Making Puppets	Inviting County Representatives to Discuss Community Problems (related to the social studies pupils have studied)
	Creating A Diorama (Third-Dimensional Scene)	
	Creating Songs related to Information Obtained on Social Studies Unit	

often complex. They will gradually understand, however, how the presence of a harbor or the ocean affects people who live there. They will understand, too, why living near mountains presents different opportunities to people for things to do. Another important quality to remember about children's learning is that even if they do not seem to understand a concept for the first time, it does not mean the time was wasted. Our measurement techniques are not sensitive enough to tell us how much the children understand. The first time they hear about a concept often becomes part of a foundation for the next time.

The crucial points in young children's education involve the need to provide exposure to many different activities which can yield knowledge. They learn in a variety of ways. They are attracted to different forms of knowledge. A classroom, although it must be organized, has to have many objects, activities, and experiences available for children. Various kinds of audiovisual materials can facilitate learning. Films, filmstrips, pictures, resource people, or artistic materials create novel situations for learning. They should be used. Children should be given an opportunity to say what they think about them so that the teacher knows what they understand and whether they have misconceptions about some of the generalizations in subject matter.

Thus, some of the most important goals of the social studies for young children in a democratic society are to help them learn how to function effectively as contributing and satisfied members. They are expected to learn about its governmental framework so that they can function as well-informed citizens when they vote. They are also expected to learn about their society so that they will not abuse natural resources in it. Last, but among the most important of goals, children should learn how to safeguard their own lives as well as the lives of others.

Developmental Activities in the Social Studies for Young Childen

Developmental activities in the social studies refer to providing experiences for young children that are equitable or compatible with their singular levels of development, academically, physically, emotionally, socially, and psychologically. The teacher has to know her pupils well and observe their behavior daily in order to judge their abilities in various subject matter areas and in these growth levels.

These ages are not always easy to discern. The teacher can, however, notice the child who cries at the slightest provocation, and who seems constantly fearful, defensive, unable to laugh and play with at least someone in the class. Typically, the child who is ready to run to the teacher complaining about others, and about mistreatment, real or ima-

These girls are using the animals of the zoo to create their own zoo, a topic of the social studies (above).

Decisions, decisions, decisions! These girls are trying to decide which of the zoo animals would be happiest in adjoining cages.

gined, is the one who is obviously having the most difficulty interacting with classmates.

The child who reflects problems either in himself or intellectual matters has to be given added attention by the teacher. Many times she can help him so that he shows constructive changes within a few weeks. This is one of the most exciting aspects of working with young children. Their behavior is not always as permanently symptomatic as it might seem. Specific children must be given attention, however, so that they are not further frustrated by thinking that nobody cares what happens to them.

Experiences for children in nursery school can include studies of the community. They may go for walks or visit the library, supermarket, fire station, and commercial agencies that are amenable to having little children on the premises. Teachers have to have other adults helping them share the responsibility for transporting pupils, especially young ones. Groups of children outside the school room need more supervision than usual so they will stay together as a group for their own protection and safety.

These visits or field trips are discussed when pupils return to school. The children draw or paint pictures about what they saw. They compose a note saying, "Thank You," to the hosts of their field trip. They may thank the firemen for letting them visit their station. Stories with pictures illustrating what they saw or liked best are usually a delight to the people who receive them. Pupils learn that it is polite to thank people when they do something for you.

In the process of learning about the fire station itself, they are learning how people interact with community agents who protect the local community. They learn what firemen do to put out fires and also how they spend their time at the firehouse maintaining fire equipment.

They are learning to understand why this occupation is important to any community. They are also discovering what firemen are like as individuals with families and children. They are learning to respect firemen as people trying to do their jobs well, not sentimentalized but valued as important members of a community.

Children hear recordings and stories about fire stations, equipment, means of receiving alarms for fires, and modern means of putting out fires. Teachers bring pictures to the classroom to illustrate various relationships in fire equipment, their uses, and the training of firemen for their jobs. Health standards are often introduced here, indicating how important it is to eat the proper foods, exercises, and take various precautions to protect one's health. Firemen have to be strong and healthy to do the things needed for their jobs. Children are also told about fire hazards in the home and how fires can be prevented.

Social studies provide many kinds of opportunities for learning in various subject matter areas. Pupils learn about health, safety, and science in the context of studying the fire station, causes of fires, the firemen's job and what it involves. They have esthetic pleasure in portraying pictures of their thoughts in relation to fire safety or the firemen's home life. The teacher notes the children's interest in various activities and provides materials to satisfy their interests at the moment. Other community problems, jobs, or events are pursued in a similar manner. Books, stories, esthetic activities, field trips, songs, or recordings can be obtained in relation to most topics selected for study.

Children in kindergartens can do the same but at a higher level of understanding. Their span of interest can be sustained for longer periods of time than is true of nursery school children who are three to four years old. Their units on the fire station could be combined with protective services in the community. A single unit may be studied for a period of two or three weeks. This depends on the amount of materials that the teacher has to support the children's interest and ability levels of understanding.

Block play is one way of manipulating materials that can be used to

This boy has built a totally enclosed area. Now he is testing an idea related to an archway. He concentrates on placing those blocks in just the position that will permit them to lean against each other and remain standing. If this doesn't work, he will experiment with another way of creating that arch. Hand-eye coordination is an essential aspect of child development at this point.

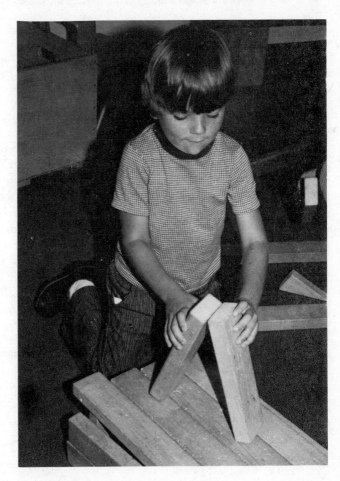

This boy is constructing a tunnel wide enough for several trucks, cars, and buses. He tests it every once in a while for adequate measurement. Social studies include tunnels, roadways, highways. The child needs to use his ingenuity to build transportation facilities of any kind.

show a fire station or various buildings in a community. Blocks used in the kindergarten are of long lengths and short, not necessarily small cubes. They are intended to represent building materials. Children build tall structures, gasoline stations, library buildings, or whatever they are studying. Many books are needed in kindergarten to provide information or details for children. Pictures, dolls or toy people, toy transportation vehicles, and recordings supplement the pupils' ideas for their structures.

Specific experiences designed for pupils may be found in various books and pamphlets on the social studies. Once the teacher understands the major ideas underlying the social studies as a field of instruction, she can apply many different activities to those principles and not have to rely on specific instructions for each program. The outstanding teacher has confidence in her ability to be creative, to originate, to initiate ideas. She has enough of a foundation and reservoir of accurate data to plan activities for children and know that she will be including valid theoretical bases and viable instructional ideas to provide children with excellent experiences. She knows how to judge individual differences among pupils. She recognizes learning in each of the children, and she is also familiar with the substantive data needed as content in the curriculum. It is very important that teachers of young children know their own strength in the knowledge of their craft, their art, and their sciences.

The teacher of young children has to be academically informed and

This boy uses the floor as a road and decides to have a few ramp facilities accommodate car usage at various heights and levels. He brings the small car to the top of the ramp and lets it go down on its own power to see how it meets the test of its own momentum. While social studies involves transportation and buildings, it also includes principles of physics or science.

has to know more than she is transmitting to the pupils. She must be informed as an adult and a professional person who has respect for the subject matter or discipline and also has enough respect for the children to give them accurate information, nothing less.

As teachers of young children become known for having a solid foundation in the disciplines, they will be respected by more people in other fields. Just because the teacher works with young minds that cannot challenge her or cannot be critical of her knowledge, does not mean that the children should be sold short by having a teacher who is not well prepared.

The teacher can upgrade her knowledge in the social studies by doing what is needed to be well informed and by reading the most recent articles in the field. She is not satisfied with outmoded techniques or reports of older articles on social studies, but rather likes to have

When several children work on a structure together, it usually becomes much larger than one planned by one child. These boys are building a large enclosure, starting with an interesting wall design.

current information that is stimulating to teach. Reading newspapers, listening to commentaries on the television news, listening to debates whenever possible and responding inwardly with one's own informed views while listening, can help the teacher not only by increasing her knowledge of social studies. She will also become more alert to daily events, and may experience greater feelings of participation in a controversial world. When a teacher knows that she is well informed she is better able to sustain a lively atmosphere for learning in the classroom because this interest in life somehow transmits itself to pupils.

Children in the kindergarten talk about current problems. They hear their parents discussing high taxes, costs of living, energy problems and the need to conserve light, heat, fuel or gasoline. These are not deep issues but children should be encouraged in this awareness of social problems by talking about them at school.

In the first grade, the teacher can develop a unit that involves greater depth and understanding. Pupils have a longer attention span. They can remain with the subject matter presented in different forms (reading, filmstrips, recordings, art forms) for a longer period of time than they could at earlier ages. Some can read simple passages and are interested in testing their own reading skills. This is true the higher one goes in the primary grades.

160

SOCIAL STUDIES UNITS IN THE PRIMARY GRADES FOR CHILDREN
WHO ARE SIX-, SEVEN-, AND EIGHT-YEARS OLD—
PART OF EARLY CHILDHOOD

If the teacher is given the opportunity to develop her own social studies unit for her grade, she may want to use the guide recommended here. Starting with this guide, the teacher can add her own ideas and expand on certain parts of it that seem best to maximize the children's learning. The guidelines given below are meant to suggest a way of trying to study a group of people, be they people in a city, a country, a region, or a continent. One of the strongest reasons for using this approach is that many of the interests of the children can be satisfied. It is a comprehensive approach and provides opportunities for using many of the technical skills and abilities of the children.

All the children are not held responsible for learning each dimension on the guideline to the same degree of depth as those who will be doing extensive work on part of it. Groups of children or individuals choose to study certain parts of the social studies unit and are responsible for bringing to the class a report on what they have found. The teacher provides many types (in terms of difficulties in reading levels) and kinds of materials that help children find answers, but the teacher does not obtain answers for the child. He searches for himself (note activity types in Figure 5.4).

If some children are involved in studying the recreation of the people, for example, and some are studying religious beliefs or sources from which the people obtain their beliefs (this can be reflected in myths that younger children can read or listen to as they are read), their sources are endless. When they are finished with one, there are others; sources such as the *National Geographic Magazine* and many newspapers and articles in various journals make it an endless search. The children do not read the *National Geographic,* of course; they use the pictures. The teacher brings to the classroom materials that she knows the pupils can use; pictures give clues too. The children and the teacher do not exhaust the sources available for information on people from societies all over the world. Their own time and energies, however, will limit their search for data.

When a teacher has never-ending resources from which the children and she can obtain information needed for a social studies unit, the children will also have an ongoing feeling in their work. The lesson plans can end with decisions to check on more clues or resources even though some tentative conclusions were made.

The teacher does not end a lesson with, "There's nothing else to do," (as was once observed by a supervisor listening to a student teacher work with children in a social studies activity). After a major assignment in the

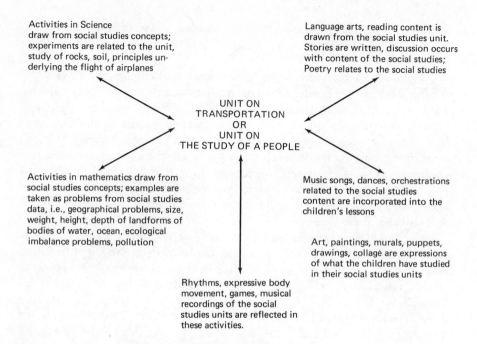

Activities in Science draw from social studies concepts; experiments are related to the unit, study of rocks, soil, principles underlying the flight of airplanes

Language arts, reading content is drawn from the social studies unit. Stories are written, discussion occurs with content of the social studies; Poetry relates to the social studies

UNIT ON
TRANSPORTATION
OR
UNIT ON
THE STUDY OF A PEOPLE

Activities in mathematics draw from social studies concepts; examples are taken as problems from social studies data, i.e., geographical problems, size, weight, height, depth of landforms of bodies of water, ocean, ecological imbalance problems, pollution

Music songs, dances, orchestrations related to the social studies content are incorporated into the children's lessons

Art, paintings, murals, puppets, drawings, collage are expressions of what the children have studied in their social studies units

Rhythms, expressive body movement, games, musical recordings of the social studies units are reflected in these activities.

figure 5.4
Pupils Learn about the Social Studies, Facts, Concepts, and Generalizations by Having Experiences that Are Related to the Unit of Work in the Social Studies

social studies had been completed by the children, the student teacher did not know how to bring the children beyond that point. The sequence of lessons had not been considered or planned. If it had been, she could have gone on working with the children. They could have at least been questioned for purposes of review or in anticipation of and preparation for next steps in the study.

Guidelines That Can Be Used for the Study of a People

Children are provided with materials, resources, films, books, recordings, which will help them discover for themselves the answers to the following questions.

PEOPLE SURVIVE IN RELATION TO THE ENVIRONMENT
IN SPECIFIC WAYS

1. How do they earn a living?
2. How do they rear their young? What values are important in that concept?

3. How do they meet their needs for food, shelter, and clothing?
4. What are the religious beliefs that are important to them?
5. How do they meet needs that give them ego satisfaction in a socially accepted sense?
6. How do they govern themselves to see that the needs of individuals and the group are met? Do they have a body of written laws?
7. What kind of art forms do they produce? Music? Art? Dance? Theater? Ceramics? Literature? Sculpture?
8. How do they obtain recreation?
9. What kinds of acts of other people cut into or lower their sense of dignity or self-respect?
10. What kinds of disciplinary measures have they prescribed for members of their own group?
11. What are the modes of orientation that guide them? What are their values? What do they work toward with a sense of challenge and commitment?
12. What are their modes of dress? What are the materials made of? Do they use a mass production process? Are their fabrics and materials made mostly by hand?
13. What sorts of ornamentation do they wear?
14. What is their language? Do they have a written language or literature that originated in their own country or with their own people, or do they share their language and forms of communication with another group larger than their own?
15. Do they export objects or consumer goods to other people in other lands?
16. What forms of transportation have they devised for themselves?
17. What forms of barter, trade, or money exchange do they use?
18. Which groups of people are given prestigious positions, high rank, added respect or deference when they are in the presence of others?
19. What are the family customs? What are customs that are related to marriage patterns? What are the living arrangements of family units— nuclear family or extended family groups? Of what does a family consist?
20. How are children brought into the adult cultural levels?
21. What rituals or rites are performed for significance ceremonies?
22. What seems most unique about their culture that differs from ours?
23. What are their means of medical protection and safety?
24. What are some of their superstitions? their fears?

PEOPLE ADAPT TO AND AFFECT THE GEOGRAPHICAL
CONTEXT OF THEIR SOCIETY

1. Are they located in a mountain region, a valley, or a desert?
2. Are their living areas in congested crowded territories?

3. Are they near oceans, lakes, streams, rivers? Are those bodies of water large enough for commercial enterprises?
4. Are they located near forests, greenery, or plateaus?
5. What kind of animals are near their settlements?
6. Are they located in regions of cold climate, the northern parts of the world?
7. Do they have an abundance of rainfall? of snow? Do they have dry seasons? What happens as a result?
8. Do they have ample transportation provided by adequate vehicles and means for thoroughfares, i.e., streets, individual carts, buses?
9. Does their soil yield food for them? Do they have adequate technical processes to give them what they need for the preparation of food?
10. What are their systems for obtaining water? for obtaining health and safety protective means?
11. What kinds of materials do they use from the earth that protect them from excesses of heat, cold, wind, or rain?
12. What products from the earth do they use for building, or for religious ceremonies?
13. Which animals from their environment do they eat or use as beasts of burden?
14. What birds do they use as symbols of values their people have? Do they use their feathers for adornment?
15. What parts of their environment seem most precious or valuable to them?
16. Are there parts of the environment that they will not touch, dig, or use because they consider them sacred?
17. Are there animals, birds, insects that they fear or are in awe of for religious reasons?
18. Are there ceremonies that involve the land, the vegetation or its waters?
19. What materials do they use from their environment to express themselves artistically?
20. Are there land or water boundaries that hinder or facilitate means of travel in and out of their territory?

EVERYONE PARTICIPATES IN THE SOCIAL STUDIES UNIT,
AS INDIVIDUALS AND AS PART OF A GROUP

The teacher divides the study of a unit in ways that are appropriate to the children's interests, abilities, and individual attitudes. It really represents a type of division of labor in which everybody is doing something of interest to him or her. A task is selected by the child or possibly urged by the teacher if a child appears uncertain of what he wants. In some cases children need the teacher's suggestion to help them get started in an activity. The teacher tries to help the child become involved in an aspect of study that will interest him and will keep him interested for an extended period of time, about a week or so, depending on the age of the child and how much material is available on the subject at his ability level. For example, some children may want to study the land, the bodies of water surrounding it; some may want to study the people, their jobs, and occupations. Some may want to study the children, and their education.

The process of working in the social studies brings the pupils into every other subject matter area and the techniques of those areas—language arts, reading, writing, keeping records (see Figure 5.4). Science can be used in relation to the people and the land they occupy and the things that people do to care for the land so that it produces food, or healing substances. If airplanes are related to a unit the children can study the principle that enables the airplane to stay in the air.

Language arts and reading use the content of the social studies and read about, discuss, and create stories about the particular social studies content selected for study. All the elements of the language arts—poetry, prose, listening, speaking, reading, writing, creativity—are involved in any social studies unit. The children must do all the work needed to obtain facts for the unit by using the communicative arts.

Mathematics is a subject that is important to counting materials involved in the social studies; it is involved when the children measure something they are making. It is involved when they compute any problems that arise in their studies of people from another country. Kindergarten children who may be studying an airport, for example, may make crude airplanes out of wood. They would have to measure, with the teacher's help, how long the fuselage or body of the airplane would be; they have to measure the wing span, the tail, the ailerons, and so on. A great deal of estimation, too, goes on when the children are deciding where the tail will be nailed on, how high it has to be in relation to the rest of the plane. All this involves measurement, judgment, relationships of size, length and depth. While it may not be an exact product in relation to proportions, it is approximate. The child is having the opportunity to see how important mathematical properties are to the utility of the product. This begins to build an appreciation for the exactness of mathematics as a system.

Body movement, rhythms, physical education, sports, and dances are very appropriately involved in the study of a people. The kinds of dances, sports, and exercises that they do for which their society will pay to see performed well, are studied by the children. Pupils can learn some of the movement and sports that are familiar to children of other nations. This contributes to the pupils' knowledge of attitudes developed by people who are unfamiliar to them. The fact that some children can grow up with a love for certain national sports that are not as familiar to American children as their own football, baseball, and basketball, introduces an appreciation of differences in a compatible sense. As children are guided by their teacher to note similarities in strong desires for certain sports, whether or not those sports are the same ones, an expansiveness in their outlook develops. At least this is what is hoped for as the teacher works with children in social studies.

Children who are learning about the feelings, desires, and sensitivities of others are learning about other people as well as those in their own society. Those differences and similarities symbolize the variety of ways that humankind meets its needs. In the process of comparing one group to another or one person with another, one learns as much about one's self or one's own group as about the other. This produces sensitivity, awareness, and objectivity at least in a small sense.

The music and art forms of another people are fascinating for many reasons. The children learn specifically about the principles of music and art as separate fields of study in themselves. They also learn, however, what the symbolism of other human groups is. People release some of their deepest emotions in art forms. Intimacy is established in art and music. They are considered universal forms of expression. Since they deal with emotions that involve feelings toward an object or idea, the esthetic experience establishes a bond. This can encourage compatibility with another human group.

The children also learn about the musical instruments that are valued in another culture. They learn how these instruments were created and the kind of musical scale preferred in that society. Oriental scales differ in terms of emphasis from those in the United States. The minor key is stressed for the most part. When the children are taught by a capable teacher who has accurate information (and is enthusiastic about it) on musical differences from country to country, the children enjoy it. They can benefit from this information early in life. It gives them an excellent foundation for more complex information they may obtain later in school or at concerts. In essence, it is the teacher's skills that make the difference between whether the children will benefit or not from what happens in the classroom. Few children dislike music when it is presented well.

The principles of visual art are thoroughly enjoyed when they are set into meaning and activity for young children. Shape, form, line, color, space, mass, volume, perspective are labels, it is true. They are concepts that young children are able to learn. Young children use them willingly and with ease when they know where to apply them appropriately. They like to show adults and older friends and siblings what they are capable of knowing, therefore they enjoy knowing the terms used for certain things that they do.

It must be kept in mind that the children do not learn these ideas from the teacher in the form of a lecture. Projects intended for the children's involvement include the ideas mentioned earlier. The teacher

Many cultures have masks of various kinds in ritual dances or general art forms. These children did paper bag puppets in the form of animals that appealed to them. The pupils were encouraged to create individual ideas, not to copy from someone else. Conformity in art expression is discouraged.

mentions a term when it is appropriate to the children's level of understanding and the activity that interests them at the moment. Instruction for young children occurs very often in an informal manner. The teacher looks for those teachable moments and gives the children distinctive data that she knows enriches what they are doing at the time. A knowledgable teacher has acquired a great deal of academic information on a sophisticated level; when it is used with children it is explained simply and accurately. Thus, when a teacher comments on a child's work, the terms such as line, color, shape, form, space, strength, lightness can be used to describe what he has done. The child will then use the terminology and become accustomed to its meaning.

Awareness, sensitivity, perceptiveness are heightened with studies of other cultures, other people, other customs, and other human ways of reacting or responding to one's environment. Whether a teacher chooses to have the children study people, such as the Israelis, the Brazilians, the French, or the Swedish is not as relevant to the fact that they will be learning to use technical processes in that pursuit. They will in the heightened perceptiveness about people also be learning to read, to write, to speak, to express esthetic ideas in the context of social studies.

The children use techniques of science, of mathematics, of physical education, of art, of music to exchange ideas and learn about various people, even those in their own society. When they study their own community services, its people, its preferences, its government, and other characteristics related to it, they are learning about the reading, writing, and mathematics of their own contemporary society. This is accompanied by the general principles regarding the subject matter or content (the substantive data, i.e., facts, generalizations, and concepts about the social studies unit) of the community being studied. Thus, the social studies unit goes hand-in-hand with the subject matter techniques of reading, writing, mathematics, science, art, music, body movement, esthetic expression in dance, physical education, sports or health education.

Social studies opens the way for exploration, creativity, and individualistic satisfaction. It is rarely the same from term to term for the teacher, because each group of children and their unique abilities and interests take the study in different directions and concentrated areas.

Different sets of children contribute different ideas to each social studies unit. The stories that they write describing people they are studying, and the esthetic forms or murals they do, individually or with other children in the class, are always different from those made by children who have done the unit before them. The creativity expressed by pupils is often unknown to adults who have not worked with young children, and they are usually pleasantly surprised at the concepts that are reflected in the work. Children can capture in art forms the subtle feelings of people from another culture that they have studied.

Social studies arouses, it excites, and draws everyone's interest into a common area of study. Some children tend to be interested in one of the subareas and pursue it cautiously or hesitantly (a subarea of recreation, games, or how people earn a living, for example). Some pupils leap into it immediately and begin to pursue several areas of content with gusto. In any case, everyone benefits from a class project in common pursuit of data needed to answer intriguing questions about a people.

Whatever the teacher's orientations are about the social studies, it must be recognized as a significant approach and outstanding mechanism for meeting the individual needs of all the children in the room. If a child does not have high intellectual ability in an area, the teacher can steer him or guide him toward an activity in a level or area that will not be too challenging for him and will not discourage him from further learning. The teacher adjusts the task for learning to the appropriate level of child involved. This can be done easily when the teacher knows the child's ability levels and knows the subject matter well enough to make suggestions for the child's further inquiry.

Everyone is busy simultaneously because everyone has something to study at his own level and feels the responsibility of contributing to the class project. He is finding information for others that they cannot have the time to do because they are also studying something else that they will report to the class. It is a mutual job for classmates. Each job, regardless of how small, needs to be done, and each is contributing to the total body of knowledge for the class. The child of lesser ability in certain intellectual categories has an opportunity for eventual recognition from his peers for completing something needed for the facilitation of an entire unit.

At the close of the unit, after the children have studied the materials related to it and the teacher feels that they have obtained the majority of information to be found, and maintained their interest at high levels, they plan a summary or closing activity. This is often called a culmination. It involves the children in preparing highlights of their work, art, stories, writing, or musical representations reflecting the social studies subject matter. The class will invite parents to see what has been done. Pupils may prepare food representative of the people they have been studying and serve it to the parents. They arrange the room environment with their products, clay, mural, or clothing worn by the people with whom they have begun to sense a bond of understanding. Pictures, books, posters, recordings, musical instruments and other objects or realia used by the people in their life's activities are displayed. Other classes in school are often invited to see the work and displays, which often represent many weeks of serious activity by the pupils. After the children's products have been displayed for a few more days, they take them home. Typically, the work they do in these groups means a great deal to them. They do not forget the experience.

The culmination of a unit is used as part of an evaluative means of assessing the children's work during the period of study. The subject areas such as science, mathematics, language arts, reading, art, and music, and geographical understandings are classified and considered individually. The teacher evaluates the children in terms of their own progress. Their skills, attitudes, habits observed during their work periods can be appraised at the end of the social studies unit. The next section deals with types of evaluation used for children's developmental progress.

Evaluation of Children's Experiences in the Social Studies

Evaluation procedures are significant to a teacher's knowledge of whether the "best laid plans" have been what they were expected to be relative to the children's maximum learning development. Sometimes the most sophisticated programs do not fit the range of comprehension skills of the children in the class. Thus, the materials are beautiful in their schematic and logical form but seldom used. They remain clean and sterile, but unfortunately they are untouched by the children's hands. If the children's levels of development, emotionally, intellectually, and academically, are not considered in planning programs and materials, the programs are useless to them.

Since little children are not sophisticated in the ways of test taking and are not sure how they are expected to respond, it is more important to devise the kind of evaluation procedures that are comprehensive in an approach to the children's knowledge. The teacher cannot use paper and pencil group-administered tests with them as with older children. For this reason, teacher observations, or daily notes on a child's performance or reactions to certain problems, are very helpful to a final assessment of the child's work.

The children's general approaches to materials, to experiences that are new to them, or to their peers in the classroom give the teacher clues as to what their progress is. The teacher saves products made by the children by storing them in a folder at the beginning of the term to the end. It is easier to see the progress they make in a period of time. Some materials, however, can be taken home by the child. Younger pupils in particular enjoy taking their work home to show to their parents. It is lucky for the child who has an appreciative parent. Parental approval and interest in the child's work goes a long "educational" and "inspirational" way toward helping the school child develop a favorable self concept.

Evaluations are made typically in the middle of the term. A teacher who is sensitive to the children will attempt to observe them daily and keep notes to this effect. Thus, when parent conferences are planned, the teacher has ready information at her fingertips. These daily notes are very helpful in refreshing the teacher's memory on the child's work. It also is a form of documentation, more dependable than memory, in relation to exact time. It also reveals patterns of behavior that give the teacher some clues as to how the child is responding to school work and his peers.

In the four-year-old group of children, which may be the nursery school period for young fours, the teacher simplifies tests by asking the children questions and writing down their responses. In the kindergarten, the teacher would have to validate verbal responses by having the children point to the objects represented by certain words. Their knowledge of the objects would be tested by questions. Such questions would be, "What does it do for us?" "How do people use it?" "Why do we like it?" There are standardized tests of this type. More have been devised since the need to know how young children are learning and at what rates, has become of concern to many psychologists and educators.

In the first grade, children can circle objects or sets of objects to demonstrate their knowledge of a concept. In the second grade, they are able to respond in more ways; they read with greater facility. In the third grade, they are still more able to take tests in writing, circling pictorial or numerical responses. Of course a teacher has to realize all the time that children's abilities in a classroom vary either way by as much as three years. A child in the second grade may respond as though he is four years old or as though he is ten instead of the actual normal chronological age of seven. Social, emotional, psychological, and academic behaviors seem to vary in wide degrees. The teacher is aware of this and accounts for it when doing any evaluation on a child. She does however realize, after several evaluation procedures are conducted, where the children need added help.

When a teacher knows what kind of social studies units will be studied, she uses the data that she expects the children to obtain as part of simple tests that can be given periodically. Responses to three simple questions in a specific area may be sufficient to test their knowledge. The more accustomed they become to simple tests of that kind, the better it is for them when tests that will become part of a significant set of classroom scores are given. Norms are developed from typical scores received by groups of children. Sometimes these norms are used for comparison and become standardized. These standardizations can become city-wide, state-wide, or nation-wide, depending on the focus or the importance of the material studied. National norms exist for mathematical or reading knowledge and often the specific schools or school districts count heavily on satisfactory scores to show how the children are learning. They hope of course that their schools can show up well in the tests. This too is part of a national concern for accountability to the public for the school's work with children.

A simple test for social studies however can be used to ascertain what children in a specific classroom have learned.

The _____ people like to:

eat _____, work with _____, teach their children

to _____.

Draw a picture below of the tools that the _____ used when they planted seeds and when they picked the crop out of the ground.

Tests can be used in formats similar to those used in follow-up seat work that children did when they circulated in reading groups. Since they had the opportunity to practice matching pictures and word-pairs with similar sets of associative objects, drawing lines from one word to another connecting meanings, these techniques may be used in testing procedures.

Check-lists can be used with the children in which they show how effectively they work with others, obtained pertinent information and materials, listened to and participated in group discussion, and used other skills needed in acquiring social studies data. Writers of books on social studies give interesting forms of simple tests that are enjoyable for children to take.[3] The teacher however must create them to fit the levels of the children being taught. Most books on social studies concentrate on elementary grades rather than only the kindergarten and the first three grades.

Prior to the initiation of any social studies unit the teacher should give a simple test of about six or seven items to determine how much the pupils might already know on the topics planned for investigation. This pre-test provides a tentative base-line so the teacher can know at what point the children are starting out in the acquisition of new facts, generalizations, and concepts.

Packaged programs that are available such as the Taba series of social studies units [4] or *The Social Sciences Concepts and Values* [5] include evaluation processes that the teacher can use or at least adapt to the pupils in her class. Teachers can easily adjust these suggestions and recommendations to their own needs. Imagination, ingenuity, and a desire to help the children enjoy the process of testing can ease tensions typically experienced in evaluation procedures.

summary

This chapter focused on social studies as an important area of study needed by young children in order to know the dynamics of their culture and their society. Children in nursery school, kindergarten, and the primary grades are exposed to knowledge about their community, their society, and their world by hearing stories about people in different lands, seeing films and film-strips about them, and also seeing books that refer to people in local communities and the services they give. Children learn about their immediate world through studying people they know and see in their own communities. They also begin to build foundations for knowledge about other societies. They become familiar with what children in other countries do and how they live or are educated at school.

The teacher has the responsibility for providing children with accurate information which is given to them through activities they can understand and in which they are able to participate. She observes their behavioral responses astutely so that she knows where they are in relation to understandings of the concepts in the social studies. For young children, only

---

[3] John Jarolimek, *Social Studies in Elementary Education* (New York: Macmillan Publishing Co., Inc., 1971), pp. 485–499. See also Lavone A. Hanna, Gladys L. Potter and Neva Hagaman, *Unit Teaching in the Elementary School* (New York: Holt, Rinehart and Winston, Inc., 1963), pp. 404–428.

[4] Mary Durkin, Alice Duvall, and Alice McMaster, *The Taba Social Studies Curriculum* (Reading, Mass.: Addison-Wesley Publishing Co., Inc., 1969).

[5] Center for the Study of Instruction. *The Social Sciences. Concepts and Values*. (New York: Harcourt Brace Jovanovich, Inc., 1970).

general ideas will be understood. Analytical or critical thinking of any depth comes later in the primary grades.

The teacher has to provide materials for the children which will not be frustrating or dull; individual differences and abilities have to be considered in the broad variety of materials available on the subject matter. Typically the teacher who has the kind of activities for pupils that challenge them and which they can master after time is spent with them, is the one who is sensitive to their needs and who has very few problems with children who seem distracted and disinterested at school.

topics for discussion

1. In what ways does the social studies as a broad area for investigation offer the use of other subject matter skills and techniques?
2. Create a social studies unit that you would like to teach in the kindergarten. Give a rationale for your topical choice, indicating what you hope that the children will gain from doing the study. Plan it as one that might run for about four weeks in your total semester plan for the children's involvement in it. Use the guidelines given in the chapter. Indicate how you would evaluate their work at the end of the unit, assuming of course that you are also doing so daily as you observe them.
3. After observing in a classroom that you think has an excellent teacher, note the social studies unit the children are studying. Describe the highlights of it in relation to outstanding work that the children have accomplished. Discuss the immediate short-term goals and also the longer-term objectives that you think the children are beginning to attain.
4. How can the art and music of another culture enhance a child's learning? What are some of the most important aspects that are transmitted from one culture to another through its art or esthetic forms?

selected bibliography for teachers

Association for Supervision and Curriculum Development. *Education for an Open Society.* Washington, D.C.: Association for Supervision and Curriculum Development, 1974.

Clare, La Verne H. *They Sang for Horses.* Tucson: University of Arizona Press, 1966.

Colton, Harold. *Hopi Kachina Dolls.* Albuquerque: University of New Mexico Press, 1959.

Crosby, Muriel, Ed. *Reading Ladders for Human Relations.* Washington, D.C.: American Council on Education, 1963.

Dempsey, Joseph H. *This Is Man.* Teacher's Edition. Morristown, N.J.: Silver Burdett Company, 1972.

Dietz, Betty and T. C. Park. *Chinese, Japanese, and Korean Folk Songs.* New York: John Day Co., 1964.

Dietz, Betty, and Olatunji. *Musical Instruments of Africa.* New York: John Day Co., 1965.

Durkin, Mary C., Alice Duvall, and Alice McMaster. *The Taba Social Studies Curriculum.* Reading, Mass.: Addison-Wesley Publishing Co., 1969.

Easton, David. *A Framework for Political Analysis.* Englewood Cliffs, N.J.: Prentice-Hall, Inc., 1965.

Engle, Shirley H., and Wilma Longstreet. *A Design for Social Education in the Open Curriculum.* New York: Harper & Row, 1972.

Estvan, Frank J. *Social Studies in a Changing World.* New York: Harcourt, Brace Jovanovich, 1968.

Faking, Mary K., and Eleanor Merritt. *Subject Index for Primary Grades.* Chicago: American Library Association, 1961.

Glubok, Shirley. *The Art of the North American Indian.* New York: Harper & Row, 1964.

Goodman, Mary Ellen. *The Individual and Culture.* Homewood, Ill.: Dorsey Press, 1967.

Greene, Maxine. "The Arts and the Global Village," *Educational Leadership,* Vol. 26 (1969), pp. 439–466.

Hanna, Lavone A., Gladys L. Potter, and Neva Hagaman. *Unit Teaching in the Elementary School.* New York: Holt, Rinehart and Winston, 1963.

Hartshorne, Richard. *Perspectives in the Nature of Geography.* Chicago: Rand McNally, 1962.

Hill, Wilhelmina, Ed. *Curriculum Guide for Geographic Education.* Norman, Okla.: National Council for Geographic Education, 1963.

Hofman, Charles. *American Indians Sing.* New York: John Day Co., 1967.

Jarolimek, John. *Social Studies in Elementary Education.* New York: Macmillan Publishing Co., Inc., 1971.

Jarolimek, John and Huber M. Walsh, Eds. *Readings for Social Studies in Elementary Education.* New York: Macmillan Publishing Co., Inc., 1974.

Kenworthy, Leonard S. *Social Studies for the Seventies.* Waltham, Mass.: Blaisdell Publishing Company, 1969.

King, Edith W. *Worldmindedness.* Dubuque, Iowa: William C. Brown Company, 1971.

Merriam, Alan P. *The Anthropology of Music.* Evanston, Ill.: Northwestern University Press, 1964.

Michaelis, John U., Ed. *Teaching Units in the Social Science: Early Grades.* Chicago: Rand McNally, 1966.

Michaelis, John U. *Social Studies for Children in a Democracy.* 4th Ed. Englewood Cliffs, N.J.: Prentice-Hall, Inc., 1968.

Michaelis, John U., Ruth H. Grossman, and Lloyd F. Scott. *New Designs for the Elementary School Curriculum.* New York: McGraw-Hill Book Company, 1967.

Pelto, Perti J. *The Study of Anthropology.* Columbus, Ohio: Charles E. Merrill Publishing Company, 1965.

Rose, Caroline B. *Sociology: The Study of Man in Society.* Columbus, Ohio: Charles E. Merrill Publishing Company, 1965.

Sorauf, Francis J. *Political Science: An Informal Overview.* Columbus, Ohio: Charles E. Merrill Publishing Company, 1965.

Stark, Richard. *Music of the Spanish Folk Plays of New Mexico*. Sante Fe: Museum of New Mexico Press, 1969.

Tooze, Ruth, and Beatrice Krone. *Literature and Music As Resources for the Social Studies*. Englewood Cliffs, N.J.: Prentice-Hall, Inc., 1955.

Wright, Betty. *Educating for Diversity*. New York: John Day Co., 1965.

Zintz, Miles. *Education Across Cultures*. Dubuque, Iowa: William C. Brown Company, 1965.

books for children

Adler, Irving and Ruth Adler. *Irrigation: Changing Deserts Into Gardens*. New York: John Day Co., 1964.

Aguirre, A. J. M., and F. Gocio. *A First Look at the Earth*. New York: Franklin Watts, 1960.

Aguirre, A. J. M., and F. Gocio. *A First Look at the Sea*. New York: Franklin Watts, 1960.

Bannon, Laura. *The Other Side of the World*. Boston: Houghton Mifflin, 1960.

Bothwell, Jean. *The Animal World of India*. New York: Franklin Watts, 1961.

Caldwell, John C., and Elsie F. Caldwell. *Our Neighbors in Brazil*. New York: John Day Co., 1962.

Caldwell, John C. and Elsie F. *Our Neighbors in Japan*. New York: John Day Co., 1961.

Cavanna, Betty. *Paulo of Brazil*. New York: Franklin Watts, 1962.

De Angela, Marguerite. *Jared's Island*. Garden City: Doubleday, 1947.

Farquhar, Margaret. *Colonial Life in America: A Book to Begin On*. New York: Holt, Rinehart and Winston, 1959.

Goetz, Delia. *Island of the Ocean*. New York: William Morrow Company, 1964.

Hays, Wilma P. *Christmas on the Mayflower*. New York: Coward-McCann, 1956.

Jordan, Phillip D. *The Burro Benedicto*. New York: Coward McCann, 1960.

Lauber, Patricia. *Icebergs and Glaciers*. New York: Scholastic Books, 1965.

Marcus, Rebecca. *The First Book of Cliff Dwellings*. New York: Franklin Watts, 1969.

Pine, Tillie S., and Joseph Levine. *The Egyptians Knew*. New York: Whittlesey, 1964.

Pine, Tillie S., and Joseph Levine. *The Chinese Knew*. New York: McGraw-Hill Book Company, 1958.

Sakade, Florence, Ed. *Japanese Children's Favorite Stories*. Rutland, Vermont: Tuttle, 1958.

Sasek, Miroslav. *This Is Israel*. New York: Macmillan Publishing Co., 1962.

Schloat, G. Warren, Jr. *Conchita and Juan: A Girl and Boy of Mexico*. New York: Alfred A. Knopf, 1964.

Schwartz, Julius. *The Earth Is Your Spaceship*. New York: McGraw-Hill Book Company, 1963.

Yamaguchi, Tohr. *The Golden Crane: A Japanese Folk Tale*. New York: Holt, Rinehart and Winston, 1963.

Chapter 6

Mathematics in Children's Lives

To count, to measure, to figure—
So many numbers to learn;
Do you think I'll be able to do it
With only ten fingers to turn?

Young children become familiar with counting and with fractions at an early age. They learn their own ages; they sing or say simple counting rhymes; they are given a piece of cookie. They discover from babyhood that things are counted and that they are measurable. They become immediately sensitized to a lot or a little in terms of crude impressions. When they come to school, however, they begin to learn it in a systematized sense.

The school's programs for young children attempt to provide the most palatable means for learning. The scientific objectivity of mathematics does not rule out the means of instructional activities which can be very enjoyable and game-like in format. A complex society involves a need for knowledge of techniques that instruct the individual in computing, measuring, assessing, judging and deciding how to spend one's money. Young children must learn as much as they can about the skills for mathematical facility. When they learn about them at an early age and in a satisfying context (an effectively functioning classroom), they are better able to build complex concepts on top of that early foundation. They learn them easily when they are presented well by the teacher and when the teacher understands the intricacies of children's learning processes.

Purposes and Goals in Mathematical Programs for Young Children

Mathematics as a system is not unlike reading as a form of interpretation of symbols devised by society. "Like man's verbal language, mathematics consists of arbitrary symbolic forms with rules of construction and interpretation." [1] Its place in elementary school is central to the means through which children may learn to reason in a logical system. Among four objectives suggested by one author, the major thread is obvious; that of providing children with experiences in mathematics so that they will understand, appreciate and enjoy mathematical processes. [2]

The advantage of working with young children provides the opportunity for the teacher to surround the pupils with many kinds of activities involving discovery of relationships among sizes, amounts, capacities, and labels. The teacher has to be constantly aware of the opportunity to give children names for the shapes around them—triangles, squares, rectangles, and oblongs. Opportunities to do this not only arise during lessons in mathematics but also during transition periods when children are completing one activity and preparing to do another, or when they are getting ready to go home.

Among the basic ideas and concepts that children must learn are the quality and nature of numbers, measurement, space, size, sets or groups, position of objects, and mathematical processes—both applied and abstract. Young children begin to recognize what the numeral 3 represents through its use in concrete situations. They know about number concepts in relation to their own age and their brothers' or sisters' ages. Their concept of number has to be established with objects they can feel or touch. They can understand five or six or ten more effectively when they count sticks or napkins or other common objects. Numbers have less meaning for them in abstract terms.

One group of writers suggest that helping children understand number concepts, structure of number systems, relationships and the like, they should also be able ". . . to perceive and understand structure in mathematics: concepts, relationships, principles, and modes of reasoning." [3] After the child has had many experiences with mathematical operations, manipulating numbers of objects, he will be able to understand how certain patterns of computation and structure emerge. The constant manipulation of $2 + 2$, and $1 + 1 + 2$, and $1 + 3$ and $4 - 3$ enables the child to understand numbers in abstract terms.

[1] John U. Michaelis, Ruth H. Grossman, and Lloyd F. Scott, *New Designs for the Elementary School Curriculum* 2nd ed. (New York: McGraw-Hill Book Company, 1975), p. 262.

[2] Leonard M. Kennedy, *Guiding Children to Mathematical Discovery* (Belmont, California: Wadsworth Publishing Company, 1970), pp. 1–2.

[3] Michaelis, Grossman, and Scott, op. cit., p. 262.

All books on mathematics emphasize that children should be able to enjoy the subject and have positive attitudes toward it. Teachers are asked to motivate the children so that the children will appreciate mathematics as something useful. The practical aspects are stressed. It is particularly easy to make games out of children's activities where mathematics is concerned. There are flannel boards and representation of objects out of flannel that children enjoy using. It helps the child understand the nature of mathematical systems when he can move objects around, count them, subtract and the like. The young child has to have a great deal of practice in these movement and arrangement processes.

Numerical concepts are easy to represent by objects used in the kindergarten—e.g., food, toys, forks, spoons, cups, saucers, napkins, and the like. Thus, it is easy to establish pleasant attitudes toward mathematics and counting. After experiences with real objects that the child places in different positions as he likes, and that he matches in a one-to-one relationship (one cup to each child, one napkin for each child), he is able to understand the abstract number one. The teacher shows children two cups and two cups and counts them so that children begin to acquire the concept of 2 plus 2 = 4. Gradually the mathematical equation will mean something to them. But they first must have experiences that make sense to them as a reality. It is difficult for the teacher to know when the child is ready to move from the concrete stage (or tangible level) of understanding a concept to the abstract level. For this reason, the teacher continues to use tangible examples whenever possible. The abstract must be buttressed by the real.

When authors in mathematics advocate programs to help children develop positive attitudes toward the subject, they refer to the manner of presentation. Children must be provided with experiences that are at their level of understanding. These are followed by experiences that represent a challenge to them, that are slightly more difficult. A teacher must be careful, however, not to frustrate the child so that he feels inept at the start. Some children will not have the desire to persist. The teacher has to acquire a pattern of introducing materials that can be mastered easily, permitting the child to continue with them for a while, then introducing them to more difficult concepts. Attitude development in mathematics is important as one of the major goals in any early childhood program.

Some writers suggest that mathematics consists of the discovery of relationships and a symbolic means to express those relationships in the process of communication.[4] It was also suggested that children will learn those relationships and their expression only if they participate in such

---

[4] *Mathematics in the Primary Schools.* Curriculum Bulletin No. 1 Second Edition (London: Her Majesty's Stationery Office, 1966), p. 9.

These boys are obviously ready to meet the challenge of a chess game. You always have at least one heckler, however, to check your moves and make you feel uncertain and uncomfortable.

activities.[5] They do not learn mathematical concepts quickly; it takes more time than adults expect.

The purposes and goals of mathematics include an awareness of measurement; of number; of proportion; of order in addition, subtraction, multiplication, and division; fractions; of classifying objects and materials; and of classifying sets and relationships among them.

Children have experiences with objects that are quantitatively and qualitatively identifiable from the time of their birth. Until they begin to speak and learn how to relate objects in their environment with mankind's system of abstracting those ideas, they will not be aware of what they see in terms of a conceptual framework of the symbolic world made up of their surrounding society. Each society has a different set of symbols, of language and symbols that represent ideas of importance to them. Children have to learn those ideas and symbols as they advance in school and have to relate important ideas to words and signs as their parents

[5] Ibid., p. 9.

and teachers, peers, relatives, or friends show them what those relationships are.

Just as there are reading readiness programs in preparation for children's learning about the "discipline" of reading, that is, its patterns for pronunciation, order, and meaning of symbols, so it is important for children to have a mathematical readiness program that continues throughout the school day. Of course children have an exposure to mathematical concepts all around them. They need, however, to be helped in understanding what is in essence mankind's efforts to systematize in a meaningful way numerical proportions, sizes, weights, and measurements.

Children enjoy using objects that they know—toy cars, miniature objects representing fruits, baseball bats, hats, pencils, crayons, or any objects familiar to them that they can count, add, subtract, divide and multiply, and thereby make mathematics enjoyable and meaningful to them. Some teachers use tiny plastic shapes, cardboard facsimilies of objects or toys. There are many ways to create representative objects that can be manipulated. They should appeal to the children in terms of the theme of those objects. Young children enjoy handling tiny racing cars, airplanes, helicopters.

Children do not have to use a pencil or workbook to be involved in mathematics. They use the objects to help them count and to help them affiliate objects with numbers—one-to-one correspondence in rote counting. Later, when they match the written numeral 3 to three objects they begin to understand the concept of three. They need many experiences manipulating objects and classifying them into sets of two or three or four. They begin to accept the addition of $2 + 2$ or $1 + 3$. They may make the association when they see the numerals representing those operations and the addition symbol after many occasions that involve these ideas. It becomes "internalized" after repeated experiences. They respond automatically to the meaning of the symbol. It does not happen at the same time for all children, of course. The teacher is very much aware of differences in the pupils and their gradual acceptance of mature processes of learning.

The purpose of mathematics for young children is to have them learn to compute with facility. They learn to see how objects in their own environment (and later in environments with which they do not have a contact) are placed into a quantitative context. A quantitative framework provides ways to measure, add, subtract, and divide with numerals that represent abstract ideas. The individual who has had many substantial experiences can later be able to manipulate more complex numerals. Figures that are obtained by finding their square root, or by raising them to a 25th power, involve an understanding of operations that can not easily be duplicated by quick manipulation of objects. Children who have had many experiences enjoying mathematical operations in the kindergarten and early grades may welcome and be thoroughly intrigued by challenging mathematical problems given to them in later grades at school.

In any case, the emphasis in mathematical goals is as much enjoyment of the development of mathematical skills as it is an understanding: not mere memorization of set operations but a broader comprehension of what the system is all about. Correct or incorrect answers are less an issue than an acceptable understanding of the processes of mathematics. Teachers are then occupied with promoting basic understanding rather than inculcating rote mnemonics. These do not replace the skills needed for mature developmental processes of learning.

Developmental Activities and Basic Concepts for Younger Children's Mathematical Programs

One of the most satisfying aspects of working with young children is that they are relatively free of erroneous concepts of the past and are open to new ideas. Most ideas are new to them. This does not mean that children do not have misconceptions about their world, about what they see and how they interpret it. Their general knowledge has to be guided into a framework of the discipline, mathematics. Children have ideas and they are for the most part very creative if they are not squelched in their effort to express them. It is when education has to compartmentalize the children's ideas and associate them with principles of subject matter areas that children become blocked. They have to learn which labels and concepts are to be used to describe their thoughts.

Children's hesitance in stating what they mean comes about when a teacher inhibits expression of their thoughts. But when children are given opportunities to put into mathematical expression what they know and have experienced, learning about mathematics makes more sense to them. They can build on this foundation of meaning.

The purpose of developmental activities is to provide concepts of a discipline that are new to the child when he is ready to cope with them. The child uses what he can from the systematized format of the discipline and transfers those concepts to his own way of perceiving life. Counting, measuring, ordering, estimating size, judging placement of something in a space—such as fitting a chair or table in a certain part of the room—all require a simultaneous judgment of space and memory. The judgment of the size of the object to go into the space involves mind-juggling of abstract ideas. While the chair and the room are not abstractions, they become so when considered in relation to space.

Activities planned for young children must be designed with the children's levels of readiness in the mind of the teacher. The children's abilities where certain skills are concerned—and a certain degree of readiness to consider fractions, parts, adding, subtracting from a larger

The teacher helps the child in counting pegs on the pegboard. This helps the child to see the quantity that is related to numerals, a process that will become more difficult later in the child's school career.

This kindergarten child is working with various geometric sizes and shapes (mostly diamond shapes in this picture) and learning how they lend themselves to his particular placement of them. They are made of a light weight wood, polished tan, and are easy to manipulate.

whole—all these considerations contribute to the teacher's understanding and expectation of the children's execution of those ideas. The activities should be designed to fit into those expectations, level by level. This does not suggest that the teacher can by analytically correct processes measure the skills of the child, but it does mean that the teacher can be generally familiar with each child's ability where the skills needed to tackle new concepts are concerned.

The teacher does not give the children something that is too difficult or too easy. The child needs an adequate amount of practice, of challenge,

Putting puzzle pieces together provides one of the earliest opportunities for children to develop a sense of spatial relationship between space and object-size.

of review. Some writers indicate that it is better for a child to underpractice than to overpractice. To do something over and over again to the point of its becoming extremely dull turns the child away from the subject matter. He expects nothing from it and subsequently gives nothing further to it.

It is neither necessary nor practical to describe here the many possible ideas that are available to teachers working with young children. Needless to say, they could not be contained in one book. The suggestions made in the next few pages, however, are only representative in that they recommend certain levels and approaches to the ways teachers can work with little children. Teachers have to consult the many books written on mathematics in elementary schools and note their suggestions for children at each grade or age level.

Activities may be described as those for the kindergarten, first grade, second grade, or third; but it is wise to remember that their appropriateness to age and grade level will overlap. Competent children in the kindergarten find it easy to do some work assigned to children in the first grade, and in like manner some children in the first grade can do second- or third-grade level work, especially in certain subject matter areas. A child may be advanced in mathematical understanding, but not as quick

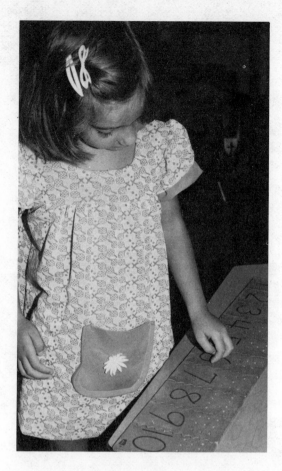

This child is becoming familiar with the figure seven by counting the number of holes at the top of the board. She should begin to make relationships between the figure and the amount that it represents. Gradually she becomes sensitized to the concept of seven.

in learning to spell. The reason, however, that some kind of designation is made regarding difficulty in subject matter is that it helps the teacher know how to adjust the work given the child. Tasks are given in terms of certain sequential levels of conceptual development.

Children in the nursery school are hearing references to number most of the day. Two children are permitted to go to a certain table to do their work. Two children are asked to go to the principal's office to deliver a note. They are exposed to counting whenever the teacher deliberately stops and does this with them prior to any experience that could "naturally" involve counting. These are functional and attractive opportunities to use counting because the situations are real and fulfill an obvious need for the children.

This game is going well. Some of the children are filling their cards. This is encouraging in learning numerals.
The children have to listen closely and see what the caller is holding up during the number game.

Teachable Moments for Purposeful Counting

When children are preparing for snack time, they are asked to count the napkins, individual cups of juice, crackers, chairs that have to be set out for each child in the group.

When children collect books that they have been using during the period they are asked to count the total number.

When boxes of crayons are collected after children have used them, the children are asked to count them.

When the teacher has collected money from the children for a gift the class counts the money together.

When pencils are distributed or returned they are counted by the group.

As the teacher counts out the number of sheets of paper the children need in order to do their work, the class counts them with the teacher.

The teacher asks the children to count the number of children who are absent.

The teacher asks the children to count the days of the calendar—
    until the end of the week,
    until a new chick is expected to hatch,
    until a school vacation.

Teachable Moments for Purposeful Measuring

Children measure their own height.

Children measure the growth of a plant.

Children measure the length of their fingers and compare them to their peers.

Children measure the length of someone's hair.

Children measure their own shoe size.

Children measure the height of the bookshelf.

Children measure the height of a table.

Children measure the height of a block structure they have made.

Children measure their housekeeping (or playhouse) area.

Children measure a chair they want to bring them home to place in their school room.

Teachable Moments for Purposeful Weighing

Children can balance weights on a scale, heavy and light.

Children can weigh heavy articles, metal, nails, and other heavy metal objects.

Children can weigh light articles that are familiar to them.

Children can weigh sand, sugar, salt, or flour in small plastic packages.

Children can weigh a cup of water—the teacher would have to help them understand that the cup was being weighed too and that they would have to subtract the weight of the cup from the total amount.

Children can weigh something they carried to school, i.e., their lunch, a toy car, a book.

Children can weigh a paper weight, plastic, wood, or metal and compare the weights to each other.

Children can weigh packages of grocery objects such as jello, cereal, or rice.

Children can weigh beans before they are cooked and afterwards to compare differences in weight.

Children can weigh packages that the teacher has prepared to mail to someone as a gift; reasons for the post office having to charge by the ounce and pound may be discussed at this point.

Teachable Moment for Purposeful Calculating

Children can subtract the number of pennies from a dime to show how much is left when three pennies are taken from ten pennies.

Children can add three more places at the table to accommodate three more children.

Children can count the number of people who need cookies and have not been served.

Children can decide how many paint brushes are needed for five cans of paint and place them where they belong.

Children can decide how many sponges are needed to be used by five children.

Children can decide how many of the 25 children are left in the classroom after six of them choose to go to the library.

Children can decide if a child who has 23 pieces of candy has enough for 25 children; they can be asked if 23 is more or less than 25.

Children can be asked if 10 is less than 5 or more than 5.

In the nursery and kindergarten grade levels, the children sing counting songs, "Ten Little Indians," "Ten Little Blackbirds," one flew away and then there were nine. Children use their fingers to show the number they have. It is permissible in the academic sense to do so. Teachers can make felt birds pasted to tops of tongue depressors and have children use those to demonstrate counting. They put one down when they show the subtraction of a bird. This song permits children to see and to manipulate objects and associate them with numbers and counting. It begins to reinforce ideas, numbers, visual, auditory, and tactile discrimination in their own thinking.

As children progress through the first, second, and third grades, the concepts exposed to them become more difficult. The teacher is the best judge of what the children are able to do. Although some school systems have adopted the "systems" approach to mathematics, some are still without it. It is extremely important in either case that the teacher understand the basic ideas underlying mathematics, and that she be able to fill in the knowledge for the child wherever she sees it lacking. Nothing can

The teacher knows what the children need to practice and prepares exercises on the board for children to do at their seats.

replace an excellent teacher. Research has substantiated that the teacher is the one in the final analysis who is the key element of the program. She is the one who helps the child develop his competencies regardless of the materials involved. A dedicated teacher can make the crucial difference as to whether a child becomes adept in any subject matter skill.

Children in kindergarten have a set of cards with numerals 1, 2, 3, 4, 5. They should match the numeral to the correct number of objects in a set of which the teacher has held pictures in front for them to see. They learn to match the correct set that the teacher has in her hands. They learn the term, equivalent sets, for equal groups of objects enclosed in a circle. They learn the term, nonequivalent sets, for sets of objects that are not equal to each other, that do not have the same amount of objects in them. Magnetic boards or flannel boards are an easy device to use. On them, the children and the teacher can place the number of objects desired for use in an example. The advantage of this is that the children can manipulate, can move the objects around and not worry about the accuracy of reproducing them as one would in the case of drawing them free hand on a blackboard. Children can easily see what it is they are moving around. The magnetic board or flannel board permits them to erase (take away) the object and place it in another part of the board and to add new objects merely by taking them out of the box that contains all the objects.

When children see a circle with no objects in it, they are expected to call it an empty set or a zero set. Since zero occupies an important place in the number system, children should become used to calling the numeral "0" *zero* instead of *nothing*. Children in kindergarten can learn and understand the concept of zero through 9 and they should be given opportunities to continually handle objects that indicate the significance of these numerals.

The difficulty that many children encounter is the progression from 9 to 10. Children need to be taught to think of 10 as one set of 10 and no 1's when they view it symbolically. If they read 10 as one zero, they will learn to perceive it as one set of 10 and no 1's. By using disks or pennies or cardboard cutouts that resemble pennies, children can learn to represent one set of 10 and show how one dime represents ten pennies. Children can learn that two dimes represent two sets of 10, that another name for them is 20 pennies or 20 cents. The mathematical concept and the monetary concept are given two different names. These names refer to the same amount of pennies but to a definite concept in the number system.

Children can learn that the equal sign means *the same as;* they can also learn inequality symbols: <, meaning *less than,* and >, meaning

The teacher attempts to help the children associate a given number of objects with the figure or numeral. The children need to learn that a numeral may be applied to many different objects.

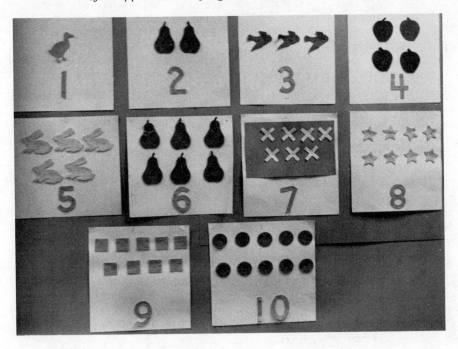

more than. But this comes gradually as they use them in their routine work experiences with mathematics.

Many pupils learn to count by rote before they come to school. This does not mean that they understand the meaning of those numbers. They may not know that 8 comes after 5 in the number sequence of the system from 1 to 10. They learn to count in a somewhat conditioned sense, the same way people respond automatically to a stimulus. It has often been observed that when teachers ask a child to show the class five buttons, or which set has five buttons in it and which set has eight, the child does not know. The child may be able to count up to 10 and even 20, yet not understand the concept of those numbers and their symbolism. Memorizing 1 to 10 does not confirm an understanding of the amounts represented nor an understanding of more and less, in the symbols of those figures. The child may not even know the relationship between the numerals and the number of objects represented by them. This is why children's responses have to be tested in many ways. Giving the correct response to a

Matching objects to numerals can be fun when a pupil has enough space and time to work at the process.

This child is absorbed in her arithmetic game, placing the correct card showing the corresponding number of objects under the appropriate numeral. The teacher will see if it has been done correctly, when the pupil is finished.

numeral and calling it by the correct name does not necessarily mean the pupil has the comprehension skills suggested by a knowledge of the terms used to refer to an idea.

Pupils in the kindergarten and first grade enjoy repeating certain counting exercises. The teacher has to vary those exercises by using different objects, be those objects small boxes, toys, cars, trains, trucks, or even children themselves. The children enjoy being correct and the teacher can help them in being successful.

Fractions can be learned easily by young children when they see one cookie broken into two equal parts and they are told that now the cookie represents two halves. When a cookie is cut into three equal parts, each part is called one-third. The teacher uses a circle cut out of flannel, cuts it into two equal parts and shows two halves. The teacher can do this with clay pieces too. Anything that is tangible and makes sense to the children can be shown to them to help them understand the concept of 1/3, 1/2, 1/4, 1/5, any idea that can be demonstrated with the concrete object (or real object) itself to the abstract way of referring to it.

Children can be shown the triangle and be given its name. They can learn to recognize a rectangle and a square and give each its correct name.

Pupils in the first and second grades learn how many parts of a given number are in a meter by using a large number line or a centimeter ruler of about 20 centimeters long. They can be shown how many fractions or halves, fourths, or fifths there are in a centimeter ruler. By marking this off on a large number line, the children can also learn which fraction is less than (see Figure 6.1) or more than another within that span of centimeters.

Using the same idea referred to in Figure 6.1, children may view that magnified centimeter in terms of fifths. They can see 1/5, 2/5, 3/5, 4/5, along the centimeter line and then determine whether 1/5 is less than 4/5, or 2/5 < 4/5.

Many opportunities to practice the same concept in different ways strengthen the children's chances of knowing the concept well. The more experiences he has with objects, things he can touch, move around on a flannel board, a magnetic board, or a table, the better. The more children see that mathematics has a purpose, in that it ensures greater precision, exactness, and accuracy, the better they will be able to accept and want to use the symbolic interpretation and manipulation which has come to be designated as a shorthand means for using quantitative and qualitative ideas. Mathematics serves humankind. It is a tool planned to assist people in doing more effectively what would otherwise be done in random fashion.

Young children can learn how to tell time, to know how to read the hands of the clock, but they can do so mainly in connection with time that is significant for them. (See Figure 6.2) As they associate what the clock looks like with important times for them in their daily routines, they begin to remember where the hands of the clock are supposed to be for their eating, recess, school time, time to go home, and other necessary routines of the day.

They can also learn to read the thermometer when they know that it has significance for heat, cold, and typical weather designations. Stories are written for children in which the weather, readings of the thermom-

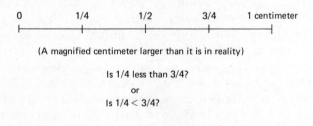

(A magnified centimeter larger than it is in reality)

Is 1/4 less than 3/4?

or

Is 1/4 < 3/4?

On the ruler a real centimeter is this big.

figure 6.1
Fractions in Measurement

These children are creating geometric structures that require thoughtful construction with tiny sticks and ties.

With three people helping, this structure is beginning to develop well. It involves mathematical knowledge, measurement, spatial relationships, judgment, and estimation of size and shape to be developed (below).

eter, barometers, and other instruments created for indicating differences in the weather are explained. Freezing temperature, boiling points, and

The boy watches eagerly as a feminine hand assists in the lightweight geometric construction.

the like are pointed out to children and they can remember these points.

Children in the primary grades are introduced gradually to more difficult concepts as the teacher observes that they understand the less difficult ideas. Because quantifiable data are difficult for young children to understand and to relate to what they actually do with materials, it requires ample time for them to have many experiences with both the materials and manipulation and the relationship of that manipulation to the symbolism of the mathematical system. Teachers may provide experiences for pupils, but it is equally important that they realize why they are doing it and how they should be associating what they are doing with the symbolic system.

Teachers have to remember that since quantifiable data are not used as often as children use verbal messages in communication with others (see Figure 6.3), it is more difficult for them to master symbols that indicate or represent measurement, weights, time measurement, mathematical measurement of squares, rectangles, circles, and the like. Children's conceptual development in regard to meanings built on their daily experiences, layer upon layer, the precision required in a knowledge of numbers and measurement is only attained after repeated first-hand or direct experiences with the raw data of reality. From early childhood on through

194

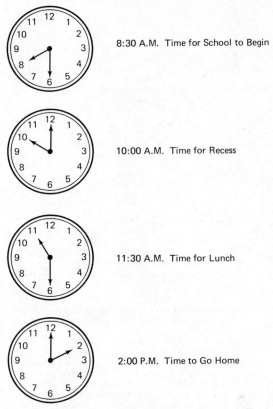

8:30 A.M. Time for School to Begin

10:00 A.M. Time for Recess

11:30 A.M. Time for Lunch

2:00 P.M. Time to Go Home

figure 6.2
Significant Clock Readings for Children

the elementary grades, the child is acquiring experiences that are significant for him. These experiences acquire meaning only as they are set into a framework of words, objects, symbols. As the teacher shows how certain ideas, words, or symbols are associated with what the child is doing, the child begins to accept those meanings for his internal "thinking system." Associating one's experiential background with new learning is emphasized in Wittrock's studies on generative processes of memory.[6] He indicates that children retain subject matter best when they create their own images in representing a definition for a new word they have learned. This can be applied to new concepts or new symbols. When children are

[6] M. C. Wittrock, "The Generative Processes of Memory," U.C.L.A., in *Educator* Issue on: "Education and the Hemispheric Processes of the Brain" Vol. 17 (Spring, 1975), pp. 33–43.

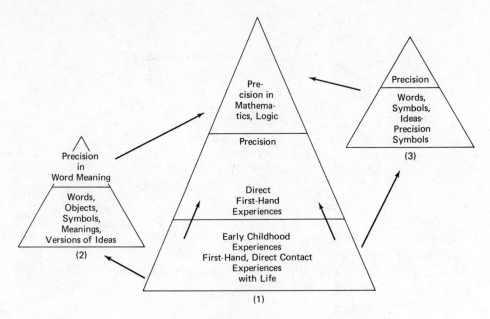

(1) The young child experiences many aspects of reality; it makes sense to him as he learns words to describe those direct experiences
(2) He receives versions of ideas from words that are subject to varied interpretations
(3) Words, symbols, objects built layer upon layer of ideas and first-hand experiences lead him up toward the most difficult concepts of preciseness. An external specificity has to become internal after years of experience with the raw data or substance of life's experiences

figure 6.3
The Acquisition of Precision in Thinking

asked to draw a picture of what it means to them when they learn the new concept, they bring their own particular idiosyncracies to it and consequently are able to remember it well.

Noting Figure 6.3, one senses the difficulties involved before a child finally attains precision in thinking. Precision in relation to an understanding of ideas or concepts is the highest form of matching the internal thoughts with the external system devised by humankind. Earlier in life, the child senses the raw stuff of life; his first-hand experiences provide him with a kind of knowledge. His culture, however, gives him words that provide him with versions of ideas that are significant for that culture. As the child matures in the elementary school, he begins to associate or tie together the words, ideas, and precision symbols. The precision symbols are the last that he learns. They are most heavily tied into an external form of measurement. He has to make those general symbols his own so that he responds almost automatically to the use of them.

Teachers and studies have verified children's difficulties in the process of learning to understand concepts of time. Yesterday, tomorrow, two weeks ago are extremely difficult for a child to judge. How does one compare a concept of two weeks when one is preparing to go on a much-desired vacation, and a concept of two weeks when one is expecting to go to a hospital for a dreaded operation such as a tonsillectomy? A dreaded experience affects his impression of whether the time sequence is long or short. In his mind, when he tries to imagine the length of time for waiting, a two-week period is "measured" differently, more in relation to his psychological perceptions than the objective calendar.

In general, the teacher of young children attempts to utilize to the maximum degree all opportunities and situations to enhance a child's knowledge of mathematical aspects of his life. Children hear mathematical terms in ordinary language usage. The teacher can list for them the kind of words that indicate measurement. It is only a beginning. Experiences upon experiences will help the children accept the abstractions underlying the meanings of those terms.

Measurement Words

longer	taller	more than
shorter	tallest	many times more
fatter	small	fewer times
thinner	smaller	more often
higher	smallest	less often
lower	less	greater than
slim	little	fewer than
fine	bigger	
thick	biggest	

The teacher bears in mind that activities can be implemented in the classroom in relation to the purposes of mathematics:

1. Children should have ample opportunity to learn about concepts of number.
2. They should learn about counting, the one-to-one correspondence of number to object.
3. Children need to learn the names of shapes, objects and forms.
4. Children need to learn qualities of arithmetical operations such as adding, subtracting, dividing and multiplying.
5. Children need to have many opportunities to estimate sizes and compare shapes.

6. Children need to learn about the properties of groups or sets of objects, intersecting sets, and the like.
7. They need opportunities to measure liquids in containers of different sizes.
8. Children need opportunities to weigh and balance objects, to compare heavy and light sizes.
9. Children need to be given the opportunity to judge positions of objects, e.g., between, above, below.
10. Children need ample opportunities to hear stories about counting toys, animals, people, food, cookies.
11. Children need to associate counting with the rhythm of marching, a drum beat, clapping hands.
12. The children need practice in telling time—significant for them.
13. The children need to have opportunities to sing counting songs.
14. The children need to have simple cooking experiences that allow them to associate measurement with daily realities—making cupcakes, jello, pudding, soup, salads, or whatever seems appropriate.
15. The children need opportunities to measure heights of people, of each other, of blocks on top of each other, of plants they grow at school.
16. They need to measure pieces of wood needed to build an airplane, a boat, a house.
17. Children need to deal with fractions in measurement so that they will understand them in an abstract sense.

Evaluation of Children's Progress in Mathematics

Some of the best means of evaluation of young children's conceptual understanding of mathematics lies in a sensitive teacher's observations of the pupils' responses every day. Systematic test taking is effective, but the teacher who "catches" children's responses and sees how they reflect evidence of the children's understanding of concepts does much in completing the impressions that test takers are trying to ascertain in a child's abilities. The teacher who notices that children recite numerals but do not know how to identify that number of objects is recognizing confusion in the child's thinking.

Many kinds of tests can be made to assess children's knowledge of certain skills. The systems of mathematics programs represent an attempt to measure skills at their very limited specifications. Each part of a skill is defined, and children are expected to achieve each of them. It represents a comprehensive analytical perception of all parts of a skill.

Teachers can devise their own tests. For kindergarten children, the teacher can place cards and objects in front of a child and have him manipulate the items. It can also be done on a flannel board or a magnetic one upon which objects can be placed and removed easily. In the first, second, and third grades, paper and pencil tests can be devised. The teacher should know the children well enough so that the tests are not misconceived in terms of what is fair to them. The children should be given ample review opportunities to demonstrate what they do and do not know.

The test should be considered as much an evaluation of the teacher's performance in class as the children's. It requires judgment by the teacher to assess deficiences wisely in a child's understanding of a concept.

One of the most noteworthy changes in educational attitudes from years past is that tests are not planned to test children's knowledge of unusual or obscure items but to help the teacher and the pupils know where the child needs help and in which skills he needs to improve. Tests are viewed as techniques and tools to provide diagnosis of a child's needs and the teacher's planning for the next few weeks for that child. The results are not an object of interest in relation to marking the child at a specific position of ignorance, such that the child senses derision. Children are very sensitive and for this reason the teacher should be careful in the way she interprets the test results to them.

The terms summative and formative evaluation are recommended to distinguish between short- and long-term learning goals.[7] The writers indicate that the formative kind of evaluation processes can be used to determine the child's degree of mastery of certain subject matter concepts; the summative can be used to assess a child's overall ability in a given area. The formative type assessment is used to pinpoint where a child is in his sequential development so that the teacher knows what next steps to take. The summative gives a report to parents or others as to what the child's general aptitude seems to be so far in his studies.

Sequential development or analyzing the next steps to be taken in the child's development of certain conceptual knowledge must be weighed in the balance of review, practice, repetitiousness. Practice is done in the form of activities that hold the child's interest, that are novel to some extent. The teacher must judge when a child has had enough review to manage without extreme frustration to meet another challenge. The attempt to analyze children's individual differences in learning styles received most emphasis in the 1960's with greater awareness of curriculum deficiencies, where slow learners or poor children who live in low-income neighborhoods were concerned. The "slow learners" were in part a result of curriculum activities which were inadequately planned or at least inappropriate to the children's levels of skills. Instructional materials can create the downfall or the success of a child's learning development.

[7] Benjamin S. Bloom, J. Thomas Hastings, and George F. Madaus, *Handbook of Formative and Summative Evaluation of Student Learning* (New York: McGraw-Hill Book Company, 1971).

Children, therefore, cannot be called slow learners when the materials are not properly adjusted to their levels of readiness. It is the educators who are at fault in using poor judgment. Many books on educational theories or educational psychology prior to the 1960's presented data on differences in the way individuals learned, but the ideas were not really taken seriously or implemented properly in the curriculum and testing until the 1960's. Somebody is listening at last.

The concern for not damaging a child's self-concept has become an important focus in evaluation. Teachers are expected to help the child in evaluating his own work in such a manner that the child understands that the evaluation is done to help him become competent—for his own sake, not to compete with others. The emphasis is on self, on using the self as one's own most important resource in learning, to realize that one can do many things, can become very accomplished if he will try. The teacher tries in every way to minimize in the child the feelings that he is inadequate. Evaluation is perceived more as a diagnostic instrument relative to the next steps in the child's learning schedule. The teacher knows what to give the child next and encourages him to move as fast or as high as he can. She must have enough knowledge of the field to know what the child can manage in his learning experiences consistent with his abilities at a given level. His capability influences the direction of learning planned for him. The subject matter elements of learning are not seen as a rigid format which every child has to follow at the same rate and with the same degree of competence. It simply does not happen that way. The time is gone when the teacher says she has to "cover" a given absolutistic quantity of stuff. The teacher may give a certain quantity to the children and feel she has "covered" what she had intended, but she will be surprised when she sees that the children were not with her in this coverage. They really did not understand or retain the materials.

Mental health of children is a significant problem area. Teachers need to protect the child's potential for sound habits in learning and encourage this in every way possible. Fear or intimidation used as motivation in learning at school do not help the child enjoy learning, nor does it help him jump out of bed in the morning eager to come to school. He cannot contribute as much to his classroom group if he is fearful of making mistakes. His relationships to people in the classroom can be far more vital and helpful as an individual in his total development, if it is based on a genuine desire to be a part of the group. The teacher tries to convey to him the feeling that he is worthy as an individual and has something to contribute in that sense. To feel that he is stupid or incompetent not only blunts an eagerness to contribute, but also creates other kinds of undesirable behavior such as ridiculing and mimicking others and complaining about other children he might envy. In the earlier grades especially, the teacher can show each child that she cares about him.

Evaluation is a delicate area of judgment to be used in ways that can be helpful to a child. Many tests are suggested with materials of instruction, with packaged types of curriculum activities, or commercialized kits. The manner in which the tests are given and the data are interpreted are the most crucial aspects to the degree of helpfulness that results in the children's behalf.

Facing reality, as many psychologists recommend, should be considered in terms of the child's ability to accept it when he hears it from his teacher. The young child does not find it easy to accept criticism from a person who means a great deal to him. The pupil in the teacher–child relationship who experiences a teacher bent on giving him the cold truth in a dispassionate manner (believing that she is helping the child in facing reality) is not fortunate. The child who has a teacher who helps him with his skills in a context of moral support and kindness will grow. Evidence of this fact is confirmed daily in the classroom with teachers who have built bonds of trust with their pupils.

summary

While mathematics is an exacting science, it nevertheless involves young children who respond to it in a flexible sense. Children should be involved in measuring, in dividing cookies, cake, cups of milk; they are aware of ½ pints of milk or juice. They are cognizant of mathematical effects even though they do not know the mathematical measurements themselves in the technically sophisticated sense.

Almost all the books dealing with instruction of mathematics emphasize the importance of children having many experiences with mathematical concepts in relation to real objects in their environment. When the children reach the point of identifying measurements and show the relationship between objects and measurement, they can be assumed to have an understanding—in part—of symbols used in mathematics. For this reason alone—the fact that children need many experiences with concrete objects and their qualities and characteristics—teachers and others who work with young children should realize how important it is to provide them with many objects and a wide variety of activities.

This chapter dealt with the simple terms that children can be taught to use and understand in relation to quantitative symbols. Suggestions were given for appropriate or teachable moments that can be used to advantage when opportunities are taken for the instruction of mathematical knowledge in a "natural" context that meets functional needs for pupils. Teachers are expected to become sensitive to ways of capitalizing on events of the classroom (the unexpected and the occasional routines as well), so that pupils obtain information in spontaneous, unplanned, and novel ways when it is appropriate.

Even though new types of techniques or systems are used for purposes of analyzing children's conceptual mastery at given levels of development, teachers are the most important aspect of influence in the child's development at school. Whether the systems analysis pinpoints the child's abilities in certain subjects or not, the effective teacher typically observes pupils carefully enough to be aware of these levels of development. Specificity of evaluation helps in the teaching process to some extent, it is true; but the outstanding teacher of young children who knows her subject matter is an unusually intricate and sensitive machine. She can surpass the systems approach in her judgment of the child's needs. This touches on whether teaching is a science or an art. It should be both.

topics for discussion

1. Create a chart for children in the kindergarten that would use quantitative words and associate them with pictures of objects children know. How would you use this with pupils to demonstrate linkage of mathematical terms with their everyday lives?
2. How and why have mathematical programs for young children changed in the last twenty years? Give specific examples of this by bringing into the discussion, units that are available in nearby schools, and commercial evidence of it as well in professional journals.
3. Demonstrate ways that mathematical learnings would be included in a social studies unit for children in the first grade. What considerations would you as a teacher have to make before you brought certain concepts and symbols in to the classroom?
4. Make three activities for children (in the three- to five-year age range) in which they can participate to increase their level of mastery in the understanding of any mathematical principle you choose. State the principle and give the directions for using the activities and the ways a teacher would want to explain them to young children.

selected bibliography for teachers

Beard, Virginia. "Mathematics in Kindergarten," *The Arithmetic Teacher*, Vol. IX, No. 1 (January, 1962), pp. 22–25.

Biggs, Edith E., and James R. MacLean. *Freedom to Learn*. Ontario, Canada: Addison-Wesley, 1969.

Bjonerud, Corwin E. "Arithmetic Concepts Possessed by the Preschool Child," *The Arithmetic Teacher*, Vol. VII, No. 7 (November, 1960), pp. 347–350.

Bouwsma, Ward D., Clyde G. Corle, and Davis F. Flemson, Jr. *Basic Mathematics for Elementary Teachers*. New York: Ronald Press, 1967.

Brace, Alec, and L. Doyal Nelson. "The Preschool Child's Concept of Number," *The Arithmetic Teacher*, Vol. XII No. 2 (February, 1965), pp. 126–133.

Buffie, Edward G., Ronald C. Welch, and Donald D. Paige. Mathematics: Strategies of Teaching. Englewood Cliffs, New Jersey: Prentice-Hall, 1968.

Byrne, J. Richard. *Modern Elementary Mathematics.* New York: McGraw-Hill Book Company, 1966.

Churchill, Eileen. *Counting and Measuring.* Toronto, Canada: University of Toronto Press, 1961.

Copeland, Richard W. *Diagnostic and Learning Activities in Mathematics for Children.* New York: Macmillan Publishing Co., Inc., 1974.

Copeland, Richard W. *How Children Learn Mathematics.* New York: Macmillan Publishing Co., Inc., 1974.

Courant, R., and H. Robbins. *What Is Mathematical?* Fair Lawn, N.J.: Oxford, 1961.

Davidson, Patricia, Grace Galton, and Arlene Fair. *Math Bibliography.* Growth Activity Products, Inc., Box 637, Newton Lower Falls, Massachusetts, 1971.

Deans, Edwina. *Elementary School Mathematics: New Directions.* Washington, D.C.: U. S. Government Printing Office, 1963.

Dienes, Z. P. *An Experimental Study of Mathematics Learning.* London: Hutchinson, 1963.

Dunkley, M. E. "Some Number Concepts of Disadvantaged Children," *The Arithmetic Teacher,* Vol. XII, No. 5 (May, 1965), pp. 359–361.

Dutton, Wilbur H., Colin C. Petrie and L. J. Adams. *Arithmetic for Teachers.* 2nd ed. Englewood Cliffs, N.J.: Prentice-Hall, Inc., 1970.

Dwight, Leslie A. *Modern Mathematics for the Elementary Teacher.* New York: Holt, Rinehart and Winston, 1966.

Educational Services Incorporated. *Goals for School Mathematics.* Boston: Houghton Mifflin, 1963.

Fehr, Howard F., and Thomas J. Hill. *Contemporary Mathematics for Elementary Teachers.* Boston: Heath, 1966.

Fehr, Howard F., and Jo McKeeby Phillips. *The Teaching of Mathematics in the Elementary School.* Reading, Mass.: Addison-Wesley, 1967.

Ginsburg, Herbert, and Sylvia Opper. *Piaget's Theory of Intellectual Development.* Englewood Cliffs, N.J.: Prentice-Hall, Inc., 1969.

Grossnickle, Foster F., Leo J. Brueckner, and John Reckzeh. *Discovering Meanings in Elementary School Mathematics.* 5th ed. New York: Holt, Rinehart and Winston, 1968.

Gunderson, Ethel, and Agnes Gunderson. "Fraction Concepts Held by Young Children," *The Arithmetic Teacher,* Vol. IV (October, 1957), pp. 168–173.

Hart, Richard H. "The Nongraded Primary School and Arithmetic," *The Arithmetic Teacher,* Vol. IX, No. 3 (March, 1962), pp. 130–133.

Higgins, James E. "Mathematics. An Alternative Approach, *Instructor,* Vol. LXXXIV (November, 1974), pp. 64–65.

Hollister, George E., and Agnes G. Gunderson. *Teaching Arithmetic in the Primary Grades.* Boston: D. C. Heath & Co., 1964.

Howard, Charles F., and Enoch Dumas. *Teaching Contemporary Mathematics in the Elementary School.* New York: Harper & Row, 1966.

Huey, J. Frances. "Learning Potential of the Young Child," *Educational Leadership,* Vol. 23 (November, 1965), pp. 117–120.

Johnson, D. A., and R. Rahtz. *The New Mathematics in Our Schools.* New York: Macmillan Publishing Co., Inc., 1966.

Kennedy, Leonard M. *Guiding Children to Mathematical Discovery.* Belmont, California: Wadsworth Publishing Co., Inc., 1970.

Lane, Lola June. *Teaching Mathematics in the Elementary School.* 2nd ed. New York: The Free Press, 1974.

Lovell, K. *The Growth of Basic Mathematical and Scientific Concepts in Children.* New York: Philosophical Library, 1961.

Marks, John L., Richard Purdy, and Lucien B. Kinney. *Teaching Elementary School Mathematics for Understanding.* New York: McGraw-Hill Book Company, 1965.

McClintic, Joan. "The Kindergarten Child Measures Up," *The Arithmetic Teacher,* Vol. XV (April, 1968), pp. 26–29.

McFowell, Louise K. "Number Concepts and Preschool Children," *The Arithmetic Teacher,* Vol. IX, No. 8 (December, 1962), pp. 433–435.

Michaelis, John U., Ruth H. Grossman, and Lloyd F. Scott. *New Designs for the Elementary School.* 2nd ed. New York: McGraw-Hill Book Company, 1975.

National Council of Teachers of Mathematics. *Topics in Mathematics for Elementary School Teachers.* Twenty-ninth Yearbook. Washington, D.C.: National Council of Teachers of Mathematics, 1964.

National Council of Teachers of Mathematics. *Mathematics Learning in Early Childhood.* Thirty-seventh Yearbook. Reston, Virginia: The National Council of Teachers of Mathematics, Inc., 1975.

Piaget, Jean. *The Child's Conception of Number.* London: Routledge & Kegan Paul, Ltd., 1952.

Sears, Pauline S., and Ernest Hilgard. "The Teacher's Role in the Motivation of the Learner," in Ernest R. Hilgard, Ed. *Theories of Learning and Instruction.* Chicago: National Society for the Study of Education, University of Chicago Press, 1964, pp. 182–209.

Schlinsog, George W. "More About Mathematics in the Kindergarten," *The Arithmetic Teacher,* Vol. XV, No. 8 (December, 1968), pp. 701–705.

Scott, L. F. *Trends in Elementary School Mathematics.* Chicago: Rand McNally, 1966.

Sharp, Evelyn. *A Parent's Guide to More New Math.* New York: E. P. Dutton and Co., 1966.

Spitzer, Herbert F. *Teaching Elementary School Mathematics.* Boston: Houghton Mifflin, 1967.

Spitzer, Herbert F. *Practical Classroom Procedures for Enriching Arithmetic.* St. Louis: Webster Publishing Company, 1956.

Swain, Robert L. "Modern Mathematics and School Arithmetic," *Instruction in Arithmetic.* Twenty-fifth Yearbook. Washington, D.C.: The National Council of Teachers of Mathematics, 1960.

Swenson, Esther J. *Teaching Arithmetic to Children.* New York: Macmillan Publishing Co., Inc., 1973.

Tyler, Ralph *et al. Perspectives of Curriculum Evaluation.* Chicago: Rand McNally, 1967.

Ward, M., and C. E. Hardgrove. *Modern Elementary Mathematics.* Reading, Mass.: Addison-Wesley, 1964.

Welch, Ronad C. " 'New Mathematics' in the Primary Grades," *Primary Education: Changing Dimensions.* Washington, D.C.: Association for Childhood Education, 1965.

Welmers, Evert T. "Arithmetic in Today's Culture," *Instruction in Arithmetic.* Twenty-fifth Yearbook. Washington, D.C.: The National Council of Teachers of Mathematics, 1960.

Westcott, Alvin M., and James A. Smith. *Creative Teaching of Mathematics in the Elementary School.* Boston: Allyn & Bacon, 1967.

Williams, Alfred H. "Mathematical Concepts, Skills, and Abilities of Kindergarten Entrants," *The Arithmetic Teacher,* Vol. XLL, No. 4 (April 1965), pp. 261–268.

Wittrock, M. C. "The Generative Processes of Memory," U. C. L. A. *Educator,* Volume 17, No. 2 (Spring, 1975), pp. 33–43. Los Angeles, California: Graduate School of Education, 1975.

Zweng, Marilyn. "Division Problems and the Concept of Rate," *The Arithmetic Teacher,* Vol. XI, No. 8 (December, 1964), pp. 547–556.

Chapter 7

Science Satisfies and Stimulates Children's Curiosity

Red, green, yellow—
A color spectrum view
Sea shells, sky, rivers and mountains—
How does one study these things?

When I am in school
And I want to know
What will my teacher say?
Will she say, "Yes, I will help you find
    your answers"?
Or will she turn me away?

There is no better audience than a group of young children who are enthusiastic, eager, and driven to know everything around them. The world is new and fresh to them. They enjoy the attention of any interested adult who is willing to give them the time and thought involved in explaining their surroundings.

It makes a difference in the child's life as to whether anyone else has devoted time to explain the why's and how's of objects and events around him. The willingness of children to reach out and become a part of their world is evident from the time they are born. What adults are busy doing most of the time is preventing the child from touching things around him, things that are dangerous and risky.

Experience with scientific phenomena is present in every child who comes to school. An explanation of these phenomena however (What makes rain? What are clouds made of? What makes the ocean move?) are not present in the background of each child. He may have heard thunder, but not had it explained to him. He may have seen or felt snow but not been told how it occurs. Children do not always have adults around them who know how to give a scientific explanation for what is happening or even where to go to obtain this information. This is not expected to be available to every child. It can happen to one who lives in a family with professional people. It may also happen when an adult is specifically interested in acquiring information the child needs and in helping him know how and where to go for it. A professional person in a family is not the only source of "wisdom" by any means. Many adults who do not have college degrees have educated themselves by reading extensively. These adults can be an inspiration to children.

Purposes and Goals in Science for Children

The field of science is one of the most highly respected of all fields because of its basic purpose—the search for truth in the nature of phenomena (events, interaction, matter, energy) of the world. When one considers how many diseases have been counteracted through vaccines, antibiotics, and other discoveries, it is easy to realize how much humankind owes to science. Objectivity guides the scientist in one of the most serious searches for truth.

Science commits itself to the most scrupulous seeking of accurate data. It entails endless hours of careful searching for definition, for analysis, for clear description of findings, and for the justification of predicting future events. Science tries to analyze findings in research so that future problems may be mediated or obviated. It represents efforts to determine the qualities, characteristics, and elements that underlie what appears to be unfathomable events or phenomena. It explains otherwise mystifying occurrences.

Since young children see many activities and events around them that they do not attempt to explain or make sense of to themselves, they need to be given reasons for what they see. They need to understand why and how certain phenomena occur. They need to know why clouds appear, what they are, why they form, why claps of thunder make an ear-deafening noise.

Children need to know causes and effects of events, natural or otherwise. Hurricanes, tornadoes, earthquakes, floods, natural effects of weather, geological foundations and land erosion can be explained. Earthquakes are related to landforms, hurricanes are related to weather conditions. Even though there is a great deal of information on these natural causes of devastating effects in people's lives and homes, young children are given only simple answers. The answers are accurate because the teacher of younger children has an important obligation to provide early answers which will be given later support in the endless search for truth. Children recognize a teacher who respects them and tells them only information that she knows is true, factual, accurate. Legends, stories, fiction have their place in literature, not in the period devoted to science.

If children see the ocean, and see the sand that builds up and diminishes with each wave that comes to the shore, they can talk about why this happens. They can learn what the causes are for certain phenomena. Cause and effect, truth and appearance of curious effects that can sometimes obscure truth need to be explained to young children. This does not destroy a love for or an appreciation of fantasy; there is a need and a specific place in the school curriculum for that. It happens in a different part of the school day.

Creativity, dreams, pretending that certain acts can occur—e.g., the talking beast that children enjoy hearing about in a story, the giant that can cover seven miles in one step—are ideas to be treasured and enjoyed by children (and the teacher). They are not to be confused with a scientific search for truth. Fantasy and imagination are needed to stir creativity, and often to stimulate the scientific mind. Imagination should not be squelched. It contributes to the scientific mind that is curious, imaginative, willing to deviate from accepted truths. The teacher simply has to know which materials and books are appropriate to certain subject matter periods planned for the child.

Children can be told that one area is pretense or "make-believe"; another is realism. Life has both, fortunately. Ironically, scientific discovery involves a somewhat visionary leap from the truth. The scientist may have to take an intuitive hunch and act on it even though it appears to be totally unrealistic.

Children learn that most living things need air, water, food of some kind. They learn through observation of pets, flowers, trees, and birds that care is needed to protect them. Since children have in one sense a strong desire to nurture things that are smaller than they are, they are amenable to caring for and feeding pets such as goldfish, puppies, or certain plants. They have also been known to be cruel by pulling a dog's tail or a cat's, or teasing animals generally. This behavior requires adult supervision and instruction about the importance of being considerate. Children have a sense of sympathy which can be aroused by a love for pets or animals. In doing this, they are learning to be more sympathetic and to identify with the pain of others. Empathy, identification with others, the desire to treat them the way one wants to be treated, can begin as soon as the child listens to the adult.

There are certain goals in science intended to direct children's thinking. Their specificity and the attempt to define the characteristics of objects and the nature of phenomena help the child think in analytical

This boy in the third grade takes the hamster out of its cage for an "airing." Several children are responsible for the proper care of any pets brought to the classroom. It is an excellent opportunity for learning about animal life as well as understanding the needs of the pet.

terms. The scientific view engenders clear thinking, logic, and dissatisfaction with unanswered questions. The desire to make order out of chaos is a natural one; however, it is not always easy, especially when data are needed to document certain findings or statements. Children have to be helped in learning to become analytical and clear in thinking. Suggestions for supporting these goals are:

Children need to learn how to classify objects, to note similarities among a group of objects.

Children need to identify characteristics among objects and to name those characteristics, e.g., something that is hard, soft, readily · dissolvable or soluble, liquid, and so forth.

Children need to note the processes that occur in the case of one object changing from one form to another, e.g., melting ice, hardening liquid.

Children need to learn to recognize cause and effect in certain processes: heavy object on top of lighter one causes both objects to fall over.

Children need to identify different odors or smells that are significant in different liquids, e.g., vinegar, cider.

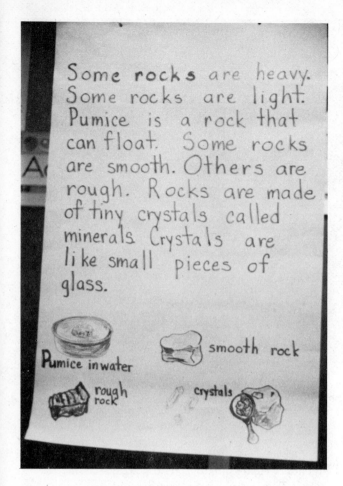

Some rocks are heavy.
Some rocks are light.
Pumice is a rock that
can float. Some rocks
are smooth. Others are
rough. Rocks are made
of tiny crystals called
minerals Crystals are
like small pieces of
glass.

Pumice in water

smooth rock

rough rock

crystals

It is extremely important to help children identify types of rock and to introduce them to words that describe their characteristics.

Children need to recognize differences in sizes.

Children need to recognize differences in shapes.

Children need to recognize differences in color; the color wheel or disks can demonstrate differences when these disks are superimposed on each other.

Children need to recognize how absorbency works as a process in a sponge or a sheet of blotting paper.

Children need to know how electricity works; they need to know what an actively charged wire is by understanding the nature of plugs and switches.

Children need to know how simple machines work, such as a pump, a lawn mower, a lever, a pulley.

Children need to know how weights offset each other as in the balance weights on a scale, the seesaw.

Children need to learn how a fire may be caused by careless behavior.

Children need to know how scientific information is acquired, i.e., the process of obtaining data that people accept as truth.

Children need to learn that scientific information is checked out and verified over and over again by many people.

Children need to learn that what is considered fact one day may be disproved and changed another day, that science is a continual process of seeking truth or for fact finding.

Children in the four- and five-year-old age group are learning about science through opportunities with materials that are safe for them to use. The teacher can introduce scientific concepts each time the children are involved in cooking, baking bread, making salads, or mixing ingredients for anything. The children learn that materials change their form and shape when they are added to other mixtures. Flour loses its distinctiveness once it is mixed with butter and milk. It contributes to the texture, the thickness of the batter, but it cannot be restored to is original characteristics once it has been mixed with other ingredients.

Children in the four- and five-year-old age range can see how the seesaw works when a heavy child is at one and a much lighter one is on the other: the fulcrum has to be adjusted. They learn this very easily. The teacher does have to explain why the fulcrum is moved and how it displaces the weight of one child and substitutes it for the other. The teacher is constantly alert to the opportunity to show the child how scientific principles affect our lives.

Children in the primary grades can be shown more complicated experiments. Six-, seven- and eight-year-old children are ready to comprehend increasingly more complicated work with scientific materials. But their guidance toward focusing sharply, observing and measuring accurately, respecting an exact analysis of what is seen, subjecting experiments to hypothetical tests and procedures, helps them appreciate the scientific process. They take certain steps, abide by certain rules of an experimental procedure. They record (or write) their observations and the time it took to do the test after which they summarize their conclusions. They offer other hypotheses (or ideas) for testing, and they realize that science is created by man in an attempt to be accurate in the examination and investigation of items, materials, or events. They learn that the experiment itself must be reproducible by someone else who should also be able to reach the same conclusions as those reached by the first experimenter. One of the values generated by scientific investigations, is the quality of predictability. Humankind can minimize the recurrence of diseases or epidemics because science has helped to uncover the causes, and prevention of them has been made possible.

Various science units have been created by companies or others who have done research on activities for primary grades children. Projects have been written to help pupils enjoy science and to develop favorable attitudes toward it as a subject matter area. While it is an unbending discipline in its techniques related to specificity, its orientation toward testing and measuring items is a dependable one.

Generally, the purposes and goals of science for children are directed toward an appreciation for accuracy and for the instruments that can obtain dependable data, and should be promoted in every classroom.

Developmental Activities in Science for Young Children

There are many activities for children in the search of observing differences in objects and phenomena around them. Children's awareness of natural phenomena, the earth, the trees, flowers, animals, water, and weather all contribute to their foundational preparation or readiness to discriminate among various environmental conditions and materials. They learn to perceive differences among phenomena when these differences are given the appropriate labels. They begin to see distinguishing characteristics between the stems and leaves of flowers and the buds or the

This kindergarten pupil is studying a plant under a magnifying glass. He is also observing the quality of soil and other small particles of life in the plant's setting.

blossoms. They see them with their eyes, but the differences in perception have to be taught in terms of the proper labels or concepts to describe a particular stage of development of a flower or tree.

Children should have experiences with magnets, attracting metallic objects, discovering that magnets do not attract certain soft non-metallic materials. They also have experiences with objects that sink to the bottom of a container of water and with objects that stay floating at the surface.

Most books on science or projects for children recommend that the teacher try to involve the pupil as much as possible in the search for answers to his own questions. The teacher should elicit answers from the children. Asking pupils why they think a certain event occurred or a certain result was found can help reverse the questions back to the learner. The teacher should ask the child how he can find the answer and where he can find it; if the child needs more help, more ideas may be suggested to help him find the answer. Discovery, participation, and the child's becoming part of the process of learning—accepting the burden of learning for himself—is the emphasis desired in the teaching–learning situation.

The earth, the sky, bodies of water, the elements of rain, snow, fog, and other interesting aspects of weather in certain regions of the world provide rich resources for children to study. The depth of study in each of these areas depends to a great extent on the complexity of the material in relation to the complexity in children's stages of development for understanding the material. Simple explanations can be given to younger children of nursery and kindergarten ages. Primary grades children are able to understand explanations that are more involved, of greater depth, and of greater complexity.

Since materials or concepts that are too difficult for young children can have negative effects on their desire to learn, the teacher is careful to keep learning materials at a simpler level so that the children's interest will be maintained. If individual pupils have the conceptual understanding to proceed beyond others in the class, the teacher can provide advanced work for them.

Children in the primary grades are not given chemicals for experimentation. The teacher cannot risk any of the children being hurt from mishandling the materials. The school in which a science supervisor or consultant is available can supplement the teacher's work with the children. Specialists are often invited to the classroom; both the children and the teacher can benefit from such a visit. At that time, experiments of a more challenging nature can be given.

Using the Smell Board (shown in Figure 7.1), the children can select from a group of cards which have words such as sweet, bitter, sour, alcohol, vinegar, perfume, garlic, and discriminate among the odors. Olfactory discrimination—as one of the five senses—is important to highlight as an area of sensitization. Smells can be pleasant, as certain perfumes are

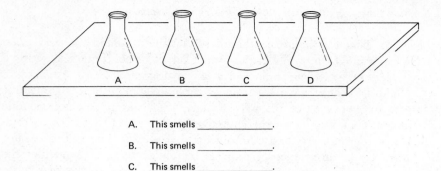

A.   This smells _____.

B.   This smells _____.

C.   This smells _____.

D.   This smells _____.

figure 7.1
The Smell Board

to people. They can also be a warning of danger. The smell of smoke, of spoiled food, of contaminated water, can be a warning signal. Children should be encouraged to associate various smells with pertinent meanings.

The Touch Board (shown in Figure 7.2) permits children to choose words such as sharp, rough, smooth, and soft as they touch a square of material or object in the left-hand margin. They begin to see the importance of using the appropriate word to describe what they feel. These spaces and words can be changed to give the children a wide variety of experiences that help them learn to be discriminating in a tactile sense.

sand-paper	This feels _____.
fur	This feels _____.
felt	This feels _____.
hard plastic	This feels _____.
velvet	This feels _____.

figure 7.2
The Touch Board (or Texture Board)

The children learn about weather from a television weather man. They also learn how to make a weather vane so that they can test its efficiency when they go outside.

Clear bottles can be shown filled with various shades of soil from nearby areas around the school, around their homes, around the ocean shore. Children can compare various colors of natural earth, sand, and soil. Seen next to each other in small vials corked securely and sealed with glue or sealing tape, the children can handle the bottles and see how nature has affected various shades of earth. The children can discuss the various forms and colors they see in their environment where subtle shading is obvious. They can discuss various colors of flowers, trees, their blossoms, stages of blossoming, and cycle of life.

Pupils can learn the scientific attitudes mainly by the way the teacher asks questions. This is extremely important. How can we find out? What do we need to do in order to find out what we want to know? What kind of things do we need in order to measure what we want to know? What ways can we use to find out what we want to know? Have we chosen an appropriate way to do this or to get this information? Is it dependable?

Often some of the most difficult aspects of a teacher's job in school with young children are: (1) to discover what some of the children's misconceptions about life are in terms of subject matter or scientific phenomena in this case, and (2) to help children learn to respond to these phenomena or events in a different way. Although learning is often defined or referred to as changed behavior in some way that is congruent with correct information the school has offered the pupils, the teacher often has first to attempt to have the children relearn (or unlearn) a response. She has first to rid the child of an incorrect bit of information regarding a specific event or idea.

Children may be familiar with sand, for example. They may have gone to the beach with their parents. They may not know, however, about the important classifications of sand—their properties, reactions to weather, to water, to various elements. Qualities, characteristics, reactions to other chemical qualities, appearance of different types of sand, shape, size of individual grains: these factors are studied at school. Sand is compared with salt, sugar, dirt. Pupils ". . . find ways to sort sand. They use sand to time, count, measure, and weigh. They explore color and texture in the making of pictures, sculpture, and jewelry." [1] Children of any age in the kindergarten-primary block of grade levels enjoy projects with sand. Colored sand is used in artistic ways, placed on a wood background— either temporarily to see its effects or glued to its surface. Time is needed for units on sand (not just ten minutes in a period) because the use of it seems to have a therapeutic affect. The children like to experiment with it and do not like to be hurried. They like to remain with the activity for a while.[2] They become absorbed in the way it feels and the creations that can be made from it.

The age of children specifically can influence the activity used with them in science. The academic and intellectual ages affect the degree of complexity of materials and concepts the teacher can provide for them; but by the same token, the teacher can have many levels of materials and ideas available to them for selection. They merely have to be told how to be cautious with materials. In the sand activity, the children have to be warned of the abrasive quality of sand. While it is soft to the touch and while it pours easily through one's fingers, it is scratchy and sharp if it gets in the eyes. It can tear soft membranes in the eyes. In this sense, the level of children's abilities and understanding must be known by the teacher. One does not simply turn loose in the hands of children any kind of material to use without giving them directions and warnings for their use. This means that they have a respect for the qualities and the nature of various objects—they do not need to be frightened by them. They need to understand them and know how to deal intelligently with them.

The recent trend in many classrooms is toward team teaching or the open school (not that the two are the same). They do, however, suggest

---

[1] David P. Butts, *Teaching Science in the Elementary School* (New York: The Free Press, 1973), p. 100.
[2] Butts, op. cit., p. 103.

that more people are involved in the instruction of a large group of children. Children of various age groups are placed together at different times of the day. Cross-age grouping, peer teaching (children instruct each other or those of greater ability teach those who have not understood a certain concept), and differential grouping has taken place to a greater extent in the last five years than ever before. This means that the teacher must—even more than was true in a self-contained classroom of children who were chronologically the same—be aware of wide ranges of abilities and skills among pupils. More materials, more books, more items to use at work have to be available. Grouping becomes more of a strategic device in instruction. Grouping properly can provide for greater individual differences than teaching to a total classroom group.

Grouping, individualization of learning activities and experiences places a greater burden on the teacher for having a wide variety of information and depth of knowledge in subject matter areas. It does not mean that she gives those answers to the children but she has to recognize when a child is ready to deal with more complicated information. And in

The carcasses and skeletal structures of animals are intriguing to these children in the science corner. It leads to further study of the animals they represent in life. Books are read, stories are written, and art work is produced because of them.

These girls are investigating accurate information on a project they have selected about animal life. An interesting and perceptive teacher is helping them find the correct facts for themselves. They need to enjoy the satisfaction of discovering knowledge in the appropriate books. The teacher asks them questions that will facilitate their search.

that sense she must have the materials ready. If she were not well informed or aware of the child's potential abilities in certain subjects, she could not recognize readiness in the child to meet a greater challenge. There is a difference between knowing the science principles themselves and knowing that a child is ready to tackle new and more difficult ideas. This is why materials, books, and filmstrips are important.

In each classroom, there should be a table devoted to different science projects—periodically changed to stimulate the children's interest. Most classrooms have a terrarium, either made by the teacher or with the children's help. A plastic container of individual small plants provides excellent opportunities for watching the growth of a variety of plants. Children also enjoy observing fish in a fish tank and like to be responsible for feeding them.

A magnet placed on a table with items that are attracted to it and items which are not, give children many opportunities for observing the properties and characteristics of materials and relationships among them. Color disks that can be placed on top of each other creating new colors give children individual control over experimenting with things not usually found in their own homes. Containers that show objects in water that sink to the bottom or float on top allow the child to test properties of materials and to become familiar with weights in relation to water.

Animals or poultry can be borrowed from a central science center in some cities. Some school systems have sources from which a teacher may borrow a sheep or a goat for a few days. This would have to be kept in a yard and penned in with the proper food available and instructions for the animal's care. Sometimes, eggs ready for hatching are given to the classroom. The teacher shows the children how they have to be protected and kept warm with a light in its box. The children count the days on a calendar, watching eagerly for the time when the chicks will be emerging from the eggs. It is an exciting time for them. The teacher can arrange to have science projects going on continuously in the classroom and periodically to have special ones that need more supervision.

Bird seeds have been planted in moist absorbent cotton and have sprouted in a short time within a few days. This is very pleasing to young children who have each planted their own in separate small plastic containers or in cut-down small cartons of individual (half-pint) size planting cups.

Most classroom groups that can have an allocated space outside their doors for a small garden find it very satisfying. To prepare the soil and to study what is needed to create a successful garden is an important prerequisite to the activity itself. This project requires more time and planning than those mentioned earlier. But the teacher needs to have both. Smaller ongoing activities that provide experimentation, manipulation, close observation for the child, and also the larger activity that is to be extended for a longer period of time and which requires closer supervision by the teacher, have their place in the science curriculum. The classroom never needs to be without one or two science activities.

Teachers have borrowed objects from museums to keep in the classroom for a period of time. The children need to be given instruction on how to treat those borrowed objects. Pupils are often chosen to serve as monitors or overseers of borrowed materials to see that the objects are handled carefully, since they must go back to the museum in good condition. It is wisest, however, that the teacher judge the children's abilities to cope with fragile objects and that she not invite problems if the children are not sufficiently experienced to exercise proper control in handling the item. One teacher, who had borrowed a stuffed bird from the museum, placed it in a large box and permitted the children to see it through a hole that was cut into the box. In this way, the children did not handle the object directly. This protected it. The children enjoyed the surprise effect of seeing it there when the outside of the box gave no clue as to what was in it.

Skeletal heads, dental evidence in fish jaws, as well as sea life are displayed in the science corner to motivate the children's interest. The children handle the items carefully and learn about the qualities of life around them. They learn that people can study characteristics of animals even after the animal is no longer alive.

In general, even though the teacher receives from the school some books that can be used with children in the first, second, and third grades about science, she should not depend on them as the only source of the curriculum. She can instill in the pupils an attitude toward the subject that can carry them a long way toward appreciating it as a living and significant area of study. Some schools bring health education into the science aspect and consider it as part of the science curriculum. Some, however, treat it separately and subsume it under the physical education component of their program. It can be part of both areas, the science program and health education.

Evaluation of Children's Progress in Science

Evaluation of children's progress in science is another opportunity for the teacher to judge the pupils' mastery of certain concepts and simultaneously become familiar with what appears to be the children's readiness to move on to more difficult work. One of the concerns of the teacher— who knows how different children are in the ways they learn and their capacities to learn—is to try to do justice to each child's pace and style in the learning process. This means that she has to have at her fingertips resource materials that can be used for children who need more help and also those who are ahead of others most of the time.

If evaluation is done in part to determine what the next steps are in a child's learning development, the teacher is more likely to notice what the child is doing and how well he seems to understand it. The child's progress is far more integrated than is usually true when the teacher does not have that kind of motivation. The teacher is also seeking many more activities to fortify the child's progress. She finds things that the child is able to master. She provides him with experiences that he can find satisfying.

The teacher helps the children think in terms of self assessment. The attitude that they should be developing is one that encourages the willingness to test one's self, to see how one is faring in his own progress. One group of writers discuss at least eight kinds of desirable attitudes that should be encouraged in the pupil as he goes through his science classes.[3] They are curiosity, rationality, objectivity, suspended judgment, critical-mindedness, open-mindedness, honesty, and humility. These qualities can be encouraged in the classroom. The teacher shows that they are valued and that they have to be developed constantly in the individual. To be honest, self-critical, and willing to be open-minded enough to permit new information to change one's mind, are part of the educational process. These qualities not only help the individual in reasoning but also help him to overcome stereotyped thinking. This kind of thinking, or critical awareness, compels the student to search his own set of premises not only about objects but about people.

While it is true that young children have difficulty in critical thinking, the teacher keeps in mind that it is a goal or direction. Many attitudes that the teacher tries to develop in children may not be apparent to the extent she would like. She must, however, continue to work toward their development. Working with young pupils is a unique experience, in that they are in the earlier stages of personality development. Negative results should not be perceived as final. Children are very resilient and will change, particularly when people working with them seem to care about those changes.

Evaluation goes on continuously as the teacher observes the children. She observes them while they are working and while they are interacting with their peers. She listens carefully to what they say in order to determine their interests, degree of knowledge in certain areas, and their false assumptions as well. This is a type of informal evaluation that does not involve paper and pencil tests or timing of responses to a given test. These

---

[3] Ronald D. Anderson, Alfred DeVito, Odvard Egil Dyrli, Maurice Kellogg, Leaonard Kochendorfer, and James Weigand. *Developing Children's Thinking Through Science* (Englewood Cliffs, N.J.: Prentice-Hall, Inc., 1970), pp. 238–239.

informal evaluation processes sometimes include a checklist that the teacher has devised or has taken from a book; it includes anecdotal records of pupil behavior and it is used at any time the teacher finds it convenient. Informal evaluation processes are an important component in record-keeping.

Some writers suggest questions that the teacher may use in order to assist her in gathering needed evidence.[4] The questions to guide the teacher include noting the quality of the child's observation and how he expresses what he has seen. The teacher should note whether the child sees beyond the surface, whether he states carefully what he has seen, and is not careless or too general when a specific answer is needed. Is the child able to stay with the point being discussed? Can the child realize a cause-and-effect relationship when it is appropriate? Since the process approach is emphasized in science as well as in other areas, is the child able to explain why he reached a certain set of conclusions? Can he give adequate reasons for thinking as he does about a certain problem?

Young children find it difficult to think in sequential order. Many writers who have studied children's thinking processes have explained this. Children's thinking is qualitatively different from adult's. Children can classify, but they need help in discovering relationships, cause-and-effect events. Children under five are famous for *non sequiturs*. They think that—as an omniscient adult—the teacher knows what they are thinking. It is difficult for them to take a frame of reference of the other person who is listening. Comments without reference to context fly every which way. Scientific and sequential thought or relationships that are logical to each other do not develop until later primary grades. Piaget has given us rich data on this.[5] For this reason the teacher is patient, providing specific objects and data to help the children understand relationships. Pupils need to be shown and to be shown very often what the content of subject matter is intended to convey.

Pictogram tests that require pointing to the correct answer or explaining reasons for what is happening in the picture help young children who are not able to read test items. Many tests for the three- to six-year-old have to involve performance, manipulation of objects, pointing to pictures, charts, and other devices that do not involve reading.

Children take a series of four pictures in their hands and show what happens in a sequence and in that activity the child demonstrates his understanding of cause-and-effect relationships. Many kinds of performance-based, manual manipulation tasks can be used to show what a

[4] Louis I. Kuslan and A. Harris Stone, *Teaching Children Science: An Inquiry Approach* 2nd ed. (Belmont, California: Wadsworth Publishing Company, 1972), pp. 394–398.

[5] Note earlier chapter on child development and intellectual development of young children.

child knows. The test should not place a child in an unfair position of surprise. Many teachers give the children opportunities to try doing what would ordinarily be required of them in a testing situation—not the actual items themselves, of course. This would not be honest nor a fair test at such time that the child actually took the officially prescribed standard test. The children are given sample tasks that are similar in principle to ideas that are typically included in most evaluation processes. This helps them become accustomed to testing experiences. Young children in particular are not as knowledgeable as their older schoolmates about taking tests; for this reason they need to have some familiarity with its expectations before they actually encounter it.

One author in a discussion of evaluation processes needed to test children's knowledge of science, indicates how the emphasis has changed from a traditional one to a more practical kind of consideration.[6] As science has matured in certain fields and has met certain politically oriented needs of the nation, it has also attained great social significance.[7] The space sciences, earth sciences, and biochemistry have taken on greater meaning in public life. They are referred to and are available for closer examination in newspapers, journals, television, and books. The child of the 20th century consequently knows science in ways that are very different from those of earlier generations. The sources from which they have obtained their information are different, as well as the forms of their sources.

Science has moved from a position of classical interest and a field available to an intellectual elite to a field that is open to a much broader public. The emphasis in science has been to show its functional contributions to the nation and to individual members of society. It makes sense that with the desire to foster rational behavior and thought in humankind (and in schoolchildren) comes the desire on the part of educators to bring science "home" to the individual, so to speak.

With the practical emphasis on science as a field needed by everyone comes a different stress on test items. Knowledge, facts, and comprehension are important. But they represent only a part of what children need to know. The process of certain elements in their interaction with each other—e.g., how the weather affects the earth, growth, decomposition, decay, erosion—are equally important to a child's understanding of his world. The teacher of young children does not attempt higher, complex, or sophisticated levels of understanding with them because these are often too abstract, not connected closely enough with the children's real experiences in life. She does, however, show how and why it is important to

[6] Leopold E. Klopfer, "Evaluation of Learning in Science," in *Handbook of Formative and Summative Evaluation of Student Learning*, Benjamin S. Bloom, J. Thomas Hastings and George F. Madaus, eds. (New York: McGraw-Hill Book Company, Inc., 1971), p. 561.

[7] Ibid.

know both kinds of information, the factual content, and what happens as a result of certain chemical reactions when two elements are brought together in a given way.

Critical thinking, the separation of fact from opinion, the knowledge that some phenomena can be proved and some cannot, is introduced to young children. The teacher can say, "We do not have enough information on that yet to be sure of our thinking on that subject." It can pervade the total program in early childhood education. The teacher need not wait for the science period to help the children learn how to distinguish truth from fiction. They can learn how to ask the most effective questions to obtain the best and most accurate answers. They can be taught to suspend judgment on a given idea until more information is acquired to provide more insight on the solution of a problem. Again these are attitudes, directions, orientations that the teacher takes with the children. In early childhood years, the pupils are not expected to produce fully developed, refined perfectionistic ideas. For this reason, evaluation processes check mainly a direction, progress, a point along the way in a child's growth cycle. A score does not represent a crystallized position that should be associated with a child's total development as a final or complete entity. Our testing procedures are not that sophisticated. Perhaps we should be grateful for knowing that. They are often relied upon more heavily than they should as true indicators of an individual's "worth." The knowledge that measurement is crude, at least encourages us to look for more information on better ways to perceive people.

Many tests come with commercialized kits on science for young children. The items themselves and the directions for administering the tests are very specifically defined. The teacher will not have any problem knowing what the designers of the kit feel are important information items to test. As the teacher becomes more experienced, however, she is better able to evaluate the children in many different ways. She can depend more on her own impressions and supportive data that she acquires for herself by using the books and her own background knowledge of educational psychology.

summary

This chapter dealt with the importance of science and scientific inquiry in the curriculum for young children. Nursery schools, kindergarten, and primary grades offer effective scientific subject matter by providing what children can understand at their levels. It is important that they learn to understand the nature of living things—e.g., plants, animals, birds—and what they need in order to live. Young children enjoy science when the teacher herself enjoys the children's excitement and curiosity about life and its unusual creations.

The child who can experiment with ideas and statements that begin with, "Let's suppose that —" or "What would happen if —" can do much to improve his own reservoir of knowledge. The teacher, however, has to be willing to allow these intellectual push-ups for the child and to show an enjoyment of it with him, not to stifle this process of toying with cause-effect ideas.

Children in kindergarten may be able to describe what keeps an airplane up in the air because the teacher has demonstrated this principle. The concept of jet plane propulsion can be explained and how it is different from the propeller-type plane. The missile and its trajectory can be discussed in its simplest forms by pictures and clear explanations. If the teacher does not feel knowledgeable enough to do so, an instructor in science can be invited to speak to the class. A resource person such as an engineer or a pilot who understands the system well and who likes to speak to young children can be asked to talk to them. The teacher often provides questions ahead of time so that the visitor knows what the children want to know. The point is that any of these ideas can be described in a somewhat simplistic but honest manner by someone who understands the subject matter well. Usually too, this kind of individual has materials that he can bring with him to clarify difficult points.

As the children progress through the primary grades, they are exposed to more difficult materials in science. So much of what they can learn is all around them: plants, animals, flowers, bodies of water, mountains, rivers, colors, cooking, foods, body parts that are responsible for our senses of smell, of sight, of sound, of touch, of taste. The glory of the human machine and brain can be shared with children through the analytically sensitive area that science was designed to be. What is mainly needed is an enthusiastic and vibrant teacher. This kind of person knows where to obtain information that children need and when they are ready to learn new facts and processes.

topics for discussion

1. What are some of the major differences in science units taught in the kindergarten and those taught in the third grades? Do you remember some of your own experiences in science that you had in the primary grades? Did they facilitate or inhibit your present attitudes toward science?
2. Visit a primary grades classroom and observe the children involved in a project or lesson in science. Note the way the teacher motivates or guides them in their work, and whether she provides individual levels of abilities and interests in the activity, and whether this lesson or project is part of a longer term one. Give your overall impressions of the effectiveness of the lesson.
3. Plan an ideal science program for children in kindergarten. Indicate your

goals, objectives, procedures to be involved and finally how you will evaluate the children's progress in it.

4. Is science taught to three-year-old children? How? What materials are used with them? What major attitudes would you want to transmit? Why?
5. Develop a science unit on a single theme or concept and indicate the purposes, goals, and activities that would be included for children in nursery school, kindergarten, first, and second grades.

selected bibliography for teachers

American Association for the Advancement of Science. *Description of the Program: Science—A Process Approach.* New York: Xerox Educational Division, 1967.

Anderson, Ronald et al. *Developing Children's Thinking Through Science.* Englewood Cliffs, N.J.: Prentice-Hall, Inc., 1970.

Atkin, Myron. "Behavioral Objectives in Curriculum Design—A Cautionary Note," *The Science Teacher,* Vol. 35, No. 5 (May, 1968).

Blough, Glenn O., and Julius Schwartz. *Elementary School Science and How to Teach It.* New York: Holt, Rinehart and Winston, 1974.

Brandwein, Paul F., and Elizabeth K. Cooper. *Concepts in Science.* New York: Harcourt Brace Jovanovich, 1967.

Butts, David P. *Teaching Science in the Elementary School.* New York: The Free Press, 1973.

Craig, Gerald. *Science for the Elementary School Teacher.* 5th Ed. Waltham, Mass.: Blaisdell Publishing Company, 1966.

Croft, Doreen J., and Robert D. Hess. 2nd Ed. *An Activities Handbook for Teachers of Young Children.* Boston: Houghton Mifflin Company, 1975.

Esler, William K. *Teaching Elementary Science.* Belmont, California: Wadsworth Publishing Company, Inc., 1973.

Fowler, William. "Developmental Science Learning for Disadvantaged Children," *Elementary School Journal,* Vol. 68, No. 2 (November, 1967), pp. 76–87.

Gagne, Robert M. *The Conditions of Learning.* New York: Holt, Rinehart and Winston, 1970.

Gale, Frank C., and Clarice W. Gale. *Experiences with Plans for Young Children.* Palo Alto, California: Pacific Books Publishers, 1971.

Gans, Roma, and Franklyn M. Branley, Eds. *Let's Read-and-Find-Out Science Books.* New York: Thomas Y. Crowell Company, 1971.

Haupt, George W. "First Grade Concepts of Hot and Cold," *Science Education,* Vol. 33 (October, 1949).

Hess, Robert D. and Doreen J. Croft. *Teachers of Young Children.* 2nd Ed. Boston: Houghton Mifflin Company, 1975.

Hurd, Paul D., and James Gallagher. *New Directions in Elementary Science Teaching.* Belmont, California: Wadsworth Publishing Company, 1968.

Karplus, Robert, and Herbert D. Thier. *A New Look at Elementary School Science.* Chicago: Rand McNally & Company, 1967.

Klopfer, Leopold E. "Evaluation of Learning in Science," in *Handbook of*

Formative and Summative Evaluation of Student Learning. Benjamin S. Bloom, J. Thomas Hastings, and George F. Madaus, Eds. New York: McGraw-Hill Book Company, Inc., 1971, pp. 559–641.

Kuslan, Louis, and A. Harris Stone. *Teaching Children Science: An Inquiry Approach*. Belmont, California: Wadsworth Publishing Company, Inc., 1972.

Michaelis, John U., Ruth H. Grossman, and Lloyd F. Scott. *New Designs for the Elementary School*. New York: McGraw-Hill Book Company, Inc., 1967.

National Society for the Study of Education. *Rethinking Science Education*, Part I. Chicago: University of Chicago Press, 1960.

Reiger, Edythe. *Science Adventures in Children's Play*. New York: The Play Schools Association, Inc., 1968.

Victor, Edward. *Science for the Elementary School*. New York: Macmillan Publishing Co., Inc., 1975.

Vivan, Charles. *Science Experiments and Amusements for Children*. New York: Dover Publications, Inc., 1963.

books for children

Allen, Gertrude. *Everyday Trees*. Boston: Houghton Mifflin, 1968.

Baker, Jeffrey J. W. *Patterns of Nature*. With photographs by Jaroslav Salek. New York: Doubleday, 1967.

Bendick, Jeanne. *What Made You You?* New York: McGraw-Hill Book Company, 1971.

Bendick, Jeanne. *All Around You*. New York: McGraw-Hill Book Company, 1951.

Bendick, Jeanne. *What Could You Be?* New York: McGraw-Hill Book Company, 1957.

Blough, Glenn O. *Who Lives in This Meadow?* Illustrated by Jeanne Bendick. New York: McGraw-Hill Book Company, 1961.

Branley, Franklyn M. *Flash, Crash, Rumble and Roll*. New York: Thomas Y. Crowell, 1960.

Bullia, Clyde Robert. *A Tree Is a Plant*. Illustrated by Louis Lignell. New York: Thomas Y. Crowell, 1960.

Conklin, Gladys. *I Like Caterpillars*. Illustrated by Barbara Latham. New York: Holiday Press, 1958.

Fisher, Aileen. *I Like Weather*. Illustrated by Janina Domanska. New York: Thomas Y. Crowell, 1963.

Gans, Roma. *It's Nesting Time*. Illustrated by Kazue Mizumura. New York: Thomas Y. Crowell, 1964.

Hutchins, Pat. *The Wind Blew*. New York: Macmillan Publishing Co., Inc., 1974.

Kanzer, Herman C. *Nature and Science Activities for Young Children*. Jenkintown, Pennsylvania: Baker Publishing Co., 1969.

Kinney, Jean. *What Does a Cloud Do?* Illustrated by Cle Kinney. New York: William R. Scott, 1967.

Lowery, Lawrence F., and Evelyn Moore. *I Wonder Why Readers*. New York: Holt, Rinehart and Winston, Inc., 1969.

McClung, Robert M. *Ladybug*. New York: William Morrow, 1966.

McNamara, Louise Greep, and Ada Bassett Litchfield. *Your Growing Cells*. Boston: Little, Brown and Company, 1973.

Nitkin, Jerome J., and Sidney Gulkin. *The How and Why Wonder Book of Beginning Science*. Columbus, Ohio: Charles E. Merrill Books, Inc., 1960.

Piltz, Albert et al. *Discovering Science. A Readiness Book*. Columbus, Ohio: Charles E. Merrill Publishing Co., 1968.

Schwartz, Elizabeth. *When Animals Are Babies*. Illustrated by Charles Schwartz. New York: Holiday Press, 1964.

Selsam, Millicent E. *The Carrot and Other Vegetables*. Illustrated by Jerome Wexler. New York: William Morrow and Company, 1971.

Selsam, Millicent E. *Peanut*. Photographs by Jerome Wexler. New York: William Morrow and Company, 1969.

Showers, Paul, and Kay Sperry Showers. *Before You Were a Baby*. Illustrated by Ingrid Fetz. New York: Thomas Y. Crowell Company, 1968.

Showers, Paul. *Your Skin and Mine*. Illustrated by Paul Galdone. New York: Thomas Y. Crowell Company, 1965.

Showers, Paul. *Find Out By Touching*. New York: Thomas Y. Crowell Company, 1961.

Zim, Herbert. *Your Stomach and Digestive Tract*. New York: William Morrow and Company, 1973.

Zim, Herbert. *Bones*. New York: William Morrow and Company, 1969.

Zim, Herbert. *What's Inside of Me?* Illustrated by Herschel Wertik. New York: William Morrow Company, 1952.

Chapter 8

Art and Young Children

To splash with paint
And puddle with color,
Thank goodness for crayons
   and paper,
The things I can make
Will be endless to see—
My school is a fun place to be!!

Children have within them an unspoiled reservoir for the expression of spontaneous ideas in art forms. They are eager to express themselves when given the opportunity. In fact, the adult artist tries to retain the freshness, simplicity, and "natural" spontaneity that young children have. The work that appears most uninhibited and honest is typically the product that is admired the most.

Teachers, in their zeal for order and sequenced levels of instruction, can sometimes demand neatness too soon in young children's art. Experimentation is not neat. It is often blurred, messy, and hesitant until the student is sure of what he wants.

In a concern for order and step-by-step learning, teachers can destroy the very quality they want to preserve in young children: creativity. Children's desire to paint ideas they have about color, size, shape—what they think about their surroundings or what ideas they have when they see the paint and the brushes—can be inhibited by too much talk from the teacher, too much instruction about neatness and dipping the brush into the paint. This does not suggest that there aren't any teachers who do permit the children to try something without a detailed line of action or directions before they are allowed to start work. It does mean, however, that the teacher who feels she must constantly be directing the children is not permitting them the time to move along in their own way.

Ideas flow when children are given the opportunity to let them come. Thoughts to be expressed are blocked by negative directions and by comments that specifically repress what the individual is trying to do. It is just as frustrating to the person who wants to create to be kept from doing so because he has been given so many explicit instructions, as it is to have the working materials before him with his hands tied behind his back.

Again the teacher of young children must remember that habits are being developed and attitudes are being formed. The child has had experiences before coming to school, it is true. His own family, friends and other relationships outside the school have helped in shaping his attitudes. The teacher, in a somewhat more formalized setting, is influencing new attitudes that may remain with the child consciously or subconsciously for a long time. This is why the teacher must be aware of the impact her comments, negative and positive, have in helping or hindering the child in developing to the best of his ability.

The watchwords recommended at this point for working with young children in art education are the following:

1. Retain a balance of perspective where giving directions are concerned. Try to give an appropriate amount, and those that are not too complex; sometimes no comment is needed.
2. Give the children an opportunity for experiences in which they can express themselves through media which are not too difficult to use. Adapt the materials to the children's age levels, physically, emotionally, and socially. Some children have low threshold levels of tolerance and become frustrated easily if products do not turn out as they expect.
3. Encourage the children to try new ideas. Try not to praise someone's work in a manner that suggests that the child has done the only acceptable product that the teacher likes.
4. Seek different types of activities for the children in order to help them build a background of art experiences that they can enjoy and build on as they progress in school (or outside of it as well).
5. Help children adopt an attitude of enjoyment where art activities are concerned. Help them acquire an attitude of self-confidence in their own preference of materials, ideas, colors, techniques.
6. Help the children develop an attitutude of willingness to experiment.

Avoid the hurried feeling of finishing a product. Encourage them to attempt different forms, directions, colors in their work.

7. Provide ample space and a pleasant atmosphere for working in art. Crowded working space often results in accidents such as spilled paint or jarring the efforts to create a smooth line in a product. Space and low noise level help in concentrating on one's work.

8. Help children learn the correct terminology in art. When commenting on their work remark on the strength of the line, the choice of color, the direction of a form, the lightness of mood in the product, the wise use of space in the pictures, the dynamics of shapes against each other, the shadows or light and dark areas in a picture, and the interesting theme of the product or painting.

9. Encourage the child to create something himself whenever possible, i.e., a birthday card, a mother's day or father's day card, an uncle's or aunt's birthday card, any product that expresses his own feeling instead of looking to commercial products to do it.

10. Help children notice the beauty of shapes and line in the objects they see around them every day, the texture of fabrics, of wallpaper, the bark of a tree, an animal's skin or fur.

It is not difficult to clean up after an art activity when everything is close at hand to do it properly.

11. Help children discern shading in color and the ways that darkness of day affects the appearance of color and also the way sunlight washes into color effects.

12. Help children adopt a playful attitude toward their work; this alleviates the tension of concern for perfection and also produces beautiful products.

13. Help the children achieve an attitude of matter-of-factness in the process of planning how to clean up after themselves and in putting things back in place on shelves or storage areas.

14. Continue to seek new ideas to use with children and continue to study children in relation to new research data in the current literature. Update knowledge of techniques, of classroom attitudes of teachers and children, and of contemporary art forms. Do not permit static impressions to remain for a long period of time.

Purposes and Goals for Art Education of the Young

As one might expect, the purposes and goals for young children's education in art vary in terms of which author, artist, or educator is asked about it. One type of response is highly symbolic, that is, that art is a form of expression generally. Another kind of response is that art is an everyday living experience. Art is a way of perceiving the world. It is true that among the many views that artists and educators have about art, the broad symbolic view is the most comprehensive.

Art is a way of life. Children can be encouraged to see the world around them in artistic ways, in analytic ways that sharpen their sight and image as it is transmitted to the brain. How much better it is to see shapes, colors, line, form, rhythm in all the objects that surround us rather than flatness and dullness. How much better it is to appreciate the beauty of various forms around us. How beautiful it is to know that people can enhance their lives by creating forms and objects in various media. One form becomes another. Life is transformed. An idea is expressed; what was internal is combined with the external.

The functions of art in young children's education are many. They include a means through which children develop an esthetic sense. Esthetic development involves an expansion of individual awareness of the physical and artistic properties of things and people and events in one's environment. It involves a means through which children are able to express what they see.

Art contributes to a child's use of his imagination. As a child is given materials to express an idea, the images that go through his mind and become transformed on paper through his own planning permit him to materialize what has occurred internally. He learns that the external

These art productions showing young children's impressions of flowers in a vase are hanging up to dry in their classroom. Each one is different. The teacher encourages differences in the children's art work.

These kindergarten girls are eagerly starting their work with crayons. They sometimes like to stand as they draw. As they become more involved with certain areas they sit down and proceed slowly.

These girls are starting their work independently. They are not interested in copying from each other. They have faith in their own ideas. This is as it should be.

expression of an idea can be very satisfying. He will repeat the experience when he realizes the transaction of art, a transaction between himself and the environment.

Art contributes to self-knowledge. A child can discover his own abilities and thoughts as he sees them visually presented before him in full knowledge that it came from his own resources. Self-awareness is part of the development of identity. It is essential at all levels of growth in the child.

Art contributes to a child's awareness of what is involved in the use of various materials. He develops an appreciation for the difficulties involved in handling paint, clay, paper forms, and their placement on a background. He needs these experiences.

Art experiences can impress the child with his own uniqueness. A teacher who points out the individualistic qualities of a child's work can help the pupil become aware of the elements of his own work that are not present in other children's work. This means that the teacher must be perceptive and sharply aware of differences in the best sense of those observations. It also means that the teacher is motivated to help young children early in life to build an honest and socially acceptable appreciation of the self and one's abilities. Uniqueness supports self-appreciation. Self-appreciation builds a healthy self-concept which in turn permits an appreciation of others and their abilities as well. Knowing what is involved

These girls have stopped doing their crayon work for a moment to discuss an important point.

in creating a lovely painting, or a sculptured piece, arouses feelings of identification with the other person in appreciation of the work and skills involved in the creation of it.

The art experience in education highlights an awareness of artistic elements in life in the way people walk, in the way they move, in the way they describe events and materials in routine experiences. It enhances children's abilities to use terms from the art field which more accurately describe the qualities of shape, dynamics, shadow, light, dark, pale, intense, and any qualitative term.

Children's sense of well-being can be enhanced through the artistic experience. The sense of achievement in a creative form and one which is admired by others contributes to their awareness of an inner resource that gives pleasure to others as well as to themselves. Anyone who has experienced the admiration and approval of friends upon completion of a beautiful product of some kind is well aware of the stimulating effects it can have. Children like to repeat successful experiences of this nature.

Some people have the impression that because children are young and unsophisticated, they do not need to have art exposure of high quality. Just because children are not discriminating enough to know how to be critical is the more reason that teachers need to take it upon themselves to be committed to high-quality materials. Children can appreciate artistic products of fine line, color, shape, and form. This applies to beautiful photographs and illustrations, too.

235

This child seems to be having difficulty starting his work. His teacher approaches, sits near him, and talks casually about what he might like to do.

The teacher's encouragement helped this kindergarten child start his work. He seems to feel happier at this point.

This little boy has finally produced what he wanted to do and seems to be very proud of it.

The art experience in which beautiful products are shown for purposes of exposing children to quality, is not to be confused with sophisticated discourse above the children's levels of understanding by the adult who is working with them. Pupils can enjoy the visual experience with suggestions as to what they should look for when they observe. The more a teacher knows about art and some of the basic principles in its visual and creative aspects, the more she should be able to present materials and ideas to young children with directness, candor, and beauty. Children respond extremely well to this kind of approach—one of integrity.

One of the most highly motivating factors in young children's enjoyment of art is the teacher's pleasure in wanting to help children share her love of and commitment to the artistic experience. Children are typically prone toward imitating the teacher's behavior and attitudes. This applies to the negative aspects as well as the positive. The teacher of young children tries to capitalize on this tendency. She is highly aware of the fact that she is a model for children; consciously or not, the children observe, consider, imitate. They are not as critical of the teacher as they will be in later grades. The children's tendency to imitate can become an important vehicle for instruction of a very subtle nature. The teacher's manner of accepting others, of trying to use constructive criticism, of not belittling others, of admiring skillful efforts toward achievement, conscientiousness, of demonstrating concern for the feelings of others, can be taught in this semi-informal manner.

Since the artistic experience or product is not well understood among many parents who view their children's work and seek identification from the child as to what it represents, it is very important that the teacher provide support for the child at school in regard to his painting, clay product, collage, or whatever. The teacher has to provide the words that describe the effective work of the child. She says that a painting or drawing shows the way we feel about something. A child who is asked, "What is it?" from his parent or sibling can answer, "It shows the way I feel," or "It shows what I was thinking about when I did it." In that way embarrassment can be avoided in situations when the parent or sibling says the child's product does not look like a house, a dog, or whatever answer the child felt obliged to give to the question, "What is it?"

Impressions of art have undergone major changes as far as children's education is concerned. In past years, art was considered an esoteric experience for the few who had the capacity to "appreciate" it. Contemporary art, however, has taken on a more personal quality. Everyone is expected to have esthetic tendencies. All children have creativity within them until it is repressed at school by some teachers asking for conformity in children's work.

Developmental Activities for Young Children

Children in nursery school and kindergarten enjoy art experiences in finger painting, clay modeling, painting with tempera (water-soluble) paint and large brush at an easel, sponge painting (small cubes of sponge dipped into dry tempera and starch), collage, string painting, and many subcategories of these media or processes. They enjoy making decorative cards on birthdays, for Mother's or Father's Day and other celebrations such as Easter, Christmas, or Hallowe'en. They like to make practical or useful things for gifts that can be functional—e.g., pencil containers, ashtrays, attractive objects out of clay, *objets d'art*. They like to bring home shadow prints of themselves or pictures they have painted of their mothers or others in their families.

The materials pupils use may also be used by adult artists. Children can, however, despite a lack of adult perceptiveness express their own ideas and abilities and have an honest experience with art materials. The teacher has to permit the child to attempt his own expression with art media. She does not do it for him in the interests of having him make something that "looks like something." This is not the purpose of a developmental activity for the child. This may help develop the teacher, but it does not focus on the child's learning progress.

Young children must be encouraged to experiment with media, to

These two kindergarten girls were painting at their easels, which were side-by-side. The girl with the brush in her hand said she was going to paint something for her mother.

The child started her work, painting a picture that she said she knew her mother would say was beautiful.

develop a curiosity about seeing what happens when brush and paper meet. Many children have been squelched by brothers and sisters who poke fun at their paintings and other efforts in art. Realism is only one dimension of the art world. Children's work is not expected to be a replica of a photograph. Teachers who have not had a background in art themselves are looking for different products from the children than those who are specialists do. Their inexperience in the art media influences their errors in expecting certain products from the children. This is unfair.

The teacher has to continue to encourage pupils to experiment with ideas and to be unafraid to express them. They should not be exposed to criticism too soon or too harshly. If the teacher has an image in mind that

Before the person in the picture was finished, the little girl decided to place the ground or floor in her painting. She was happy with the results of her work when she showed it to her teacher. "My mother will say, 'It is bee-you-tee-full!'"

she wants them to create, this can inhibit their own spontaneity in expression of an idea. If the teacher adopts the attitude that art expression develops from the children's minds and it is their privilege to express their ideas in the medium given to them, then she will allow them to experiment with it while keeping her images to herself. Teachers are often surprised at how well the children do when they are permitted to work their own ideas into a product.

At the same time that the children are learning to respect their own work (through the teacher's way of responding toward it), the children are also learning to respect the work of their peers. They learn that they do not touch the work of others, that they do not approach someone else's painting, drawing, or clay piece and start adding their own touches to it.

Children should be encouraged to try different media. Although they sometimes become comfortable with one kind and will want to remain with it, they should be exposed to different kinds and shown how to experiment. This experimental attitude is important to develop in esthetic areas; otherwise, it encourages the child to repeat the same procedure

This little kindergarten girl enjoyed experimenting with clay forms, rolling them and trying to push them into place. She considered adding more on to her project.

over and over again. One experiment with young pupils involved them in using tree branches as "brushes"—the paint was made by squeezing berries taken from nearby bushes. The effects were beautiful. The emphasis on the process—on the children's absorption in working with materials—is more important than the final product. Process effectiveness carries the child over to wanting to do more of the same thing. It has longer-range effects. It also removes the focus and pressures from an excellent product. For the child who is concerned about perfection, there is far more leeway for him in playing with the process.

The teacher helps the pupil in his progress with the painting or drawing by asking questions that can move it along. She can help him when he draws a tiny house in one corner of the paper by asking who lives in the house and what is around the house—are there other houses near it or is it alone with miles of grass around it?—and so forth. This stimulates ideas for further work in the drawing without saying specifically what the child might draw or paint.

In all of the art activities, the child is learning how to manipulate materials. Clay involves different handling; crayons as well. Collage

These kindergarten children enjoy the feeling of molding clay into tiny pieces and rolling them into tiny fruits for a basket.

introduces different qualities of control and manipulative skills. The child forces materials to form in ways that muscle constraints will allow. For a fine discussion of children's stages of development from scribbling stages to representational attempts, see Lowenfeld and Brittain.[1]

The teacher encourages the child to respect his own work by commenting on strong aspects of it, enjoying it with him and appreciating his efforts and thoughts in its implementation. By retaining a portfolio of paintings, drawings, and other products of the child, the teacher and child and parent can see the developmental patterns.

Teachers can meet with parents before the school year and indicate that they plan to keep a record of the child's work. Parents can be given some background at that time about the scribbling stages—the pre-schematic stages of a child's work—so that they too can appreciate how the child is developing throughout the year. Many parents unaware of what is involved in an art program insist on asking the child *what* his pictures are supposed to be. Pictures represent ideas. They do not have

[1] Viktor Lowenfeld, and W. Lambert Brittain, *Creative and Mental Growth*, 5th ed. (New York: Macmillan Publishing Co., Inc., 1970), pp. 103–188.

The teacher knew that her presence could provide the support needed by these kindergarten children. She encouraged the little girl to proceed with her work and to try different ideas with her clay. An unhurried pupil begins to relax and concentrate on the work instead of feeling anxious about finishing quickly.

to have the likeness of objects. The parent or siblings should not ridicule the child in any way or laugh at his work. This discourages the child from trying to perform other kinds of art activities. He will think that they will be laughed at every time. We have seen children who hide their work and will not let anyone see them start even their first stroke. This response reveals the fact that the child has already had unsatisfactory experiences in relation to his art work.

Parents of young children need some background information on the way children's art develops. If they have this, they can be very helpful in supporting the child's efforts and can see how the child is maturing in the process. The teacher and parents both want what is best for the child: the freedom to grow and benefit from experiences at school. Many parents are not aware—nor can they be expected to be—of the fact that they can damage the child's self-concept if they respond unfavorably when a child brings something home from school. The child is associating himself with his work. If he feels that his work is rejected or ridiculed, he himself is rejected as well. These little elements build up to larger effects which result in the development of more permanent feelings about the child's self-image. They do not add up to self-trust or self-confidence.

DEVELOPMENTAL ASPECT OF CHILDREN'S PARTICIPATION IN ART
EXPERIENCES IN RELATIONSHIP TO OTHER FACTORS OF GROWTH

Five-year-old children do not automatically acquire greater control over their muscles in the first few weeks before they become six and are in the first grade. They are gradually developing insights, psychologically, and are also developing the ability physiologically to maintain control over their muscle movement (or control of small muscles, not to press hard at certain times, to make light dots or strokes with certain materials).

As they progress or move ahead in the first grade, learning to read, learning to respond to more organized instruction, they begin to conduct themselves in a more responsible manner. They are aware of themselves as individuals who are expected to produce, are expected to learn, are expected to be discriminating.

Five-year-old kindergarten children and six-year-old children in the first grade have much in common. Their preferences are similar to those they had in kindergarten and those same preferences are not fully dropped in place of others. Gradually, however they acquire depth in painting. For example, they may still like finger painting. They may enjoy working with clay a little more than they did formerly and may spend more time concentrating on an object in developing it more, in refining certain lines or shapes a little more than they had before.

Seven-year-old children who are typically in the second grade acquire still more control over the media they use in art. They are able to bring more to an experience; they have had broader experiences in life by the time they are seven. Their perspective toward objects, relationships of those objects to each other, the color, shape, form, line, that they perceive in life situations and events around them change to some degree. If they have had a teacher who helped them see more in life's shapes, colors, and objects, they are lucky. If they have been taught to look at the colors in the bark of a tree to see that not only browns and dark greens could be seen in it, but also colors that are reflected in the sunlight, they have been fortunate indeed. This amalgam or blend of a teacher's highlighting what they see around them with their own view and perceptiveness—particularly when the teacher values their point of view as well—will change in the way they administer color, line, shapes and dynamics of space, light and dark, and perspective generally.

Eight-year-old children who are typically in the third grade are becoming mature in the early childhood phase. They will be moving soon into the prepuberty years and into the intermediate grades of fourth, fifth and sixth years at school. They have been secure to some extent in their routines at school. (They are somewhat veteran pupils by that time and have some idea of what to expect from the school situation. They have also had the frustrating situations of adapting to different teachers' value systems and have tried to come out ahead in the guessing game.) The parents sometimes have a very difficult time in the first couple of years when their child meets a teacher about whom the child tearfully complains, "She doesn't like me!" It is extremely difficult for the parent to accept the stories of conflict related by the child about his "mean teacher."

The child in the third grade typically knows something about school routines, the expectations that are associated with test-taking, reading assignments, writing, spelling, reports to the class, and what is expected of them by their peers as well as their teachers. At this age too, being liked by one's peers is very important. Where the approval of their teacher was one of their major considerations in nursery, kindergarten, first and second grades, the ages of seven and eight become the age of concern about how one stands in the approval of one's peers. About the middle of the second grade—typically at the age of seven—the children are developing awareness of the popularity concept.[2]

Teachers who are working with children in the seven- and eight-year-old groups will recognize a beginning of sophistication. The children want to be understood; they want to be part of a group. They want to be able to have the skills needed to be successful at school. The children have at this point many competing groups outside the school, such as the Brownie troops, clubs, dancing lessons, various kinds of extracurricular activities in which parents like to see their girls and boys participate as part of growing up.

Art experiences should not be gimmicky types of activities but rather experiences that can be part of a foundation for the appreciation of quality art. Experiences that demonstrate the excellent materials and media for expression of beauty, of emotions—e.g., anger, hate, envy, heaviness, gentleness, enthusiasm, "walking on air," bounciness, floating on a cloud. All these emotions materialized into an art form carry a forcefulness with them and a beauty about being human that cannot be demonstrated in any other way. The product that represents an arrest for a moment (or the capturing of) an emotion—not only for the individual who has produced it, but also for others who may enjoy it or empathize with it because they have had similar feelings—is an element in human life that transcends many others.

The human experience is evident throughout children's products in early childhood education and particularly in the opportunities to create art forms. Paintings, pictures for mother, father, uncle, or grandparent are treasured. Clay products are cherished for life when a child has worked conscientiously. Baking children's clay products in a kiln can immortalize

[2] Edythe Margolin, *Awareness of Criteria for Achievement, Social and Academic, Implicit or Explicit, Among Children in Kindergarten, First, and Second Grades.* 1965. Mimeographed Report, University of California, Administrative Grant #2109, 1965.

an experience. Many mothers and grandmothers can attest to this as they proudly show others what their young child did many years ago. It is a unique way of keeping a record of a child's development at any given time, and to be looked back on in later years.

For children in the age range of four through eight, a broader variety of materials should be available. Paints, clay, collage, scissors, paste, leaves, string, objects that can be flattened into clay to provide textures and impressions, are invaluable to art experiences for children. Imprinting with cut sponges or other interesting household or small kitchen utensils that have been dipped into tempera and starch produce unique designs that are very much enjoyed by children.

Pupils should have ample space to conduct their work; they should have adequate areas and materials to use in cleaning up after their work is completed. They should be shown how to store clay that is unfinished, covered with a damp cloth and placed in a dark area. There are fine clay cabinets that have snug lids and retain the temperature needed to keep the sculptured piece from drying before its creator is finished with it.

Children in kindergarten begin to have greater control over scribbling. They emphasize in their paintings things that are important to them by making them larger or brighter than other parts of their pictures. Their work is fascinating to see and more, to hear them describe as they refer to different symbols in their paintings.

In grades one and two, children may relate color to what they see; they may paint a red flower red in their own pictures. They may also place objects on a base line.[3] A vase may be placed on a table; a tree may be placed on the ground.

In the third grade, some children are able to demonstrate in their work an awareness of the joints of the body and the way they move.[4]

Children are given experiences in which they can sense feelings as they respond to the touch of something that is harsh, coarse, or as they touch fur or velvet. These feelings are reproduced in the art forms they create. In the use of clay, brush strokes, or imprinting give the clay surface an interesting texture. Collage is an opportunity to introduce various textures. Everything from sandpaper to absorbent cotton, feathers, cork, sponge, various materials, and wallpaper textures help the children become more conscious of differences in textures.

Children can be shown many booklets that can be made of pictures of their pets, animals they like, or birds that they see. Flowers, brush strokes, different colors, shapes, and forms that are presented in separate sheets, on construction paper, flannel, various materials for background

---

[3] Edith M. Henry, "Selection of Art Experiences," in *Art Education in the Elementary School*, Mary M. Packwood, ed. (Washington, D. C.: National Art Education Association, 1967), p. 49.

[4] Ibid.

and bound into a booklet tied together with yarn or chenille, create a beautiful original work that remains for years to come as evidence of a child's creativity and care in making it.

Young children like to make puppets of many kinds. Puppets out of small, medium, or large paper bags that have faces pasted on the bottom part of the bag (and placed right side up) can be made in various ways. Clothing for the puppet can be made out of construction paper and pasted on the body part. Ears are often placed above the face; even a hat or headdress is perched askew to give the puppet a unique character. Some children enjoy making puppets out of popsicle sticks.

Young children also like to take very small boxes (e.g., emptied raisin boxes of the tinest size), covering them with construction paper or painting them and making cars, trucks, and animals out of them by adding paper, ears, wheels, and string to pull them along. Some have made trains that follow a locomotive, all made out of different size empty boxes. When the author was in Italy visiting a Catholic school of little three- and four-year-old children, they were working on these tiny objects and made fascinating toys with them. Children there are taught at a very early age to work with tiny bits of paper, about 1/16 of an inch in size, to make collage assemblages, and to paste tiny parts to boxes that formed little toys. In the United States, the idea that children need to use large muscles at ages, three, four, and five is the reason that large brushes are given to them for painting large crayons for drawing. Children in America typically do not make things with small muscle involvement until they are older. That is, they are not asked to do this at an early age because research has shown that they should not. The notion is that precision builds up in the child, that it is a somewhat sophisticated talent (using small muscles with preciseness of intent) and requires time and skill to develop. Most children in Europe and in the Orient are exposed—or asked to work with—tiny paint brushes, tiny bits of paper to use in mosaic designs, and other intricate art activities when they are about two-and-one-half years old. Their products are beautiful.

It is odd that children are not asked to use small muscles in intricate work. Since the time they were infants they were picking up tiny objects or pieces of scrap found on the floor, pieces that miss the adult's eye. Their tiny fingers typically show great skill in manipulating small toys. Perhaps we need to reassess the things that we think they can and cannot do.

Children in the first and second grades in American schools make detailed products with crayons, paints, and paper. The art materials given to them when they are seven and eight are presented along with interesting techniques. Crayons are not an easy medium to use, but children are given these when they are very young and scribble or make pictures that are symbolic. Crayon or pastel techniques are a sophisticated kind of art medium and especially impressive when they are used properly. The children in second and third grades are more perceptive and more observant. They have noticed more differences in objects, pets, and human beings. The teacher can have an excellent file of study prints which a child can use to help him think of the color of foliage, of birds, of animals, and other objects of interest to him.

The teacher stimulates the pupils' use of his imagination along with help to his imagery or memory by providing him with pictures in an exciting file of various scenes, emotional expressions on people's faces, airplanes, rockets, missiles, or animals of the zoo. This is done instead of the teacher's having to draw these things on the board as examples of ideas. Children would immediately copy the teacher's work, behavior which is not desired at all. It is the children's work that is valued; their efforts are more valued than a perfect product.

Children make fascinating products with materials that create intricate kinds of collage or assemblages. Contemporary pop art often is of this type. Their work has at times a motivating theme such as Valentine's Day, foods, people, noses, mouths, eyes, clocks; there are endless motifs for collage creations. Some of them take on the qualities of a Salvador Dali creation in their unusual array and placement of objects superimposed upon objects in a flight-from-reality manner. The children can frame the work with fringe that has been cut out of construction paper. Fringe can also be used in many ways as part of somebody's eyelashes pasted to an eye (of a human being or an animal) on the construction paper background. Third dimensional work is intriguing and very effective. Even the tiniest touch of superimposed bits of paper or other articles create eye-catching effects. The children's work often looks like professional products.

Children's appreciation of art will grow from preschool to the third grade if a skillful teacher provides them with materials and books that represent some of the best that art has to offer. Since art is an area that involves personal preference, it is open for the enjoyment of many. It is not a science in the sense that only one answer may be correct for the most part, (even though there are some situations in which science has several best answers). Exactitude is less crucial in this area than in careful scientific method.

Art involves the appreciation of balance, appropriate use of color to create the effect desired by the artist or creator, and the use of many different techniques as preferred by the individual employing those techniques. Emotions, expression, individuality, uniqueness, honesty of expression are sought in fine art. The teacher helps the children capitalize on their own individual differences. She helps them learn to appreciate their own ideas, and not feel that other children's work always surpasses their own. She helps them value what they can do for themselves and to

These children were experimenting with Q-tips dipped into various shades of foodcoloring, and creating soft, intricate designs on paper. These could be used as covers for birthday cards or booklets.

take pride in it. To develop one's own skills is important, not to copy and continually prefer those of others.

Teachers can obtain illustrations of fine art forms, of paintings, outstanding sculptured pieces, third-dimensional art of plastics, metal, unusual kinds of sculpture of paper and other materials. Children have to see these things which have to be discussed by the teacher to bring out the fine points of the work. In that process, the teacher uses the correct terminology used by sculptors and artists. No matter what the children's age—whether three or eight—they can hear and learn to understand the artist's terms.

The teacher has to be aware of the materials (see Figure 8.1) that can can be used effectively with young children. The fundamental media include clay, tempera, paste, scissors, papers of various kinds (tissue, rice, construction), string, cord, wire, sandpaper squares, cardboard. The children are also taught to use material with thought and physical care. They also keep them properly so that they are stored in a way that will help them remain in good condition and appealing to use when pupils are ready to do so.

The room environment is important in preparing children for their art experiences. Materials have to be ready for them. The teacher cannot stop and get them out of the cupboard when she has already started to discuss what they are going to do. It breaks into the motivating period and mood, and distracts the attention of the children. The materials have to be placed where they will be ready for use by the teacher and the children. Any

249

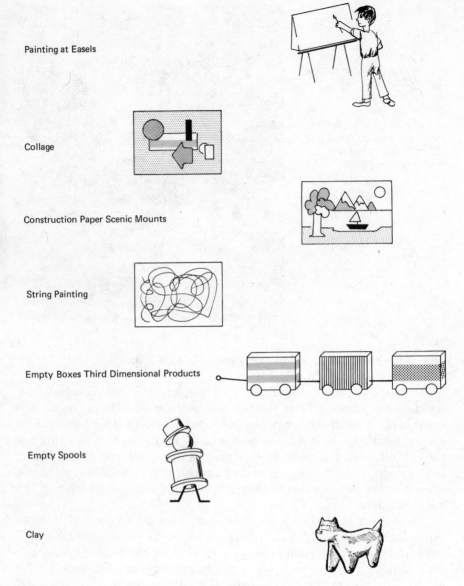

Painting at Easels

Collage

Construction Paper Scenic Mounts

String Painting

Empty Boxes Third Dimensional Products

Empty Spools

Clay

figure 8.1
Basic Items that Are Enjoyed by Young Children in Art Experiences

motivating objects or materials that have to be observed prior to the pupils' involvement with their own work should be in easy view of everyone.

Materials that are needed to assist the children in cleaning up after they are finished need to be out where they are ready to be used. The children should not have to bunch up in a small area in order to get to

250

the material—e.g., sponge, water, wipe-up rags in order to clean their own small work area. Many teachers are not aware that if the cleaning materials are made attractive and are set out near pans of water with drying cloths available, that children enjoy doing a thorough job. This also avoids discipline problems. The teacher's planning and organization strongly affects the number and kind of control problems that occur in the classroom. Skillful planning on the part of the teacher or the kind of planning that anticipates the needs of the children as they proceed in the school day obviates many unhappy situations for the children and the teacher. So often the teacher creates the problems herself. Crowded areas of work, inadequate materials for the children, insufficient activities to meet the needs of various pupils, poor organization of space for work and for cleaning up after their work is finished: these are problems that arouse irritation and argument among the children.

The children should have ample space to walk around others who are working so that they do not in their absorption with their own work bump into others and spoil their work or interrupt their concentration. There should be ample items of equipment for the class; if not, the children should not have to wait too long to use an item that someone else is using when they need it. This is when discipline problems arise. A child waiting to use another color paint or a different size brush becomes impatient, irritated, then distracting to others in some way; an altercation follows with either one or more children. These conflicts can be anticipated and avoided.

Children's work should be displayed. Every child should have the opportunity to see his work on a bulletin or display board, in the school corridor, the principal's office, the reception office, lunch room, wherever others may see it. The teacher should be aware of children who have not yet had an opportunity to have their work displayed and should retain a record of it if necessary to help her remember. Clay products, hand or bag puppets, anything that shows a child's work to advantage should be displayed at one time or another. Cards, birthday or invitation, should be displayed to let the child know that other people appreciate his work.

The teacher is a guide, an inspiration, a facilitator who can bring out the best in the child. There isn't anyone who does not need this at some time or other, and also need it at some times more than others. It is essential to human growth. Some children are given confidence they need by their teacher, not their families where it should be started and often is not. Parental problems or having many jealous siblings can squelch the bit of self-pride a child may have. The teacher can be a great source for the encouragement needed by a pupil. Art work often becomes a reason and a vehicle for that encouragement. Each child needs to know that he does something well and that he is appreciated for what he knows or what he produces. The teacher must be an empathic person and must be able to identify with the individual who is not receiving the encouragement he needs to survive and to thrive in a competitive world.

Evaluation of Young Children's Experiences in Art

Evaluation procedures in any subject matter area are crucial to the way a child will perceive himself in relation to it. Not only is his self-concept affected but also his impressions of whether that subject is an area for his pursuit of happiness—whether he should make the effort to spend time in developing his abilities along those lines.

In art, especially, children will be self-conscious about their efforts if they think that what they do is not valued in some way. They will take this as a true statement representing their actual ability in it. This is why the teacher's comments about their work so vitally affect whether they will proceed in it. They may stop trying. They accept negative comments as a real appraisal of what they can do in art experiences. Often the teacher is not equipped, intellectually or in terms of psychological sensitivities, to know how to evaluate the children's work. This is grossly unfair to children.

The danger of influencing a child's arrested development in art is greater among children in the early grades because the impressions made at that time are strong. The children's impressions of how they are doing, what they are doing, and how well they are doing it seriously affects whether they will continue to work in that area or not. In reading, writing, and mathematics, there is no question that they have to continue to develop. The decision is not theirs to make. They know they have to do it whether they like it or not. The areas of reading, writing, and mathematics involve cognitive skills that are needed as essential functions in the child's life through school and thereafter. Parents and the nation, generally look to the results of those skills which are later to be used to help a child not only succeed at school but also to help him function in an occupation or profession.

The importance of certain skills is taken for granted by everyone. Instruction in those areas are of highest priority. They will be offered as compulsory parts of the curriculum. Art experiences, on the other hand, are not pushed. Children have the freedom to make a choice in that area. If they do not feel that they are adept at it, they may not want to participate. They show this in their attitudes of withdrawal when materials are presented to them. They unwillingly draw lines, model with clay, take up the pastel chalk, or dip into the finger paint. Their reluctance prevents them from doing well. Feelings of ineptness block the activity and pleasure they should be having in their involvement. As opposed to reading, writing, and mathematical skills, they stop trying in the art area if the teacher comments negatively on their work. This is extremely important for the teacher to realize—the sensitivity children have about art experiences, and also the damage that can occur if a child takes a negative comment to be an accurate appraisal of his abilities. And most children think that the teacher is absolutely infallible in her judgment of their work (even when she may be wrong in the way she judges art).

The child does not know that art is a very personal matter. It is subjective. A child's work can be praised by one art educator and disliked by another. There are too many people with different opinions to permit one teacher's judgments about a child's work to represent an authoritative one. Yet the child accepts the teacher's comments as true. He accepts them as true about his own abilities. Worse, the parents often accept it too. This prevents further attempts on the part of the child. When he is expected to produce as he proceeds through school to the intermediate grades, it is obvious that he has already been deflected in his desires.

The teacher has some ideas as to what the child should be able to achieve. One of the most important aspects of an art experience is that the child learn to express what he feels or thinks in ways that represent those feelings as honestly as possible. One writer indicates that children in the first and second grades, for example, should be able to "recognize and use a variety of color hues, values, and intensities." [5] Children should be able to attain greater control over the use of materials and tools.

Broad goals can be defined for the child in art. The child should show greater abilities in deciding on his own use of color, form, shape, and style. He should grow in making decisions regarding what he does and how he does it. His skills in planning what he wants to produce, its means of execution, and his placement of objects and ideas in a product, should have grown from prekindergarten to the third grade.

The period of four-through-eight represents growth of a unique type. It represents an ingenuousness in ideas and their implementation, grown in a climate of encouragement and pleasant experiences. It represents an attitude of wonder, awe, expectancy, beauty and fulfillment in the art expression. (It might have also represented the opposite if a teacher was negatively oriented to the child's work.) The four- through eight-period of a child's development is when the child has grown from open vulnerability to a somewhat controlled condition of being able to handle his ideas and thoughts and imagination, having the courage to put them down in the form best expressed on paper, in clay, in paint, with scissors, and paste. The arrest of time occurs, a moment, a space, a feeling, in

[5] Kenneth M. Lansing, "Evaluation," in *Art Education in the Elementary School*, Mary M. Packwood, ed. (Washington, D.C.: National Art Education Association, 1967), p. 73.

combination with human efforts. Young children have no means of comparison of work they have done before and an appreciation of their own growth. It does not mean to them what it means to an adult. They enjoy doing and moving along.

The uniqueness of early childhood years as distinguished from later years is that this new introduction to life and its various experiences does not carry with it any promise of perfection or success. The child is not concerned with success. He wants to accomplish, to do, to move, to be where he has not been. While the safety of familiar objects is valued, he is at the same time restless to try new things. But he wants to know that he has the reassurance of supportive adults nearby to rescue him from uncertainty and faltering should this arise.

If a teacher is not sure how to evaluate a child's work or his efforts, it is best she abstain from any comment except a reassuring smile. She can do more damage than good by saying too much or making a derogatory comment. There is less chance that she will destroy a child's desire to go on participating in art experiences if she says nothing about the work than if she makes statements that do not help the child's future endeavors in art.

The teacher should work more on strengthening her own means of motivating the children's products during their involvement with them. She should note, should be perceptive as to what is needed to make the child feel more comfortable to execute his work, and be less concerned about judging it. She should also be more cognizant of needing to provide a variety of ideas and materials with new opportunities for art than on evaluating the child in his experiences with those media.

It is important to remember that people working with young children are not all art majors in their preparation for the job. They do not have at their fingertips the knowledge needed to provide a strong foundation for art. For this reason—since most teachers of young children four- to eight-years old are not specialists in art—caution needs to be exercised regarding the ways that children are evaluated.[6]

The child has to be convinced that the teacher accepts him as worthy, of liking, of caring about, of helping, and of knowing him as a person who adds to the pleasure of other people's company. It is well worth the time of the teacher to notice the children's individuality in style of working and preferences for color and technique. Art can be the subject in which a child does very well. This gives him an opportunity to be noticed and respected by his peers even though he may not do well in other subjects. The teacher should capitalize on this and give him every chance to do things needed for the class in art and in this way add to his self-identity and pride.

[6] Edythe Margolin, "Conservation of Self-Expression in Young Children," *Young Children*, Vol. XXIV (April, 1968), pp. 155–160.

summary

Art as an area of experience for young pupils in the age range of four-through-eight is extremely important to the development of their total personalities. The awareness of life, of shapes, of forms, and textures can heighten a child's sensitivity to his environment and contribute to greater enjoyment of his surroundings. It is also very helpful in his learning to read. The process of reading and recognizing new words is greatly dependent on the ability to recognize similarities and differences among letters. The tendency to be observant as one is in effective execution of art can carry over to reading skills.

Reading, mathematics, writing, spelling are compulsory areas of study at school. Art is not. For this reason, its openness to the option of the child suggests that the teacher must be careful in not dissuading the child from participating in art activities by being overly critical or too demanding about some kind of perfectionist idea. It is important that the child be encouraged to try all kinds of art activities. He should be exposed to many kinds of them and should be relatively unhampered by demands that constrict him in ideas. The assumption underlying this suggestion is that when the child becomes older, he may at least be open to the experience and can then begin to acquire finer techniques. If he has been discouraged, however, before he enters the intermediate grades, he may already have the notion that he simply should not be interested in art. Yet there are various types of art, such as the third-dimensional kind that do not involve painting or drawing. If his interest remains at that point, he can begin to develop a more concentrated orientation, and perhaps—even in the cognitive sense—begin to study art.

The area of art contributes to an emotional aspect of development in the child and is very important to his knowledge of some of the ways that humankind has chosen to express feelings acceptable to society. In spite of its richness as a field, many teachers of young children—in their lack of preparedness as art specialists—teach it in a gimmicky manner. They think of art experiences as simple little activities which the children can do if they follow a recipe like a set of directions—almost like assembling a cart when a manufacturer gives instructions to the consumer.

The purpose of this chapter is to sensitize teachers and others who work with young children toward the major elements that can be stressed in children's enjoyment of the field. One of the most strategic of those elements is to keep the pupils' minds open toward the field, so that they can develop in it to a greater degree, not only in later grades at school but also in their lives outside of school. Maturity in art will not occur if a child is given the impression early in life that others consider him inept in it. The teacher of young pupils has an obligation to give them many different media with which to experiment and to encourage growth in the art medium. This involves a delicate balance between knowing what to say (and what to avoid saying) about the child's products and also providing instructional elements on the terminology of art such as correct references to the quality of line, shape, form, color, balance, space, and the like.

topics for discussion

1. Design a sound program for young pupils in art education by including what you think are all the essential elements of art. You may choose one age group for which you want to design your program or you may plan one that moves developmentally from age three to eight. Concentrate on one medium of art if you wish.
2. Why is art education important for human development? What does it contribute to the personality?
3. Name at least five major goals for young children's art education that impressed you the most in terms of importance to esthetic development.
4. What was your own background in the kindergarten and primary grades as you remember it or as your parents might have described it to you?
5. How do the purposes of art education for young children differ from the purposes of mathematics, science, reading, or spelling? In what ways are they similar?
6. What kinds of comments from teachers can discourage young children to attempt different techniques in art? Why?

selected bibliography for teachers

Arnheim, Rudolph. *Art and Visual Perception.* Berkeley: University of California Press, 1969.

Barkan, Manuel, Laura Chapman, and Evan J. Kern. *Guidelines: Curriculum Development for Aesthetic Education.* St. Ann, Missouri: CEMREL, INC., 1970.

Barry, Sir Gerald. *The Arts—Man's Creative Imagination.* New York: Doubleday, 1965.

Bland, Jane Cooper. *Art of the Young Child.* New York: The Museum of Modern Art, 1957.

Brommer, Gerald F. *Wire Sculpture.* Worcester, Mass.: Davis Publications, Inc., 1968.

de Francesco, Italo L. *Art Education.* New York: Harper and Row, 1958.

Cole, Natalie. *Children's Arts from Deep Down Inside.* New York: John Day, 1966.

Conrad, George. *The Process of Art Education in the Elementary School.* Englewood Cliffs, N.J.: Prentice-Hall, Inc., 1964.

Eisner, Elliot W. *Educating Artistic Vision.* New York: Macmillan Publishing Co., Inc., 1972.

Erdt, Margaret Hamilton. *Teaching Art in the Elementary School,* revised edition. New York: Holt, Rinehart and Winston, 1962.

Feldman, Edmund Burke. *Becoming Human Through Art.* Englewood Cliffs, N.J.: Prentice-Hall, Inc., 1970.

Gaitskill, Charles D., and Al Hurwitz. *Children and Their Art.* 2nd ed. New York: Harcourt, Brace & World, 1970.

Gorbaty, Norman. *Print Making with a Spoon.* New York: Van Nostrand Reinhold Company, 1960.

Greenberg, Pearl. *Art and Ideas for Young People.* New York: Van Nostrand Reinhold Company, 1970.

Greenberg, Pearl. *Children's Experiences in Art: Drawing and Painting.* New York: Van Nostrand Reinhold Company, 1960.

Guyler, Vivan V. *Design in Nature.* Worcester, Mass.: Davis Publications, 1970.

Hastie, Reid, and Christian Schmidt. *Encounter with Art.* New York: McGraw-Hill Book Company, 1969.

Healy, Frederick. *Light and Color.* New York: John Day Co., 1962.

Henry, Edith W. "Section of Art Experiences," in *Art Education in the Elementary School.* Mary W. Packwood, ed. Washington, D.C.: National Art Education Association, 1967, pp. 46–49.

Herberholz, Donald W. and Barbara J. Herberholz. *A Child's Pursuit of Art.* Dubuque, Iowa: William C. Brown Company, 1967.

Hoover, F. Louis. *Art Activities for the Very Young.* Worcester, Mass.: Davis Publications, Inc., 1961.

Hopper, Grizella. *Puppet Making Through the Grades.* Worcester, Mass.: Davis Publications, Inc., 1966.

Horne, Joicey. *Young Artists.* Toronto: Longmans, Green, 1961.

Hughes, Toni. *Fun with Shapes in Space.* New York: E. P. Dutton and Co., 1955.

Itten, Johannes. *The Art of Color.* New York: Van Nostrand Reinhold Co., 1961.

Jameson, Kenneth. *Art and the Young Child.* New York: Viking Press, 1968.

Jefferson, Blanche. *Teaching Art to Young Children.* Boston: Allyn & Bacon, Inc., 1963.

Kaufman, Irving. *Art and Education in Contemporary Culture.* New York: Macmillan Publishing Co., Inc., 1966.

Karel, Leon. *Avenues to the Arts.* Kirksville, Missouri: Simpson Publishing Co., 1969.

Kellogg, Rhoda. *Analyzing Children's Art.* San Francisco, California: National Book Co., 1969.

Klee, Paul. *Pedagogical Sketchbook.* New York: Frederick A. Praeger, Inc., 1953.

Kramer, Edith. *Art As Therapy with Children.* New York: Schocken Books, 1972.

Lansing, Kenneth. *Art, Artists, and Art Education.* New York: McGraw-Hill Book Company, 1971.

Lansing, Kenneth. "Evaluation," in *Art Education in the Elementary School.* Mary W. Packwood, ed. Washington, D.C.: National Art Education Association, 1967, pp. 71–76.

Lark-Horowitz, B., Hilda Lewis, and Marc Luca. *Understanding Children's Art for Better Teaching*, 2nd ed. Columbus, Ohio: Charles E. Merrill Publishing Co., 1973.

Lewis, Hilda Present. Ed. *Art for the Preprimary Child.* Washington, D.C.: The National Art Education Association (Spring, 1972).

Linderman, Earl and Donald W. Heberholz. *Developing Artistic and Perceptual Awareness.* Dubuque, Iowa: William C. Brown Co., 1969.

Lord, Lois. *Collage and Construction in School.* Worcester, Mass.: Davis Publications, 1970.

Lowenfeld, Viktor, and W. Lambert Brittain. *Creative and Mental Growth*, 6th ed. New York: Macmillan Publishing Co., Inc., 1975.

Lowry, Bates. *The Visual Experience.* Englewood Cliffs, N.J.: Prentice-Hall, Inc., 1964.

Margolin, Edythe. "Conservation of Self Expression in Young Children," *Young Children*, Vol. XXIV (January, 1968), pp. 155–160.

Mattil, Edward L. *Meaning in Crafts.* Englewood Cliffs, N.J.: Prentice-Hall, Inc., 1971.

Mazer, June L. et al. *Exploring How a Think Feels.* New York: American Occupational Therapy Association, 1969.

Meilach, Dona F., and Elview Ten Hoor. *Collage and Found Art.* New York: Van Nostrand Reinhold Co., 1964.

Meyers, Hans. *Techniques in Art.* New York: Van Nostrand Reinhold Co., 1961.

Montgomery, Chandler. *Art for Teachers of Children*, 2nd ed. Columbus, Ohio: Charles E. Merrill Publishing Company, 1973.

Packwood, Mary W. Ed. *Art Education in the Elementary School.* Washington, D.C.: National Art Education Association, 1967.

Peterson, Henry and Ray Gerring. *Exploring with Paint.* New York: Van Nostrand Reinhold Co., 1964.

Randall, Arne W., and Ruth Elise Halvorsen. *Painting in the Classroom.* Worcester, Mass.: Davis Publications, 1962.

Read, Herbert. *The Art of Sculpture.* New York: Pantheon Books, 1965.

Röttger, Ernst. *Creative Clay Design.* New York: Van Nostrand Reinhold Co., 1965.

Schwartz, Fred R. *Structure and Potential in Art Education.* Waltham, Mass.: Ginn-Blaisdell, 1970.

Seitz, William. *Art of Assemblage.* New York: The Museum of Modern Art, 1962.

Smith, Ralph A. Ed. *Aesthetics and Criticism in Art Education.* Chicago: Rand McNally & Co., 1966.

Snow, Aida Cannarsa. *Growing with Children Through Art.* New York: Van Nostrand Reinhold Co., 1968.

Supensky, Thomas G. *Ceramic Art in the School Program.* Worcester, Mass.: Davis Publications, 1969.

Taylor, Joshua. *Learning to Look. A Handbook for the Visual Arts.* Chicago: The University of Chicago Press, 1957.

Torrance, Paul. *Guiding Creative Talent.* Englewood Cliffs, N.J.: Prentice-Hall, Inc., 1962.

Tritten, Gottfried. *Art Techniques for Children.* New York: Van Nostrand Reinhold Co., 1964.

Wachowiak, Frank, and Theodore Ramsay. *Emphasis: Art.* Scranton, Pennsylvania: International Textbook Co., 1965.

Weiss, Harvey. *Clay, Wood, and Wire.* New York: William R. Scott, Inc., 1956.

Weiss, Harvey. *Sticks, Spools and Feathers.* New York: William R. Scott, Inc., 1962.

books for children

Ayer, Jacqueline. *The Paper Flower Tree.* Illustrated by the Author. New York: Harcourt Brace Jovanovich, 1962.

Borton, Helen. *Do You Hear What I Hear?* New York: Abelard-Schuman, 1960.

Borton, Helen. *Do You Move As I Move?* New York: Abelard-Schuman, 1953.

Caudill, Rebecca. *A Pocketful of Cricket.* Illustrated by E. Ness. New York: Holt, Rinehart and Winston, Inc., 1964.

Fisher, Aileen. *I Wonder How, I Wonder Why.* Illustrated by Carol Barker. New York: Abelard-Schuman, 1962.

Fisher, Aileen. *Cricket in a Thicket.* Illustrated by Theodor Rojankovsky. New York: Charles Scribner's Sons, 1963.

Glubock, Shirley. *The Art of Africa.* New York: Harper & Row, 1965.

Glubock, Shirley. *The Art of the Eskimo.* New York: Harper & Row, 1964.

Goudey, Alice E. *Butterfly Time.* Illustrated by Adrienne Adams. New York: Charles Scribner's Sons, 1964.

Kaskin, Karla. *Square As a House.* New York: Harper & Row, 1960.

Kravetz, Nathan. *A Horse of Another Color.* Boston, Mass.: Little, Brown, and Co., 1962.

MacAgy, Douglas, and Elizabeth MacAgy. *Going for a Walk With a Line.* Garden City, New York: Doubleday, 1959.

Mead, Margaret. *People and Places.* Cleveland, Ohio: World Publishing Co., 1969.

Moore, Lamont. *The First Book of Painting.* New York: Franklin Watts, 1960.

Motsumo, Masako. *A Pair of Red Clogs.* Illustrated by the Author. Cleveland, Ohio: The World Publishing Co., 1960.

O'Neill, Mary. *Hailstones and Halibut Bones.* New York: Doubleday, 1961.

Paschal, Herbert. *The First Book of Color.* New York: Franklin Watts, 1960.

Rand, Ann, and Jerome Snyder. *Umbrellas, Hats, and Wheels.* New York: Harcourt Brace and World, 1961.

Reed, Carl and Joseph Orze. *Art From Scrap.* Worcester, Mass.: Davis Publishing Co., 1960.

Schleim, Miriam. *Shapes.* Eau Claire, Wisconsin: Hall, 1952.

Schleim, Miriam. *Heavy Is a Hippopotamus.* Illustrated by L. Kessler. New York: William R. Scott, 1954.

Selsam, Millicent. *Greg's Microscope.* Illustrated by Arnold Lobel. New York: Harper & Row, 1963.

Shaper, Fredum. *Round and Round and Square.* New York: Abelard-Schuman, 1965.

Showers, Paul. *The Listening Walk.* New York: Thomas Y. Crowell Co., 1961.

Sterling, Dorothy. *Caterpillars*. Illustrated by Winifred Lubell. Garden City, New York: Doubleday, 1961.

Weisgard, Leonard. *Treasures to See*. New York: Harcourt Brace and World, 1956.

Wolff, Janet and Bernard Owell. *Let's Imagine Colors*. New York: E. P. Dutton and Co., 1963.

Chapter 9

A World of Music for Young Children

If I could have anything
    in the world
A drum is what I'd choose;
I'd beat it, and beat it,
    and beat it—
Until my friends had
    rhythm shoes.

I'd bring it to school
And beat it all day
'Til my teacher said, "Stop!
Will you put that away?!"

But I would go on
With the beat of my drum
'Cause she couldn't hear me
If I whisper my hum.

Anyone wanting to see how young children are affected by music has only to watch the rapt expression on their faces when they are absorbed in playing an instrument in a rhythm band. Not only that, they enjoy singing catchy tunes and clapping their hands in accompaniment or for emphasis of the patterned beat. They enjoy dancing and singing simultaneously. The absorption in singing and moving to the rhythm captivates the spirit. The children seem to be off in a trance. They are hardly aware of one another. Yes, a world of music prevails, of beautiful sounds, of rhythm

It is obvious that the children enjoy many opportunities to sing and move to music. They fall into the swing and patterned beat of various songs.

that overtakes the logic and scientific orientation of thought. It is as might be expected. Instead of the emphasis on intellectual thought measurement, preciseness which must of necessity be acquired in certain school programs and for the development of academic vitality, music and its pleasurable effects permits and fully encourages "esthetic feelings" to be released.

One of the first and most important kinds of experiences a child has in the nursery school or kindergarten is in music. The spontaneity of song, of movement to music or the beat of the drum, is among the most impressive among children's experiences and involvement that can be seen by a teacher or adult interested in observing and understanding children's behavior.

Purposes and Goals of Music Programs for Young Children

Children are expected to become knowledgeable about the rhythmical beat in songs and musical recordings. It is almost natural for children to move to a certain beat; their own heartbeats are a first kind of rhythmic pattern for them. When they are infants, many of them move to the beat of music or nursery rhymes, suggesting they are aware of pattern beats. Their kinesthetic sense seems to guide them.

Each child can be successful to some measure in certain areas of musical awareness, even though not in all aspects. The teacher who is sensitive to moods and temperament of personality, as well as the mood of a particular time or day, can provide musical experiences that enhance musical richness in a child's life.

The manner in which musical activities and experiences are presented to children can make the difference between a child's enjoyment of the activity and the child's development of an attitude that makes him want to avoid anything musical. The teacher has to be very careful never to ridicule a child for not staying in tune. Embarrassment about a child's ability can leave an almost indelible stamp of shame for the child where his participation or ability in a certain musical area are concerned. A teacher must be highly sensitive to this fact. Many adults can think back to the way they felt when they had an experience in which a teacher caused them to believe they could not ever enjoy music. This is the person who was told to mouth the words when singing with the class, but not to make sounds.

Verbal facility is difficult for some children. They may not have had viable experiences prior to or concurrent with school that helped them develop verbal skills. Music provides a format for communication and the opportunity for children to express themselves. It permits them to feel a part of the total group.

Rhythm bands allow children to be productive. It thrills children to be able to use an instrument, even if it is something as tiny as a pair of finger cymbals. It begins to give them a feeling for sound productivity, a sense of establishing a beat or rhythm. They realize that they can imitate sounds. They have a comfortable feeling with the idea and will go on to do it with other kinds of instruments.

Music is important not only as a subject in itself for children to listen to and to appreciate in a cognitive and an esthetic sense, but also for use between activities. It is very helpful to have a song ready to sing, something that attracts the children's attention when they are waiting to leave the classroom or getting ready to move into another activity.

Young children, as well as older ones, become restless when they have to wait for the entire class before they can leave the room or begin another activity. When they are waiting for others to finish cleaning up after themselves or to complete an activity, the part of the class that is waiting can sing songs they have been taught or are in the process of learning. This occupies them so that they do not become restless and begin to annoy other children.

One of the most important kinds of skills that nursery, kindergarten, and primary grades teachers can have is that of keeping the children intelligently involved almost constantly. This does not mean that pupils do not have to learn to wait quietly at times. It does mean that prolonged waiting becomes a discomfort to them and can create problems. The ways to avoid incidents of children pushing each other, tattling, hitting, or pinching their peers when they think the teacher cannot see them is to have many activities readily available for spontaneous participation. While waiting, a group needs songs to sing, poems to say, and—for younger children—finger plays to sing or say. They need to be kept occupied and interested in what they are doing. Some of them are irritated, cold, warm, or have headaches. They feel as though they want to punch everyone around them. If they can be encouraged to sing songs while they wait, they will be less irritated by the people around them and their own internal problems—be these physical, mental, or both.

Children involved in a music program in early childhood education are expected to experience various beats, cadences, and rhythms in song and in instrumental activities. They are expected to recognize loud, soft, decreasing and increasing loudness. They are expected to recognize sounds that are high or low, and the strength or intensity of sounds. Many materials are available to assist the teacher in doing this with pupils.

"Teaching music has to do with concepts and generalizations of importance concerning rhythm, melody, harmony, texture, tone quality, dynamics, tempo and form. These represent conceptual approaches to selection and organization of content of the music curriculum.[1] Teachers of young children can easily include these concepts in any music program, because most children already have sensed them to some degree.

Children have from infancy onward sensed some kind of movement, from rocking, from being wheeled in a baby carriage or stroller, from riding in a car, from the rhythmic movement of an adult holding them and walking with or rocking them. For this reason the musical aspect and rhythmic sense of experiences in a child's life are already there by the time the child attends school. Music capitalizes on some of these natural tendencies.

Each child should be free to find his own tempo, his rate of walking, skipping, hopping, or jumping. Each child needs time to develop his steadiness in any rhythmic movement.

Children can slide, jump, sway, crawl, reach high, pretend they are bouncing a ball. The teacher who does not play the piano or does not have one available can use percussion instruments, a recording, or an autoharp. Anything that produces sound with a beat and pattern which indicates perceptible cadence to move to can influence children to walk, run, skip, hop.

Walking is done to 4/4 and 2/4 meters, smooth, easy and fluid tempos. Children do this without feeling self-conscious if the teacher sets the scene in that manner, also if they are asked to pretend they are animals. This means that they are matching mind imagery with a coordinated action.

Early childhood education must include the introduction of fundamental movements such as hopping, skipping, marching, all of which

---

[1] Robert Evans Nye and Vernice Trousdale Nye, *Music in the Elementary School*, 3rd Ed. (Englewood Cliffs, N.J.: Prentice-Hall, Inc., 1970), p. 109.

can be done to a drum beat, a piano, or tone blocks being struck by sticks in a rhythmic cadence. Clapping the hands to a child's movement can also indicate what kind of rhythmic pattern is occurring. Five-year-olds like to jump, to crouch like animals, skip, hop and run. They are sometimes carried away by their own enthusiasm. The teacher has to notice whether they are becoming overstimulated and has to plan activities that will slow them down.

Experiences, many of them at different times of the day when appropriate, should be offered—producing music in song, producing movement in the accompanied beat of a musical instrument or recording, listening to all kinds of music. People develop preferences and tastes for different types of music. This is fine. Children in the elementary school, however, should be exposed to different types so that they can ultimately develop preferences later.

If children are to learn how to produce songs, movement or dance accompanied by music, they need to have those experiences to accustom them to melodies, beats, variety of tempos, variety of intensities, high-low sounds. Part of the purpose of music instruction is to have children learn to enjoy the variety of music types that exist in repertoires throughout the world. Schools have music books and programs in the form of courses of study or guidelines to provide a curriculum. Publishing companies provide books for the teacher's and children's use. But the teacher also must be resourceful in finding materials on the music of other countries. Children are fascinated by oriental and African music that is culturally distinct from the American style. Television stations often have films that they will permit educators to use, and teachers can be aware of anything of that kind that will be instructive for children.

The children need to have listening experiences. They learn to recognize the beat of a march and they learn to identify a waltz, a polka, or a fox trot. Of course, the younger child does not typically recognize the polka or fox trot as such, even though he can move to it. Music is familiar to the child in so many ways. He merely has to learn what authorities and composers in the field have named certain rhythmic beats.

Meaning and music need to be brought together for young children. They need to learn the terminology used in the field. They learn what the word for the reference to timing is—*tempo*. The expression referring to the loud and soft aspects of musical works is called—*dynamics*. *Crescendo* means to become louder and *diminuendo* means to become softer. Children can only learn about these ideas if they experience them. They cannot learn about music without experiencing it any more than they could learn to swim by only reading about it and not getting into the water and doing it.

Music is associated with kinesthetics, with body feeling and physiological changes. The moods that music can introduce are evident in the effects that music has over introducing feeling states such as sadness, buoyancy, depression, optimism. Songs such as "Give a Little Whistle," are intended to give the singer and hearer of the song the feeling of optimism and to dispel feelings of fear. Music has an instantaneous effect on internal states. Some people are more susceptible to it than are others. If they enjoy music, they seem to attend to details of it and to concentrate on many aspects of it. It affects individuals in mood, temperament, and motivation.

Purposes and goals for the instruction of music to young children stem from a concern that pupils learn how to enjoy a lifetime of involvement in many kinds of musical forms. Seeing a movie or a cartoon, children are hearing the musical score with the visual elements of the presentation. They hear music in many different occasions from graduation ceremonies to informal functions such as a small social gathering for friends. They also hear music in a supermarket, the dentist's office, or in an elevator. Many of these musical worlds are created to calm a patient, a client, whomever the consumer of services or goods might be. Music is sometimes intended to soothe nerves and ease tensions. The more that children are encouraged to listen and to analyze what they hear, the better for their musical development. They learn about the mood intended for them by the writer of a song; they learn how tempos can create certain moods and how the rhythmic timing patterns affect the listener.

The goals of music education are planned in accordance with analysis, identification, conceptual development, just as those of the sciences and mathematical areas are. But the goals of music are intended to include esthetic development. Children can analyze musical patterns, beats, tempos, dynamics, and many other elements. They can also achieve an esthetic orientation which provides for individualistic enjoyment of specific kinds of musical experiences. In that sense, along with learning about the substantive elements of music as a subject, they are also learning about feeling states and how to participate in the unique expressive elements themselves. This is where the teacher's encouragement is essential in helping children value their own feelings toward music.

Children should be given choices for recordings they want to hear or songs they want to sing. This is why the teacher has to expose them to a wide variety of materials in music. The choices for rhythmic instruments should be offered too. The greater the variety that the children know about, the better for them. They learn to discriminate. It does not mean that it is given to them all at once. It does mean that they need to hear many different kinds of music within the appropriateness of the range of experiences the teacher thinks they should have.

Books and materials are available for guidance. With review opportunities and repetition, they will learn to recognize well the differences between various kinds of music. The teacher has already given them labels for recognition of differences—time, tempo, loud, soft, high, low, melody, rhythm, heavy, serious—they use labels for identification, for stating differences that they recognize. This knowledge provides an excellent base for more sophisticated work in music later in the child's life.

One of the purposes of music education is not only to help children learn how they may enjoy the many things and events around them but also to help them enjoy it to such a degree that they want to create some of their own. Songs need to be written just as bridges need to be built. People need new ideas, new songs, new themes for their own pleasure as well as for the pleasure of others who enjoy similar types of music.

One of the most glorious contributions to early childhood education is helping children find out what their abilities and resources are. They need to learn about the many skills lying dormant within them that they can cultivate and use to obtain more meaning, joy, and participation in life. Children can learn that no one can give them this outright. They learn that they have to reach out and work for it themselves. They must be the activators of their own life in socially acceptable and constructive ways, once they discover the many ways to participate in and contribute to it. Teachers in early childhood education can contribute crucial beginnings to this to this orientation for children.

The greater the degree to which teachers instill in young pupils an awareness of their own abilities to create, to become, to develop, to influence others in socially acceptable and desirable ways, the better the teacher has done her job. Music as well as other areas of subject matter learning at school can give a child an added spurt to his self-confidence, assuring him that he is capable, that he has skills or talent in an important area of learning. Recognition by others that he has abilities or resources that have the potential or power to bring joy to others is extremely important to the development of a mentally healthy personality.

Developmental Activities in Music for Young Children

Many sources are available for the effective music instruction of young pupils. They are attractively presented, informative and well-organized. They recommend various ways to fill the children's worlds of music, not only at school but at home as well. Children must be exposed to listening with intent to identify sounds, rhythms, intensities, pitch. Among the highest priorities in the development of musical sensitivities is listening. It is one aspect of the child's musical development to hear sounds; it is quite another to know how to identify them within some sort of conceptual framework related to a subject matter area.

One writer suggests that the child progresses in his listening through several stages, from a first impression of unfamiliarity with sound or music, to a gradual identification with it; to an ability to discriminate timbre, dynamics; to an awareness of form and style; to an ability to give personal expression through his voice to the music he hears; to the use of his body as an instrument for movement or some kind of creative activity; to relatedness in his response to another musical experience.[2]

In order to develop high levels of perceptiveness in listening, it is recommended that children are prepared for it by understanding that they have to give it their undivided attention. They should have all distracting things put away. No talking can go on while children are listening. They learn how to listen respectfully as well as intelligently in order to get as much as possible from the experience.

Musical abilities can carry over to language. Listening to the sound of words orients the child to hear the accent or stress on certain syllables, loud and soft tones (dynamics of music), tempo (the fast and slow parts in a word), and patterns that repeat themselves.[3]

Children are encouraged to stop during certain times of the day to hear sounds outside the school. They are encouraged to discuss sounds they hear on the way to school. This method of calling to their attention that different sounds are important to listen to helps them become discriminating, an important quality that needs to transfer to many other subject matter areas. They learn to detect differences in sounds, tempo, pattern, form, and intensity. The teacher has to give the children many opportunities to hear the tone bells, tone blocks, recorders, drums, percussion instruments of many kinds—e.g., rattles, tambourines, maracas, triangle, and autoharp—to be led to the discovery of different sounds.

When pupils are learning a new song, they have to listen with focused attention. Even though they are not expected to learn songs correctly the first time they hear them, they are expected to learn simple parts. The teachers often try simple songs with children, songs that are very repetitive. Children are able to listen and to join in at the appropriate time with a phrase, a clap, a jump-up (as in "Pop Goes the Weasel!"). They learn nevertheless that they have to come in at the correct time; if they are to be successful at it, they have to listen carefully—most of them do.

The "counting" songs are very effective with young children. They are learning in a pleasant and simple way how to count. They use their fingers as part of the dramatic effects of the song. It involves them fully as they listen, watch, and sing and reproduce sounds that match what they hear from the recordings, the teacher's voice, or other children whose voices are clear and on pitch.

While music has a certain amount of release and freedom from ac-

[2] Adeline McCall, *This Is Music for Kindergarten and Nursery School* (Boston: Allyn & Bacon, Inc., 1971), p. 7.

[3] McCall, op. cit., p. 8.

curacy of a logical or scientific nature, it does have elements in it that train the ear, that require accuracy in listening and matching tones. The need to be in tune, to match rhythm and timing, and intensity requires careful listening. The more astute the listening process of the child, the greater discrimination he will develop. His ability to be discriminating, to be able to differentiate between the tonal sounds of sharps and flats, and the ability to match accurately what he hears can be of service to him not only in the musical atmosphere but in other subjects too.

Listening well is an important requirement in elementary school. Teachers assume that a child hears directions. They assume that directions have been heard a first and second time. If the child does not respond as expected in following through on a task, the teacher often erroneously assumes that the child does not have the ability to do it. Actually, he may not have been certain of what he was asked to do. Children have not yet developed enough sophistication to know how to ask the teacher to repeat a certain part of her directions. They are usually too embarrassed and do not know how to select from what they missed.

When some teachers work with pupils, they show by their bodies, reaching high when they refer to high notes, and stooping low, when they refer to low notes. Young children like to do this, and the physical involvement showing the representation of tones helps them understand the placement and reference to them.

Since music and its terms are abstractions that are not familiar to some children, many experiences are needed to help them learn what those abstractions mean. The abstract terms need to be brought to the children's level of understanding by using something they can touch to gain greater emphasis. Educators are reminded of this by writers who say that, "Young children often confuse *high* with *loud* and *fast* and *low* with *soft* and *slow*." [4] They recommend games that can be played with the children in which they are asked to think of the musical scale in terms of a rug at their feet as the low tones and the airplane up high as the high tones. Thinking of the tone bells, the large bars are low and at the bottom, the shorter bars are at the top and are higher in tone.

Teachers find many songs that indicate the simple high and low techniques. She can also improvise the kinds of songs that emphasize slow, fast, loud and soft effects. The steps of an animal, a tiger that stalks or runs swiftly, the tiny mouse that skitters about, the staccato movements of a kangaroo. There are several films that can be obtained on the movement of animals. It is typically after that or a visit to a zoo that children are able to remember more vividly the stealthy or sleepy turning of a large animal's head (such as a hippopotamus), or the yawning of a lion and the way he turns his large and heavy head.

[4] Nye and Nye, op. cit., p. 270.

The larger bars of the instrument emit lower tones than the smaller bars. Most children enjoy playing the tone bells whether they do it for their own satisfaction or when they accompany the class singing a simple song.

The teacher can create songs as the children move around in their work, at their block building, their painting. "Johnny paints a pretty picture; He paints with lovely colors; His work is pretty; Johnny paints a pretty picture all the day." The teacher encourages the children to compose their own songs. "Fiddle dee-dee, Fiddle dee-dee; What a jumbo slide I can see;" or "Skip, Skip, Skidaddle; Skip, Skip, Skidaddle; skipperee, skipperro, skipperi; Joey skips along in his new shoes!" repeat beginning with "Skip, Skip, Skidaddle."

Teachers need to reach a compromise between bringing high-quality materials to young children and expecting them to produce high-quality responsiveness. Expectations for children's responses to music may be high as long as the teacher is not hypercritical of those responses. They need time to develop and improve certain techniques. Again, the emphasis has to be on accuracy in the teacher's knowledge and instruction to children with the notion that they need a great deal of exposure to different kinds of music. Educators want the children to remain open to learning about music and not to be turned away by premature expectations of perfection in their performance.

Developmental activities mean that the teacher observes the children carefully and presents them with materials that can be mastered to some extent. Developmental aspects of activities suggest that children are considered in terms of certain abilities and skills they are able to do at certain ages. The activities are planned in terms of the teacher's impressions of their feasibility for children at their physical, emotional, academic, and social levels. This gives the children a fair chance to succeed and in turn to think well of themselves. The teacher has to know her subject matter well enough to provide what is not too difficult for the children. She has to plan the activity in such a way that the child can succeed. Some call this child-proof or fail-safe to ensure the activity, success.

Bells, chimes, piano, finger cymbals are intriguing to young children. They like to manipulate and experiment with them. The teacher creates an environment (a classroom organization of experiences, activities and materials) that encourages children to participate. The major idea in any kind of subject matter experience is to have the children involved as much as possible. If they do not participate actively they are not learning as much as they could be.

They need the opportunity to make mistakes, to try, to create, to experiment with new ideas and generally to produce, to learn, to listen, and to respond to their own reactions.

Teachers need not be accomplished musicians. They only need to feel an obligation to expose children to as much music as they can appropriate to pupil-levels of interest. They can do this by guidance and through the use of instruments and recordings. They can ask resource people who are accomplished musicians to visit the classroom and tell the children about their work. Parents who know about music or someone in the community who is involved in a community music program or orchestra can be invited to give the children more information than the teacher can. Cities and towns differ in terms of what they have for citizens. Every town or city cannot have its own philharmonic orchestra, but for cities that do, every opportunity should be taken to ask players to visit the classroom and show the children what a musician's instruments are like and what is involved in becoming a professional player.

In order to encourage children to enjoy music, the teacher can check her own preparation in the following ways:

1. Do I have all the equipment and materials I need on hand?
2. Am I ready to introduce the children step-by-step to a new song or new activity in playing instruments?
3. Have I properly planned for enough materials so that children can have an opportunity for the experience? Do I need more of one kind of instrument than another? Can I fill in with more finger cymbals so that every child can have an instrument and participate in the rhythm band?

4. Have I properly planned for a variety of instruments so that the children are aware of different kinds?

5. Do I have ample variety for the children so that they are aware of many kinds of string instruments? (Pictures are acceptable here and they may be used with recordings accompanying them.)

6. Do I use opportunities to invite members of the community or the children's parents who can contribute effectively to musical knowledge of the children?

7. Do I plan for adequate motivation for each experience in order to whet the children's appetite and give them something to look for in any musical experience?

8. Do I have the room arranged in a way that will minimize distraction for the children and will permit easy participation in the experience?

9. Do I have an adequate number of counting songs, of songs that have a repetitive pattern, both of which are learned easily and retained well by children?

10. Do I have colorful pictures to show the children during the motivation period and during instruction of the song so that the children will enjoy it?

11. Do I have a pleasant attitude myself in the instruction process of the song?

12. Am I setting an example by my own attitude that learning a song is fun? Do I avoid the appearance of grimness during the instruction of a song?

13. Do I remember to use songs whenever a situation seems appropriate for it?

14. Do I permit the children some free improvisations? They suggest the movement and we match the music or beat to their idea of animals, or pacing in walking, marching, jumping, skipping?

15. Do I permit the children to take the lead whenever possible in suggesting the songs or dances that we will do?

16. Do I encourage children to look for musical notes, symbols, songs, tunes, melodies, instruments outside of school and to tell the class about it when asked?

17. Do I encourage the children to listen to fine music whenever a program offers it in a community function, or special presentation on television?

18. Do I encourage the children to notice the kind of music that is played with a mystery kind of picture as opposed to a love story or historical documentary?

19. Have I sensitized the children to the kind of music that advertisers have in commercials—the catchy tunes that are difficult to forget and subsequently makes the listener remember the product?

20. Do I change the moods in music either in a recording or piano to show the contrasts between them?
21. Do I provide enough of a variety of songs to give the children a broad choice of musical types that can build their knowledge and awareness of musical styles?
22. Do I provide for opportunities in which the children can create songs or rhythmic scores of their own?
23. Do I encourage the children in knowing that everybody can create a tune, however short it might be?
24. Do I help children in the realization that music has been a product of humankind for centuries?
25. Do I plan for teaching children that all people whatever their birthright produce specific styles of songs, i.e., indigenous folk music to any country?
26. Do I help children learn about the resources that are available in the community to hear music of different types?
27. Do I help children respect the preferences of others who enjoy certain types of music even though they may find it different from their own style, i.e., Oriental music is different from western country music or jazz?
28. Do I expose the children to classical music when possible so that they develop an "ear" or appreciation for it, i.e., "The Nutcracker Suite," "Peter and the Wolf"?

The teacher shows the children by placing her hands low, middle and high as they sing a song the direction she wants them to take. They also sing and move to:

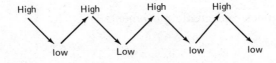

"We reach   We reach   We reach   We reach   We reach   We reach
High,   low;   High,   low;   High,   low;
                          We reach   We reach
                          High,   low."

The children move around the room to this:

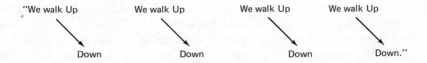

And they can move to this:

"A snake slides low,   A snake slides low,

         A giraffe walks tall;   A giraffe walks tall."

"I run up the hill, Mary runs down.   I run up the hill, Arthur runs down."
      *hi*ll, Ma-   *hi*ll, Ar-
    the   *ry*   *the*   *thur*
  up   *runs*   *up*   *runs*
 run   *down.*   *run*   *down.*
I   *I*

Various games can be played with the direction of the music, the tone bells, a tone block, or drum. Intensities of music, loud, soft, slow, fast give the clues to what the children are expected to do. They listen carefully and enjoy following the suggestions created by the sounds and beats of instruments. For heavy stealthy movements, the children can pretend they are animals such as:

Tiger—and several of them, Mother, Father and Babies

Bear—and two of them playing with each other

Lion—roaring and trying to get away from each other

Heavy footed:

Hippopotamus, rhinoceros, elephant—all of them are walking stealthily through their environment trying to find food

For lighter quick and gentle movements:

Sparrow

Butterflies

Bee

Moth

Children are encouraged to use the high, middle, and low space levels around them to help give them variety and thought in what they are doing or ways they are moving to music.

Young children learn to sing, learn about rhythm in music, song, and recordings they hear. The beat of the music is dramatized through things they have experienced and know. Dramatizing a visit to the circus and eating the popcorn, cotton candy as it sticks to their lips and cheeks, watching the clown, they match their movements to the music and improvise actions to fit the general mood of the songs or music they hear. They pretend they are getting dressed in the morning before they go to school; they may exaggerate their movements if the music is played to match their action. They may be sleepy, tired, slow. They may be excited about getting to school because of a special event that is to take place.

The pleasure that children obtain from the musical experience is more important (with a few exceptions), than any kind of accuracy they demonstrate. Most are forms, by their very nature, suggest that what the individual experienced during the process of creation is more important than the product. The more experiences the teacher provides for the children in relation to music—either singing or listening to it and moving to it—the more children will be able to find it "natural" as an activity. The child will feel less inhibited if he participates in it often.

Teaching a New Song to Young Children

MOTIVATION: The teacher discusses ideas related to the song. If it is about the ocean she talks about the sea, the beach, the sand, the shells, the smell of the ocean. She shows pictures of all of these things.

PROCESS: She asks them to listen to what the song says. She sings the entire song and asks them to tell her what it said.

Then she asks them to listen only to the first part, two lines so that they can repeat it. They do. She does this again. Then she sings the second part of the song. She asks them to listen so that they can repeat it. She sings the second part again. They follow. She repeats this. They follow her. Then she asks them to listen as she sings the first part. They repeat. She sings the second part. They sing it with her. Then she sings the entire song as they listen. Then they sing it with her.

Some of the major guidelines for early childhood education in science, in music, and in art are to explore, to manipulate, to become familiar with, to urge the children to become involved in many kinds of experiences. This period of life is not only impressionable: it is exploratory, and an introduction to skills and exciting activities that the child may engage in with greater depth later in school and in life outside of the classroom. The introduction and exposure to all these things should be open, embracing, and inviting as a participatory experience. Later perfection and refinement of techniques is built on first attempts at earlier stages. Understanding at earlier levels invites greater complexity as a challenge to the child.

The teacher has respect for individual differences in learning and in music as she does in other subject matter areas. She encourages differences of opinion, in preference to certain pieces of music remaining a constant choice. She tries to help the children learn that people like different tunes and instruments. It is important that they be helped to realize that it is all right to like different songs and recordings. Children should be encouraged rather than discouraged, and not made to feel uncomfortable if they do something that is different from group consensus.

If the teacher plans to help young children in rhythmic activities, involving them in music, in hearing recordings, in singing, in encouraging them to sing simple tunes for many things that they do during the classroom day, she is helping them to use music in their daily lives. Children are rhythmic; they are interested in music. The only time they are not is when they are made to feel that they must perform to perfection. Any time that they are disciplined in relation to it or are ridiculed because of their performance, they will develop uncomfortable feelings about it and will not want to participate in such activities. They will try to avoid them in any way they can. The teacher must be sensitive to their feelings.

Evaluation must be done in a very perceptive and empathic manner. The child can be helped in learning to improve in a certain area, but he must not be made to feel that he is inferior as an individual in any way. Some people go through life maimed as musical respondents. They become dulled or numbed to criticism in that area and avoid situations that require singing—understandably so.

Evaluation of Children's Progress in Musical Areas

Evaluation of children's progress in music is important in that it gives the teacher information on what the next steps in instruction should be. In the same objective vein, the teacher has to be aware that children cannot be dispassionate about themselves. For that reason, evaluation has to be conducted in a considerate manner. The data received in any kind of testing have to be used wisely.

The child's efforts must be valued. They must be safeguarded because of young children's vulnerability. Since they are developing patterns of responses to school, the teacher wants to ensure the overall orientation of participation on the part of the child.

Children may evaluate themselves by responding to the teacher's request to sing certain songs, to match tones, to clap their hands in time with a certain beat. They can decide with the teacher whether they are able to follow directions well and to do what is asked of them. They may decide where they need practice. Of course, the teacher is guiding them through all this toward areas in which she thinks they need help.

Tapes can be made of the children's performance. They can hear themselves in playback and indicate what they think of their voices. They may compose songs and tape them. After hearing them, the teacher can help them evaluate the songs, the beat, appropriate to the words, the intensity of loudness and softness, the pleasantness of the tune.

In the hearing of many songs, tunes, recordings, and in asking the children to indicate by a show of hands, by clapping in time to the music, or by hopping to the time of the recording, the teacher can observe whether a child hears the beat of the song or recording. The teacher should record on a card what the child is able to sing, where he may have some difficulty, and outstanding characteristics in his presentation. A check sheet can be made for this so that the teacher does not have to write out the song again and again on each card.

It is informative to have an attitude scale in which the children's preferences for certain tunes or types of music can be shown. Whether they go to the musical instruments, play the bells when they have free time, or after they have finished assigned work, whether they go to the recordings and play the records containing tunes and stories provides some information on the child's preferences. The teacher, noting similar choices, will try to introduce him to others. The teacher notes the child's behavior—to which activity does he go most often and how long does he stay (after he has completed his work). Where does he do the most creative job? Where does he go to participate most often? What does he mention to the teacher as having enjoyed the most at school, either in his assigned work or free choice? In which does he do his best work?

The teacher can devise an attitude inventory of creative work. Does the child feel free to plan new ideas? Does the child enjoy getting off by himself and become involved with a different activity or set of materials and initiate it for himself? Does he enjoy proceeding with something new? Does he enjoy telling others what he has done?

The teacher can help the child in planning next steps in what he is doing. Anything related to musical sequencing, singing simple to difficult tunes, remembering more than only a few lines of a song, and learning more difficult songs and more difficult words and rhythmic patterns. Children enjoy singing a two-part song and can do this when they have the concentration to retain their own part without being distracted by the part others are singing.

In evaluating the child, at least four major ideas should be remembered:

(1) The means implemented to evaluate the child
(2) How it is done (in a group or individualistically)
(3) How is the information on the test interpreted to the children (in conference or in writing)
(4) How are the records of the testing kept? On what forms? Where? Who keeps them? Who is responsible for keeping them up-to-date?

Various charts that indicate the skills in music that children should be learning at school can be used as checklists to help the teacher determine the children's progress. See "A Scope and Sequence Chart of Conceptual Learnings Related to the Elements of Music." [5]

Most music programs have specific sequences in concept development. One source has the songs which are recommended in terms of the various skills a child can develop when they learn those songs. The reference chart is called a "Music Reading Readiness Program." [6]

It is important after the teacher has data on the evaluation of a child to know how to report it. Some school systems have provided for conferences with parents rather than writing letter grades to assess the child's performance, especially for younger children. Whatever the way chosen to report to parents, the teacher has to consider, "How would I feel if I were that parent and my child were being dissected academically, emotionally, and socially? How would I like the information presented to me?"

University students discussing the process of evaluation have indicated that when they had parent-teacher conferences and they were the parents listening to the teacher, they were humiliated by the teacher's manner of handling the conference. Some said that after the teacher finished telling them how inept and incompetent their child was, they went home feeling exhausted, very depressed, and simply cried. They felt that they were total failures as parents. This is not what the parent conference is intended to convey. It is planned to help parents know their children's strengths, interests, and where a child may need help with books, visits to the library or museum—whatever needed to stimulate further growth. The teacher should mention the child's strong points in either personality or academic, social, and physical abilities.

Teachers can recommend to parents the kind of musical variety that children can experience at home or different musical opportunities available in the community. Parents appreciate honest recommendations from the teacher that are given with an earnest desire to help the child. This is obvious when the teacher is sincere.

summary

Music is one of the most important areas of development for young children at school. It contributes not only to listening skills, and the development of concentration but also to the pleasure of self-expression. Since young children have so much to learn about the role of being a

---

[5] Nye and Nye, op. cit. (See inside back cover of the book.)
[6] William R. Sur, Adeline McCall, William R. Fisher, and Mary R. Talbert, *This is Music for Today.* (Boston: Allyn & Bacon, Inc., 1971), pp. 186–187.

pupil, music affords the opportunity to be part of a group while expressing one's self. It gives children many experiences that allow individualistic expression, in which one is allowed to be one's self and not have to measure up to a perfectionist scale.

Since many school subjects necessary for the functioning of an intelligent member of society require diligence, exactness, and precision (such as that of the sciences), music as one area of esthetics gives children a different kind of opportunity to attain a sense of identity at school. They have a greater sense of freedom in it, because they already have experienced rhythms, music, and song before attending school; many children have experienced music in some form, if only from rattles and music boxes as well as radios and television, since infancy.

There are many materials available to teachers on musical units, recordings, books, songbooks, professional background, orchestrations, and community functions related to musical performances. The teacher has only to ask her school or nearby educational commercial sources. Many early childhood organizations have journals that supply endless sources on music for young children.

Teachers can be of great assistance in helping pupils enjoy music. Their own attitudes, a love for it, or at least a desire to expose the children to as many types of songs and instrumentations as possible in relation to the children's age levels for appreciation will do a great deal to help pupils develop a repertoire.

Evaluation of children in their performance of musical experiences has to be done with empathy and sensitivity. This can create positive or negative orientations toward music, not only in the child's present work but in the future.

topics for discussion

1. Recall your own experiences in music at school and indicate what you remember as your best and your worst memories related to skills in music.
2. Plan a curriculum for music of young children in nursery, kindergarten, and first grade. What type of experiences will you plan for them? Which skills will you consider in sequential fashion, going from simple to complex in singing, musical instruments, whatever you wish?
3. How do programs in esthetics differ from the kind requiring skills development in mathematics, reading, science, spelling, handwriting?
4. Why is an effective music curriculum essential to young children's development at school?
5. Visit an outstanding music program in an early childhood program at a school that is well-known in your area for excellence in performance. If you cannot find one, visit two schools and discuss with the teacher the contents of their music program.
6. Find five oustanding sources in music or songbooks that can help you in

planning an ideal program for young children in nursery, kindergarten, and primary grades.

selected bibliography for teachers

Aronoff, Frances Webber. *Music and Young Children.* New York: Holt, Rinehart and Winston, Inc., 1969.

Doll, Edna, and Mary J. Nelson. *Rhythms Today.* Morristown, N.J.: Silver Burdett Co., 1965.

Gary, Charles L. Ed. *The Study of Music in the Elementary School: A Conceptual Approach.* Music Educators National Conference, Washington, D.C.

Humphreys, Louise, and Jerrold Ross. *Interpreting Music Through Movement.* Englewood Cliffs, N.J.: Prentice-Hall, Inc., 1964.

Kraus, Richard. *A Pocket Guide of Folk and Square Dances and Singing Games for the Elementary School.* Englewood Cliffs, N.J.: Prentice-Hall, Inc., 1966.

Landeck, Beatrice. *Children and Music.* New York: William Sloane Associates, 1952.

Landeck, Beatrice. *Songs to Grow On.* New York: William Morrow Co., 1950.

Landeck, Beatrice. *More Songs to Grow On.* New York: William Morrow Co., 1954.

Mace, Kathrine. *Let's Dance a Story.* New York: Abelard-Schuman, 1955.

McCall, Adeline. *This is Music for Today. Kindergarten and Nursery School.* Boston: Allyn & Bacon, Inc., 1971.

Nye, Robert Evans and Vernice Trousdale Nye. *Music in the Elementary School.* Englewood Cliffs, N.J.: Prentice-Hall, Inc. 1970.

Rosenberg, Martha. "Making Music Pictures with Rhythm Instruments," *Journal of Nursery Education,* Vol. 17 (1973).

Sheehy, Emma D. *Children Discover Music and Dance.* New York: Teachers College Press, 1968.

Smith, Robert B. *Music in the Child's Education.* New York: Ronald Press, 1970.

Sur, William R., Adeline McCall, William R. Fisher, and Mary R. Tolbert. *This is Music for Today. 1.* Boston: Allyn & Bacon, Inc., 1971.

Swanson, Bessie R. *Music in the Education of Children.* 3rd Ed. Belmont, Calif.: Wadsworth Publishing Company, 1969.

Todd, Vivian E., and Helen Heffernan. *The Years Before School.* New York: Macmillan Publishing Co., Inc., 1970.

Vernazza, Marcelle. "What Are We Doing About Music in Special Education?" *Music Educators Journal* (April 1967), pp. 55–58.

Wilkin, Esther. *Baby Listens.* New York: The Golden Press, 1960.

books for children

Bertail, Inez. Ed. *Complete Nursery Song Book.* Illustrated by Walt Kelly. New York: Lothrop, Lee & Shepard, 1954.

Charlip, Remy, and Burton Supree. *Mother, Mother, I Feel Sick Send for the Doctor Quick Quick Quick.* Parent's Magazine, 1966.

Evans, Patricia Healy. *Rimbles; a Book of Children's Classic Games, Rhymes, Songs and Savings.* New York: Doubleday, 1961.

Hector Protector and As I Went Over the Water. Interpreted by pictures, Maurice Sendak. New York: Harper and Row, 1966.

Kapp, Paul. *Cock-a-Doodle Do! Cock-a-Doodle Dandy! A New Song Book for the Newest Singers.* Illustrated by Anita Lobel. New York: Harper and Row, 1966.

Langstaff, Joh. *Frog-Went a-Courtin'.* Illustrated by Feodor Rojankovsky. New York: Harcourt, Brace, 1955.

Montgomerie, Norah. Compiler. *This Little Pig Went to Market: Play Rhymes.* Illustrated by Margery Gill. New York: Franklin Watts, 1967.

Taylor, Margaret. Compiler. *Did You Feed My Cow? Rhymes and Games from City Streets and Country Lanes.* Illustrated by Paul Galdone. New York: Thomas Y. Crowell Co., Inc., 1956.

Chapter
10

Toward the Development of Joie de Vivre (Joy of Life) in Young Children: Body Awareness, Self-Image, and Health Education

The joy of life
    Although labeled a gift
Is not given to us, you see,
    It's a prize we work toward—
And strive for and love for
    To be part of its energy.

When we help children
    In the excitement of life
We help ourselves too
    In re-creating that strife
Of eager participation,
    The most worthwhile, in life.

Movement is synonomous with any young child. The healthier the child, the more active he is and the higher his energy levels are. With all the movement and energy noted in a child's behavior it is small wonder that the adult is sometimes overawed by the neverending activity a child wants to enjoy.

In recent years, more writing has been done on the perceptual motor development of young children. Its importance in relation to the way a child learns or will want to learn, and its relevance to cognitive learning and in reading, has been recognized. Perceptual motor development refers to the coordination of cognitive efforts combined with physical movement of the body. A child's body image—that is, its relationship in terms of space, the ability to move with facility, grace, and ease—affects his self-confidence in many ways. It affects his abilities in games, in social amenities, and generally in the way he thinks others see him. The child who is confident in his ability to manage himself and to help others in various ways—such as lifting objects easily, carrying things without dropping them, or opening cumbersome boxes without tearing the objects inside—is viewed as both dependable and well-coordinated.

The opportunities children have for using their bodies in various movements—crawling, sliding, jumping, hopping, skipping and dancing—involve opportunities to practice self-control and body coordination. Not only does success in those movements help them in a physical sense, but in a social and psychological sense as well. The child with apparent poise has an excellent start in his interpersonal relationships.

Children who are not part of teams, games, and other activities involving action and adequate physical coordination, miss out on many friendships that they might otherwise have if they were competent in this area. Participation in sports as an area of skills is highly respected in America and other countries throughout the world. Through this participation in sports, children gain access to many kinds of opportunities such as traveling to schools and even countries beyond their own, and wide recognition of their accomplishments through news and television media.

Very young children are able to participate when they have fine motor coordination in many kinds of activities, all of which are important to their development physically, socially, emotionally, and psychologically. Teachers who can help children in this area are doing them a great service. Purposes of participation in motor coordination activities are not purely for fun. Competence in it contributes to enjoyment of school, of friends, of a healthier self-concept plus a facilitation of skills in certain academic areas.

Purposes and Goals in Various Programs Involving Movement, Rhythms, Perceptual Motor Development, and Health Education

One writer indicates the children should have the opportunity to have rhythmic experiences which permit them "to feel free and self-directed and also give a means for *outward expression of inner feelings.*"[1] This ability to learn how to express one's self is difficult in the sense that it has to have meaning for the child and the teacher in terms of a framework of some kind. For example, it is not enough for the child to move; it has to

[1] Carol E. Clark, *Rhythmic Activities for the Classroom* (Dansville, N.Y.: The Instructor Publications, Inc., 1969), pp. 6–7. Italics are Clark's.

have a context and an element of communication underlying the action. If a child moves about in a helter-skelter fashion when the class has been given an assignment in which they are asked what they would like to be, the child's movement has to reflect meaning in terms of the assignment. He has taken an idea and acted upon it. He has made something internal become external.

Children are extremely active typically if they are healthy. They enjoy moving around. They are learning in school that many things which have been familiar are also relevant to certain concepts taught at school. This is part of the richness of life, communicating with others, communicating in various ways, talking, moving, dancing, singing, and later on as children mature, writing.

Movement and related skills involve not only skipping, hopping, walking, running, twisting, bending, stretching, pulling, leaping, and turning but also involve executing these movements in various levels of space. Children may use lower levels of space—the floor; they may use middle levels of space—from about the knee to the shoulders, and from the head to above their heads. They may use more of their movement activities at the lower levels than above their heads unless this is suggested to them as a way to use space.

Movement may be placid, slow, stealthy. It may have force behind it— propelling, pushing, quick stacatto movement. Children can experience the pleasure of this by giving them problem examples such as, "How would we show we are quietly moving along like an alligator in the sun in a muddy river bank?" The children imitate an alligator's movement by remembering what an alligator looks like from either a visit to the zoo, or by having seen it on television, or having seen one in its natural habitat, a riverbank in Florida.

A purpose of movement programs for young children is to help them become aware of the many things their bodies can do. Perceptual motor development involves a coordination of mind and body, of muscle control, both forceful and constrained. The feeling of accord in the mind-body action is very satisfying to the child. It is one of the first things he learns and tries to refine in his development. It contributes to his self-satisfaction relative to his competence.

The child is learning how many kinds of abilities he has. Movement and management of his body begin to build in the child an awareness of a reservoir of skills relative to action. He may consider that he is also able to swim, to ride a bike, to dance, to run fast, to hop for an extended distance. The awareness of skills in the child who begins to master his own body movement can do much to help him in wanting to try many other activities and be less fearful in doing so.

Children should be able to move to music in a way that suggests what the mood of the music is. When teachers play recordings of heavy bass music, a child who understands the musical mood would not skip around with the lightness of a butterfly. The child who matches the sounds of music to his own body coordination learns a kind of physiological match to the musical sounds.

Children should gain from movement activities a stimulated sense for various kinds of movement. After hearing the teacher's suggestions, they can be creative about their own ideas for the interpretation of movement. They can develop further awareness of the kinds of movement that are seen in the people around them. They can learn to note various kinds of significant aspects of movement seen in the common daily occurrences of people and things around them. They note the movement of a leaf picked up by a sudden gust of wind; they note the ripple of water in the deep puddle on the ground after a rainstorm. Their sensitivity to shapes in relation to movement, the heaviness or lightness of a mass object in the wind or on the sidewalk gives them a sensitivity to air, its effects on objects and people, and life itself—the way it interacts with space, human beings, and their capacity to resist winds, air, rain, and other elements of the atmosphere.

The purposes and goals of any movement program for young children vary to some extent. For the most part, however, they indicate that children should receive pleasure and satisfaction from participating in any such program. They should learn how to manage themselves in body movements of many kinds. They should be able to move with ease, walk, hop, jump; they should be able to move their arms with abandon. They should be able to twist the trunks of their bodies, bend, jump, lift, throw. These activities are done with music, with beats of a drum, clap of hands, or without any sounds to note the beat in body movement.

Body movement is a broad title to cover dance, rhythms, movement to music, exercises to increase perceptual motor development. It often refers to children's activities in dramatic play. Children have scarves, props, furs, hats, cummerbunds, articles of clothing that are given to them and which give them an idea as to how they want to transform themselves in a role that is prompted by the materials used. Children like to dance to music that they select by placing a recording on the phonograph. Then they wait in readiness to move to its rhythm. They wave a scarf, a streamer or two, or they don a cowboy hat which accompanies the mood as they gallop around the room slapping their sides as they go.

Health Education

Body movement is facilitated by good health—physical and mental. The individual who is in good physical condition has the vitality to produce an energetic performance with ideas he wants to portray.

Self-perception is greatly affected by one's condition; agility, ease, and grace influence a child's self-image. Physical education for young children is important in its contribution to their health and personality. A program that includes a concern for the child's diet and sleeping habits so that he knows what is best can provide an excellent foundation for him.

Children need to learn that healthful living does not simply happen. It needs to be planned and nurtured by the individual himself. It requires self-discipline and understanding. When the child realizes the importance of habit where certain bodily functions are concerned, it becomes easier for him to sustain those requisite habits. He ensures a better life for himself in that understanding and willingness to practice health care.

Effective programs in health education teach the child to avoid toxic foods and liquids, extremes in food intake, and excesses in exercise and sun exposure. Curiosity about drugs, smoking, and other palliatives intended to slow the individual down, to calm him, or to shut out hurts and anxieties perceived by the individual as existing in an external world, can do much harm to the body at an early age. Children can learn in constructive ways how important their knowledge of protecting their health can be. They learn that abuse of the body at one time of life can often leave a devastating mark on it for a long time to come.

Cleanliness which prevents infection, and enjoyment of a clean body is a valuable asset to develop. Pride about one's body and manner of dress can contribute to the enjoyment of others when the individual is in groups. These ideas are discussed with pupils, not in the sense of grim moralization but in terms of the pleasure and satisfaction that can be gained from confidence in one's health and appearance.

For young children four years old, different activities are planned to encourage them in sound health education. They are not expected to participate in competitive games. This does not help them in their emotional and social development. Competitive activities are introduced later in team-type games. They enjoy individualistic play; dances or games should not be planned for them that force them into restraining routines. They cannot accept rules very well either. Young pupils should be encouraged to participate in as many activities as possible—not to be the greatest or best in those experiences, but to become familiar with them. Refinement in doing them well comes later.

Goals in physical education which are part of health education programs planned for young children must be considered with the appropriateness of age levels in mind. "Knowledge and understanding of the general pattern or sequence of motor, emotional, social and intellectual growth are necessary in designing programs in order that children may have joy in the experience of participation in physical education activities." [2] Competition should not be stressed in young children's games.

[2] Association for Childhood Education International, *Physical Education for Children's Healthful Living.* Bulletin No. 23 A. (Washington, D.C., 1968), p. 21.

Their goals should be pleasure in moving, in running, skipping, hopping, and in obtaining an exhilarating sense of abandon in planned movement.

Physical education program goals include the importance of setting realistic objectives for the child so that he does not feel that he is expected to accomplish things that are too difficult for him. They should not be placed before him. This leads to frustration that is difficult to counteract. If the child is to learn about his own abilities, resources and skills, the teacher has to use skillful observation to understand what the child can do. If the child is given opportunities to succeed in certain skills, he can feel better about himself and be happier because of it. "Acceptance of one's own strengths and limitations is the basis for the acceptance of other people." [3] This suggests that the teacher be cautious in not overextending the child's abilities or challenges. Early childhood years are the most important ones in which these ideas are tested for the children themselves.

While the test of one's abilities is crucial at any age, the judge of what is given to the children and of which activities they should experience is always an important decision. It relates to whether a child will see himself as a successful individual or not. The child who learns early in life that he can make his arms and legs do as he desires (and then some) has a dependable start toward conquering other self-challenges. His orientation develops as one which tells him that he has the skills and can meet various situations with great success.

Children's bodies develop with frequent and more varied use of their muscles. As distinguished from machines that wear out when their parts have been used intensively and for a long time, the human body continues to become stronger. "The human body develops and grows through use and this is known as the physiological law of use. The body has its own built-in system of growth, repair and even spare parts." [4] The idea that muscles have to be used because otherwise they atrophy has been emphasized in many fields—e.g., physiology, education, medicine, physical education.

As the body is used, so its demand for use is increased. Each pupil needs many opportunities to do this. Not to give him these opportunities is to deny the pupil some degree of awareness of his body's capabilities. Unless the body is called upon to stretch itself in terms of its efforts toward increasing skills in its functions and abilities, it will be less able to respond to further challenge when it arises.

Several writers [5] suggest that the human being has built into its structure the potential for doing various things and performing many

---

[3] Ibid., p. 21.

[4] Caroline B. Sinclair, *Movement of the Child. Ages Two to Six.* (Columbus, Ohio: Charles E. Merrill Publishing Company, 1973), p. 3.

[5] Ibid., p. 32. Also see Elizabeth B. Gardner, "Proprioceptive Reflexes," *Quest,* Monograph VII (May, 1969). p. 1.

different activities. The propioceptors in the individual's neural structure are there at birth; they are genetically endowed. This is probably why many educators in the early 1900's thought that the child "unfolds"—that his powers to unfold were there at birth and just needed time to mature. Contemporary writers maintain that the individual does not merely "unfold" his powers; he must be stimulated to utilize his abilities. He must be taught certain skills and the ways to refine them. The early childhood period of life is stressed as being an optimal time to acquire a fine beginning in this path of the body's development.

Children's attempts to define their own movement facility and skills in the process of their development must have a response of social approval. They receive satisfaction themselves, it is true, when they find they can ride a tricycle, throw a ball, spin around without falling down, move with freedom and abandon as they leap into the air. Their desire to continue in developing bodily skills in relation to the use of space and their own muscles is spurred by adult praise and of course when they receive peer approval later in the group situations they encounter in the second and third grades.

Children's attempts to improve in these areas are a result of having opportunities to discover the process. The movement itself through the propioceptors and sensory nerve fibers records direction, position, tension, and force.[6] The child has this feedback to let him know how he is managing himself. But the child needs the approval of adults, too, when he has finally succeeded in something that he found very difficult to do. Everyone can think of the instance of a child seeking this praise while asking the adult to watch him skip after he has persisted in the task for many days.

Children enjoy activities involving a test of themselves in balancing on a balance board or a narrow ledge (such as a sidewalk partition). Putting one foot in front of the other, arms outstretched at shoulder level, tottering cautiously is fun to do if the child senses that it is a safe distance from the ground. This kind of balancing experience is fine for the child as long as he chooses to do it for himself and is not forced into it. Any exercise that appears too difficult to the child should not be forced on him. It creates fear rather than pleasure, satisfaction, and security in the test of his own ability.

Movement and body expression of any kind are an aspect of energy level. Children who are not in good health are not enthusiastic about movement experiences. They may be listless and uninspired by any ideas related to buoyant romping around, lifting, throwing, bouncing and just generally having fun running, skipping, hopping, or jumping energetically in space. Good health is closely related to children's work at school. A

---

[6] Sinclair, op. cit., p. 33.

teacher can recognize slow moving in the child who reflects inadequate rest, an inadequate diet, or emotional disturbances, however mild they may be. For this reason, health education is an important part of the school program as mentioned earlier in this chapter.

Health is a school subject that can be enjoyed. The teacher of young pupils can be an important element in its beginnings for them. It does not need to be administered in so moralistically a manner that the children dislike it. Sometimes, it is difficult to like something that is continually stressed as "being good for you." People seem to turn away from things that are emphasized as essential. If children could be told in ways that helped them pleasantly enjoy the worthwhileness of learning sensible health habits, they might realize the essential nature of it. They could learn about the many ways that it "pays off" or benefits them in happy good times, energy to go places and do many kinds of things, to be strong in games, and so on.

Health education is sometimes included in programs of physical education. The same people who are in charge of physical education plan materials for purposes of pupil-learning about health. Care of the body, nutrition, importance of sleep and exercise for a healthy body, are planned as part of the curriculum.

One writer suggests that at least 18 specific objectives are needed in a school health program.[7] These include not only the detection of children's health problems but also an acquisition of functional knowledge of personal and community health. The list is comprehensive and seems ambitious in terms of one of its objectives. It suggests that the school should be expected to correct children's defects. This may be more than a school can afford to do. The school may recommend parents take their child for examination to certain other sources. Funds for each case would not always be available. School health is a kind of partnership with parents, as are some of the other areas responsible for the child's well-being at school.

Teachers can help young children develop wholesome attitudes toward their bodies and the fact that good health is related to *joie de vivre*. It is difficult to derive satisfaction from life if one's energy levels are low. Energy is needed to want to compete, to want to achieve, to want to be successful in tasks. Particularly in an urban society where competition is stressed and where many opportunities are available for those who want to put some effort into succeeding in what they choose to do, it is important to have vitality.

While the school does not take the place of services provided for the youngsters by their parents and private physicians, it does have a commitment to observing problems the child may be developing. Teachers

[7] C. L. Anderson, *School Health Practice*, 5th ed. (Saint Louis: The C. V. Mosby Company, 1972), pp. 14–15.

who work with children day in and day out recognize a child having difficulty that others do not. Cases have been known in which children having problems in faulty vision and needing corrections in medical health care were unnoticed or ignored by most adults with whom they came in contact. This delayed help for them and made their problems more difficult to counteract.

The child who is chronically sad, listless, or often absent from school is the one who the teacher might recommend for a checkup by the school nurse or doctor. Many behavior problems observed by the teacher stem from physical problems. While children in low-income areas are known to be hungry because of inadequate meals, the children may suffer from physical deficiencies related to teeth, vision, hearing, and the like which may require minor or major corrections.

Mental states of the individual are crucial to the way he approaches life. He may see it as manageable and view the world as a place that is stimulating, exciting, and socially satisfying in its possibilities for worthwhile contributions. What he chooses to do, he is able to do. For the things he likes to do, he often receives attention, recognition, and social approval because he does them well. Life in general seems to give him applause after he has given of himself with some reasonable effort and persistence.

The child who sees life as an affirming experience, affirming what he is and what he can do, is the one who has had pleasant experiences. These experiences have reflected a mirror image back to him of a worthy and joyous individual. Mental health, vigor, vitality, body condition, and mind, emotional levels of highs and lows, are not only related to good health and individual habits to maintain it, but also relate to euphoric states of mind that tell the individual he *can* do, he *can* succeed in almost anything he decides to pursue. He may begin to develop realistic and inspiring levels of achievement. Fantasy achievement is not given much time in daydreaming as are the ways to achieve in reality, when the individual knows he can enjoy real success.

Health programs—whether school-wide or developed by the teacher—depend on the insight of the teacher, awareness of materials that are available, and knowing how to intersperse them with other things in the school day. This is known as incidental or informal teaching. Bringing in ideas that are related to a major concept permits the children to learn an important view in a nonformalistic manner.

A school environment that encourages vitality, exuberance, outgoingness, willingness to enjoy each other as individuals, is one of the most effective "devices" for developing students who will want to achieve. It is not this alone that will encourage accomplishment. It is this that can induce it. A child's ability in any stage of development can be encouraged to progress whether progress for him means moving slightly or leaping ahead because of an inherent ability or set of talents.

Even though school health is mentioned in this chapter, it is not intended to suggest that body movement is viewed mainly as a health or physical education component. Movement for young children is considered a program in itself. It has a broad segment emphasizing the development of esthetics. Those who want more information on the topic should consult such books. School health must be considered as part of the curriculum for young children, however; it is viewed as central to their development of habits in self-help.

A child's body image develops as he participates in experiences which give him an opportunity to find out about himself, how he moves, how he feels when he creates ideas and feelings. His facility in movement experiences greatly affects his body image. The self-concept is affected as well by whether he feels clumsy and awkward, or facile and agile, at ease when he moves either in esthetic experiences or in dance forms.

Related to the self-concept and development of body image is mental health and a sense of humor. It is difficult for someone to be light-hearted if he feels that he is not getting a "fair deal" from life and people around him. Mental health permits a sense of humor that allows one to laugh at himself—not at the distress of others but at the ridiculous things that arise in life affecting one's own goals. The person who tries too hard to please, the one who tries to be outstanding in something that is too difficult for him, the one who becomes furious at a defeat of some kind, has to be able to counteract these feelings with the ability to look at himself through a sense of humor. It is the saving grace. It allows people to get through life, particularly those who are very conscientious and who want desperately to achieve. The desire to achieve can remain, but the defeats have to be tempered with a sense of balance in order to go on, try again, and retain a sense of humor throughout it all.

Young children should be encouraged to laugh at situations that do not hurt other people's feelings. The teacher can encourage this by telling the children of times that she did something foolish and that everyone does this occasionally. She shows children that she can laugh at herself, that she does not think she is perfect. A teacher can set excellent examples for personality development that can help the child become well-balanced rather than grim, with the need to be perfect and reassured of it at all times. "To achieve the highest expressions of humor in terms of mental health, the child should learn to laugh at himself. A person who can look at himself objectively as that has the antidote for his inherent egocentricity. It is an attribute of children with the highest levels of mental health." [8]

Programs for school health include many aspects of the child's development. Since it is well-known that emotional development is affected by

[8] Ibid., p. 26.

health (and indeed vice versa), the teacher includes whenever possible the opportunities for children to test themselves, to enjoy the freedom, the practice of being involved in body movement of leaps, jumps, runs, skips, and the kind of controlled muscular movements involved in pretending that the child is a tree shaking off its leaves, settling softly to the ground. Airplanes, ships in the ocean in a storm, sailboats gliding easily along in a gentle wind, give excellent imagery opportunities for combining a motor experience and an esthetic one.

As body control builds, as the body image develops in a positive sense, as the child acquires a self-image of mastery over various experiences presented to him, he can transmit these feelings about himself to others. This is the best way for a reciprocal impression of self-confidence to build. As he lets others know by his own demeanor and general aura of feelings, "Hey, I can do many things—with ease," so it is that the mirrored image of those around him will reflect confirmation. He is accorded respect and approval. He in turn can regard others in the same way. It builds an excellent foundation for mental health and adequacy of self. Jealousy, tattling, aggression of a hostile nonconstructive nature, is held to very low levels in a child that receives so many satisfying experiences. This kind of child often becomes a model for other children who want to be like him.

Resource units for the instruction of health habits are recommended for kindergarten through third grade.[9] These units can operate at any level in terms of how ready the children are for them. They deal with qualities of personality, of friendship, of understanding others and ourselves. While recommendations are made for activities the teacher can use and the kind of objectives that should be considered, the enterprising and versatile teacher can think of activities that seem even more appropriate to her particular classroom group of children. The important part of the unit is that many exciting ideas can be implemented in an aspect of life which many of us take for granted as knowledge everyone has. This is in fact not true. Children miss out on health education in most cases if they do not hear something about it at school in the context of a formalized program.

Perceptual Motor Development. This is another aspect of movement, mental health, and learning processes. "Movement integrates the simultaneous experience of spatial and temporal dimensions, and is therefore a powerful tool in promoting the integrative processes of the brain." [10] The writers indicate that the brain is no longer as much a puzzle as it used to be, that much research has disclosed new information. "Modern neurophysiological research has demonstrated that experiences do change both the physical structure and the functioning of the human brain." [11] This

[9] Ibid., pp. 263–269.
[10] Marianne Frostig and Phyllis Maslow, *Learning Problems in the Classroom* (New York: Grune & Stratton, 1973), p. 23.
[11] Ibid., p. 24.

A sense of pride is reflected in this kindergarten boy's face as he stands high above others, even his teacher, and balances himself steadily on the ladder bar. Children need many experiences of this nature to give them an idea of their competence. They need to know how well they are able to coordinate mind and body actions.

suggests too that the simple stimulus-response pattern of learning is no longer tenable. There is a greater conglomerate of connections than was once thought and an ". . . interdependence of feedback mechanisms among the various regions of the brain." [12] This is yet another approach to the importance of mind and body coordination and its relationship to school learning processes.

The writers again suggest (as others have) that physical well-being is important as a contributor to the child's learning ability. This, as well as adequate nutrition and the avoidance of stressful situations, is emphasized.

Adequacy of skills that involve perceptual motor development is part of the underlying orientation for children's step-by-step progression in school subjects. Children who are physically and perceptually able to manage simple concepts are able to meet further challenge from the teacher. The teacher does not introduce activities that are too difficult for the child. This is what is meant by a child development curriculum. The teacher would not, for example, introduce grammatical construction

[12] Ibid., p. 24.

of a sentence if the children had not even learned the parts of speech. One considers the principles of the child's developmental age—chronologically, socially, emotionally, academically—in deciding what the child can manage in his school tasks. In this sense, the curriculum is tailor-made for each child. He does not need to experience nonsuccess to any great degree. He can meet new tasks with the assurance of his teacher, that tasks are simply that, further steps along the way to test what one can do, with success in the previous tasks leading to success in another.

The teacher is a crucial element in the child's achievement. If she knows what a child can do and in which tasks he is likely to succeed, she can "stack the cards" to his benefit. The teacher can almost guarantee success for a pupil as he progresses through the learning path. She has to know her children well to do this effectively; otherwise, she will not be helping them.

Children can become successfully aware of their own muscles, that force which their bodies create against the wind or against another object. Exercises are recommended in books devoted mainly to the subject of movement education. A few children pulling on one object sense the force of others against their own. Several children holding on to a large circular hoop running around in one direction sense balance, force, or both against the object and the results of other children holding on to it while running around in a circle.

When children are young, they can learn to walk the balance beam which helps them achieve better control over balance, coordination of arms, legs, mind. They can learn to hop, jump, skip on the balance beam when they acquire a sense of mastery in that kind of exercise.

Mathematics, language, imagery, rhythm, music are all a part of movement education. The teacher incorporates all of these whenever possible. The children run to the sixth line shown on the floor. They run backwards to the third line. What do they have left? Three lines which are not covered are left. This may be termed body mathematics.

Young children in particular need a great deal of help in channeling their "natural" tendencies toward activity and movement. They need the approval of knowing that they are able to follow directions. The joy of succeeding in an act suggested by the teacher (such as the request to move across the room in a certain way with one's body) gives the child great satisfaction. He knows how to continue to work toward achievement. He will want to improve and will welcome further challenges or tasks in the future. He turns *toward* learning rather than *away* from it.

Children need information from an informed adult to tell them what they are seeing, feeling, in terms of the language framework of one's society. It may be a view of society at large—e.g., the United States, the child's family, or neighborhood view. "To learn about the world outside, the child must have experience and must be consciously aware of what he is perceiving. When his perceptions are given a label, he is better able to store perceptions in his memory and later retrieve (remember) them." [13]

The child often bounces, flops, gallops, and skips in spontaneous movement. He is not aware that this describes his movements until he is told or is asked to do them in a certain way. The vast world around him with all its information has to be built up for him as he progresses in school. The child is usually curious. It is natural to be interested in one's surrounding world. People who are totally uninterested are ill, despondent, have been constantly denied of their desires, or have been imprisoned in some way physically or psychologically. One of these problems is just as devastating or self-denying as the other.

The blocks, puzzles, collage materials given the child in nursery school, kindergarten and the primary grades provide opportunities for the development of dexterity for different purposes.

They all involve movement; planned, controlled, and careful. Blocks involve coordination of mind, eye, and hand. The child places them as he plans. Puzzles involve the judgment of spatial relationships. The child places in the empty space the puzzle part that he thinks will fit into the appropriate area. Collage in art experiences involves the placement of various pieces of objects—be they paper, fur, feathers, sponge, or roughly textured materials—which have to be pasted on a background in a way the child desires. This involves coordination of mind, eye, and hand. It involves the judgment of spatial relationships.

Between three-and-one-half or four to seven or seven-and-one-half years, children's perceptual functions are assumed to develop to a heightened degree. From birth onward, the infant has only limited abilities to discern certain stimuli in his environment. He adapts to the world through his senses. Later his eyes and ears become receptors of greater distance and they furnish him with the major means through which he can understand his environment. This suggests that most of the child's visual perceptual abilities are in their maximum receiving state of development by approximately seven-and-one-half years of age. This period of life is indeed the crucial range of the latter part of early childhood education, the age of eight marking the child's attendance at school in the third grade.

The school-age relationship has been linked to specific kinds of learning. Many things end in this period. The child typically is viewed educationally as preparing for the next period of school life, the intermediate grades in the elementary school. This marks a point at which the child begins the later period of childhood. He has learned the pupil role to some extent. He has learned where he was able to succeed and where

[13] Ibid., p. 179.

he was not so far. The early part of his childhood has passed. "Between the ages of seven and eight-and-a-half, visual-perceptual development tapers off; in fact all abilities needed for successful school learning are in the repertoire of the six to eight-year-old child who has developed normally." [14] This statement has vast implications for the early childhood period of life and particularly for the school's obligation in the kindergarten–primary educational aspects of a child's life.

The teacher has not only to be aware of the child's need for certain kinds of development—such as motor, visual-perceptual development, and the effects of these types on the child's self-image, self-concept, and his esthetic development—but also the effects they have on cognitive development. Further, the child who has not been given time and effort in the development of those crucial areas in the early part of his life, in other words, if he is rushed too quickly in the time needed for each mastery stage, he may miss the very requirements for development essential to learning the things that provide foundation and balance for later developmental support.

The child who is not fortunate enough to be with a teacher who knows what young children need and realizes the importance of certain fundamental techniques for their growth, as well as knowing how to achieve this development in the child, may miss opportunities to strengthen his skills both affectively and cognitively. Surely, teachers of young children may feel a double commitment not only to the young children they see in their classroom every day but also to the kind of future they are creating for the children.

The message here is to urge the necessity of including certain kinds of activity in the curriculum. The teacher can find specific references to these activities in books and pamphlets written by specialists for the treatment of those learning problems. Once having seen these, the teacher can improvise activities in movement and in perceptual motor areas for her own individual pupils and classroom groups.

The teacher of young children has to be versatile in meeting pupils' needs. Since the children are at the beginning of their lives academically and affectively or emotionally, she has an enormous commitment or obligation to help them make the best of what they have. Too often, pupils are not aware of their own resources. It takes an interested and concerned teacher to bring out those skills and abilities. Thus, it is incumbent upon the teacher of young children to be informed of as many activities and experiences and curriculum ideas as possible.

No group of children is the same as another. Each classroom group has different problems. For this reason alone, the teacher of young chil-

14 Ibid., p. 112.

dren has to be a specialist of specialists. That is, the teacher has to know where to obtain the best materials as soon as possible when she needs to apply them to the variety of children in her class. Exposure to new ideas, to new experiences, to pupil self-testing is needed in the classroom. The curriculum that provides the broadest array of experiences while at the same time meeting the individual differences and needs is a satisfying curriculum for all concerned.

Developmental Activities in Movement, Health Education, and Perceptual Motor Development

One of the most important considerations in any of the areas mentioned above is the awareness of differences among the children, in the ways they learn, and in their physical coordination. Teachers who plan the kind of work the children will be expected to do, simply need to be concerned that the pupils they teach are physically and conceptually equipped to complete the tasks assigned to them.

Challenge is needed in all educational activities. This means that at times the children will not find a given task easy. It will puzzle them and they will have to exert greater effort than usual if they are to find the answers. The supreme balance between the child's management with ease in an activity and his enjoyment of a difficult assignment is not easy for teachers to reach. If, however, it becomes one of their major goals in teaching, they have gained an important turn in the right direction.

Movement Activities. Exploration in space, in movement, in low, high, and middle levels become exciting experiences for even the youngest of children, intellectually capable or not, if the circumstances are offered in an assuring environment. A pleasant adult—one that the child knows cares for his safety, ample space, nonhurried environment—encourages the child's experimentation with almost anything suggested to him. The child himself thinks of the idea; suggestions regarding a theme for movement may come from the teacher.

Activities that are appropriate to the child's age level are developmental in the sense that they provide for sequential levels of difficulty. The child accomplishes an easier form of movement before going on to a more complex one. The teacher is sensible about knowing what the child is capable of doing and knows how to lead him further in the hierarchy of difficult movement.

Movement experiences relate not only to the physical development in the child but also to his esthetic development. Movement affects his creative drives as well as having an affect on the self-image. The child becomes aware of what he is able to do and that his own powers can cause a force of some kind. His ideas are translated into movement. The action that he alone creates has an effect on his peers, his teacher, and himself.

Original efforts to develop an idea are transferred from one endeavor to another. The child who learns that he can manage his body in one area of graceful movement or of imitating an animal's movements is also learning that his mind is a powerful force. He begins to learn that the possibilities for creating ideas are endless. Adults are not the only ones who initiate ideas that are translated into acceptable communication by others. The sense of pride, of accomplishment, and of self-appreciation soars. For young children, this source of growth is essential.

As children sing songs and match their own body activity to the words of the song, they are developing another aspect of mind-body coordination. The "Looby-loo" song—which "instructs" them when the right foot goes forward, the left foot, and so on, in time to the music—is just one example of body movement that young children enjoy.

Children enjoy moving like the wind, fast, furious, then slow, subsiding, or dying down slowly, quietly. The run softly and quickly like leaves fluttering in the rain or the wind. They are not told how to do this; their body rhythms do it differently from each other. The teacher encourages the children to use their own ideas, not those of others. The imagery of their own minds creates the action. The teacher merely gives them suggested content to think of when they move. A leaf stuck to the bicycle spoke which is picked off and allowed to go free through the air suggests an idea for bodily expression. The child who has seen this happen knows how to recapture the imagery of the experience and knows how to re-live it through his own body and mind.

Pulling, pushing, thrusting, sliding back and forth are ideas that grow with the child's experiences participating in such movements. The teacher asks the pupil to do these activities by imitating the behavior of an animal, by imagining himself as a tree, a leaf, a bicycle rolling down a hill going faster and faster as it descends.

The young child who is learning to skip, who is learning how to "pump" himself on the swing, is pleased when he can master these skills. They are not easy for the four- and five-year-old child. Hopping, changing to a skip, stopping short and standing still when he has been running or leaping, are also forms of body or muscle control. Children enjoy being successful at these skills, particularly when they are done in a pleasant, accepting (not a grim, perfectionist) atmosphere.

Many books are available indicating the forms of activities that may be used. The purpose of this book is mainly to sensitize the teacher to the appropriate and general guidelines that should be used with young pupils. The teacher who has a sense of what is needed for the child knows which activities to use. Since age differences vary to such a great degree in their influences on a child's mental and physical capacities, the teacher must have a commitment to the appropriateness of activity to each child's development. The teacher must be the searcher, the scientist, the artist with vision in order to create appropriate work for the child at different age levels.

Movement as an esthetic form can be brought into the children's curriculum at every opportunity. Hopefully the teacher will enjoy it as much as they do. Not only do the pupils follow directions of some kind to "take on" an idea and transform it into bodily use, but they move; they become free, unentangled from classroom sedentary activity; they have an opportunity to become part of an esthetic experience. Too few of these opportunities are given to them because the teacher is typically more concerned with cognitive or intellectual pursuits involving paper and pencil materials. This is not to say that purely cognitive experiences are not important, but if they constitute the only kind offered, it results in an imbalance in the curriculum. Research indicates that we have neglected that part of the brain's development that is involved with spatial reasoning. "Since education is effective only in so far as it affects the working of the brain, we can see that an elementary school program narrowly restricted to reading, writing, and arithmetic will educate mainly one hemisphere, leaving half of an individual's high-level potential unschooled." [15]

Movement is an intellectual function insofar as it engages the child's mind in translating a "problem" put to him by the teacher, e.g., making one's body respond to an idea of imagined leaves lifted by a strong gust of wind, or making one's body respond to the imagery of becoming a ferocious tiger (hungry at that), stalking through the jungle. Teachers have to be careful not to separate movement activity from the curriculum, thinking that it has no useful purpose. They need to know what its purposes are so that they can explain them to parents and colleagues who ask what is included in the curriculum and why, for each of the activities that are in it.

One of the most important assignments given to students in my university class is to present a rationale for any activity in the curriculum they offer to children. They have to show why and how a certain activity that they have chosen for the children is appropriate for teaching the concept they want the pupils to understand. They have to be able to answer why a paper and pencil activity might be better to help children learn a specific bit of information than a film would, for example. Why is a film a better way to have the children learn about airplane lift than it would be to read about it? Why would movement of their own bodies in space showing what happened to a leaf by the wind be a better activity than reading about it? The reasons they give for providing children with one

[15] J. E. Bogen, "Some Educational Aspects of Hemispheric Specialization," in *UCLA Educator*, Volume 17, No. 2 (Spring, 1975), p. 27.

opportunity rather than another when they want them to learn a certain fact are important to any experiences they plan for children.

Position of up, down, low, high in space helps children orient themselves in space, a concept which is not easy to learn. Direction of right-to-left, east-to-west, north-and-south is also not easy for young children (nor adults for that matter). Practice in these activities which allows pupils to have many experiences finding their direction in songs and movement will encourage the use of such knowledge outside the school as well.

An interesting aspect of movement is that it seems to relate to many other activities. The child who is learning to coordinate movement is employing these ideas when he is working at collage, which is a cutting, pasting, placement activity as well as an art activity. The child who is singing "Ring Around the Rosy," is not only singing, but also learning to coordinate body movement with an idea, is experiencing perceptual motor development, is stretching his legs in a physical education sense, and is presumably enjoying a social experience with his peers.

In movement experiences, the teacher has plenty of scarves and odd types of materials available so that the children can improvise in graphic ways to act out their ideas. Many kinds of props are on hand to stimulate and encourage ideas that may be put to music when desired.

As the children proceed in the grades from kindergarten to first, second, and third, they are able to manage ideas in movement that are more complex. Their imagination is more sophisticated presumably because they have had richer experiences. Greater muscle control is evident in "problems" designed to have children run, skip, twirl three times to the right, stop, twirl three times to the left, stop, hop three times, settle down to the ground or floor in a loose "heap." Some children can illustrate the growth of a seed: its lifetime to the flowering process—the autumn of its days; and gradually the settling back in the earth at the end of its life.

Poems, songs, stories, music can be demonstrated in rhythmic patterns as well as represented in movement that depicts the messages or themes of the compositions. Free movement in which children's original ideas are used should be greatly encouraged. The more they exercise their imagination, the more they will have to exercise in the way of new ideas.

Children in the primary grades are better able to perform organized dances than are the children in kindergarten. Teachers can teach them short dances so that they enjoy knowing some and yet are not going through tedious rehearsals in order to learn them. As they demonstrate their understanding of the simpler dances, they can learn the more difficult ones. The timing for these learning periods has to be set in terms of the teacher's discretion and what she thinks the children are able to withstand.

When children feel uncomfortable about choosing partners in which boy-girl partnerships are requested for folk dance formats, the teacher can try to plan for many types of dances, for those that include partners and those that include larger groups at times. "A good repertoire of primary folk dances should include a number of dances which require no partners or those which require groups of threes." [16] Again it is up to the skill, vision, and perceptiveness of the teacher to plan comprehensive programs, those in which success can be ensured for the children.

Health Education. From the very simplest ideas of good health and body care to the most complex about the human body, young children can be exposed in clear elementary terms to valid techniques needed for effective body care. Children learn about the importance of brushing the teeth; what happens if one does not, is shown in various materials that are available upon request from dental associations. The importance of adequate rest, of keeping the body clean and guarding against disease, infection, or susceptibility to illness is taught to children through various means of posters, films, games, factual data presented at the children's levels of understanding.

Materials have to be appealing, factual, clear in the message they convey. Children learn that they themselves are primarily responsible for guarding their own health. They discover that the safeguards for their protection are among the most worthwhile concerns they can have. To enjoy life to the fullest, to achieve and sustain vitality, they need to be in good health. The health habits that they establish in their early years are one of their most important contributions to their own best way of life.

In the kindergarten and first grade, children enjoy making posters and decorative cards that emphasize the importance of wholesome attitudes toward health habits, such as using tissues for blowing the nose and discarding those tissues to prevent the spread of colds, flu, and other infectious diseases. They learn to place their hands over their mouths when they sneeze to prevent the spread of germs; they learn to wash their hands before they eat or before handling food to serve to others. They learn to wash their hands after micturition and defecation. If they view these habits as essential to their good health and for the protection of others around them, and the teacher involves them in activities that emphasize these points, they will adapt to these habits.

Young children make excellent murals that they work on together. A mural that portrays important health habits—one that is made of collage items of toothbrushes, food, toothpaste, vegetables, fruits, whatever the children want to use—is exciting to see. It can be completed in a few days if most of the children in the class work on it. The theme for health and body care can be suggested by the teacher, but various materials available from local or Federal organizations provide colorful recommendations for a wide range that children should be encouraged to use.

[16] Clark, op. cit., p. 39.

Dramatizations or role playing offer the opportunity to represent precautions and mistakes in faulty health practices. These can be humorously presented. Posters or dramatizations showing before-and-after behavior of the person who does not eat properly, wash properly, or receive adequate rest can be depicted in humorous ways.

Home and school safety comes under the heading of health care. The avoidance of accidents created by misplacement of materials in walkways, faulty electrical appliances, or plugs, combustible rags in the garage or back room of a home, can be studied. Children understand these problems.

Rules are created for the safe use of playground equipment. Children learn that certain precautions have to be taken when a child is using a bat, throwing a fast ball, running fast to base; young children, need to learn that their uses of swings, tricycles, and climbing bars require thought. They learn that children who are not involved in using equipment have to stand back in order to avoid being struck by someone or by an object. All these ideas are illustrated on posters, murals, and sequenced cards that are attractively displayed in the room or in the school corridor.

The teacher stands by watching the children on the bars and monitors the number of children using it simultanteously. Most schools have safety rules that apply school-wide. Some of the schools expect each teacher to create rules with the children so that pupils know why those rules are necessary.

In the second and third grades, children are able to study nutrition in a slightly more sophisticated sense than their younger counterparts. Foundational knowledge about healthful foods, their growth and care in earth that is not polluted, can give the pupils an early knowledge about ecological themes. They like to study their own community in those terms. The water supply and its sources interest them. People who are knowledgeable in these areas should be invited to the classroom to speak to them about the problems of pollution and remediation of them.

Children in the nursery school, kindergarten, and the primary grades learn about sharing, cooperation, concern for the welfare of others, trying to do one's best in working with others; this contributes toward mental health. While young children, of course, are not able to do this in full understanding of what it means to cooperate, they will imitate such behavior if it proves satisfying and productive to them. The teacher's praise and the pleasure reflected in classmates' playing or working cooperatively with each other provide an incentive to consider the feelings of others. Young children can be very considerate and unselfish if conditions are not too frustrating. The teacher who anticipates their needs and ways of meeting them has little difficulty in urging young children to be helpful members of a group.

Mental health is important in a classroom, both for the children's benefit and the teacher's. Typically, a calm approach to the children's problems with an understanding that children are human, (they are not unreasonable and do not misbehave only for purposes of attracting attention at all times), brings results that encourage a calm, business-like, and pleasant classroom atmosphere. Some teachers consider normal behavior in children annoying. They need more information on child development.

Perceptual Motor Development. This area of development typically involves specific sequences in terms of a child's accomplishments or difficulties. While all children are involved in this kind of development—mind-hand-eye coordination—some have greater difficulties than others in the ordinary course of school work planned for them—i.e., activities that concentrate on trouble spots for the child.

A child may be doing well in mathematics and science but not in reading. The teacher notes the reading skills that are causing problems for him and provides exercises that involve practice in those skills. Change in the way a child reviews those skills is needed. When something is difficult for a child, he cannot remain with it for too long. The teacher has to be sure that the pupil starts out with easier elements of skills. Younger children can be asked to walk from one letter to another; in that way, their bodies become involved in creating words. Teachers have many games that can be used for manipulating letters and words, and also for walking on floor designs that represent words, syllables, and sounds.

Pupils have to be given a variety of manipulative games that can be used individually and in groups. The more that children learn to judge where materials should be placed—the appropriate shape in the appropriate space, turn things upside down and replace them correctly, group objects in correct grouping style—the easier it will be for them to manage the next steps in the learning progression.

A child of eight may be able to perform certain activities at the level of a four-year-old. For this reason, the teacher realizes that the activities needed for her program must meet a broad range of skills appropriate to the abilities of three- through nine-year-old children. Developmental levels refer to the child's abilities in various areas rather than an age level. The teacher's readiness to recognize differences in the child's abilities to perform certain activities means that she has at hand many materials, any of which can be used to help a child in a specific skill within any given level. These are available from many sources. And once the teacher sees what those materials are, she can often duplicate them herself.[17]

Children need activities in which they can learn directionality and laterality. They have to discover which way their bodies must turn to find right, left, east, west. They need to discover which leg moves with which hand or arm as it swings alongside their bodies. Practice of these concepts in the context of a variety of experiences provide pleasure in learning. The teacher's praise when they do it correctly, and plenty of individualized activities they can do by themselves, serve as the follow-up in further direction for their learning. They can go to certain activities in which they need more practice when they are finished with other assigned work and thereby become self-directing and independent at school. This ability is excellent for their self-concept development.

Placing on correct hooks the cards on which the correct answers are indicated is one way of having children manipulate figures, cards, and spatial relationships. Answer boards with cup hooks on them along with numbers designated as the correct answers, or letters designated as the correct letter for the beginning or ending of a word, represent other ways of having children manipulate materials and concepts in a very real sense.

Whatever the activities that the teacher selects for individual children, they are intended to fit a child's needs in terms of certain strengths of the planned experiences. Along with the child's practice in certain skills, he should be learning that he is progressing in his work at school, that he is worthy of help, and that he will be able to help others as well.

The importance of relationships between adequacy of the child in this school work and the development of a zest for life cannot be overemphasized. (See Figure 10.1.) Health education in a satisfying developmental sense contributes to the vitality of spirit and the physical aspects

---

[17] See Lorton, op. cit. Teachers have made these activities and used them successfully with children.

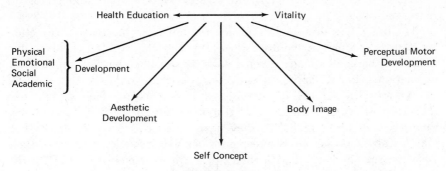

figure 10.1
Interrelationships Between Curriculum Activities and **Joie De Vivre**

of it. This affects the self-concept. Children who have healthy attitudes toward themselves will have them toward others. They become the contributors to their group. The reciprocal processes of giving and receiving are satisfying testimonies that reflect the joy of social approval.

Evaluation of Young Children's Progress at School in Movement, Health Education, and Perceptual Motor Development

The unique aspect of this kind of evaluation in young children's progress is that it is visual; it can be observed daily without any special efforts on the part of the teacher. A child's knowledge of health education is reflected in his appearance, posture, participation with others in class, and general level of energy most of the time. The teacher's awareness of the child who moves easily and is well coordinated when it comes to managing tasks that are somewhat intricate, should be developed and used continually.

One of the best ways that a teacher can evaluate a child is to take careful notes of his performance periodically, date these observations, and indicate the levels of skills and abilities achieved to that date. A card file or folder on each child can be used to retain anecdotal records of how the child is doing in his routine work. The teacher will note a pattern in the child's behavior relative to each of the subject matter areas. Studies that have been conducted to measure pupils' achievement and which have compared the investigator's data with the teacher's impressions of the same children's achievement or approximate scores on tests given in the research, indicated that the researcher's data and the teacher's judgment coincided. This suggests that when a teacher really observes the children and cares about their progress, her records (when administered objectively) reflect sensitivity and awareness relative to the children's performance.

The objectives designed in any curriculum give the teacher direction for assessment of the children's work. When the children achieve the objectives or goals of any given lesson, the teacher has information for evaluation criteria. Appraisal procedures can be done in the form of interviews with parents, questionnaires, checklists in which a child can indicate yes, no, or sometimes, as responses. Often when children assess themselves in terms of habits they have developed or precautions they take toward good health, the responses are valid. Particularly when their answers can be checked with their appearance—which can attest to the truth of their impressions—a self-checking sheet on health data can be productive in evaluation procedures.

Perceptual motor development and other forms of movement evaluation procedures can be obtained from the various sources mentioned earlier in this chapter and in the references at the end. Many excellent and simple processes have been devised for teachers of young children.[18] Authorities in the field of children's development are concerned that teachers become effective diagnosticians in knowing what kind of help a child needs. Teachers are able to conduct simple tests and to move the child on to the next steps without too much difficulty. They can discover the child's problem, diagnose it specifically, prescribe for its remediation. Some require more time than others to solve and some problems require more time for the child to improve.

The young child needs more than anything else in his early years at school the trust and endorsement of a caring adult. The pupils in such a classroom thrive; and it is obvious to others, teachers or adults, who visit the classroom that this is true. Only the teacher who enjoys nurturing and helping others grow should be working with young children. The grim humorless person who needs continuous reassurance that she is appreciated and loved—without realization between moments of those reassurances that she is in fact worthy of loving—will have a difficult time with young children. Their demands for attention and security will be too much for her own emotional instability. This kind of work would be unfair to such a person.

Evaluation can be performed with children in a non-threatening manner if the teacher will take the time to present it that way. It can be used mainly for diagnosing, record-keeping, delineation of progress in a child's work, and for providing data referred to in a parent conference or with a colleague. The teacher does this with an underlying feeling of helpfulness—not punitiveness—for the child. Fortunately, many teachers who work with young children succeed in this.

[18] Frostig and Maslow, op. cit., pp. 122–140.

summary

Movement education for young children is extremely important to their early stages of school learning. Not only does it contribute to the growing sense of body awareness and self-concept, but it also contributes to academic learning. A sense of body awareness helps the child know what his own powers are; it helps him realize the ways he can use his own powers of self-starting and initiative to externalize ideas.

As the child learns about the freedom of movement and the sense of direction he obtains from moving in space in certain ways, using his imagination and imagery to carry out an idea, he discovers that his views are powerful forms of communication to others. Approval from the teacher and his peers builds a sense of self-approval and strengthens a necessary healthy self-concept.

Perceptual motor development is extremely important to the later development of the child as he proceeds in school. Writing, reading, music, art, and mathematics can be improved by a child's sense of muscle or motor control. Since literature indicates that the child's maximal development of perceptual motor skills occur by seven and eight years, the child needs to have mastered many kinds of activities that involve motor skills and perception.

The child needs to learn not only how to sense himself as a powerful instrument of communication but also how he perceives himself as an object in space. Care for the body is relevant here. A great respect for his own body can develop with a viable education related to it at school. Respect for adequate rest, exercise, nutrition, and nonabuse of drugs can be developed at school. The wisdom of caring for one's body and being mainly responsible for giving it the best kind of care are emphasized at school. Children learn to have self-respect, respect for natural functions, caution, health, attitudes of concern for the health of others, prevention of accidents, illnesses, and the like.

The joy of living obtained when an individual is healthy and has the vigor and vitality to want to achieve, is worthwhile developing in young children. A healthy personality can respond well to the rigors of life, to frustration, to disappointment, and to the needs required in hard work. Most of all, the individual who is healthy, who is achieving as he feels he should, and is able to like himself and others, also has that most valuable of commodities: a sense of humor. This takes him through life somewhat protected from exaggerated perceptions of self-stress, or feelings of being treated unfairly. He cannot take himself too seriously for too long. He is able to laugh at himself. He has compassion for the problems of others but at the same time he sees the incongruity of situations related to himself. He is able to acquire as much needed resilience that most successful (happily so) people have. Children need this kind of person around them.

topics for discussion

1. Design what you consider an ideal program in movement education that would be used with children in kindergarten and first grade. Indicate your rationale for using certain activities; justify their uses.
2. What do you remember of your own education in health at school in kindergarten and the primary grades? What were you taught and what activities were you given in which you were expected to participate?
3. What do you think are the most important health problems that should be taught to young children in the second and third grades? Why do you think so?
4. Plan a unit for young children, four through seven years old, that would help them learn about safety in the home. Include necessary activities for them to engage in at school, visiting places that would give them information on the subject, and inviting resource people into the classroom to discuss the problem with them in an interesting and informative manner.
5. Discuss various non-threatening ways of evaluating children in movement education and perceptual motor development.
6. Visit a school in your community and observe their rhythms program. Ask teachers what their goals are for children in those programs.

selected bibliography for teachers

MOVEMENT REFERENCES

Arbuckle, Wanda Rector, Eleanor Hill Ball, and George Cornwell. *Learning to Move and Moving to Learn.* Book II. Animals. Columbus, Ohio: Charles E. Merrill Publishing Co., 1973.

Cherry, Claire. *Creative Movement for the Developing Child.* Palo Alto, California: Fearon Publishers, 1968.

Clark, Carol E. *Rhythmic Activities for the Classroom.* Dansville, N.Y.: The Instructor Publications, 1969.

Cratty, Bryant J. *Active Learning.* Englewood Cliffs, N.J.: Prentice-Hall, Inc., 1971.

Espenschade, Anna S., and Helen M. Eckert. *Motor Development.* Columbus, Ohio: Charles E. Merrill Publishing Company, 1967.

Frostig, Marianne, and Phyliss Maslow. *Learning Problems in the Classroom.* New York: Grune & Stratton, 1973.

Godfrey, Barbara B., and Newell C. Kephart. *Movement Patterns and Motor Education.* New York: Appleton-Century-Crofts, 1969.

Latchaw, Marjorie, and Glen Egstrom. *Human Movement.* Englewood Cliffs, N.J.: Prentice-Hall, Inc., 1969.

Hackett, Layne C., and Robert Jenson. *A Guide to Movement Exploration.* Palo Alto, Calif.: Peek Publications, 1967.

Harvat, Robert W. *Physical Education for Children with Perceptual Motor Learning Disabilities.* Columbus, Ohio: Charles E. Merrill Publishing Co., 1971.

Nunn, Riba R., and Charles R. Jones. *The Learning Pyramid: Potential Through Perception.* Columbus, Ohio: Charles E. Merrill Publishing Co., 1972.

Radler, D. H., and Newell C. Kephart. *Success Through Play.* New York: Harper & Row, 1960.

Rowen, Betty. *Learning Through Movement.* New York: Teachers College Press, 1963.

Sinclair, Caroline B. *Movement of the Young Child. Ages Two to Six.* Columbus, Ohio: Charles E. Merrill Publishing Co., 1973.

Singer, Robert N. *Motor Learning and Human Performance.* New York: Macmillan Publishing Co., Inc., 1975.

MENTAL HEALTH, PHYSICAL EDUCATION, LEARNING

Bernard, H. W. *Mental Hygiene for Classroom Teachers.* New York: McGraw-Hill Book Company, 1970.

Blank, M., and Solomon, F. A. "A Tutorial Language Program to Develop Abstract Thinking in Socially Disadvantaged Preschool Children," *Child Development.* Vol. 39 (1968), 379–389.

Bogen, J. E. "Some Educational Aspects of Hemispheric Specialization," *U.C.L.A. Educator,* Volume 17, No. 2 (Spring, 1975), p. 27.

Breckenridge, M. E., and M. N. Murphy. *Growth and Development of the Young Child.* Philadelphia: W. B. Saunders Co., 1969.

Clements, F. W. *Child Health.* Baltimore: The Williams and Wilkins Co., 1964.

Ellis, R. W. B., and R. G. Mitchell. *Diseases in Infancy and Childhood.* Baltimore: The Williams and Wilkins Co., 1968.

Ellis, R. B. *Child Health and Development.* New York: Grune & Stratton, 1966.

Estes, W. K. *Learning Theory and Mental Development.* New York: Academic Press, 1970.

Frostig, Marianne, and Phyliss Maslow. *Learning Problems in the Classroom.* New York: Grune & Stratton, 1973.

Frostig, Marianne. "Visual Perception, Integrative Function, and Academic Learning," *Journal of Learning Disabilities,* Vol. 5 (1972), pp. 1–15.

Frostig, Marianne. *Movement Education: Theory and Practice.* Chicago: Follett Educational Corporation, 1970.

Frostig, Marianne, D. Horne, and A. Miller. *Pictures and Patterns. Teacher's Guide to Pictures and Patterns.* Chicago: Follett Educational Corporation, 1972.

Godfrey, B. B., and N. C. Kephart. *Movement Patterns and Motor Education.* New York: Appleton-Century-Crofts, 1969.

Gibson, E. J. *Principles of Perceptual Learning and Development.* New York: Appleton-Century-Crofts, 1969.

Hanlon, J. J., and E. McHose. *Design for Health: the Teacher, the School, and the Community.* Philadelphia: Lea & Febinger, 1963.

Health Appraisal of School Children. Washington, D.C.: American Association for Health, Physical Education, and Recreation, 1961.

Johnson, D., and H. Myklebust. *Learning Disabilities.* New York: Grune & Stratton, 1967.

Keith, J. D., R. D. Rowe, and P. Vlad. *Heart Disease in Infancy and Childhood.* New York: Macmillan Publishing Co., Inc., 1967.

Kilander, H. F. *School Health Education.* New York: Macmillan Publishing Co., Inc., 1968.

Krugman, S., and R. Ward. *Infectious Diseases of Children.* St. Louis: The C. V. Mosby Co., 1968.

Lamon, W. E. *Learning and the Nature of Mathematics.* Chicago: Science Research Associates, 1972.

Nemir, Alma. *The School Health Program.* Philadelphia: W. B. Saunders Co., 1970.

Pulaski, E. J. *Common Bacterial Infections.* Philadelphia: W. B. Saunders Co., 1964.

Sabatino, D., and D. L. Hayden. "Psychoeducational Study of Selected Variables of Children Failing the Elementary Grades," *Journal of Experimental Education.* Vol. 38 (1970), pp. 40–57.

Samuels, J. "Letter Name Versus Letter Sound Knowledge in Learning to Read," *The Reading Teacher.* Vol. 24 (1971), pp. 604–608.

Schilder, P. *The Image and the Appearance of the Human Body.* New York: John Wiley & Sons, Inc., 1964.

Silverthorne, N. H., C. S. Anglin, and M. Schusterman. *Principal Infectious Diseases of Childhood.* Springfield, Ill.: Charles C Thomas Publishers, 1966.

Smolensky, J., and L. R. Bonvechio. *Principles of School Health.* Boston: D. C. Heath & Co., 1966.

Stein, A. "Strategies for Failure," *Harvard Educational Review.* Vol. 41 (2) (1971), pp. 158–204.

Stuart, H. C., and D. G. Prugh, Editors. *The Healthy Child: His Physical, Psychological and Social Development.* Cambridge, Mass.: Harvard University Press, 1960.

Suggested School Health Policies. Washington, D.C.: American Association for Health, Physical Education, and Recreation, 1962.

Tanner, L. N., and H. C. Lindgren. *Classroom Teaching and Learning: A Mental Health Approach.* New York: Holt, Rinehart & Winston, Inc., 1971.

Turner, C. E., H. B. Randall, and S. L. Smith. *School Health and Health Education.* St. Louis: The C. V. Mosby Co., 1970.

United States Public Health Services. *Teaching Poison Prevention in Kindergarten and Primary Grades.* Washington, D.C.: United States Government Printing Office, 1962.

Vannier, M. *Teaching Health in Elementary Schools.* New York: Harper & Row, 1963.

Wallis, E. L., and G. Logan. *Exercise for Children.* Englewood Cliffs, N.J.: Prentice-Hall, Inc., 1966.

Weber, E. W. Editor. *Health and the School Child.* Springfield, Ill.: Charles C Thomas Publishers, 1964.

Winnicutt, D. W. *The Maturational Processes and the Facilitating Environment.* New York: International Universities Press, 1965.

Winnicutt, D. W. *Playing and Reality.* New York: Basic Books, Inc., 1971.

Part Three

Teacher, Parent, School, Community, and World Relationships

More than ever, it has become obvious that understanding among men in all communities, both local and international, has to be maintained. With the threats, disagreements, and conflicts that frequently disrupt world affairs, the schools view their role as that of providing citizens who are well-informed and equipped to make effective decisions in mediating problems.

Young children, while not having the depth of knowledge and understanding required to grasp the seriousness of world problems, have to their advantage a desire to be approved and loved. The schools are in an excellent position to nurture that desire.

The following section emphasizes certain elements that need to be considered in relationships with parents and the community. Teachers can help their pupils a great deal by having successful conferences with parents in which more information is given on the child's background at home and with friends. The teacher who listens with empathy and understanding helps the child in his development both at home and at school.

The community that senses its own school as a place that wants to create and maintain the best in that neighborhood is willing to cooperate in many ways with the school. They need to be informed on ways that people in the area can help. When the community supports the interests of the children in school, it does a great deal to facilitate progress for all concerned. A mutual sense of cooperation on the part of parents and personnel in the school is extremely satisfying to those involved in any issue or program. Teachers who discuss parent cooperation are grateful and want to work all the more with the children of those parents. They realize how much the parents want the best for their children and will cooperate in every way with teachers and the school to bring exciting goals to fruition.

A well-informed community—one that is given facts on world events and is encouraged to think of its own problems along those lines—benefits from a school that is contemporary in its views. Parents who support the children's orientations toward reading and finding facts are providing an example for the children that will serve them in good stead in their present and future world.

Chapter
11

Teacher-Parent Relationships

Very young children in the three- and four-year-old age range are still physically dependent on their parents. The parents are seen quite often by the teacher, typically before and after school when the child is left there and picked up after school. The physical bond of the parent and child makes it necessary to view that relationship as a totality, at least where the school is concerned.

The teacher has much to gain if she tries to communicate effectively with the parent. It benefits the child's progress in the larger perspective of schoolwork and the development of his personality. Since the variety of parent personalities is as great as the variety of children's personalities, it behooves the teacher to take note of individual differences in parents as much as to observe them in their children.

Often the teacher considers parents in a large category and responds to them in those terms. Unless the teacher is a parent herself, she typically does not have as much empathy with the parents regarding problems involved in child-rearing. Many young teachers have indicated this, too. They have said that until they had children of their own, they had not been aware of what happens to the child before getting to school, of the struggling with getting up on time, washing, getting dressed in appropriate clothing for the day, having a nutritious breakfast, bringing what was needed to school, and all the other problems that go on at home prior to and after the child comes to school.

The nature of the parent-teacher relationship is a very crucial part of the young child's education. It is instrumental in creating results that can be beneficial for the child's work at school. One of the most important effects that can result because of a sound parent-and-teacher relationship is the element of trust on the part of the parent. Not only do the two begin to know each other better and know how flexible the personality of the parent is, in terms of present anxieties about the child or her family or herself, but it also permits the parent to build up a basis of trust in the teacher. If the parent thinks that the teacher is making the best decisions on behalf of her child, she will cooperate with the teacher. She will agree with the teacher's requests because she knows that they are reasonable and in the child's best interests.

The School Program and Parent Awareness

The parents need to know more about the school program than they usually do. Teachers in their closeness to the subject matter, the curriculum and routines are not aware of the parent's desire to know what is happening. The parents will not typically approach the teacher and ask this, but they should be told about the program, if only to understand better what is happening to the child during the time he is at school.

It is not usually true that children have the same curriculum that their parents had when they went to school. This alone creates some misunderstandings between the teacher and parent. The mother assumes that what happened to her at school ought to be happening to her child. If she learned to read or to write in a certain manner, she expects that her child will be or at least ought to be learning it in the same way. If the child is not successful or does not appear to be doing well at school—and the parent did do well when she went to elementary school—all the more reason that the parent wants to know why her child is not learning in the same way that she did. Many parents think the school system is inferior if the children are not receiving the same kind of instruction that they themselves experienced. For this reason alone, it is helpful to parents if they know what the schools are trying to do.

Each generation in a society goes through a different educational process. This process is based on newer findings in research and on the results of testing new procedures with children. This is particularly true in a large urban society and some rural areas that have outstanding educators at the top of their organizational systems or outstanding teachers in their schools.

As educational groups attempt to respond more effectively to what the data say about the way children learn, the more do they change their techniques in teaching. Parents are not aware of this. They are not aware of different rationales that are created each time different methods are introduced. They need to be brought up-to-date where their children are involved.

In kindergarten, for example, what appears to be toys to parental eyes are actually activities planned to evoke learning strategies in children. Puzzles involve the child's dexterity of hands, fingers, eyes, judgment of spatial relationships. When these are part of a child's curriculum activities, the parent needs to know why. It is the rationale—the reason for or the justification of an activity being offered to children in the classroom—that provides understanding for the parent.

Each of the things that children are expected to do must have been planned to bring about learning of some form; constructive learning activities are understood by the parent even though the materials appear similar to things children have at home. Even though kindergarten teachers may be aware of why each activity is presented to children as an important aspect of learning, it does not mean that the parents are aware of it. It helps parents when they know the basis for curriculum design.

Parents are excellent resources for the curriculum when the children need to meet a pilot, a nurse, a doctor, a city planner, policeman, musician, dress designer. Children learn a great deal from the people in various occupations or professions. They learn what the functions of those jobs are; they learn first-hand what some of the problems in those jobs are. This is an important part of social studies instruction. Parents can perform excellent services for the school, for their own child in the classroom when they visit the class and demonstrate their own talents or abilities as they relate to their field or even one of their hobbies such as painting, drawing, gourmet cooking, ballet. Parents can assist when something is needed at the school. (See Figure 11.1.) They can contribute to the acquisition of library books, expensive equipment (such as a television set), and medical equipment to test hearing, vision, or other senses. Parents are eager to help when they know what is needed. Scholarships for children, after-school classes in ballet, painting, and music are important to certain schools. Group attendance at a symphony, ballet, or sports event can be made possible by parents of a school.

The parents who understand the curriculum of the school find it satisfying to be a part of it. They enjoy the knowledge of newer methods or techniques, and can assist the child at home in those techniques. Even if they do not assist them, at least they will not make counteracting comments about them. It confuses the child when parents criticize the school, its methods, or the teachers.

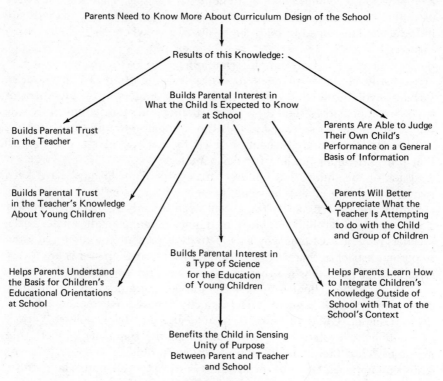

Parents Need to Know More About Curriculum Design of the School

Results of this Knowledge:

Builds Parental Interest in
What the Child Is Expected to Know
at School

Builds Parental Trust
in the Teacher

Parents Are Able to Judge
Their Own Child's
Performance on a General
Basis of Information

Builds Parental Trust
in the Teacher's Knowledge
About Young Children

Parents Will Better
Appreciate What the
Teacher Is Attempting
to do with the Child
and Group of Children

Helps Parents Understand
the Basis for Children's
Educational Orientations
at School

Builds Parental Interest in
a Type of Science
for the Education
of Young Children

Helps Parents Learn How
to Integrate Children's
Knowledge Outside of
School with That of the
School's Context

Benefits the Child in Sensing
Unity of Purpose
Between Parent and Teacher
and School

figure 11.1
Parents Need to Know More About Curriculum Design of the School

Teacher Conferences with Parents

The teacher has to be sensitive to several aspects of the parents' background when she talks to them. She has to be aware that their concerns about the child may be tinged with mixed emotions. She has to tread gently when discussing weaknesses of the child's work at school.

Some parents have indicated that, after a conference with their child's teacher, they have gone away from the school feeling like failures as parents. They felt as though they had made a mess of their child's life (already at the tender age of five). The teacher told them so much of what she thought was "wrong" with the child that they felt an irreparable injustice had been done to their child. They felt that they themselves were the direct cause of it.

When parents come to school, either after they have been asked to do so by a teacher or because they were upset about something that had happened to their child, the teacher should be prepared for knowing how to speak to them and to listen to their complaints. One way to offset parental explosion early in the school year or term is to invite all the parents to the pupils' classroom. Do this about a week or two before school begins. The parent does not feel uncomfortable about coming because she knows that nothing could have happened yet to create problems with her child. The teacher at this time discusses the school program and shows the parents what the children will be doing. She explains the routines for the school day and general activities that are offered as special events on certain days. They might have an art room, music room, or a library in the school in which the children are offered periodic activities.

The teacher explains the materials that are in the kindergarten—the blocks, how they are used, for which subject matter area they are used (e.g., social studies—how the use of those blocks include learning about size relationships, spatial relationships, building with "raw" materials, and the like). She explains the use of puzzles, painting, easels, finger painting, clay modeling, what these activities do for children's development in learning physically, and the way that sensory involvement with certain materials develops children's knowledge for understanding books they read or songs they sing. Further, these experiences provide them with ideas and sensory images that are useful for the creation of songs, stories, words, sentences, and literature.

Parents listen to this from the teacher who reflects the assumption that the parents *want* to know about their children's course of study. The reasons for using certain kinds of equipment is described to them. They have the right to know what their children are doing and what contemporary pupils are expected to learn from participating in those activities. By letting parents know that the teacher and the school realize they want to know what their children are learning and that they are respected as people who are interested in their children's progress, the parents begin to sense a partnership with the school. They do not feel as though they are being ignored and considered unimportant (and perhaps even an incumbrance) in the child's learning processes.

The teacher should be considerate of the parent, showing the mother that she is respected for her validity in perceiving problems. At times when people discuss problems with each other and one person thinks that the other person's problem is not serious enough to warrant anxieties and fears, there is a tendency to act as though the person's problems are not valid or authentic. The person responsible for making decisions in relation to that problem, however, is deeply troubled. For this reason, the teacher—while being able to reassure the parent that something can be done to alleviate the problem—should not respond to the parent as though the parent does not know what she is talking about or is foolish for having such a concern. (See Figure 11.2.)

figure 11.2
Teacher Awareness of Parental Representation

Teachers must be aware that the parent represents:

a valid personality with problems that are very real to her even though it may not be understood by the teacher

an individual who has a number of complex relationships with others in the family and neighbors and in this sense brings complexity to the child's life

an individual who may or may not understand what the purposes of certain curriculum activities in the school's programs are

an individual who is sending her child to school not because she wants to but is compelled to do so

an individual who may be having marital problems which are affecting the child's routine sleeping, eating, thinking patterns

an individual who may not feel that she can effectively cope with the problems her child is having

an individual who may have a family history of parent-child problems

an individual who is depressed about her own family problems and has already conceded defeat

a person who may feel inferior as a parent and who feels helpless in dealing with her own child

a person who has tried to do well at school herself but has not met her own goals

A mother who worries that her child will never want to learn is a case in point. She may have deeper anxieties about it because of other problems in her family about which the teacher has no information. If the teacher will relate to the mother as though she understands the various kinds of situations that can happen in a family and shows that she empathizes with the mother, the conference will move along well. The mother will feel that the teacher cares about her problems. In turn, the mother will sense some security that this kind of personality in the teacher will take good care of her child at school.

Parent-teacher conferences can be very satisfying for the parent and the teacher when the teacher adopts an attitude of putting herself in the parent's place. The teacher who can sense the parent's discomfort or embarrassment about something her child is doing at school is the one who can be of great help to the parent and the child. Identifying with the parent as an individual who knows she should be helping her child in many ways and wants her child to do better, the teacher can make much kinder remarks in speaking to the parent.

Too many teachers speak in an authoritarian tone, scolding the parent in either words or attitude for not doing a certain thing for a child. The parents who leave these conferences come away with aggravated feelings of inferiority, anger, or defeat. Furthermore, they feel more inept than before in assisting their child in any way and are more likely to feel that they don't blame their child for not doing well in that teacher's class.

One of the most important responsibilities on the teacher's part in a conference with parents is to listen to the parent, to try to read between the lines of conversation, to what the parent is trying to say, what the parent is actually saying in words, and what the parent seems to be trying to avoid saying. The teacher with insight can learn a great deal about the child through the parent's conversation. If the teacher listens more than she talks, the teacher will learn what the child's home life is like, and what the parent's orientations to life are. In any case, after the parent has been heard, the parent feels much better generally about the teacher, the school, and her child's future acceptance at that school.

An effective parent-teacher conference does not guarantee success for the child at school any more than does any single element in the child's home and school life; but it does ensure better understanding between parent and teacher, which promotes a better life for the child at school. The teacher is far better able to see the child in the context of his problems at home, and typically is far more willing to work around them with the child when he is at school. An attitude of empathy, of understanding, and almost of identification with the child because of his problems results, and the teacher—instead of perceiving the child and parent as an adversary in the classroom process—has joined their side as an ally against the problem. Personalities in the situation become secondary.

When the teacher has to give suggestions to the parents about ways to help the child at home or ways to encourage him to do better work, this can be done in a way that indicates the teacher's trust in the parent's ability to help the child in the best possible way. Recommendations should be given calmly to the parent. The teacher should not transmit feelings of irritation. (Note Figure 11.3 for general format of a teacher–parent conference and guidelines for questions and comments that may be made.)

The parent's answers to questions about the child's health habits, what he likes to do outside of school, what he likes to eat, what games he likes to play, which children he likes to play with, and so forth give the teacher some insight on the child's life outside of school. The teacher must not comment critically, then, on what the parent tells her. General comments can be made toward the end of the conference. If the teacher reacts critically toward what the parent says and interrupts her while she is speaking and gives an "instant analysis" of the child's and parent's problems, this will bring the conference to a halt. The parent will not be willing to continue talking when the teacher continually interrupts. It is too frustrating.

In terminating the conference, the teacher indicates that she is glad that the parent came to school and is happy to have had the opportunity to know the parent and child better. She also indicates that, if the parent

figure 11.3
Teacher Conferences with Parents

Individual Conferences	*Group Conferences*
The Teacher:	The Teacher:
1. asks parents how the teacher can help with the child's progress;	1. greets parents;
2. listens to the parent's concerns about the child;	2. discusses daily routines of the children;
3. tells the parents of the child's strengths at school, i.e., child's ability in certain subject matter areas, the child's talents in painting, music, physical education, leadership skills with other children;	3. describes the curriculum to the parents, gives the rationale, the how and the why of the program;
4. concludes conference by transmitting a feeling to the parent that the teacher appreciates the parent's coming to school to discuss her concerns.	4. answers the questions of the parents in a matter of fact manner, not defensively or arrogantly; and
5. Teacher and parent decide on next steps to support child's progress.	5. gives the parents the impression that their comments are valued.
	6. Last of all, the enthusiasm for working with children is evident in the parent conference so that the parents leave the conference with a sigh of relief knowing that their child is in the care of someone who wants to help their child develop to the best that is within the child.

has any questions or concerns about what is going on at school in the future, she should leave a message at the office for the teacher to call the parent or arrange a conference. The channel for communication must be kept open. The parent must feel that the teacher cares about her opinion and about the welfare of the young pupil in her class. This, in effect, is the most important thing that comes out of a conference; the parent knows her opinion is valued, as is the worth of her child at school.

It is assumed, of course, that any parent confidences given to the teacher will remain in confidence. If something needs to be disclosed to the nurse or principal, this too can be done in a professional manner. However, the parent's disclosure to the teacher does not become the common property of others in the school.

A parent-teacher conference should be held alone where others are not passing through the room. The teacher should arrange a comfortable place for them to sit, either in the classroom or an office if one is available nearby. The conference should not take place within earshot of others. It should not be done standing in the hallway or a doorway, unless of course the parent has stopped the teacher for an emergency of some kind.

The two people should be talking away from the pathway of children and other teachers. They should have a quiet area. These are important elements that can promote professionalism. The conference is only for the teacher and parent. Privacy allows greater freedom in the element of confidentiality. It also gives the parent the feeling that the teacher is giving her undivided attention to the problems at hand. The parent becomes more willing to say what she feels if time and privacy and quiet are given to her—time to allow her to say what she thinks and time to ask the teacher questions that she may not have known how to ask before meeting the teacher.

When teachers talk to parents of children in the four- to five-year-old age range, it becomes obvious that many parents are concerned not only about the present but the future of their child. They want to know if the behavior of their child now is not leading toward the development of a habit of some sort, one that may not be desirable. They are concerned about everything—from the boy who plays in the housekeeping corner with dolls and with little girls more often than he plays with other boys out in the block building area or outdoors on the tricycle or in the swings and slides, to the child who does not want to participate in group activities. The emphasis with young children is on the way that the present daily activities and behavior of the child will affect the future personality of the child. Because the children are so young, the parents are concerend to a greater extent about habit-forming behavior.

The parents of children in the six- to eight-year-old age range are also concerned about habit-forming behavior, but not in the same way as parents of younger children. About this time of the child's life in the primary grades, certain manifestations of personality problems arise. The child's adaptation to school is beginning to stabilize itself. He is familiar to some extent with the routines of school and what is expected of him from the teacher. He has learned that everyone is expected to do what the teacher says and that he has to react to his peers in different ways. He is cautious, on his guard to see what they like or don't like, and he tries to adapt to the general stream of behavior of children and to the teacher if he possibly can.

The responsibility for school and his performance there has become mainly his. He is not as much at the bridge between school and home as he was at four or five. He is across the bridge and strongly rooted in the school pattern. Much of what happens to him at home is a result of what happens to him at school. Discussions of his performance in subject matter areas and behavior at school—generally about other children that he may like or not—are a large part of home life. For this reason the child in primary grades is more like a young student learning the ways of school life and bringing it home in the same way a father brings home discussions about his work. It becomes the child's bailiwick, his cross (or not) to bear.

He is totally responsible for it. It is his private development of school life and tasks and relationships with other children. His parents are not as much physically involved in his school life as they used to be, but they are psychologically tangential to it; it takes up so much a part of each day and even the weekends at which time school or his work with others is discussed. Just as a man's thoughts about his occupation or profession do not leave him much of the time, so does the child's school life remain in his mind. It is an ongoing stream of a major part of his waking hours.

For the teacher who discusses children's progress in the primary grades with parents, the topic of conversation leans more toward progress in school subjects. While it is of interest to the parents to know that a child may be a leader among his peers—or at least cooperates and does not instigate problems—the major emphasis is on the child's abilities and skills in subject matter areas. In a parent-teacher conference, the teacher discusses the child's abilities in reading, mathematics, writing, science, physical education, music, art. The emphasis, slightly different from that in the parent-teacher conference for the children in the four- and five-year-old age range, is precisely grounded in the subject matter areas. The general orientation of the teacher toward parental concerns for the child, and the general anxieties that parents bring with them to a conference, need to be remembered. The teacher who has empathy with the parent, and can identify at least in part with the parent's feelings of responsibility for the child, brings a needed quality to the conference, and adds to the validity of the discussion.

The teacher who cares about the general feelings of ineptness that a parent may have about a child not doing well at school can do much to alleviate a parent's helplessness and frustrations about the child's progress. This does not mean that the teacher cannot give constructive criticism; it means that the teacher must be highly sensitive to the feelings of the parent. The teacher can continue to work with the child and try to do everything possible to help him at school. The teacher's attitude transmits the feeling, "I care about you and want to help you every step of the way. You need to pull your share of the load; learning is an independent process after the teacher provides the materials and direction."

The teacher who can help the child realize that—after she gives him opportunities to learn, it is his responsibility for learning—is helping the child mature in the process of self-development. It is a way of showing the child how various situations in life require self-help, taking advantage of opportunities if one is to enjoy living. Individuals make their own.

Parents should be asked to observe the child at school. Many times, parents are not aware of how their own children are when they are in groups. Parents gain insight into their own child's behavior by seeing him as one pupil among others answering questions asked by the teacher, involved in discussion and playing games. Teachers can help parents see the child in relation to others and to note the quality of his interpersonal relationships. This is typically of interest to parents. It shows them something they simply cannot know in any other way but to see it for themselves. It leads to questions and comments that can be dealt with in a parent conference when one is held. It helps the parent realize that there are times when she cannot know what her child is like; that a child behaves differently with friends or peers or in situations outside the home beyond the protection of parents.

Books on the popular market and particular journals written for women offer tips on child-rearing processes to parents. The orientation of various authors range from the permissive, open, and democratic parent philosophy to that which emphasizes greater restriction on the time and tasks of the child. Some take the position of the parent as ruler of the house, or at least the major decision-maker. Some emphasize the point of view of the child and attempt to have the parent take the imaginary place of the child, identify with him, and try to put himself in the child's shoes to adapt to the child's perspective. "How would you feel if you were your child?" is the question often posed for consideration.

Parents are more perplexed as society has become for them more analytical and complex in relation to how to raise their children. They want to be "modern" in their views rather than "old-fashioned." Teachers must understand that even when parents try to listen to "modern" views, they are not comfortable, because it places them in a position of becoming the child's counterpart. Parents can remember how they felt as a child, but their parent was different to them and the social milieu was different. In this wavering position of taking the parent view toward the child and also trying to consider the child's view against them as the parent, they become confused. They look to books, magazines, various media, and perhaps to their friends to decide what to do when certain issues arise in their family discussions or problems of conflict—the child wanting permission to do something of which the parent disapproves.

Parents who are very conscientious about their children's development of good habits and doing a laudable job in raising their children become inhibited. Those who permit their own views to guide them are less concerned about what the "authorities" say and follow their own predispositions. The attitudes of parents toward their children—whether they expect them to act "mature" or whether they regard them as babies (even when they are four or five)—makes the difference between the kind of treatment the child gets at home: whether the child is expected to do things for himself or whether the mother is always there to peel the banana for him or put his shoes on for him or to button his jacket or zip it. The parent who wants the child to be more independent and mature will urge him to do things for himself and will sometimes give suggestions for ways to do it and will praise him for his efforts.

Parents realize that the child's peers have a great effect on his behavior. The desire to be liked is strong and the child will cooperate with others when he may not with his parents. Young children are not as much concerned about peer approval as older children are—e.g., seven- and eight-year-olds. Children below seven still want adult approval. When group behavior and its competitive overtones become more important to the pupil in the second grade, then he becomes aware of popularity as a concept. Before that time, he does not seem to care about "special status." For young children, the warmth and reassurance of their teacher seems to give them a feeling of "specialness."

A concept of popularity presupposes an awareness of what it is that makes children popular in certain groups. When children know how to appeal to—and can indeed do what it is that they think is approved by —a group, they know how to become a star. Children in the second grade are aware of who does outstanding work and who is chosen most often to be on teams of various kinds. Before that time, if these ideas are not stressed (nor is it suggested here that they should be) in the classroom, the children are not aware of group goals nor of who is the "most popular." Being popular presupposes the existence of a group; and young children do not sense "groupness" among themselves, even though the teacher says repeatedly to them that they are a group. Telling them they are does not necessarily make them feel that they are.

Problems of peer relationships are constant in a classroom. The teacher is aware of this most of the time. It is not difficult for her to notice who has been accepted by other children and who is chosen most often for various teams or group functions of a special kind. Teachers can sometimes help pupils who want to be with certain classmates by sending them on an errand together. Sometimes, parents invite their child's preferred classmate to their homes after school or to stay the night.

Parents have to help children choose their companions at times. This is their prerogative. Parents can verbalize a philosophy for young children to help them in self-guidance now and in later life.

Teachers can be of great assistance in helping pupils have opportunities to be with friends they like. Particularly with younger children, the teacher can arrange pleasant relationships by having them mix paints together. She tries to help all pupils learn how to be likeable. She sets a tone for the acceptance of many kinds of people. The teacher can indicate that all people make mistakes; all people have faults of some kind; all people have moods of happiness one day, sadness or irritation another.

The teacher sets examples for her pupils by her own behavior which is perceptive and understanding of problems that hurt the feelings of others. Children should learn to empathize with people. Many incidents arise in children's lives—e.g., illness in the family, death, death or injury to a cherished pet, for which emotional support is needed. A child is often affected by something he cannot even explain; a depressed feeling often manifests itself this way. A child's mother might be seriously ill in the hospital. He may feel lost without her at home. A teacher who senses a change of mood in a pupil can be of great support to him and not only provide the solace he needs but also the help he needs for expressing the way he feels. She can help him become occupied so that he learns for the future how to involve himself in constructive activity even when he is depressed. Prolonged self-pity can be nonproductive.

The teacher of the four- and five-year-old child notices ways that the child is trying to adapt to the schoolroom situation. Older children of six, seven, and eight have begun to understand the routines. Just as they have learned that teachers are different as other people are from each other, so they have learned that school policies are different from those found anywhere else. They know that they are responsible at all times for certain kinds of behavior. They are expected to respond in certain ways at different times in the school day. They learn too that they are expected to do their best in order to please their parents and their teacher. They realize that they are the focal point between school and home.

By the time the child is eight, a year which relatively marks a period of maturity to later childhood, he is fairly aware of expectations. He senses as he approaches the intermediate span of school years, an individualistic awareness of who he is and what he is. He has some idea by this time what his abilities are and which subject matter areas give him the most pleasure. He sees some depth in certain areas such as painting, music, physical education, science, mathematics. He knows by this time when he steps into the intermediate grades what he as an individual is capable of doing. The early childhood years hopefully were not only to inform and educate him about the skills and attitudes he was to develop by the time he reached intermediate grades, but also an exposure period. It was intended to be a period of allowing him to see the various and wonderful kinds of things that could be done by anyone who wanted to get involved.

The teacher and parent can work together helping the child try various activities in the early childhood years at school. The child should be encouraged at all times to try his hand at different things. Perfection is not of concern at this time; helping the child improve in his own way is. Perfection, refinement of skills can be developed as the child shows he is ready. But if this idea is introduced too soon, the child gives up. He decides he cannot do it too soon and often never goes back to try again. He does not want to progress beyond a stopgap. It is easier to retain the impression that he cannot do it, thereby obviating the need to try and to subject one's self to possible embarrassment.

The major goals of the teacher in the early childhood education range of a child's life should be to help the child tap as many resources as he possibly can. The teacher can help the parent see that this desire to try different activities is important. Encouragement is needed more than scolding for not being perfect at an activity. Children need a sense of openness to life rather than a closure for perfection. The parent and teacher are the two people most involved with him at this period and are the two people who can create a foundation of support for him. The satisfaction for the child in this endeavor is evident to the parent and teacher and that kind of satisfaction makes their effort extremely worthwhile.

Record Keeping and Observations

It is difficult to make any statements about a child's progress if some records are not kept to show a child's work from one period of time to another. Early stages at school in which a child is introduced to the program and routines reflect different responses from him than later when he is more familiar with what he is supposed to do or the way he is expected to spend his time while there.

The most important aspect of keeping records is objectivity. The teacher has to be scrupulously sensitive to keeping records that avoid derogatory remarks or adjectives that describe the teacher's insensitivities or hostilities more than the child's actual behavior itself.

Records on the pupil's responses toward his work, toward other children at different times of the day, and toward adults can disclose patterns in the child's behavior. Those observations can be helpful in the teacher's diagnosis of the child's progress and next steps needed in his program of work at school. Ever-increasing development—not perfection, but continuing work of an upward nature—is the teachers' goal for the child: not to frustrate but to praise and to encourage the child in his increasing efforts. Plateau performance is all right for a while but not so that it discourages the child from continuing to reach and grow. This is done in the context of pleasure, enjoyment, and the teacher's continual encouragement that the child is on the right track.

There are a number of ways of observing a child. Besides the teacher seeing what a child is doing and remembering what things or activities he enjoys most and which ones he remains with, she must also write these ideas down for a continuing record. This may have to be shared with the nurse, principal, parent, director of a program—whoever is professionally affiliated with the program and the child's welfare.

One way of recording the child's progress is in the form of anecdotal records. The teacher has a card or sheets of paper kept in a folder for each child. On each card or sheet of paper is a sampling of the child's activity and behavior for one 10-to-15 minute period. This is not easy to obtain. It requires total concentration on one child for the entire time span.

The teacher cannot do this at the same time that she is in charge of the entire class. One cannot watch one child carefully and analytically while simultaneously being responsible for an entire class of 25 or 30, even more. An assistant has to be responsible for the entire class while the teacher takes time out to observe and record the behavior of one child. This should be done on each pupil in the class. The teacher can far better discuss a child's progress with the parent and far better indicate the child's general behavior at school if she has anecdotal records on him. (See Figure 11.4)

The teacher notes the time on the left hand margin that she is observing the child. An example of this would be:

9:05   Charles came bounding into the room, smiling as he rapidly looked around the room. He spotted a corner with new games in it; he ran over to it. Another boy came to the area; "Can I play with you?" Charles asked. The boy said, hesitating, "Well, O.K., if you do what I tell yuh." The two of them opened the box of tinkertoy materials and began to sort out certain pieces. They smiled at each other. "This is fun," said Charles.

9:07   Charles began to build an object while he sorted out rods and wheels from the tinkertoy box. He said, "You can't have this. This is all mine." The other child said, "I don't want it anyway."

And so it goes, the teacher observing the child until she decides she has had sufficient sampling of the child's behavior. She may have noticed, meanwhile, that Charles was straining to see a tiny piece of colored wood. She may think that his eyes are bothering him. This bit of information can be added to other things that Charles has been doing at school. He may not have been attentive when seated behind other children in the back of the room. She may decide to refer the child to the nurse because she suspects that he may have difficulty with his vision.

Many times the child goes through several grades before somebody finally realizes that he does not see or hear well. Somehow, nobody took the time to really observe the child and reactions to his schoolwork or the way he responded to other children. What was "diagnosed" as laziness or disinterest was actually the result of a child's physical disability of some kind. People were quick to designate derogatory terms to the child's behavior—not willing to cooperate, stubborn, whatever—when in fact the child was having difficulty attending to what was going on because his vision was blurred or he could not determine what the teacher was saying because he could not hear her well.

People who work with young children must be just as aware of what they see physically in the children before them as they are of what they are trying to teach. Observations of the child, his responses to others, to his peers, to adults around him, to slides, to swings, tricycles, bugs, books, tell the teacher a great deal about the child and how he feels about the school environment. Does he enjoy it? Does it challenge him sufficiently? Does he like the people around him? Do they represent a source of fun to him? Do they represent a source of satisfaction to him? Does he enjoy approaching them? Does his behavior reflect expectations of receiving affirmative responses from others? Does he sense negativism toward him from the school group? All this can be noted by the sensitive teacher. It can help the child in the long run because he has a teacher who is willing to understand him.

The teacher notes the child's physical condition and energy levels. She notices if the child is listless, lethargic. No healthy child behaves this way; it is not laziness. It is symptomatic of many things; a child may be ill, or becoming ill. He may not be motivated by the environment. A lack of stimulation causes people to behave as though they are lazy, when actually it is disinterest or lack of challenge. The pupil who is not challenged by his environment is also the one who becomes mischievous or who begins to distract or tease other children. His own responsibilities become somewhat curtailed because he does not feel involved or committed to the completion of anything in that environment. He has ruled himself out of the game, so to speak, so that what he does is not the same as what the other children are expected to do.

The teacher notes during her observation period how often the child approaches one kind of activity. She notices how often and for how long he plays with a particular child or children. She notes what his part in the play behavior is: Does he lead? Does he influence? Does he distract? Does he create? Does he contribute ideas that the other children accept? Do they ignore him? Does he respond to this? (See Figure 11.4)

The teacher observes the child in various kinds of activity if possible. For the teacher of younger children in the four- and five-year-old age range, she notices his coordination of materials, and his way of managing himself on the equipment outdoors—the way he throws a ball, rides a tricycle, skips, hops, jumps over obstacles in the sandbox or in a pathway. She tries to observe the child's physical development and progress in his facility to participate on the slides, swings, and other climbing apparatus such as the jungle gym, jumping rope, noting how the child regards himself in these activities. She also notes his attitudes in painting, working with clay, whether he is pleased with what he does, whether he creates his own ideas rather than looking at another child and copying or asking the teacher what he should do.

The teacher in her observation also writes down verbatim what the child says, making no correction in speech sounds. The child said, "Yetsch

Behavior Record of the Child

Name of School _____

Child's Name _____   Date _____

Observed by _____

Time	Situation or Activity	Behavior of Child

figure 11.4
Behavior Record of the Child

go to da cornah an det a boh," (meaning "Let's go to the corner and get a board.") It is important that the teacher learn to hear what children are actually saying instead of what she wants them to say. The discipline involved in observing what children do helps the teacher in being more discerning about the children's habits. She can become more accurate in her perceptions of the children and hopefully in turn more accurate in knowing how to describe them to the appropriate person or referral service.

The teacher uses this information not only to help her prepare a progress report for the child for the term at school but also uses it to help her discuss the child's work at school when she has a parent (or referral service agent) conference.

No observation of a child is actually complete without his products. The work that the child has done in finger painting, drawing, collage, or easel painting should be dated and retained in a folder so that the teacher has a record of the child's progress in each area. The teacher notes too— as the children participate in musical activities or dances or singing games —how they coordinate their bodies in terms of balance, movement, grace, poise, rhythm. These are noted in the children's observation folders. The folders should be kept in the teacher's private files. They are not for public view. It is for the teacher's assistance, the parents', and the administrative personnel with whom the teacher feels it is necessary to confide. It is not public domain.

One of the most difficult aspects of teacher behavior is professionalism. New teachers have a misguided sense of privacy, what it is and what it is not. They sometimes treat information about their pupils in the same way they treat information about members of a family. It becomes items for gossip or items that contribute to feelings of "holier-than-thou" to some individual's need for reducing his own sense of guilt about something. Since it is new to such teachers to have all that information about other families and children, they are overwhelmed by it.

Teachers have to learn to keep private information about children and families to themselves. Again, they need to consider those children as people who are depending upon them for help. The children are the responsibilities of the teacher. The teacher who discusses a pupil's or the family's problems without compassion or empathy is not fair to the child. It is taking unfair advantage of a professional situation in which the teacher obtained information based on parental willingness to be vulnerable in the belief that her trust in the teacher would be valid. This relationship is not too different from that of a doctor and patient. The doctor needs to have certain confidential information in order to prescribe for his patient. The child trusts the teacher and so does the parent who discusses personal feelings and information with her. The least a teacher can do is to keep it to herself. It is typically privileged information, not meant to be shared.

The teacher who is a professional person feels that her first commitment is to the safety and welfare of the child. It is for the child's best interests that the teacher consider private and personal any information about the child that the teacher has—be it family, the child's work at school, whatever. The teacher needs to learn that the child's life is not to be discussed with others. At such times that general discussion takes place with colleagues and others, the teacher may refer to children in her class or generally to children she knows; but does not give names to identify specific children or their problems.

Record Keeping for Admission Purposes at School

This varies in terms of the purposes of the school and other institutions of which it may be a part. For a pre-school or early childhood school that is administered by private foundations, the records are kept in a total reserve. These records are not part of another set of files as is true of public school records. In the public school, the child's admission records may be part of other files that were sent to the school office from another school in the same system. For the private school it depends on its own records completely without the assistance of any others.

The school office has records on the date of admission of the child and his vital statistics: the date of birth; parents' names; their occupations; addresses and telephone numbers of business and home; whom to notify in case of accident or illness; records of illnesses, contagious or otherwise; innoculations the child has been given and the dates for them; the name of a physician if the parent would want him to be called in case of accident; allergies the child has or has had; medication that the child may be taking; and other information along those lines. Other schools the child has attended are noted. Academic information includes data on tests if the child is old enough to have had them; readers the child has completed if the child is in a series used by the school. This provides some information on where the child is in his academic progress. It sometimes helps the teacher to know what kind of work to give the child, what kind would be too difficult or too easy for the child.

As long as the records and the information obtained by them are used judiciously in the child's behalf, they can be helpful. When they are carelessly used or used in ways other than being considered privileged information, then the privilege of private information on the child or his family is abused. Professional personnel should be very self-conscious about the way they disclose any private information. They should feel a serious obligation to the child and to their profession.

Medical care is indicated on the records. The series of innoculations or antibiotic shots given to a child should be kept on the records. Shots given to migrant children who move throughout the country are recorded not only in the school but in a centralized place, a computer at the University of Arkansas. This is done so that children who go to different schools are not given the same innoculations more than once in relation to the timing sequence expected in the series.

Parents often forget which child has had which shot and when he has had it. These records need to be kept. Medical information about the child is extremely important to record keeping. Also whether a child has any disorder which means he cannot receive certain kinds of antibiotic medication, or whether he is allergic to other types of medication or to any foods, are all important data that should be on his school record. A child with diabetes cannot have sugar, and certain children must avoid foods or candies that make them sick.

The teacher must be aware of allergies children have to certain foods. She and the parent explain to the child that certain foods are dangerous for him; in that way cooperation can be secured to obviate serious problems. Foods at school are an important consideration. When parents send the child to school with some kind of snack in hand, this is all right. The teacher can help children understand why they should only eat snacks their parents have given them, not other children's food.

If lunches are eaten early at the school, then snacks are not a problem. In some schools, lunches are eaten about 11 o'clock. Teachers know when children have not had breakfast because it is sometimes mentioned in total discussion when children talk about what they had for breakfast before they came to school. Teachers can also check with older brothers and sisters who bring the child to school to determine whether the child needs milk or cereal before he starts the day. She can also check to see whether the child needs rest or sleep, and permit him to rest instead of forcing him to work in other school activities.

Some schools have what are called cumulative folders, referred to as "cum cards or records." These records include some of the information mentioned earlier. The problem with cumulative records is that they can create impressions that can be harmful to the pupil and stereotype him through his school years. The teacher's notes on the pupil can be distorted by her biased feelings toward him. Is he a problem child? Is he the teacher's problem? Is he a behavior problem? The data in the cumulative folder often tell the reader more about the teacher's irritation and her idiosyncracies than the child whose folder it is. Some teachers wisely enough do not want to read the cumulative folders on a child they are going to teach for the first time, because they want to remain free from biased attitudes about the child. They want to be fair, thus they avoid reading derogatory information about him. The teacher starts out with fresh impressions this way. She is ready to establish positive relationships with every child regardless of his past negative experiences with other teachers.

Parent Education Programs And Their Development. Many programs for the education of parents have grown in the last 10 years since Head Start gave the nation an awareness of the importance of effective education for young children. Children of parents who have steady jobs and adequate incomes typically go to schools that have enough tax funds to provide at least fairly adequate equipment, books and materials for the pupils.

Low-income neighborhoods having a lower amount of tax revenue coming into the community typically have had poor equipment in the schools. A community has to support itself in the best way possible. If a community does not have a high proportion of working people living in it, its members cannot contribute much to the tax dollar of the schools. With Head Start programs and other governmental subsidies, money has been allocated to schools in low-income neighborhoods. Attempts are made to give children a fair chance at having an adequate school program. Children need not suffer from the fact that their parents have not had the money of other children's parents in wealthier neighborhoods which have had support for their schools.

There are programs for parent-education. Typically, most public schools have had parent-teacher associations that attempt to provide information about child-rearing—its psychological, medical, and sociological aspects. This would be presented in a series of lectures, panel discussions, or study groups.

Parent-education programs are sometimes planned by teachers and administrators who want parents to be aware of their children's schooling and generally what is happening at school. They do seek parental support for any plans made at school. It makes the child's life—not to mention the teacher's and the administrator's—much better when the parents support the school's goals.

Some parent-education programs are part of a larger program. Head Start is one example of that. While the program is planned mainly for the development and the progress of young children, a significant segment of the program is devoted to parent involvement. The planners devote a great deal of time thinking of effective ways to have parents become involved in assisting, in doing school-community work, and in hosting parties (expenses paid by the government program).

The purposes of some parent-education programs are to interest the parents in visting the school to see what their children are doing, to have them participate in the children's activities, and to understand why instruction is done in the way it is. For young children, it is obvious that if parents know what the school's goals are for pupils, and if the parents agree with those goals, they will endorse the school, will support it morally particularly in the child's eyes, and will praise the child's work when he brings it home. The cooperation that parent involvement can create is a valuable addition to the school's and to the child's advancement in educational life.

Programs for migrant education of young children give great emphasis, as would be expected, to parent involvement. A series of activities and pamphlets are planned to provide information about the community.

Pediatric services are available for the child and his family as well as dental services, assistance in obtaining clothing, food, and other essentials. If a child needs glasses, physical examinations at school can help the parent secure this for the child. People who have volunteered, transport parents to community agencies where the child can receive what he needs. The parents have to be given information on these services and the school sees itself as an important focal point in this regard.

Some parent-education programs plan discussion groups for parents. They wisely ask parents what they would like. They do not talk down to parents but treat them as important to the child's education. The school knows that without the parent's cooperation, the child will be in conflict between the school and the home. The more the parent feels that the school is trying to help the child and not take the child away from the parent (even though the school may be bringing the child past the parent's educational levels), the better it is for the parents, the school, and the child. Parents do have fears that their children will surpass them in educational abilities and need reassurance that their children will always want and need their love regardless of how much they progress in education. Pupils should be taught to respect their parents for being their parents and trying to provide for their support. Part of a child's self-respect is based on his warm feelings toward his parents.

Most of all, children can learn compassion. They can be taught that kindness and consideration of others is an essential part in the enjoyment of relationships with others. Teachers have to help pupils respect their parents regardless of educational levels or retaining a job. This is vital to helping the child face various interpersonal relationships with a variety of people.

Parents in low-income areas sense a loss of dignity as it is. They need to be respected as human beings. For this reason, parent-education programs must be cognizant of the uneasiness parents have in their relationships with the school. Unless administrators and teachers go out of their way to show them they are respected as people and as a crucial part of the child's rearing patterns and vital contributors to the child's educational development (if only by virtue of endorsing the school's efforts), the parents may not realize how much they are needed.

Some educational programs for parents include coffee klatches, get-togethers for parents sharing information on the best buys in food, sewing classes, helping each other plan interesting hair arrangements, cosmetology groups—whatever the parents have indicated they want to discuss. Information can be obtained from doctors and social agencies; people who sew their own clothes, or who know how to plan thrifty but nutritious foods for their families, are asked to come to the groups. For parents who work, another group of activities has to be planned; they can get together on holidays, Sundays, and in church-related activities that provide food or refreshments as part of the program.

Working parents are primarily interested in their children having a place to stay when no adults are at home. They are also interested in what happens to children at school. Some are very concerned about the child's work and want him to be successful at school. Others who may have come from a family that believed work was more important than a formal education may not be as concerned about a child's progress at school. This varies. The parents must be made to feel that their interaction with the child is important to the development of personality. If the teacher speaks to the parent indicating that she knows the parent cares and will help her in every way possible, the parent usually responds in kind.

Parents like to know how they can help their children outside of school; they like to know of places to go which will enhance a child's knowledge. They like to know how the children can obtain help from a librarian, from museum facilities, free services for recreation and the like. The schools can help in this. Any kind of intermediary service that the school can provide is helpful. Again, as stated before, the key to parental acceptance of help, or their appreciation of it, is in the teacher's attitude and the way she provides this service. It is not to be patronizing in any way.

Parents in discussion groups on the subject of child-rearing indicate that they learn a great deal from it. One of the major satisfactions they receive from discussions on parent-child relationships is knowing that they are not alone in the perceptions of irritations and frustrations inherent in any close relationship. Parents have similar problems. When they are discussed, parents are relieved to know it is not unique to only one family or one parent.

Various groups have tried to help parents in child-rearing problems. More attempts have been made to facilitate this than are evident in the literature on the subject. It comes up mainly in the context of cooperative school ventures as those for children in pre-school. Child-rearing education for parents is evident in school discussions, PTA meetings, recreation, playground, community schools, and adult education groups. As a subject in itself, it is usually treated under the topic of family development. Some sociologists have touched on studies of ways that families deal with problems. Community agencies have attempted to help women in achieving better relationships with their husbands, children, and relatives as well as ways to improve interrelationships among them.

Parent-education programs can be one of the most welcome and appreciated by the parents. When the programs are provided in the spirit of helpfulness and pleasure in working with parents, everyone benefits from it—the school, the teacher, and the children. It is worth the effort involved.

summary

This chapter dealt with teacher-parent relationships and parent education, both of which are important to young children's development. If the school's goals are not congruent with those of the parents of the children of that school, the children will sense conflict. When their parents are supportive of the school's program, it is easier for the children to follow through in their schoolwork.

Children of parents in low-income areas sometimes do not have the financial advantages of adequate food, housing, or clothing needed for various kinds of weather. Cleanliness and protection from disease is another concern in low-income neighborhoods. Some parents are unaware of the role they play in the development of their children's personalities. They are not as aware as they might be of the fact that their children need to be praised by them when they do adequate work at school. They also need to know that the comments they make to their children are affecting the personality patterns they will develop, and more important are affecting the way they will make decisions for themselves.

Several kinds of parent-education programs exist in informal and formal ways. Some schools plan specifically for parent involvement. Typically the younger the child—e.g., four, five, six as compared to children in the intermediate grades—the more the parents are involved. If the parents do not know what the school is trying to do for their children, the child will be caught in the middle of this uncertainty, not knowing when the teacher or the parent has to be his major allegiance.

Research programs that are subsidized by Federal grants often have parent involvement concepts built into them. The parent becomes an active educator in the child's life, since the parent is an important caregiver who aids the child's welfare. Follow Through programs which attempted to follow the children who had been in the Head Start programs at an earlier age have parents as aides who come to the classroom and work with the children. They are learning about children in general, about child development and general methods of education. This knowledge is used not only for their own children; many of these parents go on to school to further their own education and improve their chances and those of their families for a better life.

topics for discussion

1. What are some of the major guidelines that you feel are important to ensure an effective parent-teacher conference?
2. Present a parent-teacher conference with another person in the class by role-playing the parent who has come to school because she was upset by something her child said had happened at school. Find out what the problem was and then discuss with the parent some of the activities that children are engaged in at school.
3. Create files for anecdotal records and bring in some products of young children, four to six years old, that could be used for hypothetical records. Indicate what you think the child's work reflects in his development at school. How would you explain or interpret this to parents of the children?
4. Why is parent education important for parents of young children in the three to five year old age group? What kinds of discussion groups or lecture series do you think would be enjoyed by them?
5. What does privileged information mean in the context of a conference with a teacher? Where should conferences take place and what should the general tone of that conference be?

selected bibliography for teachers

Auerback, A. *Creating a Preschool Center: Parent Development in an Integrated Neighborhood.* New York: John Wiley & Sons, Inc., 1971.

Auerback, A. *Trends and Techniques in Parent Education: A Critical Review.* New York: Child Study Association in America, 1961.

Becker, Wesley C. "Consequences of Different Kinds of Parental Discipline," pp. 169–208 in *Review of Child Development Research,* Volume I. Edited by Martin L. Hoffman and Lois Wladis Hoffman. New York: Russell Sage Foundation, 1964.

Brim, Orville G. Jr. *Education for Child Rearing.* New York: Russell Sage Foundation, 1959.

Emmerich, W. "The Parental Role: A Functional Cognitive Approach," Monograph of the Society for Research in Child Development, 1969.

Hess, Robert D., and Virginia Shipman. "Early Experience and the Socialization of Cognitive Modes in Children," *Child Development.* Vol. 36 (1965), pp. 869–886.

Lane, Mary B. *Education for Parenting.* Washington, D. C.: National Association for the Education of Young Children, 1975.

Medinnus, G. R. *Readings in the Psychology of Parent-Child Relations.* New York: John Wiley & Sons, Inc., 1967.

Parent Involvement: A Workbook of Training Tips for Head Start Staff. No. 10. Washington, D. C.: Office of Economic Opportunity, 1969.

Yarrow, Leon J. "Separation from Parents During Early Childhood," pp. 89–136. In *Review of Child Development Research,* Vol. I. Edited by Martin L. Hoffman and Lois Wladis Hoffman. New York: Russell Sage Foundation, 1964.

Chapter
12

School–Community Relationships

Communities have a variety of characteristics. There are urban, suburban, rural, mixed, transitional, commercial types. It depends on the economic status of people who support the financial aspects of buildings, businesses, or resident areas in the neighborhoods. The character of a community— while *not* homogeneous—has certain qualities that can be readily summarized.

A community in the commercial downtown area has theaters, factories, shops, and small grocery stores. Not many residences are evident except perhaps for apartment houses, some of which may not have been built of high-grade materials. Communities in residential areas vary too. They may be well-built, have large lawns set back from the street, maintained consistently well and may reflect currently wealthy residents or those who are no longer wealthy.

The community has a variety of residents. They include businessmen, professional people, storeowners, parents of schoolchildren, parents who have children in elementary, junior or senior high school. Grandparents who have no children living at home with them are also in the community, plus people who have not had children at all. The variety of people in a community is great. Educators have to be aware of these implications for the maintenance of schools and how it affects the type and turnover of the school population.

Schools that have a community with few children needing a formal education in that neighborhood may not have adequate funding support. People in that community have to get money to support the schools, and they also have to have the desire to vote for it when the opportunities arise.

Variety of Neighborhoods and Communities and How This Affects Education

Because so many different communities and people exist in any one city, the nature and characteristics of each community are difficult to generalize into one category or type. Beyond saying that cities, towns, small towns, large suburban areas, the megalopolis or metropolitan-type cities have complexity in common, most of them differ in several ways. They differ in terms of the economy or subsistence patterns they have. The variety of community areas suggests that whenever a group of people want to do something about improving their children's education or their development in general, the problems blocking them will differ from community to community.

Many communities attempt to reach businessmen so that their support, psychologically and financially, can be won. The educational system knows that industrial components of society warrant attention as an important sector to be involved in helping children.

The community and its businessmen plus the people who belong to voluntary associations which give charitable help and which have a sense of civic pride, enjoy being a part of a successful venture for children. Their assistance can be gained often. Federal aid to provide proportional support for community efforts, the educational system can gain added support for a project from the members of their own community and those of the broader geographical regions of an outlying city when this is appropriate. One of the most important elements in acquiring support of community members is communication. When people understand what is needed to help the school and its program, they will cooperate. They are usually excited about participation in a project that enables children to have something or some kind of opportunity that would otherwise not have been available to them.

Schools have provided adult education for those who are interested in going to school. Adult community schools are available in many parts of the United States. People who have not graduated from high school (or even elementary school for that matter) may attend community schools and take classes in almost any subject. Sewing, cosmetology, cooking, photography, learning to read, write, or speak English or several other languages are offered as part of a broad range of choices in an adult educational program.

With more education and a comfortable feeling about the school, parents and others cooperate with the school in that community. A willingness to support what happens there, not being afraid of it, and wanting to have functions in it, is of benefit to the young as well as the parents or adults who are participating in the programs.

Young children are not going to receive as much help as they should if the adults in their society do not think education is an important and necessary part of their lives. When children see that adults participate in educational pursuits and they see that adults are attempting to learn just as they are, the children acquire a greater appreciation of the school as an extension of their own homes. The parents too do not feel as though their children are going to outdistance them.

Society is not built on the strength of one level of development—viz., the educational system alone cannot adjust problems of its general society, or the society that provides the context of education. The educational system is only part of a broader total entity that constitutes a society for a group of people. For that reason alone, one of being part of a broader system, the educational component of society must be aware of how it can interweave its goals, purposes, and implementation into the broader context. A single school is part of a larger system, part of its own regional or local longitudinal stream of kindergarten through secondary and higher educational levels. In that sense of interrelationships between and among its own levels, other elementary schools and higher levels of schools (middle, junior, higher educational), the educators have to be aware of the part that its own system plays in its contribution to other systems.

The elementary school programs which usually house early childhood programs (kindergarten through grade three) need to encourage an awareness of being one part of a broader system. Administrators and teachers have to be aware that the parents and other people of the community in their school's boundaries are as much a part of the lives of the children they are teaching as are the school's.

The pupils are reflecting the influence of their community when the teacher sees them in the classroom. The teacher may have ideas as to what she wants to see changed in the children, how she would like to see them develop, what and how they should be learning and the like. She may have a strong influence on them, but all of this work with them needs to be considered in that broader context of other agencies, the parents and people in that community who have something to do with the child.

The schools provide programs for parents of the community and other adults so that adults can perceive educational opportunities for what they are. They are merely techniques or devices which expose the individual to other aspects of life that were formerly not available to him. The individual may not have been interested before this period of life; he may not have had time for it; he may have been pressed into helping the family earn a living to provide for food, shelter, their very life's existence. For whatever reason, the individual did not have the inclination to take advantage of educational opportunities apparently not meant for him.

As the schools seem to become more a part of their communities, they can be of greater service to the parents and the children. The early childhood education component of a school is one of the most important to ally itself with the community. It has the youngest children. They are the least angry, destructive or defensive of any individuals. People like to protect them and enjoy their innocence, lack of guile or deceit. They are a wonderful audience for appreciating the attention of adults, particularly when they are shown something. They have seen so much less of life than the adult that many things are still a source of wonder to them.

Because of the variety of communities, each school has to look at its own and attempt to be as sensitive as possible to what is there. The way of perceiving a community influences what will actually be seen. If people go into it trying to correct what they think is there; even before they validate such impressions, they will miss the target. They really have to approach it with unbiased notions or preconceptions. Openmindedness is enriching. It gives the individual a broader and unlimited perception and sensitivity to his environment than he may ever have had.

Teachers who come into a community have to be open to what the parents are saying, what the children are reflecting of the community, and what they see physically and psychologically around that particular school. It cannot be ignored. If the teacher has a biased or distorted view of that community, she will have to make a conscious effort to make adjustments in that regard. She will not be able to function effectively in that unawareness nor will she sense fulfillment in her work.

A community may be multicultural in the number and groups of residents in that area. A teacher, then, has to know who the people are, what their feelings are toward each other, how those feelings are manifested in their interaction with adults and with children. This information does not include value judgments in terms of comparing behavior as superior or inferior (or ascribing invidious differences). It merely provides the teacher with a repertoire of data on her pupils and the kind of background that they bring to school. It is an attempt at trying to see life through the children's eyes in one sense, yet in another sense trying to understand how the parents and other adults experience life in that community.

Teachers as professional people are attempting to be fair and equitable in their way of responding to adults and children. They can—by virtue of the fact that children sometimes try to emulate their teachers—set an example for the pupils by acting toward others in ways that reflect compassion, friendliness, and trust. For this reason, it helps teachers to know the community and to understand some of the frustrating problems faced by the people and families there.

The varieties of people in communities—both in the sense of variety of personalities and in the sense of different cultural or ethnic derivations —will not be listed here. Those varieties exist in endless combinations. The talents, abilities, skills, and predispositions of people from various backgrounds, genetic constitutions and the like will also not be listed. The teachers who work with young children must learn to be prepared for those differences not only in the children but because of the differences that reflect the community.

In general, educators may view communities in terms of eight factors and the effects these factors have on the children at school (See Figure 12.1). *First,* the economic level of the community is a factor—whether the community is high-income, low-income, middle-income or transitional will affect the school and the program it can develop. *Second,* the job status of parents of the children will affect the children. Questions such as:

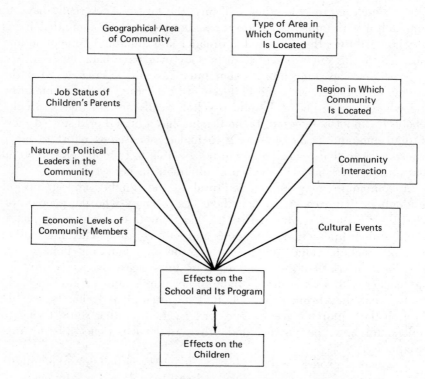

figure 12.1
School-Community Relations and Its Effects on School Children

Is the father the major breadwinner for the family? Is it the mother? Does she supplement a small part of the father's salary? Does she more or less share an essential part of the support of the family? Is the mother alone? Is she a women's lib advocate? Is she younger or older in the age range of 18–55? *Third,* the topographical nature of the community area—whether it is located in the mountains, the desert, a coastal region makes a difference. *Fourth,* is it urban, rural, suburban, isolated, or semi-isolated? *Fifth,* in what geographical part of the United States or other country is it located: Midwest, Northwest, Southwest, South, Northeast, Southeast, etc.? *Sixth,* community interaction refers to the frequency of interaction among people in it, and the effectiveness of certain groups in that community. Does the community have functions that bring them together, such as parades, street dances, or festivals? *Seventh,* a community's desire to have cultural events such as art shows, musical festivals, playhouses, symphonies; do they support them or provide them for the people in that community? *Eighth,* the nature of political leaders and influence in that community: do they lean toward conservatism, liberalism, or *avant garde* orientations?

As teachers and educators become more familiar with community types and the intricate systems of networks in them, they become more aware of the variety of ways that children may be educated. School systems do not have to be locked into certain programs. Education has made strides in some areas of the country and local communities are freer than they have ever been to develop their own ideas. When Federal funding is provided, the local areas merely have to present their ideas for the allocation of funds. This facilitates planning and conceptualizing the number and kinds of personnel that will be needed for a particular program. Thus, indications are made on paper as to how the budget will be allocated but the local community is given leeway for its own choices in implementation. In countries with centralized government (as distinguished from the federal system of the United States), local communities do not have the prerogative to decide on their own directions. In American cities, and towns, community members have far more influence than ever on the way they choose to govern themselves.

Policies planned by communities and schools are a reflection of preferences or needs of people in that particular neighborhood and school district. Each area can guide itself by solving the problems of highest priority. Monies from subsidy allocations or Federal grants are usually given in proportion to the local area's matching of funds. If the local area provides 15 percent of funds in support of a certain program, it represents their concern about it. It shows the people's willingness to bring energy and time to it in order to ensure its success.

Many people in communities still do not realize how much they can influence improvement in their own surroundings. Of course, it depends on the individuals. If a group of migrant workers go in and out of cities (and on the outskirts at that), they do not realize that they are part of it nor do they feel that they are. They are often rejected in many of them. Since one has to be a resident in order to vote, or at least to live in the community to know it for a while, they do not see themselves as having any effect on what happens there. They cannot have a sense of expansiveness for the welfare of others when they have to use most of their energy trying to take care of their own welfare, theirs, and their families. But some people who live in a community for a few years and who sense what is needed to make it a more effective living area can be of service to it. Their votes, their participation in meetings at school, their concerns do affect people who are in a position to help.

Community support for the school's programs in language development in young children can be secured. Parents whose cooperation is needed are generally pleased to do so as long as they know why—if they understand the basis of the program and what the school has planned for the children. They are usually flattered and appreciative that the school has taken the time to describe or explain the purposes and projected outcomes of the program.

When financial aspects of a program are an essential part of the discussion with parents, this presents a different problem. Their financial support is questionable. In a low-income neighborhood, it cannot be expected. In middle- and upper-level income areas, PTA functions, picnics, spaghetti suppers, sales of seats to a play or symphony, dance, or ballet, can bring in the needed monies for equipment (such as a television set or a sound system) that the school cannot supply.

Moral support for an idea that the school wants to use in a program is another type of support that parents can be asked to give. This involves mainly an explanation and an understanding of the program so that parents will permit their children to participate. It means not only allowing the children to participate but also being positive about it. When parents undermine it by grumbling about its inconveniences to them or its oddities, or are generally critical, it gives the child the feeling that the program is unimportant, not valid, unnecessary.

In any case, when the school and the community are at least in partial accord with events in the schools, this makes for the best of worlds. The schools are pleased that they are approved by the community and a sense of good will pervades the areas. The parents, too, feel that they are an important consideration to the school and they think of it as more a part of their own lives and responsibilities. They feel comfortable because the school apprises them of its current strategies and in that sense they trust it with their children. The resultant ease in working together facilitates the success of many projects and strengthens the children's development in ways that could not otherwise be accomplished.

summary

Each community differs. While problems such as financial or moral endorsement for programs may be similar among communities, the people of those communities differ. The composition of a community or what it consists of in terms of its proportions of low-, middle-, or upper-income groups affects its current life.

Businessmen, parents, other adults, and people working in social agencies of a neighborhood affect the number of interest groups and their perspectives. The points of view taken by members of a community reflect problems of certain percentages among them. If one is in a community of low-income groups—mainly of one ethnic group, their concerns will be of and for that ethnic group. This is the major point of view they can take, what happens to them is what means the most and is what they understand best. When they realize that crucial issues are advocated by people who want to advance the interests of their group, they will support those ideas. This is to be expected. Some groups strongly maintain family interests. They want their children's welfare above all. Thus a school would only recommend themes that support ideas which can promote family unity.

If a community is located in a resort town, a crowded urban area, an outlying town, an industrial city, one that manufactures cars, high-income mainly, mainly middle-, or low-income: all this affects the nature of the community in relation to its activities, problems, physical layout, and transportation facilities.

Whether a community is in a mountainous region of the country, desert area, near the ocean, seaport town, midwestern area, agricultural community, whether it is in a governmental hub, such as Washington, D.C., whether it is close to the Canadian border, whether it is in cities or towns in the lower southeastern area near the Gulf of Mexico: all these things affect the community interests they will have. The schools in those regions have to realize that their problems are unique in one sense and similar to other communities in another sense.

One of a teacher's best efforts (the school's as well) is to familiarize herself with the community. This means that she must be aware of the concerns of the people who live and work there. What goes on in those homes and buildings, in the offices and businesses is the substance of that community and where it will place its support morally and otherwise. It is very satisfying, too, to know people in that community to the point of feeling that the school is one with it. Teachers who know the community well are able to enjoy their work with people and children there.

topics for discussion

1. Describe a community using the eight factors suggested as characteristics that could be used to delineate its qualities.
2. Why and how does a community's characteristics affect the children's work and program at school in that community?
3. Does a teacher have to be a member of a given community in order to be an effective teacher at its school? Why? Why not?
4. Why is the period of early childhood education an important time for children as far as an awareness of their community is concerned? How does this emphasize the teacher's necessity for understanding and knowing something about that community?
5. How can the school be an effective agency for parents of the community?
6. Does the size, location, financial support of a community affect the number, variety and types of services that can be given to it? Why? How do these factors influence the provision of services to young, old, and in between?

selected bibliography for teachers

Fitzpatrick, Joseph P. *Puerto Rican Americans.* Englewood Cliffs, N.J.: Prentice-Hall, Inc., 1971.

Goldstein, Sidney, and Calvin Goldscheider. *Jewish Americans.* Englewood Cliffs, N.J.: Prentice-Hall, Inc., 1968.

Moore, Joan W. *Mexican Americans.* Englewood Cliffs, N.J.: Prentice-Hall, Inc., 1970.

Pinkney, Alphonso. *Black Americans.* Englewood Cliffs, N.J.: Prentice-Hall, Inc., 1969.

Wax, Murray. *Indian Americans.* Englewood Cliffs, N.J.: Prentice-Hall, Inc., 1971.

Chapter

13

International Understanding

The world outside children's homes has come within their reach far more than it ever did before in comparable groups of children in any era of history. This affords ample opportunity for children to know more about people in other parts of the world. What they see on television, in movies, on film in travelogues—whatever the format, provides them with knowledge of other cultures and societies. They also need the more systematic instruction that comes to them in school on this topic of other peoples and societies.

Helping Children Understand the World Beyond Their Geographical Boundaries

Children in any part of the United States need to know not only about children in other parts of their own city, state, and region, but also about children who live in other parts of the country and other parts of the world. One evidence of this necessity is the attempt to help nations establish peace among themselves. The establishment of a United Nations organization, the attempt to have each nation's representative sit at a conference table, is evidence of the need for national interaction among all peoples. Peace for one nation can represent peace for all nations. Wars represent a kind of insanity that occurs among men when their desires are frustrated. Men do not usually behave in irrational terms when their needs are met.

Young children in a contemporary society have at their disposal information on children of other cultures. The educational world has become more informed about other societies with the help of anthropologists, sociologists, and others who study life in various cultures. Family styles, customs, traditions, occupations of people in various cultures and how they earn a living, the food they eat, how they rear and educate their young, are all aspects of other societies that children should know. The simplicity of a society (e.g., isolated geographically and psychologically, sparsely populated, preliterate) or its complexity (e.g., highly industrialized, technological society in a densely populated, urban area) affects the view of its children. Most important, children's views and impressions and their development of a guiding philosophy (constructive or not for them), are greatly affected by the adults and siblings around them. The comments made about their experiences in that world convey impressions from others about the values that children are expected to develop in relation to certain situations, events, people, and life experiences, generally. The directions they are expected to take are implied by the parents and other supervising adults. With each of the experiences they have and their view of adults' reactions toward them, the children begin to develop a world view of their society (and themselves, as well). This gives them a sense of identity with others of their own group. They begin to associate certain kinds of behavior and certain feelings that they "ought to have" —e.g., feelings of love and appreciation for their parents.

A child from Sweden, France, or Nigeria has feelings or emotional twinges (negative or positive) about his homeland that will be similar to those of a child from other countries. It will no doubt be a feeling of belonging, possessiveness, identification. Names children hear about their country—words and labels given with places and people—provide them with a map of awareness of their context, their background, and their own identification. Stores, holidays, ways of marketing, routine of meals, school hours, days of attendance at school are some of the characteristics that define a country's "flavor."

Parents involved with young children are teaching them the values of their country simultaneously with the more personalized and idiosyncratic values of their own immediate family. No society, as an entity, is "instructed" to children in any total way since no "society" can be assimilated by anyone, except a very primitive one inhabited by a very small number of people. Each child experiences his society through his family, its experiences, his own direct experiences and because impact comes mainly through the directness of an experience, a child can only truly know his own feelings through direct experiences.[1]

[1] Edythe Margolin, *Sociocultural Elements in Early Childhood Education* (New York: Macmillan Publishing Co., Inc., 1974).

Whatever children learn about their own country, they need eventually to sense that they are similar to children in other countries. While parents may not do this deliberately, teachers need to do this as an essential part of the school program. They are educated to see things in a broader academic and systematic context than parents. This does not mean that the parent who had traveled extensively could not also provide her own child with excellent international information.

As more sociological and anthropological data are available, teachers can update their own knowledge to use with young pupils (See Figure 13.1). Pupils are very responsive to customs and traditions of other cultures, their beliefs, their way of life, their perspectives toward the world, marriage, child-rearing, and schooling of children. In general, children acquire this information from the teacher through social studies. This is one reason why the social studies can provide a crucial base, not only academically but psychologically, for young pupils' first introductions to and understanding of international cultures.

Early childhood is an impressionable time and it is ideal for instilling values that help young children appreciate people of different cultures. Their lives will be richer because of it. Ethnocentric people (those who think that their own culture is the only valid one and which has the best set of values and beliefs for its people) close off other points of view in their thinking. It prevents them from enjoying different people and viewing them in positive terms. It does not mean that children should want to emulate the habits or customs of other cultures. It does not mean that children should want to negate their own culture or not feel a sense of pride in it. It does mean that they expand their ability and capacity to appreciate other people who have grown up in a country different from their own.

More materials are available for teachers of young children to help

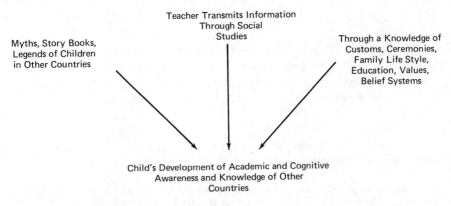

figure 13.1
Children Learn About Other Cultures

them with accuracy in presenting activities that will transmit an appreciation of other societies.[2] Note references in the chapter on social studies in this book. Many materials and resources are noted in books, articles, journals on social studies. Literature of children in other lands is also an important source of information. Its myths, legends, and stories give children in this country ideas as to what the beliefs of the country are, what legends are important to the adults and children in those places. It gives colorful impressions of the people, their history, values, view of life, death, moral orientations, virtues or honor.

In books for young children, illustrations of contemporary clothing of people in those countries, give children living in the United States a picture of what their counterparts in other cultures are wearing. Some people in those cultures wear the same styles of clothing as people in the United States. As individuals visit other countries, fashions in clothing are brought from one place to another. Paris notes American styles; Americans note Parisian and Italian clothing. Imports are considered valuable and prestigious. What comes from another country is appreciated because it is different from most of the things in one's resident country.

Children see people of other societies when they see travelogues on television. Some of the cultures are isolated to some extent. The clothing worn by the people on islands separated from the continents may differ. Their livelihood is maintained differently from people living in a city. Handwork, hand carvings, provide a "living" for some people. Food is acquired by groups for its own groups. There is not the large surplus supply or division of labor that occurs in a complex city where millions of people work in specialized jobs. People who work in clothing supplies have to buy their food from those who specialize in the selling of food or who conduct a business in marketing food supplies.

Games, songs, singing games of children from other countries help pupils understand what brings pleasure to those children. It creates a kinship between them. They see what other children their own age enjoy even though they are an entire continent away and are separated by an ocean.

Dances that children from other cultures have known from the time they were babies, give pupils in the United States an appreciation of the themes or dances that are important to other children's background. Esthetic appreciation can build on the intellectual and emotional elements of the dances.

Celebration of holidays in other cultures is another way to know the children of those cultures. What kind of gifts they enjoy, cakes, candies, meals, in what ways they celebrate their birthdays, provide information

[2] Association for Childhood Education International, *Children and Intercultural Education* (Washington, D.C.: Association for Childhood Education International, 1974). Bulletin #72–97348.

that all children appreciate. Do children in other lands celebrate holidays with a picnic, decorating a tree, with their own family or with groups of children their own age?

Real clothing, objects used by people in other cultures, realia (the tools actually used by people in other societies, clothing actually worn by them, their flags), pictures, art work, musical instruments: all these lend reality and vivid impressions of other people and their lives. Children gain from this. They feel almost as though they know the people intimately.

The food they like in other cultural groups, special treats, special gifts, or what other cultures recommend for their children's development of sensible health habits, are important facts revealing intimate details about other people and countries. Besides the foods of children in other countries and their impressions of health and how it is obtained and maintained, pupils in America need to know about the fears and anxieties of children in other cultures. They need to know what preoccupies children's minds, what the children prize, what dreams or goals they have. This bond between children here and an understanding of the feelings of children in other parts of the world, create closeness that is not only prized but really necessary as the world contact becomes closer, and as military technology have emerged with atomic bombs and life-snuffing-out capacities. People need more and more to understand one another if they are to enjoy each other with all the differences that can enrich people's lives. Young pupils can achieve this easily through effective reading, sensitive, and empathic and knowledgeable teachers.

Childen learn about themselves, the personalities they are, the characteristics their parents value in them, what their peers admire, and the characteristics their "country" admires in people. They discover this through literature, other communicative media, and through their own books at school. All children learn through compliments or derogatory remarks what most people in their own nation admire.

Children learn about themselves through their own immediate family (see Figure 13.2). They find out how they are expected to behave, what they ought to do, what they ought to want to do (e.g., love their parents, respect their elders, to be generous, kind, fair, equitable, and so forth). They learn most about how they are expected to act from their parents in the home setting. As they mature, children in their neighborhood implicitly teach them what is expected of other children their own age. They learn through media about their city and also by traveling around in it what their city is like, what is in it, what kind of institutions, agencies, theaters, symphonies, department stores, restaurants, hospitals, colleges, universities, libraries and museums it has. They hear about and may go to those places; they may participate in them in some way, too.

Knowledge about a child's state reaches him through his books at

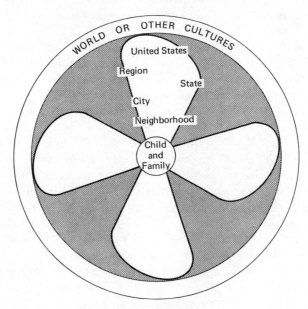

figure 13.2
Inroads of the World into the Child's Awareness of Self and
Personality Development
(Relationships to Other Parts of the World Outside His Own Family)

school, media, television, and in various written forms through parents
and teachers' information to him. This does not come to him every day,
necessarily, but periodically he hears about it: state licenses on cars, state
taxes, state laws regarding health. In general, a child hears about the
state and learns about it vaguely as a governmental institution, but he
becomes familiar with the term and concept through laws or policies that
govern his school or institutions (a state hospital, for example).

Knowledge about the United States, as a governmental body, reaches
him at least through the pledge of allegiance to the flag of his country.
He gets some impressions on what the United States comprise as a
democratic unit. He begins to acquire strong feelings about his country
through association with other children in the United States. This knowledge does not come to him consciously every day in the same way that
his parents' interaction and information come to him (regarding how he
is expected to act and what kind of characteristics he is expected to incorporate into his personality to please his parents). He learns about "his"
country in conscious or explicit ways every once in a while.

His knowledge about the world and the way he relates to it periodically
acquires greater significance for him. Looking at Figure 13.2 one sees

how the world outside is the farthest point from the child's "central being." It is with him as he sees television, sees presidents and prime ministers of different countries speaking at formalized gatherings, negotiating peace, and negotiating help. He begins to differentiate himself from other countries, aware that he is an American citizen, differentiating himself from an Egyptian, Syrian, Israeli, Norwegian, Russian, or Belgian.

The pupil develops an awareness of who he is, what his country is, what it believes, what its government stands for, and hears about its history at an introductory level. Tradition is reflected in the celebration or observation of holidays. He learns about significant elements of his country in part by those traditions and the reasons for their celebration. Inroads into his consciousness are made periodically. The farther away geographically that the bodies of government are, the less often do they intrude into his consciousness. The day-to-day contact with his parents, family, friends, and school are the strongest interaction elements that affect the creation of his personality.

Teachers can be very instrumental in helping children develop a healthy awareness of themselves in relation to the country in which they live. They can help pupils learn not only about their heritage and the books available to describe it, but also the endless variety of other fascinating interests enriching to their personalities, and which can be pursued at school.

Early Childhood Education's Responsibilities for World Affairs

Early childhood education as a field affects pupils at an extremely important time in their lives. They are highly susceptible to learning. The way they will learn, however, depends on a particular set of adults who are skilled and who care enough to provide them with many materials and objects worthy of use—worthy of being investigated, manipulated, turned, pushed, pulled, examined, turned upside down.

People in the field of early childhood education have an optimum opportunity to affect young children as future citizens to understand and enjoy the world. To teach young children empathy, understanding—in an emotional and an academic sense combined—is one of the most satisfying jobs a teacher can have. To perceive others in ways that arouse feelings of identification (in spite of not knowing them personally) becomes more important as the world comes closer to one's own.

Sociologists have noted that many Americans are philanthropic as a people. When someone has problems of illness, when flood overtakes a region, when there is a plea on television or in the newspapers about a person with a terminal illness (especially a child), people who do not know the individual personally send help in the form of money, cards of good luck, prayer, flowers, or whatever. They are touched and concerned. They empathize with others' problems. Young children can learn to appreciate these concerns.

It may not be a guarantee for sound adulthood that young children be given the best opportunity to develop empathy with and understanding of the problems of other people, but it is to their own great advantage if they are with teachers who can help them in this development. A sensitive teacher can help the children become sensitive to the hurts, fears, and disappointments of others. She can help the children learn to become perceptive about the problems of others by discussing them with the class when the problems occur. Literature or stories can also be used in strengthening empathic feelings with other people, other children, and particularly those in other countries.

If children realize that other people have problems similar to their own, that other children have disappointments, that their pets die, that gifts cannot be purchased because of a lack of money, hopes, goals for winning something—a game, a prize, or whatever—children can develop a capacity for identifying with the feelings of others. Putting one's self in the shoes of another, so to speak, inside the skin of another, transcends the feelings of jealousy, envy, or anger. Placing one's self in someone else's position helps the child perceive the effects of another person's problems as though they were happening to him.

Pupils can be shown films, filmstrips, of children from other lands. Plays can be part of the class's efforts in literature or in language arts activities, after the class studies the country's myths, beliefs, customs, and means of celebration. They may, if they wish, use a fine classic or a story that they enjoyed and dramatize that. A play usually provides a sense of aliveness for pupils. It encourages imagery, planning, and satisfying modes of creativity while simultaneously using the knowledge gained from reading about other cultures.

Music of other cultures and societies can be learned. Dances and festivals can be planned. Children enjoy those productions. It has to be simple for young pupils. Scarves, paper hats made by them, scenery, similar to a mural form can be made by them too. These ideas arise as the teacher discusses with them the many things that they may do. She tries to amplify their own ideas.

The obligation of early childhood education to international understanding proceeds from cognitive, emotional, and empathic views. The schools have materials that can give the children insight and information about other cultiures in a contemporary sense. Adults who do not travel or have not watched films of people in other lands usually have a distorted impression as to what other countries are like. They have had sparse information in school about other countries, the people, how they earn a living, their government, their holidays, and beliefs. In the past, social studies were not taught with the social science orientation it has now. Children learn about other cultures mainly through studies of social scientists. Educators use the data and integrate it with school experiences.

The field of sociology was not a thriving one until after World War II. Anthropologists had information even before that time, which could have been useful to educators, but their information remained mainly with other anthropologists. Somehow, the fields of anthropology, sociology, and education did not intersect then in ways that were later discovered to be of benefit not only to social understanding in society, but also to young children's development of knowledge and personality. As the years progressed, however, more people learned to understand the value of anthropology and realized how it could be applied to education. Sociologists' data have also been invaluable in this context. Their studies in the area of social class (or social stratification) and its relationships to other aspects of society such as education and political power have done a great service. As more of their contributions are brought into educational literature and applied by curriculum writers, administrators, and teachers, children, too, will benefit from it.

Teachers need to strengthen their professional information from fields outside of education. They should acquire as much as they can from newspapers, television, news media, or political science articles if they have predispositions in that direction.

Any of the social sciences, contemporary literature on other countries, or journals such as *National Geographic* have pictures and articles that are very informative. Teachers have to digest and interpret them to children. Pictures in authentically written journals are valuable in themselves, because they reflect an attempt to be accurate and not exaggerate cultural traits or characteristics, territory, and homes of the people being studied. As teachers show children those pictures, a discussion is held on the implications evident in them—e.g., what it means if people live in the desert in terms of livelihood, food-gathering, clothing, and the shelters they will devise from the only available materials in their environments.

Teachers gather data in the form of books, journals, and filmstrips for the children. The children assimilate, relative to their age or developmental level, what they can from it. They can understand a great deal in the cognitive sense about the fact that people have to earn a living for their families even though their ways of doing it are different. Ideas such as these are not far removed from contact with their own parents and problems related to working. Children are educated differently from those in American territory, but they are educated in some way. In this sense, children begin to conceptualize broad differences as well as similarities in the ways that people of different cultures seek satisfaction from foods, comfort, shelter, security (whatever security may mean to people in another culture), beauty, satisfaction from self in terms of pride about certain characteristics they have developed.

If young children can learn early in life that they are part of a wide spectrum of human beings, having various characteristics and are loved, depending on the people around them, they will learn a great deal. Teachers have a responsibility to the young. They can also help children appreciate the work of people who have developed some of the outstanding technological products in their country. Living in a country that tries to be as technologically efficient as the United States, is a compelling fact. It emphasizes the importance for young pupils to learn very early how to live with international neighbors.

Airplanes, television media, newspapers, and journals have facilitated almost instant communication and knowledge between nations and people. To see as it occurs what happens to people in the Middle East, to watch television press coverage of Presidential visits, to watch a Secretary of State negotiate peace agreements with other countries is almost overwhelming to the older generation. Yet to children in contemporary times it is not amazing at all. They are in fact growing up with all these things and take them for granted. What they cannot know unless they are taught, however, is that rapid communication media and the closeness of one nation to another means that the countries and people must remain on relatively good terms.

The technology of firearms, atomic warfare and the like has introduced the awareness that a few people can destroy much that has been done of a progressive nature in the world. It means that the idea of peace must be protected constantly.

What one generation fights to win, another generation cannot possibly appreciate because they were not without the objects fought for. That which one does not have to strive for, is typically not considered important. Teachers however can help the children realize how important good relationships with all countries are. They can also stress the fact that a peaceful status between or among countries can never be taken for granted. It has to be watched, nurtured, and protected. Without being sentimental about it, pupils can learn that unless peace is nurtured, its loss will destroy millions of people along with much that has been admired as constructive, brilliant, and creative as well. The teacher can help children understand how ridiculous it is that only a few men for whatever reason can create such widespread problems as mental illness, epidemics, or a high percentage of deaths.

A skillful teacher and a sensitive one can easily establish the groundwork for a broader understanding of people in different parts of the world. The way in which it is done is crucial. It can be done with respect for the individual, with concern for the welfare of all human beings, and also with the underlying orientation that it is extremely satisfying to sense a oneness with other people, regardless of whether we know them personally or whether we live in their land.

summary

The teacher and other adults who work with young pupils are in an optimal position to impress them with an awareness and appreciation of all people throughout the world. Not only can the pupils be impressed with the interesting varieties of cultures throughout the world, but they can also be led to the enjoyment of those differences.

Schools have an obligation to help young children become aware of the cognitive knowledge in relation to world cultures as well as to develop an empathic capacity with people of those cultures. The openness of young children to new ideas, to sympathetic understanding of children's problems in other lands, and the willingness to listen to the intriguing patterns of life different from their own, provide the maximum lead to educational development. Teachers can take advantage of this crucial time when the pupil is susceptible to learning and willing to abandon himself to powerful forces and compelling ideas.

The more one reads the newspapers and watches television, the more one sees the necessity of young children learning how to understand their neighboring cultures, societies, and countries across the ocean and within the same continent. The problems encountered each day, relative to exports and imports, energy, oil, and ecology, are ample testimony to the importance of developing a new citizenry that will have to monitor its own future world and will have to be well "schooled" in how to live in it.

Even though teachers of young pupils in a contemporary society cannot prepare them fully for the world of tomorrow, because no one knows what it will be like, teachers can prepare them with specific knowledge about the world of today that provides some import of tomorrow. Pupils can be provided with flexibility, stamina, and knowledge that seem appropriate to the problems of today, i.e., scientific, mathematical, and humanistic knowledge, adaptability, and creativity. They can be taught to read the newspapers with perceptiveness so that they can vote intelligently, note what the government is doing, have an awareness and a sensitivity to what is happening. Ultimately, they must realize that they have to accept the responsibility for all of this.

No one is going to force the pupil. He has to develop this depth of consciousness within himself at the same time that teachers sense their obligation for the children's welfare and viability in a future society of their own making.

topics for discussion

1. Why is it important for teachers of young children to expose them to a knowledge of people of other cultures beyond the boundaries of the United States as well as in it? How would you transmit this important information to young children? What would you use to do it?
2. How do teachers as adults learn about other cultures? How have they usually learned about them in their early school years?
3. How does ethnocentrism relate to a lack of knowledge about other cultures?
4. What kind of social studies units can children in kindergarten and primary grades study in order to acquire adequate information about other cultures and other people?
5. How is the United States different from the geographical context of each of the European countries? In what ways do the United States and the separate countries differ from each other?

selected bibliography for teachers

Association for Childhood Educational International. *Teaching for Social Values in Social Studies.* Washington, D.C., 1974.

Association for Supervision and Curriculum Development. *Curriculum Materials.* Washington, D.C., 1974.

Brown, Ina Corinne Brown. *Understanding Other Cultures.* Englewood Cliffs, N.J.: Prentice-Hall, Inc., 1963.

Kenworthy, Leonard. *The International Dimension of Education.* Washington, D.C.: Association for Supervision and Curriculum Development, 1970.

King, Edith W. *Worldmindedness.* Dubuque, Iowa: William C. Brown Company Publishers, 1971.

King, Edith W., and August Kerber. *The Sociology of Early Childhood Education.* New York: American Book Company, 1968.

Margolin, Edythe. *Sociocultural Elements in Early Childhood Education.* New York: Macmillan Publishing Co., Inc., 1974.

National Association for the Education of Young Children. *Multi-Ethnic Books for Young Children.* Washington, D.C.: National Association for the Education of Young Children, No date. Order from Publications Department, National Association for the Education of Young Children, 1834 Connecticut Avenue, N.W., Washington, D.C. 20009.

Ward, Martha Coonfield. *Them Children.* New York: Holt, Rinehart and Winston, Inc., 1971.

Wolcott, Harry F. *A Kwakiutl Village and School.* New York: Holt, Rinehart and Winston, Inc., 1967.

Index